Madagascar

Northern Madagascar
p143

Western Madagascar
p118

Eastern Madagascar
p181

Antananarivo ⭐
p38

Central Madagascar
p60

Southern Madagascar
p89

Anthony Ham

Stuart Butler, Emilie Filou, Helen Ranger

ALLÉE DES BAOBABS P138

HELMET VANGA P269

CHRISTIAN NILSEN/SHUTTERSTOCK ©

AGAMI PHOTO AGENCY/SHUTTERSTOCK ©

ON THE ROAD

Contents

SPECIAL FEATURES

Welcome to Madagascar

Lemurs, baobabs, rainforest, desert, hiking and diving: Madagascar is a dream destination for outdoors enthusiasts – half the fun is getting to all these incredible attractions.

Wild World

Madagascar is unique: 5% of all known animal and plant species can be found here, and here alone. The island's signature animal is the lemur of course, but there are many more weird and wonderful creatures and plants: baobabs, insects, sharks, frogs, orchids, palms, birds, turtles, mongooses. The list goes on. Much of this biodiversity is under threat, from climate change and population pressure, giving each trip a sense of urgency but also purpose: tourism can truly be a force for good.

Epic Landscapes

The remarkable fauna and flora is matched by epic landscapes of an incredible diversity: you can go from rainforest to desert in just 300km. Few places on earth offer such an intense kaleidoscope of nature. There are sandstone canyons, limestone karsts, mountains, fertile hills cascading with terraced rice paddies, forests of every kind – rain, dry, spiny – and a laterite-rich soil that gave the country its nickname of 'Red Island'. With 5000km of coastline, the sea is never very far, turquoise and idyllic in places, dangerous in others.

Island Adventures

Making the best of Madagascar can be challenging (and expensive): it is the world's fourth-largest island and its roads are dismal. For those who relish an adventure, however, this is a one-of-a-kind destination: the off-road driving is phenomenal, there are national parks that only see a few hundred visitors a year, regions that live in autarky during the rainy season and resorts so remote you'll need a private plane or boat to get there. There are also more activities than you'll have time for: hiking, diving, mountain biking, kitesurfing, rock climbing, you name it. Oh, and there are plenty of natural pools, beaches and hammocks on which to recover, too.

Cultural Insights

Madagascar has been populated by successive waves of migrants from various corners of the Indian Ocean. It is unlike anywhere else in Africa or Asia. There are fantastic sites where you can discover this unique history, but also numerous opportunities to meet local people and immerse yourself in their world: in village stays, long-distance trails, festivals, *taxi-brousse* (bush taxis) and Friday-night discos.

Why I Love Madagascar

By Emilie Filou, Writer

Madagascar is unlike anywhere else I have been to – fantastically beautiful, amazingly diverse for its size (similar to France) and surprisingly resistant to change. Nothing comes easy, save perhaps a chat with the locals: Madagascar is undoubtedly one of the friendliest places I've been too. That's why I keep coming back. Plus the fact that after a day of bumping around in a dusty 4WD, or fighting off leeches on muddy trails, you can be served a meal worthy of a fine-dining restaurant anywhere in the world, capped with exquisite rum – that's definitely my kind of travel!

For more about our writers, see p320

Above: Fianarantsoa (p76)

Madagascar

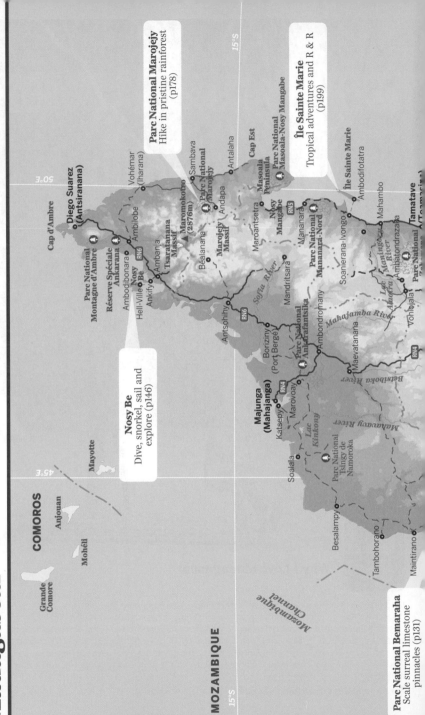

Parc National Marojejy
Hike in pristine rainforest (p178)

Île Sainte Marie
Tropical adventures and R & R (p199)

Nosy Be
Dive, snorkel, sail and explore (p146)

Parc National Bemaraha
Scale surreal limestone pinnacles (p131)

COMOROS

Grande Comore

Mohéli

Anjouan

Mayotte

MOZAMBIQUE

Mozambique Channel

Cap d'Ambre
Diego Suarez (Antsiranana)
Vohémar (Iharana)
Cap d'Ambre

Parc National Montagne d'Ambre
Réserve Spéciale Ankarana
Ambilobe
RN6
Ambanja
Ambodibonara
Hell-Ville Nosy Be
Ankify
Tsaratanàna Massif
Maromokotro (2876m)
Parc National Marojejy
Sambava
Marojejy Massif
Béalanana
Andapa
Antalaha
Cap Est

Masoala Peninsula
Parc National Masoala-Nosy Mangabe
Maroantsetra
Nosy Mangabe

Antsohihy
RN6
Mandritsara
Sofia River

Boriziny (Port Bergé)
Parc National Ankarafantsika
Ambondromamy
Mahajamba River
Mananara
Parc National Mananara-Nord
Soanierana-Ivongo
Île Sainte Marie
Ambodifotatra

Majunga (Mahajanga)
RN4
Maevatanana
Betsiboka River
Mahambo
Mangoro River
Lac Alaotra
Ambatondrazaka
Parc National
Tamatave (Toamasina)

Katsepy
Maroovay
Lac Kinkony
Mahavavy River
Vohibinany
RN4

Soalala

Parc National Tsingy de Namoroka

Besalampy

Tamboharano

Maintirano

15°S
45°E
50°E
15°S

200 km
100 miles

N
0
0

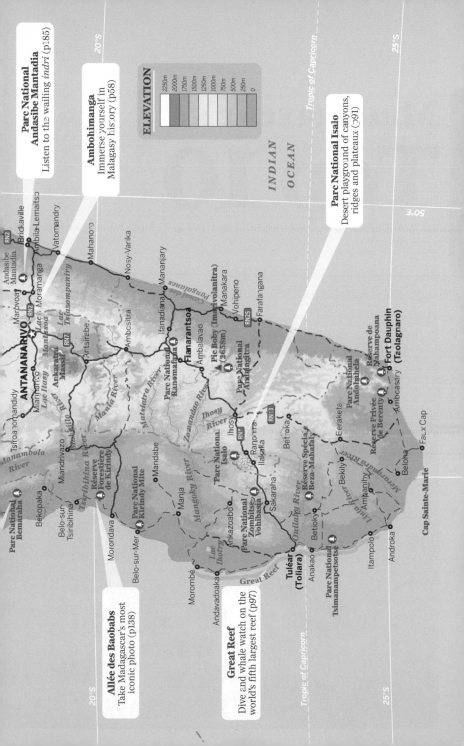

Parc National Andasibe Mantadia (p185)
Listen to the wailing *indri*

Ambohimanga
Immerse yourself in Malagasy history (p58)

Parc National Isalo
Desert playground of canyons, ridges and plateaux (p91)

Allée des Baobabs
Take Madagascar's most iconic photo (p138)

Great Reef
Dive and whale watch on the world's largest reef (p97)

ELEVATION

2250m
2000m
1750m
1500m
1250m
1000m
750m
500m
250m
0

INDIAN OCEAN

20°S
25°S
Tropic of Capricorn
30°S

Parc National Bemaraha
Bekopaka
Belo-sur-Tsiribihina
Mandrivazo
Tsiroanomandidy
ANTANANARIVO
Marianao
Lac Itasy
Ankarana Massif
Andasibe Mantadia
Marovoay
Moramanga
Lac Mantasoa
Lac Tsiazompaniry
Brickaville
Ambila-Lemaitso
Vatomandry
Mahanoro
Nosy-Varika

Morondava
Belo-sur-Mer
Réserve Forestière de Kirindy
Parc National Kirindy Mite
Mandabe
Manja
Ankazoabo
Parc National Zombitse-Vohibasia
Sakaraha
Parc National Ranomafana
Fianarantsoa
Ambalavao
Pic Boby (Imarivolanitra) (2658m)
Parc National Andringitra
Ifanadiana
Mananjary
Grand des Pangalanes
Manakara
Vohipeno
Farafangana

Andavadoaka
Morombé
Anakao
Tuléar (Toliara)
Great Reef
Parc National Tsimanampetsotsa
Betioky
Réserve Spéciale Beza-Mahafaly
Ilakaka
Ranohira
Parc National Isalo
Ihosy
Betroka
Bekily
Ampanihy
Itampolo
Androka
Beloha
Cap Sainte-Marie
Faux Cap
Ambovombe
Réserve Privée de Berenty
Ambosary
Parc National Andohahela
Réserve de Mahampoana
Fort Dauphin (Taolagnaro)
Eeraketa

Tropic of Capricorn
20°S
25°S

Madagascar's
Top 10

Parc National Isalo

1 It's not just because of its epic desert landscapes – canyons, ravines, gorges, savannah-like plains and their numerous ochre hues – that Isalo (p91) is so popular, it's also because there is so much to do here: hiking, via ferratas (fixed cable routes), horse riding, mountain biking, 4WD circuits and swimming in natural pools. Let's not forget lemur- and birdwatching, nor admiring the technicolor sunsets and exquisite clarity of the night skies.

Lemurs

2 Seeing lemurs in the wild is a must-see for most travelers to Madagascar, and with good reason. This is the only place to see them, and they are simply wonderful: cute, agile, graceful, loud, elusive, weird – there are more than 100 species, all different and captivating in their own way. You'll see different species in different parks but the Andasibe area (p185) is probably one of the best. Not only is it home to half a dozen lemur species, including the wailing *indri*, it also mixes national parks with excellent community-run reserves. Sifakas (p257)

JORDIEASY/GETTY IMAGES ©

LOUIELEA/SHUTTERSTOCK ©

Sunset at Allée des Baobabs

3 Few things say Madagascar more than this small stretch of the RN8 between Morondava and Belo-sur-Tsiribihina. Lined with majestic baobabs (p138), it comes into its own at sunset and sunrise when the trees cast their long shadows on the red sand and the sky lights up with orange and purple hues. In addition to the Allée, you'll find plenty more baobabs across southern and western Madagascar. Some live for up to 1000 years and reach epic proportions: Majunga's sacred baobab measures 21m around its trunk!

Île Sainte Marie

4 How this little gem of a tropical paradise has managed to remain so unspoilt is a wonder: Sainte Marie (p199) is quite simply heavenly. There are whales and turtles, beaches you could only dream of and kilometres of tracks accessible only to hikers and quad bikes. Île aux Nattes, the tiny island at its southern tip, ups the ante on the Robinson Crusoe dream: you go there by pirogue (traditional dugout canoe) and simply walk around. No cars, no tuk-tuks. Bliss.

Parc National Bemaraha

5 There is nothing else on earth quite like the jagged limestone pinnacles of Parc National Bemaraha (p131). A Unesco World Heritage Site, the serrated, surreal-looking peaks and boulders are a geological work of art, the result of millennia of water and wind erosion. Just as remarkable is the infrastructure the national park has put in place to explore this natural wonder: via ferratas, rope bridges and ladders, with circuits combining forests, caves, pirogue trips and even abseiling.

Diving & Snorkelling at Anakao

6 Madagascar boasts the world's fifth-largest coral reef – 450km of fringing, patch and barrier reefs from Morombe in the north to Itampolo in the south. Work with local communities and marine conservation areas have helped maintain the reef's health despite increasing pressure. Anakao (p109) has some of the best infrastructure on the reef, with the added bonus of whale watching in winter. Other spots that will blow you away are the 'cathedrals' at Ifaty and Mangily and the serene village of Ambola.

Humpback whale (p273)

GABBRO/ALAMY STOCK PHOTO ©

Tropical Haute Cuisine

7 The freshest of ingredients combined with traditional and colonial culinary influences have produced a divine strand of fusion cuisine. Zebu meat rivals beef in succulence and tenderness, spices add piquancy to sauces, and the tropical sun-ripened fruit can be found in sorbets and macerating in rum, amongst other things. Antananarivo has the best selection of restaurants (p46), but Mad Zebu in Belo-sur-Tsiribihina (p131; pictured above), La Table d'Alexandre in Nosy Be and Chez Samson in Île Sainte Marie are other establishments worth seeking out.

Ambohimanga

8 This is Madagascar's only cultural site on Unesco's World Heritage list, and with good reason: Ambohimanga (p58) was the seat of King Andrian-ampoinimerina, the Merina sovereign who decided to unify the warring tribes of the island so that his kingdom would have no frontier but the sea. The cultural significance of the site goes beyond history: Ambohimanga is revered as a sacred site by the Malagasy, who come here to invoke royal spirits and request their protection and good fortune. Gateway to Rova (p58)

Parc National Marojejy

9 With its pristine mountainous rainforest, thick root-filled jungle and waterfalls, Marojejy (p178) is a primordial place, where the 'angel of the forest' (the endemic silky *sifaka*) inhabits misty mountains, and spectacular views of the Marojejy Massif open up through the canopy. A superb trail crescendos through the landscape over two days, climaxing with a tough climb to the summit (2132m). The nearby Réserve Spéciale d'Anjanaharibe-Sud is well worth visiting too: travellers will be rewarded with the wail of the *indri*.

Nosy Be

10 The 'big island' (p146) is a dream destination: you could spend two weeks here and in the surrounding islands and still feel like you haven't had enough. It's not just the world-class diving and snorkelling, the turquoise sea, the exquisitely soft light and arresting views; you can also visit vanilla and ylang-ylang plantations, explore kilometres of inland trails, see fabulous wildlife in the marine and nature reserves, feast on an abundance of seafood and sail to small islands nearby.

BY VALET/SHUTTERSTOCK ©

Need to Know

For more information, see Survival Guide (p281)

Currency
Ariary (Ar)

Language
Malagasy, French

Visas
All visitors must have a visa to enter Madagascar.

Money
ATMs (Visa and MasterCard) are widely available in large towns and cities. In rural areas, cash rules. Euros are the easiest foreign currency to exchange.

Mobile Phones
Local SIM cards can be used in European and Australian phones; other phones will have to be set on roaming.

Time
East Africa Time (GMT/UTC plus three hours)

When to Go

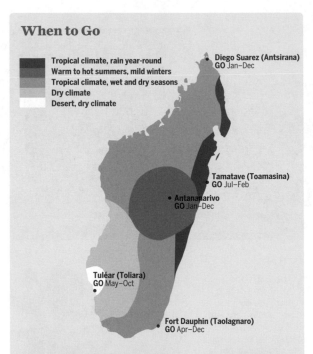

Tropical climate, rain year-round
Warm to hot summers, mild winters
Tropical climate, wet and dry seasons
Dry climate
Desert, dry climate

Diego Suarez (Antsirana)
GO Jan–Dec

Tamatave (Toamasina)
GO Jul–Feb

Antananarivo
GO Jan–Dec

Tuléar (Toliara)
GO May–Oct

Fort Dauphin (Taolagnaro)
GO Apr–Dec

High Season
(Jul & Aug)

➡ Especially busy because of European school holidays.

➡ It's winter – balmy temperatures by day, cool nights (cold in the highlands), stormy seas and rain on the east coast.

➡ There's also a spike of high-season activity at Christmas/New Year.

Shoulder Season
(Apr–Jun, Sep–Dec)

➡ The best time to go: warm temperatures and fewer visitors.

➡ Some areas don't open fully until April or May if the roads haven't dried up from the summer rain.

Low Season
(Jan–Mar)

➡ Cyclone season: all coastal areas are susceptible.

➡ Rainy season everywhere – some areas inaccessible.

➡ January and February are some of the best months for wildlife viewing.

➡ Discounts available in many hotels.

Useful Websites

Lonely Planet (www.lonely planet.com/Madagascar) Destination information, hotel bookings, traveller forum and more.

Madagascar National Parks (www.parcs-madagascar. com) Detailed background and practical information about Madagascar's national parks.

Madagascar Tourisme (www. madagascar-tourisme.com) National tourist-office site, with lots of info and great photographs.

Wild Madagascar (www.wild madagascar.org) Background information, conservation news.

Important Numbers

Madagascar's country code	☏261
Landline prefix	☏020
Mobile prefix	☏032, 033 or 034
Police	☏117
Fire	☏118

Exchange Rates

Australia	A$1	Ar2515
Canada	C$1	Ar2790
Eurozone	€1	Ar4080
Japan	¥100	Ar3390
New Zealand	NZ$1	Ar2360
South Africa	R10	Ar2500
UK	£1	Ar4765
US	US$1	Ar3690

For current exchange rates, see www.xe.com.

Daily Costs
Budget: Less than €60

➡ Basic double (shared facilities): €7–12

➡ Meal at *hotely* (local restaurant): €2.50–4

➡ *Taxi-brousse* ticket: €4–12

➡ National park admission and guide: €25

Midrange: €60–150

➡ Double room (mostly en suite): €12–25

➡ Meal in good restaurant: €10

➡ Car and driver, per day: €35–50

➡ Half-day excursion or activity: €35

Top End: More than €150

➡ Accommodation in boutique hotel: €100

➡ Private 4WD, per day: €60

➡ Internal flight: €120

➡ Half-day diving: €65

Opening Hours

Shops geared towards tourists tend to open longer at the weekend.

Banks (Antananarivo) 8am to 4pm Monday to Friday

Banks (rest of the country) 7.30am to 11.30am & 2pm to 4.30pm Monday to Friday

Bars 5pm to 11pm

Restaurants 11.30am to 2.30pm & 6.30pm to 9.30pm

Shops 9am to noon & 2.30pm to 6pm Monday to Friday, to noon Saturday

Arriving in Madagascar

Ivato Airport (Aéroport d'Ivato) Taxis cost Ar60,000 during the day, Ar80,000 at night for a 45- to 120-minute ride to the city, depending on traffic. A number of hotels in Ivato offer complimentary airport transfers.

Getting Around

Madagascar is a huge place, the roads are bad and travel times long, so be realistic about how much ground you want to cover or you'll spend every other day in the confines of a vehicle.

Private vehicle If you can afford it, this is the best way to explore Madagascar. You'll be able to go anywhere, whenever suits you. The off-road driving can be great fun too.

Taxi-brousse (bush taxi) Slow, uncomfortable and not always safe, but they are cheap, go (almost) everywhere and you can't get more local than that.

Premium buses A definite upgrade in comfort and punctuality on the *taxi-brousse* but they only ply the routes between Tana and big cities.

Plane Huge time savers, but expensive.

For much more on **getting around**, see p289

What's New

Musée de la Photo

This amazing museum (p40) in Antananarivo opened in 2018 and is a great addition to Madagascar's cultural scene. It showcases archive images retracing Madagascar's history and offering a window into the country's past and its culture.

Kitesurfing in Les Trois Baies

With reliable wind for eight months of the year, and near perfect sea conditions, it was only a matter of time before this area became a kitesurfing mecca. There are now a number of hotels and kitesurfing schools (p168) offering packages, with accommodation in or near the Trois Baies or shuttles from nearby Diego Suarez.

Whale Sharks in Nosy Be

Nosy Be, it turns out, is something of a whale shark hotspot. Handily, the wonderful Baleines Rand'Eau (p147) organises tightly regulated boat excursions to observe them as well as humpback whales and turtles depending on the season. It respects codes of approach and has specialist guides on board.

Proper Hostels

At long last Madagascar has hostels worthy of the name: cool places to hang out, with good dorms, and a good restaurant/bar where you can meet other travellers and swap tall tales of *taxi-brousse* (bush taxi) mishaps and crater-sized ruts. Hello Madagascar Underground (p45), Chez Nath (p206) and Tamana Hostel (p151).

LOCAL KNOWLEDGE

WHAT'S HAPPENING IN MADAGASCAR

Anthony Ham, Lonely Planet writer

The last few years have been tough on the good people of Madagascar. Political instability, economic hardship and a natural world seemingly on the brink of environmental catastrophe have all taken their toll. Long-term concerns over climate change are often drowned out by the daily difficulties of drought and other challenges. And with 75% of Madagascar's population living on or below the poverty line, most people are just struggling to make ends meet and give their kids a good education. These difficulties are not to be underestimated. And yet, there is a palpable sense of optimism at large on the streets of most Madagascan towns. Democracy is holding, if fragile, and while not everybody likes their young president, they're proud that he was elected through the ballot box. The economy is on the upswing and people here are cautiously hoping that Madagascar's incredible natural resources and increasing tourism popularity can trickle down in some meaningful way to the ordinary person.

Shopping in Diego

The shopping has become rather good in Diego Suarez since the cruise ships have started calling into town. There is phenomenal jewellery (p165), fine chocolates (p165) and beautiful handicrafts.

New International Airports

Both Ivato (Antananarivo) and Nosy Be airports have received major facelifts, with better/larger terminals, better shops and smoother departure and arrival formalities. There are also an increasing number of international connections to neighbouring Indian Ocean islands, Africa, Turkey and Europe.

Staying in Ivato

Traffic between the village-suburb of Ivato, where the airport is located, and Antananarivo is now so bad that an increasing number of people now opt to stay in Ivato if they only have a day or night between flights. It's no hardship though: there are a couple of great attractions and some fantastic hotels and restaurants too.

LISTEN, WATCH & FOLLOW

For up-to-date news and inspiration, visit www.lonelyplanet.com/madagascar/travel-tips-and-articles and www.lonelyplanet.com/news/madagascar.

Madagascar Tourisme (www.madagascar-tourisme.com) Countrywide info with great images.

Wild Madagascar (www.wildmadagascar.org) Madagascar's natural story.

Madagascar National Parks (www.parcs-madagascar.com) Madagascar's national parks, at once inspirational and practical.

Real Travel Madagascar (https://realmadagascar.com/blog/) Blog by tour operator with a focus on conservation news.

Wildlife Conservation Society (@WCS_Mada on Twitter) Up-to-the-minute environmental news.

BBC News (www.bbc.com/news/topics/c1038wnx0llt/madagascar) The latest stories on Madagascar as they happen and with a good archive.

FAST FACTS

Food trend Gourmet chocolate – boutiques can now be found in all big cities

Length of coastline 4828km (3000 miles) – the longest in Africa

Forest cover 21.5%

Population 26.7 million

population per sq km

MADAGASCAR SOUTH AFRICA UK

≈ 45 people

Accommodation

Find more accommodation reviews throughout the On the Road chapters (from p37)

PRICE RANGES

€ less than Ar60,000 Simple room, often with shared facilities, normally with fan and mosquito net, where needed.

€€ Ar60,000–Ar120,000 A notch above budget in decor, rooms are generally en suite, though hot water does not always work. Air-con may be available.

€€€ more than Ar120,000 All mod cons, good hotel facilities – pool, wi-fi etc. Prices quoted in euros in most upmarket establishments.

Accommodation Types

Bungalows Ubiquitous standalone structures, often wooden, always atmospheric. The style changes with the region. They range from basic to luxurious and they're especially popular in seaside locations and scenic areas.

Hotels Many are made up of bungalows, but not all, especially in cities. They range from simple guesthouse to boutique/luxury affairs. Hot water is rare in budget accommodation, hit-and-miss in midrange places, but reliable in top-end places. You'll have to make do with extra blankets to keep warm. Air-con is only really necessary in summer months (December to March).

Camping Available in most national parks and the default option on multiday treks; operators can usually provide all the gear. Facilities vary, from showers, toilets and well-equipped cooking areas, to nothing more than a cleared area of bush and a long-drop toilet.

Homestays In rural areas you can sometimes arrange a homestay by politely asking around a village for a place to sleep. Pay a fair fee – about Ar20,000 to Ar30,000 per couple is appropriate. If you can, bring some rice (the main staple) too.

Best Places to Stay

Best Overall

Madagascar's portfolio of places to stay just gets better with each passing year. Although things are improving steadily down at the budget end of things, the number of high-end places is growing. Some of these are temples to stylish living in some of the most beautiful places on the island. These are among the best of the best.

➡ Auberge Peter Pan (p110), Anakao

➡ Sakatia Lodge (p158), Nosy Sakatia

➡ Samaria (p205), Île Sainte Marie

➡ Mantadia Lodge (p184), Andasibe

➡ Le Soleil des Tsingy (p132), Parc National Bemaraha

Best for Budget

It used to be that budget travellers didn't have much choice in Madagascar. Not any more. True budget choices – with simple, clean accommodation, travel-savvy staff, and cool hang-outs where you can meet other travellers – are increasingly the norm. For now, the better choices are restricted to major tourist areas, but expect that to change over the coming years.

➡ Chez Sica, Île Sainte Marie (p208)

➡ Tamana Hostel, Nosy Be (p151)

➡ Madagascar Underground, Antananarivo (p45)

➡ Chez Billy, Antsirabe (p65)

➡ Le Bon Endroit, Île Sainte Marie (p205)

Best for Families

If you plan your trip carefully, Madagascar has all the makings of the family trip of a lifetime. And the accommodation here is every bit a part of the mix. Activities to enjoy, attention to detail for families, hotel swimming pools and rooms that keep families together without sacrificing on comfort – they're all possible across the island.

➡ Chez Aina, Antananarivo (p45)

➡ Mantasaly Resort, Les Trois Bales (p169)

➡ Andilana Beach Resort, Nosy Be (p156)

➡ Cap Kimony, Morondava (p135)

➡ La Pirogue, Mahambo (p198)

Best for Luxurious Isolation

Madagascar does luxury particularly well, and everything just seems that much more comfortable when your vantage point is an untrammeled stretch of gorgeous coastline or pristine arc of rainforest. There are so many opportunities for deep immersion in quite stunning surroundings all across the country. Here are some of our favourites.

➡ Masoala Forest Lodge, Parc National Masoala-Nosy Mangabe (p215)

➡ Eden Lodge, Nosy Be (p155)

➡ Iharana Bush Camp, Réserve Spéciale Ankarana (p174)

➡ Anjajavy, Anjajavy Peninsula (p130)

➡ Isalo Rock Lodge, Parc National Isalo (p94)

➡ Olo Be, Andavadoaka (p107)

Anjajavy hotel (p130)

Booking.com (www.booking.com) A vast range of hotels and other accommodation.

Lonely Planet (lonelyplanet.com/hotels) Find independent reviews, as well as recommendations on the best places to stay – and then book them online.

Booking

Accommodation in Madagascar is affordable compared to Europe or North America, but not as cheap as you might perhaps expect. You should book ahead during winter months (July to September) and around Christmas and New Year.

Airbnb (www.airbnb.com) Search online for homes, apartments and other private accommodation with real-time availability.

Practicalities

Few hotels (except in Nosy Be and Île Sainte Marie) have official low-/high-season prices, although many offer discounts in quiet periods, notably during the rainy season (January to the end of March).

Because of the depreciation of the ariary, an increasing number of hotels (even midrange ones) are quoting their prices in euros.

The *vignette touristique* is a tax applied to hotel stays; it's charged per night per room and is usually not included in room rates.

If You Like...

Wildlife

Famed for its wildlife, Madagascar is to nature lovers what France is to foodies. But you'll have to be patient, time your visit right and have Lady Luck on your side to see the best it has to offer.

Indri Madagascar's largest lemur is easily seen – and heard! – around Andasibe. (p185)

Fossa This strange-looking animal, Madagascar's top predator, is a rare sight everywhere, except in Kirindy. (p139)

Iconic baobabs Most commonly found in the southern half of the country, the collection on Allée des Baobabs has become one of Madagascar's signature views. (p138)

Turtles Beloved of divers and snorkelers, turtles thrive all along the Malagasy coast but are best spotted in the turtle sanctuary of Nosy Sakatia. (p158)

Chameleons There are big ones, tiny ones, expert camouflage artists and technicolor pros. Andasibe is probably the best for the photogenic Parson's chameleons. (p185)

Humpback whales Every year from July to September, hundreds of whales make the long journey from Antarctica to mate and give birth in the warmer waters of the Indian Ocean and the Mozambique Channel. (p214)

Beaches

With two oceans, 5000km of coastline and dozens of islands, Madagascar's beaches are one of the country's top attractions. Many rival the beauty of traditional beach destinations, with the added bonus of fewer visitors.

Anakao A perfect arc of white sand, turquoise water and laid-back atmosphere; the pearl of the Great Reef. (p109)

Anjajavy Only accessible by private plane or boat, the beaches on Anjajavy Peninsula bring a whole new meaning to the word remote. (p130)

Île aux Nattes (Nosy Nato) A classic tropical island, with curving white-sand beaches, reclining palms and the most inviting sea. (p207)

Salary Just one resort for 7km of beach, this is what exclusivity feels like. (p106)

Nosy Iranja This postcard-perfect duo of islands becomes one at low tide, when a slim sandbank emerges. Tour companies in Nosy Be arrange day trips. (p159)

Diving & Snorkelling

Madagascar is home to the world's fifth-largest coral reef, which partly explains why diving here is so good. The fauna is exceptional, with sharks, turtles, whales and rays.

Nosy Be Dozens of dive sites within half an hour's boat ride, with a huge variety of seascapes, from shipwrecks to reefs and spectacular drops. (p146)

Nosy Tanikely Now a protected marine reserve, Nosy Tanikely is one of the best and most accessible snorkelling spots in Madagascar, with turtles guaranteed. (p156)

Ifaty & Mangily A great range of dives, including the famous 'Cathedral', a network of stunning rocky arches. (p103)

Anakao The best spot on Madagascar's southern reef, with good snorkeling, even better diving and great accommodation to boot. (p109)

Hiking

With such an alluring shoreline, it's easy to forget that about 70% of Madagascar's land surface sits at a

lofty 1000m to 1500m above sea level. Cue superb mountains, extinct volcanoes, dramatic peaks and, ergo, fabulous hiking.

Massif de l'Andringitra World-class trekking, a hardly visited national park and wonderful accommodation options. (p84)

Parc National Marojejy A trek through the primordial rainforest of the Massif de Marojejy progresses from scenic walk to full-on climbing expedition; if you're not up for a challenge, stop at Camp 2. (p178)

Parc National Bemaraha Scale the weird and wonderful *tsingy* (limestone pinnacle formations) along the park's sensational via ferrata (mountain route; p131)

Parc National Isalo Southern Madagascar's trekking destination par excellence, with stunning canyons and gorges. (p91)

Parc National Masoala-Nosy Mangabe There are short and long-distance trails through this pristine primary rainforest. They are hard work, but worth it for the exceptional wildlife. (p213)

Food & Drink

Madagascar is a culinary delight. Thanks to a mix of cuisines and prime fresh ingredients (plentiful seafood, succulent zebu meat and fruit and vegetables bursting with flavour), you're certain to eat well wherever you go.

Camarons Try the Malagasy prawn (there are saltwater and freshwater varieties) for a fraction of what you'd pay back home.

Société de Rhum Arrangé Flavored rum is the red island's signature drink. There are dozens to try (and take back home), from

Top: Rova (p40), Antananarivo
Bottom: Camarons (Malagasy prawn)

vanilla to lychee, chocolate or ginger, at this shop in Nosy Be. (p153)

Domaine d'Ambohimanitra Vanilla and a host of spices grow in abundance on the northeast 'vanilla coast'. See how it's done at this wonderful plantation. (p177)

La Chocolaterie Robert Madagascar's best-known chocolatier has shops all over the country. Buy a few to eat on the spot or a bundle to take home. (p52)

History & Culture

Although many come to Madagascar for its incredible nature, the island has a rich and diverse culture, influenced by the waves of migrants who gradually populated the island and the colonial powers who hoped to control it.

Ambohimanga The most sacred of Antananarivo's 12 sacred hills and the long-standing home of Malagasy royalty. (p58)

Rova It may be a shadow of its former self, but the queen's palace in Antananarivo's Haute-Ville is steeped in history. (p40)

Famadihana Visitors are often welcome at traditional exhumation ceremonies – an opportunity to re-assess our own beliefs about life and death. (p65)

Île Sainte Marie's pirate cemetery Overlooking the Baie de Forbans, where many pirates lived, this cemetery is a fascinating reminder of the island's lawless past. (p202)

Creature Comforts

If you've had enough of trekking, diving, wildlife seeking and bumping around in a 4WD, put your bags down for a few days at one of these wonderful retreats.

Tsara Komba The jewel in the crown that is the tiny island of Nosy Komba, this is one of the finest lodges in Madagascar. (p157)

Princesse Bora Lodge & Spa Pirogue (traditional dugout canoe) tubs in the spa, suspended beds in the bungalows and a dizzying wine list...this is as close to perfection as you get. (p207)

Nosy Be Hôtel & Spa Stunning and highly original decor, three pools, a private beach and a spa make this a winning destination for R & R. (p156)

Le Relais de la Reine An oasis of luxury in the surreal landscapes of Isalo, the perfect place to come back to after a day under the hot sun. (p94)

Five Senses Lodge Infinite horizons, contemporary design and one of the best restaurants anywhere along Madagascar's coast. (p106)

Shopping

Finding souvenirs is no hardship in Madagascar: there are woven baskets, gemstones, spices, clothes, rum, silk, leather goods and much more.

Lisy Art Gallery This Antananarivo boutique is like a shopping kaleidoscope of Madagascar. Pretty much everything you have seen in the country is available here at reasonable (fixed) prices. (p52)

Soalandy Finding silk at such low prices back home is unthinkable, so make the best of the local product in Ambalavao (and watch the production process, too; p83)

Le Jardin des Sens Essential oils, spices and beauty products in lovely premises in Nosy Be. (p152)

Couleur du Monde You'll come in for the chocolate and come out with shell jewellery, a bag of spices and a few more bits and pieces... (p165)

Epic Off-Road Journeys

If this were a TV program, it would open with 'don't try this at home'. Far from putting travellers off, though, the challenge that is Madagascar's roads is something many revel in, so here are our favourite boneshaking, tyre-bursting, vehicle-bashing road trips.

RN5 from Maroantsetra to Soaniera-Ivongo Depending on how you look at it, this is either the country's worst road or its best off-road adventure. Motorbikes or very sturdy 4WD only. (p198)

Coastal road from Morondava to Tuléar The highlights of this journey are the northern end of the Great Reef and an overnight stay at the serene village of Belo-sur-Mer, ensconced in the dunes. (p140)

Month by Month

January

This is the beginning of cyclone season, which runs until March. Cyclones affect both the west and east coast. Most areas have received some rains by now, turning arid landscapes numerous shades of green.

🎆 New Year Celebrations

Like the rest of the world, the Malagasies welcome the new year with much partying on New Year's Eve and New Year's Day.

February

The weather may be sweltering and humid, but for those who do make it at this time of year, the wildlife rewards are unique. Summer is also cruise-ship season from Tamatave to Nosy Be.

👁 Reptiles & Amphibians

After many months of hibernation or reduced activity, snakes and frogs come out in force in the hot and humid summer climate. This is the best time of year to admire their colourful displays and incredible variety.

👁 Orchids

Madagascar has more than 1000 species of this delicate plant, 90% of which are endemic. Many are endangered, however, so being able to see these floral works of art in the wild is an increasingly rare experience.

April

Many areas that were inaccessible during the rainy season are starting to reopen. Be prepared for slower travel times, however, and copious amounts of mud.

🎆 Easter

The main festival of the Christian calendar is fervently celebrated in Madagascar. Extended families gather, wear their best clothes, attend Mass together (sometimes twice on Sunday) and share a meal.

⭐ Nosy Be Jazz Festival

Started in 2017, this relatively new festival (p149) is already hugely popular, attracting artists both local and international. Concerts are held all over the island.

May

In the north, the wind has picked up and will blow until the end of the year. Tourism starts picking up again.

🤸 Kitesurfing

A combination of fantastic wind and good surf has turned Baie de Sakalava and Mer d'Émeraude (northern Madagascar) into the Malagasy capital of this extreme sport. Tuition and equipment are available and hotels offer special kitesurfing packages.

🎆 Zegny'Zo Festival

For a shot of artistic zing, head to Zegny'Zo, an international street-arts festival with a carnival-like atmosphere in Diego Suarez.

⭐ Donia

Held at the end of May or the beginning of June, the week-long Donia in Nosy Be is Madagascar's most high-profile arts festival. It is primarily a music event, although the fringe also involves a carnival and various sporting events. (p150)

June

The last few inaccessible roads start opening up. Humpback whales begin arriving along the western and eastern coasts to give birth and mate. Tourism season is well on its way.

✿ Fête de l'Indépendance

Madagascar's independence day is a big deal. The official celebrations in Antananarivo feature military parades, speeches, shows and much flag waving. Elsewhere, there are street celebrations, themed parties in nightclubs and a profusion of red, green and white decorations.

July

It's winter and temperatures regularly drop below zero in the highlands at night. Bring a very warm sleeping bag if you're camping, and some layers for the evenings.

✿ Famadihana

The 'turning of the dead', or exhumation, ceremonies to commemorate ancestors take place in the highlands from July to September. The practice is common from Antananarivo to Fianarantsoa and is an important celebration. Foreigners are sometimes invited.

✕ Vanilla Season

The country's flagship plant is harvested between July and October. It is a labour-intensive process, as vanilla pods mature at different times. Flights are full to the vanilla-growing northeast region at this time of year, so book ahead.

August

With school summer holidays in full swing in Europe, August is peak tourism season in Madagascar. Book ahead for the most popular trips and in areas with limited accommodation, such as Parc National Bemaraha.

◉ Whale Watching

Humpback whales migrate annually from their feeding grounds in Antarctica to the warm waters of the Indian Ocean and Mozambique Channel to mate and give birth. Famed for their spectacular breaching (jumping), they can be observed all along the coast from July to September.

☆ Hira Gasy

Enjoy an afternoon of *hira gasy* – traditional storytelling narrated through dancing, singing and oratory jousting. Shows take place year-round but are especially popular in winter, when it's not too hot.

September

With spring under way, this is the perfect time of year to come to Madagascar. Temperatures are pleasant, there is little rain and there are no school holiday crowds.

◉ Birdwatching

Dry, deciduous forests are at their barest at this time of year – a godsend for birdwatchers. Deprived of their usual camouflage, Madagascar's 280 bird species, a third of them endemic, are easier to observe. Don't forget your binoculars.

October

As with spring all over the world, there is stunning blossom, birth and mating – a great time of year to admire wildlife. Temperatures are also at their best – warm but not stifling.

✕ Mango Season

The delectable mango bursts onto the scene, inundating market stalls and roadsides and making its way into every dessert and fruit salad. The green fruit is picked in August and September to make *achards* (a pickled condiment) and savoury salads.

◉ Jacaranda Blossom

The exquisite purple blossom of the jacaranda tree is a sight to behold: its delicate colour contrasts beautifully with urban greys and country greens, while petals carpet the ground like a technicolor version of snow.

◉ Fossa Mating Season

The normally elusive fossa, Madagascar's biggest predator (and the baddie in *Madagascar* the cartoon movie), makes quite a show of its loud nuptials. It's best observed in the Réserve Forestière de Kirindy in western Madagascar.

☆ Madajazzcar

Going strong for more than 25 years, this annual jazz festival in Antananarivo taps into Madagascar's rich musical tradition and brings together local and foreign jazz performers. Many of the events are free.

November

This is a lovely time of year, with visitor numbers petering out and the weather warming up. It is prime diving season, too.

👁 Baby Lemurs

If you thought lemurs were cute, wait until you see the babies, clinging to their mother's fur or being carried by the scruff of the neck. The entire troop generally looks after the young.

🍴 Lychee Season

Madagascar provides around 70% of the lychees consumed in Europe, but fear not, there are plenty left in the country to gorge on. The season lasts until January and lychees are a favourite Christmas food.

December

Christmas is a low-key event for Malagasies: families go to Mass and share a meal. Tourism peaks briefly around festive celebrations, with many Europeans enjoying the warm weather and tropical showers.

🏃 Diving

It is the height of summer, with great visibility and calm seas, ideal for diving, be it in Nosy Be, Île Sainte Marie or southern Madagascar.

Top: *Hira gasy* performance (p41), Antananarivo

Bottom: Orchids

Itineraries

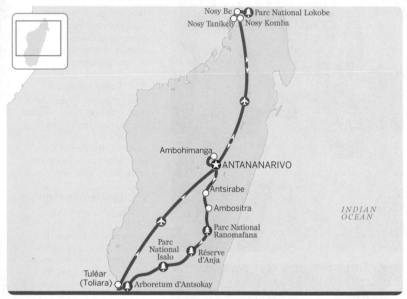

2 WEEKS Essential Madagascar

A combination of the classic RN7 with some island R & R in glorious Nosy Be.

On day one, head from **Antananarivo** to the highland town of **Antsirabe**, with its wide colonial streets and colourful rickshaws. On day two, wind your way to Ranomafana through the highland's scenic landscapes, stopping en route at the arts-and-crafts capital, **Ambositra**. Then spend day three hiking and searching for lemurs in the rainforests of **Parc National Ranomafana**.

On day four, drive to the superb **Parc National Isalo**, stopping in **Réserve d'Anja** on your way to see the oh-so-cute ring-tailed lemurs. Spend the next two days exploring Isalo's stunning desert plains and canyons.

On day seven, head to **Tuléar**, making sure to stop at **Arboretum d'Antsokay** on your way. On day eight, fly to **Antananarivo** (Tana) and then on to **Nosy Be** the next day. Enjoy some beach R & R on day 10. The next day, take a day trip to **Nosy Komba** and **Nosy Tanikely** for unrivaled snorkeling. On day 12, visit **Parc National Lokobe**. Fly back to Tana on day 13. Take a day trip to **Ambohimanga** for your last day, or shop for souvenirs.

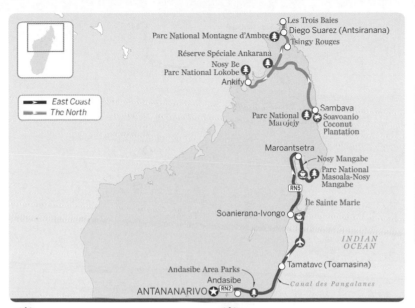

 ## The North

Northern Madagascar offers rainforest hikes, spectacular rock formations and tantalising white beaches.

Fly to **Sambava**; the next morning, visit the **Soavoanio Coconut Plantation** to learn more about the region's signature products before heading to **Parc National Marojejy**. Spend a couple of days trekking on this sensational massif. It's a day's drive from Sambava to the beautiful **Réserve Spéciale Ankarana**, a wilderness of caves, pinnacles and dry forests. Spend a day here and continue on to the northern belle of **Diego Suarez**, with a stop at the terracotta-colored **Tsingy Rouges** on the way.

Take a day to discover Diego's heritage and explore the wild coastline of **Les Trois Baies**. Take another day trip to the mountainous **Parc National Montagne d'Ambre**.

From Diego, it's a six-hour drive to Ankify where you'll board the boat for **Nosy Be**. Spend three or four days enjoying its coral reefs and beaches, putting a day aside for the fabulous **Parc National Lokobe**. Fly back to Tana from Nosy Be.

 ## East Coast

Exploring this coast is challenging but by no means impossible, though budget travellers will balk at the cost of heading beyond Île Sainte Marie, since Maroantsetra is hard and expensive to get to.

Head east along the RN2 from Antananarivo to charming **Andasibe**, jumping-off point for the luxuriant, misty rainforests of **Andasibe Area Parks**. Spend a couple of days waking to the cries of the legendary *indri* (Madagascar's largest lemur), hiking and birdwatching before winding down the RN2 to **Tamatave**, gateway to the waterways and lakes of the Canal des Pangalanes. Allow three or four days for this aquatic wonderland.

Back in Tamatave, fly to gorgeous **Île Sainte Marie**. Tour the island by quad- or motorbike and take a whale-watching trip (July to September) or go snorkelling/diving (October to January). If you relish a challenge, take a boat to **Soanierana-Ivongo** and drive (4WD/motorbike only) the infamous RN5 to **Maroantsetra**; minimum two days. Spend a night at **Nosy Mangabe** and a couple of nights in **Parc National Masoala-Nosy Mangabe**. Fly to Tana from Maroantsetra.

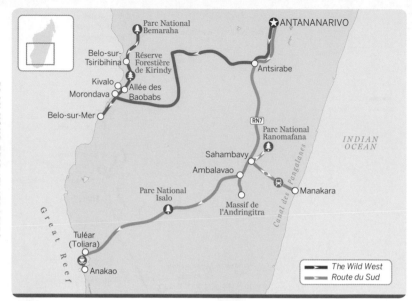

The Wild West
Route du Sud

 ## Route du Sud
2½ WEEKS

This classic route will whisk you from **Antananarivo** down to Tuléar along the famed RN7.

First stop is **Antsirabe**, where you should visit some of the town's famed artisans. Drive to **Sahambavy** and its glorious tea-plantation landscapes. The next day, hop on the scenic FCE train to **Manakara**, where you can tour the Canal des Pangalanes.

Drive to **Parc National Ranomafana** and hike in the park's rainforest. Time your visit to the highland town of **Ambalavao** to coincide with Madagascar's largest zebu market, then allow three or four days to explore the spectacular **Massif de l'Andringitra** with its granite peaks, phenomenal hikes and wonderful lodges.

Further south is the fantastic **Parc National Isalo**, with jagged sandstone massifs, cool canyons and delightful natural pools. Two days will do it justice.

You'll then be on your way to the perfect beaches of **Anakao** and the Great Reef, via speedboat from **Tuléar**. Once you've had your fill of white-sand beaches, fly back to Antananarivo.

 ## The Wild West
2 WEEKS

This itinerary features some of Madagascar's most iconic sights; it requires a 4WD for the whole journey and a fair amount of driving.

It's a long day's drive from **Tana** to the laid-back seaside town of **Morondava**. The next day, take a day trip to the beautiful village of **Kivalo** in the mangroves; tours are organised and led by the local community. You'll get to see the iconic **Allée des Baobabs** on your way there and back. The following day, head to **Parc National Bemaraha**. It's about a day's drive through scorched landscapes to get here, but the reward will be lunch at the amazing Mad Zebu in **Belo-sur-Tsiribihina** on the way. You'll need at least two days to explore the national park. Head back down towards Morondava, this time stopping at **Réserve Forestière de Kirindy**, home to the elusive fossa and the giant jumping rat. Make sure to go on a night walk.

Head straight to the fishing village of **Belo-sur-Mer** for a couple of days where you can enjoy some well-deserved R & R. You can then drive on to Tuléar (during the dry season only), or go back to Morondava and fly or drive back to Antananarivo.

Plan Your Trip
Activities

Madagascar is an excellent destination for sporting activities. Climbing, diving, hiking and canoeing/kayaking are all in plentiful supply. Whatever activity you embark on, pick a reliable operator, especially with high-risk activities such as diving, kitesurfing and rock climbing. Check the operator's affiliations, the instructors' qualifications and inspect your gear.

Hiking

Madagascar has some wonderful hiking opportunities. Trails traverse the country's slew of national parks - unlike on the African mainland, hiking is the best way to get around with no dangerous animals to fear – and the standard of guiding is excellent. Although some walks are dedicated hiking expeditions of varying length, many combine exercise with the opportunity to track down lemurs, chameleons and birds.

Where to Hike

With such an alluring shoreline, it's easy to forget that about 70% of Madagascar's land surface sits at a lofty 1000m to 1500m above sea level. Cue superb mountains, extinct volcanoes, dramatic peaks and, ergo, fabulous hiking.

Multiday treks (three to 10 days, such as Maroantsetra to Cap Est, Ambalavao to Manakara, the Razafimaniry villages, Isalo and Makay etc) are becoming more popular and are often the highlight of a trip.

For day hikes, just about every national park has superb trails and plenty of guides on hand to take you out into the wild. Our pick of the hiking destinations include the following:

Massif de l'Andringitra (p85)

Parc National Marojejy (p178)

Parc National Bemaraha (p131)

Best Activities

Ultimate Hiking Experiences

Massif de l'Andringitra (p84)

Parc National Marojejy (p178)

Parc National Bemaraha (p131)

Parc National Isalo (p91)

Best Wildlife Watching

Indris and Parson's chameleons: near Andasibe (p185)

Aye-ayes: Aye-Aye Island (p209)

Fossas: Réserve Forestière de Kirindy (p139)

Whale watching: Île Sainte Marie (p199) and Anakao (p109)

Green turtles, Nosy Sakatia (p158)

Best Diving & Snorkelling

Parc National Marin de Nosy Tanikely (p156)

Île Sainte Marie (p199)

Anakao (p109)

Ifaty & Mangily (p103)

Best Alternative Activities

Cooking course (p44), Antananarivo

Village visit (p137), Kivalo

Day spas (p41), Antananarivo

Parc National Isalo (p91)

Parc National Masoala-Nosy Mangabe (p213)

Parc National Ranomafana (p71)

Parc National Montagne d'Ambre (p170)

Parc National Andohahela (p113)

Parc National Ankarafantsika (p126)

Practicalities

Longer, multiday trips require advance planning (for reservations and equipment to bring). A few tips:

➡ Operators can usually provide all the required equipment for camping, cooking etc; you'd be advised to bring your own sleeping bag however, or at the very least a sleeping liner, if you want to avoid bed bugs.

➡ Check the difficulty of the trek with your operator: some treks are notoriously hard (Maroantsetra to Cap Est, Marojejy etc) and require good physical condition as well as a love of challenges. Others treks, such as Razafimaniry villages, are accessible to anyone with a modicum of fitness.

➡ You'll likely go to the most remote spots on your trip whilst you trek; make sure you have a decent first-aid kit, water-purifying equipment (such as LifeStraw or chlorine tablets) to minimise plastic waste, and a good torch. A battery pack to be able to keep charging phones and other electronics is also handy.

Diving & Snorkelling

Much of Madagascar is surrounded by coral reefs – the Great Reef in the southwest is the world's fifth largest. And it's no coincidence that those areas with offshore reefs are the epicentres of the country's tourism industry. Added to the natural beauty is a highly professional diving industry.

Where to Dive & Snorkel

There are three main diving/snorkelling areas in Madagascar: Nosy Be (p146) and the surrounding islands; Île Sainte Marie (p199) in the east, and the Great Reef, which stretches from Anakao (p109) to Andavadoaka in the southwest; Ifaty and Mangily (p104) are the main diving hubs.

Nosy Be is generally considered the best all-around, with good conditions year-round and a phenomenal marine biodiversity, including turtles, rays, whale sharks, humpback whales, coral reefs, myriad fish species and hammerhead sharks. Parc National Marin de Nosy Tanikely (p156) is especially good.

Practicalities

Although diving takes place year-round, the best time everywhere is usually between October and January.

Note that the only decompression chamber is located in Nosy Be.

Consider the following tips when diving and help preserve the ecology and beauty of reefs:

➡ Don't touch living marine organisms or drag equipment across the reef. If you must hold onto the reef, only touch exposed rock or dead coral.

➡ Be conscious of your fins. Even without contact, the surge from fin strokes near the reef can damage delicate organisms.

ALTERNATIVE ACTIVITIES

For a break from looking for lemurs, lazing by the beach or high-energy hiking or diving, here are some lesser-known things to do:

Tana Kitchen (p44) Madagascar's very first cooking school, in Antananarivo, is a glorious introduction into Malagasy cooking.

Spas (p41) Pamper yourself in one of Antananarivo's excellent day spas.

Kivalo (p137) Spend a day immersed in local culture with a visit to a local village and ecotourism project close to Morondava.

Rando Raid Madagascar (p64) Mountain biking, among other activities.

Rent 501 Madagascar (p134) Explore the national parks of the west on a quad bike.

Fishing in Nosy Be (p147) Tussle with a giant trevally out on the open sea, from March to June and October to December.

Hiking, Parc National Isalo (p91)

→ Take great care in underwater caves. Spend as little time within them as possible as your air bubbles may be caught within the roof and thereby leave organisms high and dry.

→ Resist the temptation to collect or buy corals or shells.

→ Do not feed fish, even if operators offer it.

Wildlife Watching

Lemurs are found nowhere else on the planet, and with dozens of species, each with their own landscape niche, all across the island, the possibilities for watching wildlife are epic. Other wildlife prizes include the fossa (Madagascar's only large carnivore), a rich portfolio of chameleon species, abundant birdlife, and a host of marine creatures, from turtles and migrating whales to astonishing fish populations.

Most wildlife watching is year-round, but the time for seeing whales runs from July to September.

Where to Watch Wildlife

Everywhere that there's a national park, you're likely to find lemurs (of both the daytime and nocturnal persuasion) and guides adept at tracking them down.

Each park has a handful of different lemur varieties so do your research before setting out – *Lemurs of Madagascar* (2010) is an outstanding resource, while our coverage of national parks throughout this guide lists which species to see in each park. Other highlights among many include the following:

Parc National Mantadia (p187) and Parc National Analamazaotra (p186): *indris* and chameleons.

Parc National Masoala-Nosy Mangabe (p213), Aye-Aye Island (p209) and Parc National Montagne d'Ambre (p170): aye-ayes

Réserve Forestière de Kirindy (p139): fossas

Île Sainte Marie (p199) and Anakao (p109): humpback whales

Nosy Sakatia (p158): turtles

Plan Your Trip
Family Travel

Travelling in Madagascar can be a memorable experience for the adventurous family. Fantastic wildlife that's nothing like the movie, a host of fun activities, glorious beaches and opportunities for genuine cultural immersion – Madagascar has fun for all the family.

Keeping Costs Down

Eating

Children's menus are rare, but they do exist in tourist areas and resorts, as well as in Antananarivo. Elsewhere, try asking for smaller serves – some restaurants are happy to oblige.

Sleeping

Ask about discounts for children if an extra bed is required; those sharing beds with their parents will generally stay for free.

Sightseeing

When entering national parks, children under 12 pay around half of the adult rate – the actual amount varies from one park to the next. At other sights and attractions, such as arboretums, expect children to pay between one-half and one-third of the adult admission price. In Antananarivo, there is no discounted rate for children at museums.

Transport

Domestic airlines usually offer discounted fares of around 25% for children aged between two and 12, while infants (two years and under) most often travel free. If renting a car or 4WD vehicle, the rate offered will be for the entire vehicle rather than per person.

Children Will Love...
Watching Wildlife

Indri Madagascar's largest lemur is always a highlight at Parc National Mantadia (p187), both for seeing and hearing their unearthly cries.

Fossa Look under your bungalow at Réserve Forestière de Kirindy (p139) and you might just see the elusive fossa.

Turtles Sightings of green turtles are almost guaranteed at Nosy Sakatia (p158).

Chameleons Ranomafana Arboretum (p69) is *the* place to see the lovely and large Parson's chameleon.

Ring-tailed lemurs Madagascar's most charismatic and photogenic lemurs are easy to see at Parc National Isalo (p91).

Activities & Beaches

Nosy Be (p147) Go snorkelling to enjoy some of the Indian Ocean's richest marine life.

Anakao (p109) Enjoy perfect (and blissfully quiet) beaches with snorkelling and whale watching possible.

Île aux Nattes (Nosy Nato; p207) Beaches don't come any more beautiful than this classic tropical island with curvaceous white sand and stunning palms.

Vohémar (p174) One of the most sheltered beaches in northern Madagascar, with interesting local villages and a hint of vanilla in the air.

Thermal baths (p64) Soak in natural hot water in Antsirabe for fun or medicinal purposes – kids love it.

Cultural Immersion

Village visit Learn about the lives of locals with a welcome ceremony, crab fishing and tree-planting at Kivalo (p137).

Zafimaniry culture Dive into the wonderful world of the Zafimaniry villages (p71) of Central Madagascar, and live for a day like a local.

Royal palace Explore the Rova (p58) and listen to tales of kings and queens at Ambohimanga.

Cooking class Shop for local foods in the market, then learn to cook like a Malagasy chef in Antananarivo (p44).

Spice gardens Inhale deeply as you wander Millot Plantations (p159) with its spices, essential oils and cocoa plants.

Strange Trees & Landscapes

Allée des Baobabs (p138) Come for a sunset promenade down one of Madagascar's most celebrated (and most beautiful) avenues; don't miss the nearby, entwined Baobab Amoureux (p138).

Parc National Bemaraha (p131) Landscapes don't come any weirder than the *tsingy*, strange, jagged limestone towers that seem to spring from a child's imagination.

Jardin Tropical (p161) Crocs, chameleons and porcupines in a lovely forest setting.

Arboretum d'Antsokay (p99) Marvel at how the trees of Madagascar's wild and arid south seem to come from another planet.

Réserve Spéciale Ankarana (p171) Lose yourself in caves, canyons, grottoes and that bizarre freak of Madagascar's natural world, the *tsingy*.

Region by Region

Antananarivo

Tana has very little to entertain the kids, although the food is excellent, some restaurants have children's menus, and you can always thank them for their patience by a trip to La Chocolaterie Robert (p52). A cooking class at Tana Kitchen (p44) could also be fun.

In the surrounding highlands, attractions include Lemurs' Park (p56); Le Village (p56), where they make model ships; and the Croc Farm (p57).

Central Madagascar

Madagascar's Central Highlands have a handful of kid-friendly attractions. Road conditions are generally better and distances shorter than other corners of the island.

Attractions include chameleons and lemurs at Parc National Ranomafana (p71), ring-tailed lemurs at community-run Réserve d'Anja (p82), and papermaking workshop (p83) at Ambalavao. Other highlights include a cultural visit to the Zafimaniry villages (p71), and paddling a pirogue along the Canal des Pangalanes (p74).

Southern Madagascar

As long as you stick to the RN7 and Great Reef, Southern Madagascar has much appeal for families. The Parc National Isalo (p91) is good for lemurs and weird-and-wonderful rock formations, while Anakao (p109) is perfect for a beach holiday. In Tuléar (Toliara), the Arboretum d'Antsokay (p99) makes Madagascar's botany fun.

Western Madagascar

Western Madagascar can be a challenge for travelling families – distances can be daunting and road conditions can be appalling. If you make it out this far, the ample rewards include the *Lord of the Rings*-esque limestone pinnacles of Parc National Bemaraha (p131); the beautiful baobabs at Allée des Baobabs (p138); the chance to see fossa at Réserve Forestière de Kirindy (p139); the ecotourism excursion to Kivalo (p137); and the natural swimming pools of the Grottes d'Anjohibe (p119).

Northern Madagascar

In the north, the proliferation of tourist resorts and attractions brings many great opportunities for a fun family holiday. Nosy Be (p146) in particular has plenty of activities. Elsewhere, snorkel the Parc National Marin de Nosy Tanikely (p156), find black lemurs and boa constrictors at the Parc National Lokobe (p154), or learn all about vanilla at Domaine d'Ambohimanitra (p177).

Eastern Madagascar

Eastern Madagascar can feel like Madagascar's wildest corner and getting to some places can be a challenge. But places like Parc National Mantadia (p187), to see the *indri*, or Île Sainte Marie (p199), with its whale watching and natural swimming pools, are both accessible and worth reaching. Kids also enjoy the solar-powered boat rides at Lac Ampitabe (p189), and the snorkelling and swimming at Île aux Nattes (p208).

Good to Know

➡ Look out for the 👪 icon for family-friendly suggestions throughout this guide.

➡ Distances can be large and road conditions appalling, so plan to spend a few days in each place and don't try to be too ambitious. Consider flying between each stop.

➡ Many hotels provide *chambres familiales* or double rooms with an extra bed (single or double) geared for use by parents and children. You'll only find travel cots in some midrange and top-end hotels.

➡ Disposable nappies and infant milk formula are available in Antananarivo and other large cities, but are hard to find elsewhere.

➡ Some midrange and top-end hotels/restaurants have high chairs and games or play areas for children. Some also have dedicated children's menus.

➡ Some tour operators have children's car seats – inquire when booking.

➡ Some exclusive top-end resorts and hotels are adults only – check when making your reservation.

➡ Some activities have a minimum-age requirement.

Useful Resources

Lonely Planet Kids (www.lonelyplanetkids.com) Loads of activities and great family travel blog content.

First Words French (shop.lonelyplanet.com) A beautifully illustrated book introducing the French language for ages five to eight.

Wild Madagascar (www.wildmadagascar.org/kids/) An excellent overview of Madagascar's history, culture and wildlife.

Kids' Corner

Say What?

Hello.	Bonjour. bon·zhoor.
Goodbye.	Au revoir. o·rer·vwa.
Thank you.	Merci. mair·see.
My name is ...	Je m'appelle ... zher ma·pel ...

Did You Know?

- Madagascar is nicknamed the 'eighth continent'.

- There are 111 different species of lemur here.

Have You Tried?

Koba Roadside snack of ground nuts, rice flour and sugar, wrapped in a banana leaf.

Regions at a Glance

Madagascar is the world's fourth-biggest island, and with its huge size comes a huge amount of diversity.

Central Madagascar is the most accessible part of the country, with the paved RN7. Western Madagascar, with its national parks, beautiful coast and 4WD trails, will delight those in search of something a little different, while southern Madagascar will appeal to divers and snorkellers, although much of the interior is off-limits. Beach bums will be better off in Île Sainte Marie in the east or Nosy Be in the north.

Eastern Madagascar is the most remote region, but those who make it there will be rewarded with pristine environments.

Antananarivo

History
Food
Shopping

History & Culture

The development of a Malagasy identity is intimately linked to the emergence of Antananarivo (Tana) as a capital: this is the home of the kings who brought together the island's tribes.

Gastronomy

Foodies of the world, rejoice; Tana's got fusion cuisine down to a T. Imagine French gastronomy, prepared with the freshest Malagasy ingredients, add a soupçon of Creole, a smidgen of Indian and voila!

Retail Therapy

Tana is a potpourri of arts, crafts, clothes and deli shops. Hard-nosed bargain hunters head for the markets, while more conventional shoppers love the well-stocked boutiques.

p38

Central Madagascar

Culture
Trekking
Artisans

Malagasy Life

Travellers often start their trip in Madagascar with the highlands, and what an introduction to Malagasy life: accessible homestays, colourful markets (including the country's biggest zebu market) and colonial architecture.

Amazing Treks

Massif d'Andringitra is in a trekking league of its own. The trails are challenging, the views breathtaking and there's good infrastructure.

Arts & Crafts

Much of Madagascar's signature arts and crafts – raffia work, woodcarvings, miniatures, silk weaving – originate from the highlands and visiting artisans' workshops and purchasing unique souvenirs is part and parcel of the destination.

p60

Southern Madagascar

Diving
Beaches
Trekking

Great Reef
It is the world's fifth-largest coral reef, ergo a great diving destination. There are multiple dive sites all along the reef and many professional outfits to choose from.

Remote Beaches
Malagasy beaches rarely suffer from overcrowding, but many southern beaches are so off the radar that the likelihood of your having the beach to yourself is actually quite high.

Scenic Treks
Madagascar's southern hinterland is a paradise for hikers. Parc National Isalo offers numerous circuits, including via ferratas, in its scenic desert canyons. For more of the same, but with even fewer crowds, head to Massif du Makay.

p89

Western Madagascar

Baobabs
Seafood
Scenery

Magnificent Giants
The Malagasies call them 'roots of the sky', after their crooked branches, and in western Madagascar they come in all guises: in majestic avenues, intertwined, straight or bottle-shaped.

Fabulous Seafood
Foodies will rate the region for its cheap and outstanding seafood, including lobster and crayfish as well as fish, often prepared with a divine blend of local spices.

Photogenic Landscapes
From meandering rivers to immense beaches, arid plains to deciduous forests, serrated peaks to undulating sand dunes, western Madagascar is easy on the eye.

p118

Northern Madagascar

Activities
Islands
Plantations

Diving & Trekking
Adrenaline junkies, look no further. Here, you can trek in mist-shrouded rainforest, scale rock cliffs on deserted islands, kitesurf along unspoiled beaches and dive with whale sharks and rays. Oh, and beachcombing counts, too.

Paradisiacal Islands
It's a cliché but the islands around Nosy Be are more than live up to it. Crystalclear waters, shades of turquoise, fine white sand, exquisite light: yes, this really does exist.

Vanilla & Spice
If you've ever wondered where the delectable vanilla comes from, what a pepper plant looks like, or how fruity cocoa beans become chocolate, visit plantations to find out.

p143

Eastern Madagascar

Whale Watching
Rainforest
Islands

Humpback Migration
Île Sainte Marie and Baie d'Antongil have been the nursing and mating grounds of humpback whales since time immemorial. Take to the water to admire these endangered giants in all their breaching glory.

Unspoiled Rainforest
Eastern Madagascar is one of the last areas in the country where huge tracts of rainforest remain. Explore it on foot or by boat on the Masoala Peninsula.

Tropical Islands
For sheer escapism, you can't do better than idyllic Île Sainte Marie and Île aux Nattes. Both cater admirably to those in need of R&R, but Sainte Marie also holds the promise of adventure in the north.

p181

On the Road

Northern Madagascar p143

Western Madagascar p118

Eastern Madagascar p181

Antananarivo p38

Central Madagascar p60

Southern Madagascar p89

Antananarivo

POP 1.39 MILLION

Best Places to Eat

➡ La Varangue (p48)

➡ Le Saka (p46)

➡ Toko Telo (p46)

➡ Nerone Ristorante Italiano (p46)

➡ Pâtisserie Colbert (p49)

➡ Lokanga (p48)

Best Places to Stay

➡ Grand Hotel Urban (p45)

➡ Madagascar Underground (p45)

➡ Citizen (p45)

➡ Lokanga (p45)

➡ Chez Aina (p45)

➡ Hôtel Niaouly (p45)

Why Go?

Tana, as the capital is universally known, is all about eating, shopping, history and day trips. The town centre itself, with its pollution and dreadful traffic, puts off many travellers from staying, but bypassing the capital altogether would be a mistake: Tana has been the home of Malagasy power for three centuries and there's a huge amount of history and culture to discover, as well as some unexpected wildlife options.

In the city itself, the Haute-Ville, with its beautiful colonial buildings, steep streets and cool climate (average altitude in Tana is 1400m), is a great place to wander about. There are also some excellent markets and shops that stock products and crafts from across the country at very competitive prices. Finally, Tana is *the* place in Madagascar to treat yourself to a fine meal: some establishments rival Europe's Michelin-starred restaurants, but without the price tag.

When to Go
Antananarivo

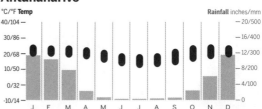

Jun–Aug Winter season in Tana, when night temperatures drop below 10°C.

Jul–Sep *Fama-dihana* season, when families exhume their ancestors' bones.

Oct The purple blossoms of jacaranda trees lines the shores of Lac Anosy.

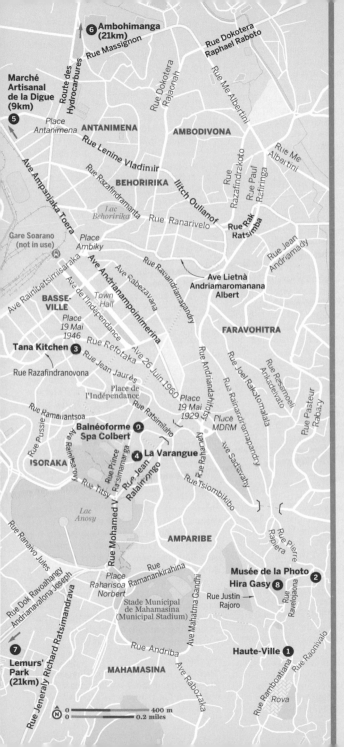

Antana-narivo Highlights

① **Haute-Ville** (p40) Visiting the historical monuments that crown Antananarivo's lovely upper town.

② **Musée de la Photo** (p40) Taking the time to explore Madagascar's past in Antananarivo's best museum.

③ **Tana Kitchen** (p44) Learning the fine art of Malagasy cooking and having loads of fun in the meantime.

④ **La Varangue** (p48) Discovering why Malagasy cuisine is so rightly celebrated.

⑤ **Marché Artisanal de la Digue** (p52) Shopping till you drop (and haggling all you can) at the city's best handicrafts market.

⑥ **Ambohimanga** (p58) Spending an afternoon in the spiritual home of Malagasy identity.

⑦ **Lemurs' Park** (p56) Ticking off the lemurs you missed elsewhere in Madagascar.

⑧ **Hira Gasy** (p41) Attending an afternoon of music, dancing and storytelling spectacles in Tana, or in one of the surrounding villages.

⑨ **Balnéoforme Spa Colbert** (p41) Treating yourself to a massage with Malagasy essential oils.

History

The area that is now Antananarivo was originally known as Analamanga (Blue Forest), and is believed to have first been populated by the Vazimba, ancestors of today's Malagasy, about whom little is known. In 1610 a Merina (a tribal group) king named Andrianjaka conquered the region, stationed a garrison of 1000 troops to defend his new settlement, and renamed it Antananarivo, 'Place of 1000 Warriors'.

In the late 18th century Andrianampoinimerina, the unifying king, moved his capital from Ambohimanga to Antananarivo, where it became the most powerful of all the Merina kingdoms. For the next century Antananarivo was the capital of the Merina monarchs and the base from which they carried out their conquest of the rest of Madagascar.

Tana remained the seat of government during the colonial era, and it was the French who gave the city centre its present form, building two great staircases to scale the city's hills, and draining swamps and paddy fields to create present-day Analakely. In May 1929 the city was the site of the first major demonstration against the colonialists.

Today the greater Antananarivo area is Madagascar's political and economic centre.

◉ Sights

Central Tana is relatively compact, which means that it's easily explored on foot. The catch is that it's hilly, with *plenty* of stairs. The Haute-Ville, with its numerous old buildings, is a great place to explore.

★ Rova
HISTORIC BUILDING

(Palais de la Reine; Map p42; ☑034 05 520 49; Rue Ramboatiana; Ar10,000, guide Ar20,000; ⊙9am-5pm) Tana's *rova* (fortified palace), known as Manjakamiadana (A Fine Place to Rule), is the imposing structure that crowns the city's highest hill. Gutted in a fire in 1995, it remains under endless restoration but the compound can be visited. The palace was designed for Queen Ranavalona I by Scottish missionary James Cameron. The outer stone structure was added in 1867 for Queen Ranavalona II, although the roof and interior remained wooden, much to everyone's regret in 1995...

The palace gate is protected by a carved eagle, the symbol of military force, and a phallus, the symbol of circumcision and thus nobility. Succeeding rulers built (and destroyed) a number of other palaces on the premises; there are ruins scattered about. There is also a replica of King Andrianampoinimerina's palace at Ambohimanga.

The Rova is the resting place of the country's greatest monarchs: the most imposing stone tombs are located left of the main gate. The plain grey ones are those of kings, while the queens' are painted red (red was the colour of nobility).

Remember that it is *fady* (taboo) to point your finger directly at the royal tombs or the palace itself. The Rova, which can be seen from almost anywhere in Tana, is at the very top of Haute-Ville, with wonderful views from the grounds.

Despite what they tell you at the gate, a guide is not compulsory.

★ Musée de la Photo
MUSEUM

(Map p42; ☑032 88 871 81; www.photomadagascar.com; Lalana Andriamanalina, Anjohy; Ar10,000; ⊙10am-5pm Tue-Sun) Opened in early 2018, this fabulous photography museum is Antananarivo's best museum. There are four small rooms showing films (in French, English or Malagasy) that offer a fascinating window on Madagascar's past using archival photos – subject matter includes the history of Madasgacar's seven largest cities, important Malagasy identities from the 19th and 20th centuries, a look at the work of an early Malagasy photo studio, Saklava burial traditions, child rituals and other themes.

Upstairs are exhibits on the role of the zebu in Malagasy life and walls filled with Polaroids covering modern life in the capital. There are good views from the pretty garden, a small but good shop at the entrance and an excellent cafe.

Musée Andafivaratra
MUSEUM

(Map p42; Ar10,000; ⊙9am-4pm Tue-Sun) Housed in a magnificent pink baroque palace, this museum is the former home of Prime Minister Rainilaiarivony, the power behind the throne of the three queens he married in succession (Rasoherina, Ranavalona II and Ranavalona III) between 1864 and 1895. The museum's collection is a spare, dusty assortment of memorabilia from Merina (a tribal group) kings and queens, but the upper floors remain closed and labelling is poor.

Presidential Palace
HISTORIC BUILDING

(Map p50; Rue Rainilaiarivony) This beautiful 19th-century manor was an official French residence for many years. It became the Malagasy presidential palace in 1975 and remained so until president Didier Ratsiraka decided to build a more modern complex about 15km south of the capital in 1991. The mansion remains an official residence but is generally quiet. No photos allowed.

Parc de Tsarasaotra　　WILDLIFE RESERVE
(Lac Alarobia; Ar15,000; ⊘6am-6pm) Lake Alarobia may be located at the heart of Antananarivo's industrial area, but it is a vital refuge and nesting site for 14 threatened endemic bird species such as the Madagascar pond heron, Meller's duck and Madagascar little grebe. The site is classified Ramsar (International Convention on Wetlands), a treaty that highlights the importance and fragility of wetlands and protects key sites. Unless you're a birder, the place will have only limited appeal.

Gare Soarano　　NOTABLE BUILDING
(Map p50; Ave de l'Indépendance) Tana's old train station doesn't see much passenger traffic these days, so the lovely building has been converted into a small, upmarket shopping centre. There are regular art shows of works by Malagasy artists, as well as chi-chi boutiques and a couple of more prosaic shops (airlines, telecoms etc).

Lac Anosy　　LAKE
(Map p42) Antananarivo's heart-shaped lake lies in the southern part of town. It's particularly lovely in October, when the jacaranda trees lining its shores are covered in purple blossoms. On an island connected to the shore by a causeway stands a large golden angel on a plinth, the Monument aux Morts (Monument to the Dead), a WWI memorial erected by the French. It is currently not advised to walk in this area so the best way to appreciate Anosy is from the viewpoints in the Haute-Ville.

Analakely Market　　MARKET
(Map p50; Ave Andrianampoinimerina; ⊘6am-5pm) Antananarivo's main market is a shadow of the former *zoma* (market), for which the capital was legendary, but you'd only realise this if you came back in its glory days. It's still a packed, teeming place, selling clothes, household items, dodgy DVDs and every food product you could imagine, plus a few you probably couldn't. Don't bring any valuables with you.

Musée d'Art et d'Archéologie　　MUSEUM
(Map p50; Rue Dok Villette; ⊘9am-4pm Mon-Sat) `FREE` This small, dusty museum in Isoraka gives an overview of archaeological digs around the island, including displays of grave decorations from the south (known as *aloalo*), rotating exhibits on Malagasy life (cooking, music etc), and a few talismans and objects used in traditional ceremonies. A tip for the guide (if there is one) is customary. There was a minor facelift happening in part of the building when we visited, so hopefully the experience will improve.

HIRA GASY

Traditional Malagasy performances of acrobatics, music and speeches, *hira gasy* events are held most Sunday afternoons in the villages around Antananarivo. Check newspapers for details: entry is generally very cheap (around Ar1000), and the experience is great fun.

Tana's regional tourist office Ortana (p54) also organises a *hira gasy* (2pm to 5pm Sunday, August and September). Check the venue. In 2019 it was held in the grounds of the Rova in the Haute-Ville in an effort to revive the tradition. It is free to attend, although spectators normally throw small notes (Ar100 or Ar200 for instance) to show their appreciation.

🏃 Activities

Spas, massages and treatments are good value in Tana, and there are plenty of options to choose from.

Balnéoforme Spa Colbert (Map p50; 📞020 22 625 71; www.hotel-restaurant-colbert. com; 29 Rue Prince Ratsimamanga, Hôtel Colbert; Ar75,000; ⊘6.30am-8.30pm Mon-Sat, from 10am Sun) For a truly indulgent experience, try this fantastic spa with a mosaic swimming pool, Finnish sauna and Turkish bath. The entrance fee also gives you access to the gym. For additional pampering, there is a treatment list an arm long. It's not cheap (Ar50,000 to Ar150,000), but worth it if you've just arrived back in Tana after some hard hiking.

Le Royal Palissandre Spa (Map p50; 📞020 22 605 60; www.hotel-restaurant-palissandre.com/spa; 13 Rue Andriandahifotsy; ⊘9am-9pm) A gorgeous spa, with a beautiful heated outdoor pool and a hammam (Turkish bath); a number of treatments such as massages, scrubs and facials are available (from Ar90,000).

Antananarivo

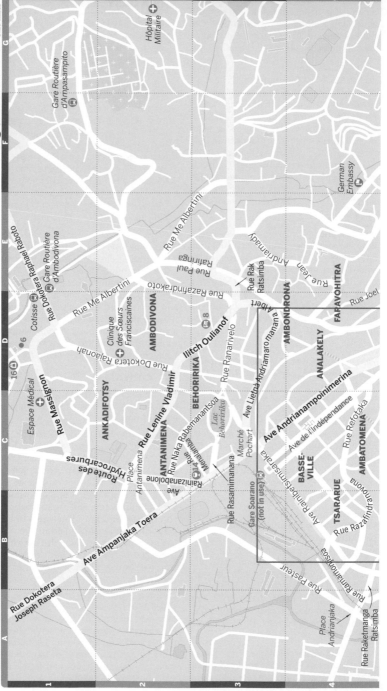

Rue Dokotera Joseph Raseta

Ave Ampanjaka Toera

Rue Raketmanga Ratsimba

Place Andrianjaka

Rue Ramamonjisoa

Rue Pasteur

Gare Soarano (not in use)

Rue Rasamimanana

Ave Rainizanabolone

Rue Naka Rabemanantsoa

Metallurgie

Place Antanimena

Route des Hydrocarbures

Rue Lenine Vladimir

ANTANIMENA

ANKADIFOTSY

Rue Massignon

Espace Médical

Cotisse Rue Dokotera Raphael Raboto

Gare Routière d'Ambodivona

Rue Me Albertini

Clinique des Sœurs Franciscaines

Rue Dokotera Rajaonah

AMBODIVONA

BEHORIRIKA

Lac Behoririka

Ilitch Oulianof

Rue Ranarivelo

Rue Razafindrakoto

Rue Paul Rahiringa

Rue Me Albertini

Gare Routière d'Ampasampito

Hôpital Militaire

German Embassy

Rue Rak Ratsimba

Rue Jean Andriamady

Rue Joel

FARAVOHITRA

AMBONDRONA

Albert

Ave Lietna Andriamaromanana

ANALAKELY

Ave Andrianampoinimerina

Ave de l'Indépendance

Marché Pochart

Ave Rainibetsimisaraka

BASSE-VILLE

Rue Refotaka

AMBATOMENA

TSARARUE

Rue Razafindriovona

Rue Razafindri

N

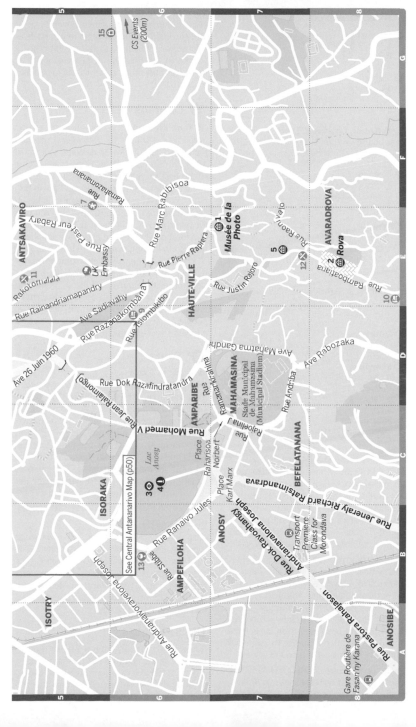

ANTANANARIVO

ISOTRY

ISORAKA

Ave 26 Juin 1960

Rue Andrianjafinjavelona Joseph

AMPEFILOHA

See Central Antananarivo Map (p50)

Rue Dok Razafindratandra

Rue Razanakombàna

Rue Rainandriamapandry

Ave Sadiavahy

ANTSAKAVIRO

Rakotomalala

UK Embassy

Rue Pasteur Rabary

Rue Ramahazomanana

Rue Marc Rabibisoa

Rue Pierre Rapiera

HAUTE-VILLE

Rue Justin Rajoro

Musée de la Photo

AVARADROVA

Rova

Rue Raonijo

Rue Ramboatiana

Rue Islombikibo

Rue Mohamed V

AMPARIBE

Rue Ramanankrahna

Rue Rajoelina

Ave Mahatma Gandhi

MAHAMASINA

Stade Municipal de Mahamasina (Municipal Stadium)

Rue Andriba

Ave Rabozaka

BEFELATANANA

Rue Jeneraly Richard Ratsimandrava

Place Norbert Raharisoa

Place Karl Marx

ANOSY

Rue Dok Ravoahangy Andrianavalona Joseph

Transport Premiere Class for Morondava

ANOSIBE

Rue Pastora Rahajason

Gare Routière de Fasan'ny Karana

Lac Anosy

Rue Ranaivo Jules

Rue Stübe

AMPEFILOHA

CS Events (200m)

Antananarivo

Vaniala Natural Spa (Map p42; ☑020 22 207 71, 034 49 151 70; www.vaniala-naturalspa. com; Antsakaviro; ⊙9am-6pm Mon-Sat, to 1pm Sun) Vaniala has the full range of beauty treatments, massages and natural products. There are a number of outposts around the city, but this one, close to the German embassy is reasonably accessible.

ArômBio (Map p50; ☑034 21 295 53; 54 Rue Ramanantsoa; ⊙8am-6pm Mon-Sat, 8.30am-12.30pm Sun) As well as selling local oils and bath, spa and spice products, ArômBio offers massages (30 to 90 minutes, Ar35,000 to Ar90,000), facials, scrubs, reiki, manicures and pedicures. Standards have slipped a little after a change in name and management, but it's still an OK choice.

Homeopharma (Map p50; ☑034 49 150 58; www.facebook.com/homeopharma.mg; 47 Rue Ratsimilaho; ⊙8am-6pm Mon-Fri, to 5pm Sat)

The state-approved natural-health chain Homeopharma has outlets all over Tana and throughout the country; many, such as this branch, which was undergoing renovations at the time of our last visit, offer massages and other treatments (Ar15,000 to Ar20,000).

🎓 Courses

⭐**Tana Kitchen**   COOKING
(Map p50; ☑032 05 145 00; www.tana kitchen.mg; 2nd fl, Rue Jean Jaurès; adult/child Ar150,000/60,000; ⊙10am-2.30pm Mon-Sat) One of the best ways to spend time in Tana, this small cooking school teaches you how to prepare, cook and eat three Malagasy dishes. If you arrange with them in advance, you can, for no extra cost, join them at 10am for a trip to a local market for the necessary supplies – itself a fascinating insight into local life.

Landy is an engaging and knowledgeable teacher, and enlivens the lunch with descriptions of local culinary and family traditions. Classes can be in English, French or German, and families are welcome. A minimum of two people are required, but they may be able to add you to an existing group.

🧭 Tours

Tany Mena Tours   TOURS
(Map p50; ☑020 22 326 27; www.tany mena-tours.com; Ave 26 Juin 1960) This agency specialises in sustainable tourism and offers highly original tours around Antananarivo. Tours combine history and culture, such as visits to local villages or traditional artisan workshops, *famadihana* (exhumation and reburial, literally 'the turning of the bones') ceremonies etc (from €40 per person per day). Most tours are led by trained historians or anthropologists (some English-speaking).

Boogie Pilgrim   TOURS
(Map p42; ☑020 22 248 47; www.boogie pilgrim-madagascar.com; Tana Water Front, Bâtiment Trio Property, Ambodivona; ⊙office 8am-noon & 1-5pm Mon-Fri) Adventurous ecotours and camps in several places in Madagascar, including Parc National Andringitra. English and German spoken.

🛏 Sleeping

Accommodation in Tana is pricier than in the rest of the country, but quality is generally high across all price categories, less so at budget level. Advance bookings are recommended. A number of hotels offer 'day rates', which allow guests to keep their room until early evening, as many flights out of the country leave late at night.

★ **Madagascar Underground** HOSTEL €
(Map p50; ☏ 034 29 909 07, 034 20 019 83; www.madagascarunderground.com; 18 Lalana Rainitovo; dm €8, d €18-22, d bungalows €20, f €25; ☏) Budget travellers rejoice! This brilliant Australian-Malagasy hostel fills a long-empty niche in the city, with excellent rooms, male and female dorms and a real hostel buzz utterly unlike anywhere else in Madagascar. The restaurant (mains from Ar6000), open to nonguests, serves good Mexican food, including a mean breakfast burrito, and there's live music many nights from 7pm.

Hôtel Moonlight HOTEL €
(Map p50; ☏ 020 22 268 70; hasinaherizo@yahoo.fr; 62 Rue Rainandriamapandry; r Ar24,000-44,000; ☏) This budget stalwart is an excellent option in a lively part of town. Rooms have brightly coloured walls, parquet floors and new bathrooms (most rooms have showers but share toilets; just a couple have private bathrooms). The staff is friendly and there are two large communal terraces from where you can watch the world go by. It's often full.

★ **Hôtel Niaouly** HOTEL €€
(Map p42; ☏ 020 22 627 65; www.niaouly.com; Rue Tsiombikibo; r Ar48,000-72,000; ☏) Between the beautiful Haute-Ville and the trendy bars and restaurants of Isoraka, the Niaouly punches well above its weight for the price. The rooms are pretty with polished wooden floors, Malagasy crafts and modern bathroom (the cheaper rooms are very dark, however) – the more you pay, the better the room and view. There's a panoramic terrace and good restaurant.

Hôtel Tana-Jacaranda GUESTHOUSE €€
(Map p50; ☏ 034 22 562 39, 020 22 694 63; www.tana-jacaranda.com; 24 Rue Rainitsarovy; dm €8, s €10-15, d €14-22, f €33; @ ☏) Rooms at this superfriendly, family-run hotel are simple, quiet and clean. There is also a tip-top dining room with fabulous views of the Rova (p40) and the Haute-Ville, piping-hot water in the showers, good wi-fi, a guest computer and wonderfully helpful multilingual staff.

Chez Francis HOTEL €€
(Map p50; ☏ 020 22 613 65; hotelchezfrancis@yahoo.fr; Rue Rainandriamapandry; d Ar45,000-60,000, f Ar75,000; ☏) This great-value establishment hasn't changed much in years,

and we're not complaining. While the rooms are a little tired, that's easy to ignore in the west-facing rooms, which have what could be Tana's best views, and small balconies from which to enjoy them. The family rooms are larger, so might be worth reserving even if there's only two of you.

Le Karthala PENSION €€
(Map p50; ☏ 020 22 248 95, 033 11 971 56; 48 Rue Andriandahifotsy; s/d/tr incl breakfast €21/24/31; ☏) The Karthala's motto is 'a little bit like home', and Arianne and her family certainly have a way of making guests feel welcome. The rooms are well kept and homely, there is a gorgeous roof terrace on which to relax or sip a drink, and guests can use the kitchen.

★ **Grand Hotel Urban** BOUTIQUE HOTEL €€€
(Map p50; ☏ 020 22 209 80; www.grandhotelurbanmadagascar.com; 12 Rue Lalana Tsiombikibo; d €93-126; ❋ ☏) Easily one of Tana's best hotels, Grand Hotel Urban has stunning white rooms, most with glorious views out over the city. An excellent restaurant, bar and supremely comfortable rooms with all the amenities round out an outstanding package.

★ **Citizen** BOUTIQUE HOTEL €€€
(Map p50; ☏ 034 05 720 60; www.citizen-guesthouse.com; 12 Rue d'Angleterre, Isoraka; r/ste €65/78; ❋ ☏) With just three rooms and a palpable sense of quiet sophistication, the Citizen has gorgeous rooms lightly sprinkled with antiques and each with a balcony overlooking the lake. There's a terrific on-site café-restaurant, service is attentive and there's real attention to detail.

★ **Chez Aina** GUESTHOUSE €€€
(Map p42; ☏ 034 12 188 12; www.chezaina.com; Ilitch Oulianof; r €26-52; ❋ ☏) This place is a real find. Inhabiting a traditional Malagasy home, the five rooms are individually (and beautifully) decorated and there's a gorgeous garden. It serves delicious Malagasy meals and has strong roots in the local community. Aina is a delightful host.

★ **Lokanga** BOUTIQUE HOTEL €€€
(Map p42; ☏ 020 22 235 49; www.lokanga-hotel.mg; Haute Ville; r from €105; ☏) This superb 1930s house, a stone's throw from the Rova (p40), has been lovingly renovated by owner Fabiola Deprez and furnished with exquisite taste (many of the antiques belonged to her family). There are just five rooms, each with a theme and sweeping views of the city from the shared terraces.

Le Pavillon de l'Emyrne
BOUTIQUE HOTEL €€€

(Map p50; ☑020 22 259 45; www.pavillonde lemyrne.com; 12 Rue Rakotonirina; s/d/ste incl breakfast from €69/79/109; ✳@🛜) In a beautiful 1920s house, the Emyrne has a handful of rooms with an exclusive feel. Each has been individually decorated with a refined mix of vintage and modern. Some rooms have their own garden or veranda. Those on the lower ground floor are a little dark, however. Rates also include complimentary massages.

Hôtel Sakamanga
BOUTIQUE HOTEL €€€

(Map p50; ☑020 22 358 09; www.sakamanga.com; Rue Andrianary Ratianarivo; d €21-52, ste €60-81, apt €105; ✳@🛜🏊) A perennial favourite, the Sakamanga offers fantastic accommodation for both midrange and top-end travellers who set store by a friendly atmosphere, varied rooms, characterful decor and comprehensive services. The intriguingly mazy layout (with enough artefacts in the corridors to stock a museum) leads to an unexpected pool with bar and terrace. Reserve well in advance, as it is often full.

Résidence Lapasoa
BOUTIQUE HOTEL €€€

(Map p50; ☑020 22 611 40; www.lapasoa.com; 15 Rue Réunion; d Ar157,500-192,500, ste Ar245,000; ✳@🛜) The exquisite Lapasoa is a modern twist on colonial decor: there are polished wood floors, beautiful wooden furniture (including stunning four-poster beds in some rooms), colourful fabrics and light flooding in from skylights and big windows. The top-floor rooms, with their high, sloped ceilings, are the loveliest. The same owners run the superb Kudéta (p48) restaurant next door.

🍴 Eating

⭐Toko Telo
MALAGASY €

(Map p50; ☑034 10 763 79, 020 24 657 47; 2nd fl, Rue Jean Jaurès; mains Ar8000-18,000; ⊙9am-5pm Mon-Sat) Run by Landy, the teacher at Tana Kitchen (p44) cooking school with which this restaurant shares premises, Toko Telo is our pick to try expertly crafted Malagasy specialities. In addition to soups, there are pork, zebu, seafood and chicken mains, as well as sorbets (try the baobab flavour) and pastries. For a real local delicacy, try the *zanadandy,* fried local caterpillars.

L'Orient
ASIAN €

(Map p50; ☑034 36 788 88; Rue Andriandahifotsy; mains Ar12,000; ⊙noon-8pm Mon-Sat) Fabulous pan-Asian fusion in a casual cafe setting make L'Orient a real find. Dumplings with ginger, creative salads and terrific rice and noodle dishes – it's all good and our pick in Tana for Asian food.

Mad'Délices
MALAGASY €

(Map p50; Rue Ramanantsoa; mains Ar5000-8500; ⊙6am-6.30pm Mon-Sat; 🍴) This cheerful little restaurant in the heart of Isoraka serves hearty Malagasy meals such as pork with greens, zebu stew and omelettes. It's also a good place for breakfast: the pastries are excellent and there is an espresso machine. It doesn't look like much, but it's all about the food.

Saka Express
CAFE €

(Map p50; ☑020 22 358 09; www.sakamanga.com; Rue Andrianary Ratianarivo; mains Ar8000-18,000; ⊙11am-9pm; 🛜🍴) The snack cafeteria and takeaway outlet in Hôtel Sakamanga is the best place in town for lunch on the go. There are pizzas, kebabs and sandwiches, all bursting at the seams with fillings. There are a few tables inside, which fill quickly at lunchtime. Delivery to nearby hotels is possible.

Leader Price
SANDWICHES €

(Map p50; ☑034 47 177 33; www.leaderprice. mg; Ave Rabehevitra; cakes/sandwiches from Ar3000/6000; ⊙9am-7.30pm Mon-Sat, to 1pm Sun; 🍴) This supermarket chain churns out excellent (and great-value) sandwiches, quiches, tarts and cakes; take away for a picnic or eat in the cafe upstairs.

⭐Le Saka
FUSION €€

(Map p50; ☑020 22 358 09; www.sakamanga. com; Rue Andrianary Ratianarivo, Hôtel Sakamanga; mains Ar15,000-32,000; ⊙noon-3pm & 6.30-10pm) Striking the perfect balance between gastro French and straightforward local cooking, Le Saka is a Tana institution. The restaurant is housed in a gorgeous wooden house full of old black-and-white photos and local artwork. The chef whips up some mighty desserts using Malagasy chocolate. Make sure you finish your meal with a house rum or coconut punch. Booking essential.

⭐Nerone Ristorante Italiano
ITALIAN €€

(Map p50; ☑020 22 231 18; www.facebook.com/ neroneristoranteitaliano; Rue Ratsimilaho; mains Ar16,000-26,000; ⊙noon-2pm & 6.45-10.45pm) Tana's best Italian restaurant is one of those places you'll find yourself coming back to time and again. Artful Italian cooking of pasta, pizza, meat and fish leave plenty of room for

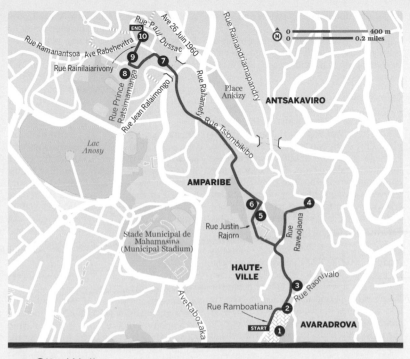

City Walk
Antananarivo Walking Tour

START POINT DE VUE DU ROVA
END PL DE L'INDÉPENDANCE
LENGTH 2.5KM; ONE HOUR

This walk starts at the viewpoint below the Rova, so you could combine it with a visit to the palace or come straight here by taxi (Ar20,000 from the centre). Security in the area has improved markedly in recent years, but ask locals or the tourist office about the current situation. The views from the lookout below the **1 Rova** (p40) make it clear why the city's rulers decided to build their palace here: the Malagasy landscape unfolds for kilometres in every direction.

A few hundred metres downhill, on your right-hand side, you'll find a **2 bas-relief** (1940) by Malagasy artist Charles Rabemanantsoa that tells the history of Madagascar. Rabemanantsoa trained at the school of fine arts, which used to be in what is now **3 Musée Andafivaratra** (p40), the magnificent pink baroque palace of Prime Minister Rainilaiarivony (r 1864–1895). From here, wend your way north down the hill, detouring en route 100m east to the excellent

4 Musée de la Photo (p40). Return the way you came, then down to the reconstruction of **5 Jean Laborde's house**, a beautiful wooden building that served as Madagascar's first French consulate. At the end of the street is **6 Cathédrale de l'Immaculée Conception**, which was built on the spot where Queen Ranavalona I ordered Christian martyrs to be thrown from the cliffs. From here, amble down through the Haute-Ville's quiet lanes to **7 Rue Ratsimilaho**, famous for its jewellers. Turn left on Rue Prince Ratsimamanga to have a look at the old **8 Presidential Palace** (p40), with its white, green and red sentry boxes that match the Malagasy flag colours; at night, the fountains at the front are lit with multicoloured spotlights, adding a trendy touch to the classic facade.

Head up Rue Rainilaiarivony, where you'll see a **9 memorial** to the victims of the 7 February 2009 riots, which eventually led to Andry Rajoelina overthrowing president Marc Ravalomanana. Finish your walk on shady Pl de l'Indépendance – the friendly **10 Buffet du Jardin** (p49) is the perfect place to relax with a THB (Madagascar's signature beer).

choice, the dining area is stylish and softly lit, and the service friendly.

In fact, we can't think of a reason not to come here, and locals agree – it's become something of a meeting place for Tana's young and cool.

Cafe du Musée   CAFE €€

(Map p42; ☑ 032 07 090 40; Lalana Andriamanalina, Musée de la Photo; mains Ar17,000-33,000; ⊗ 10am-10pm Wed-Mon; 🖘) This excellent place next to the entrance of Musée de la Photo (p40) has soft lighting, assured cooking and friendly service. The menu is predominantly French but has a few Malagasy and vegetarian options, ranging from stuffed crab, lobster curry and seared duck breast with chocolate sauce and caramelised apple to pork with crushed cassava leaves.

Le Phare   FRENCH €€

(Map p50; ☑ 020 26 323 28; Rue Rakotonirina, Isoraka; mains Ar8500-21,000; ⊗ 11am-3pm & 6-10pm Tue-Sun) For a real slice of France down the lower end of Isoraka, this Breton crêperie does all manner of savoury galettes and sweet crêpes, allowing you to take care of all of your cravings in one place. Ingredients range from quality French cheeses to zebu.

Grill du Rova   INTERNATIONAL €€

(Map p42; ☑ 020 22 627 24; Rue Ramboatiana; mains Ar12,500-28,500, Sun menu Ar45,000; ⊗ noon-5pm; 🖉) Not content with having one of the loveliest locations in town (just 100m from the Rova (p40), with great views), Grill du Rova serves delicious food, including homemade pasta, brochettes, vegetarian dishes and Malagasy specialities such as *romazava* (beef and vegetable stew) and tilapia. It's especially popular on Sundays when it sometimes has live music and dancing (set menu only).

Chez Sucett's   CREOLE €€

(Map p50; ☑ 020 22 261 00; 23 Rue Raveloary; mains Ar18,000-30,000; ⊗ noon-2.30pm & 7-10pm Mon-Sat, 7-10pm Sun) Sucett's popularity has somewhat slipped recently, but it's still a good choice. The Malagasy and Creole (a blend of African, Asian and European influences) dishes are still good but steer clear of the Asian dishes that aren't as well executed. We enjoyed the duck with olives and Creole sauce and looked longingly at the zebu steak.

La Terrasse du Glacier   MALAGASY €€

(Map p50; www.hotel-glacier.com; Annexe Le Glacier, 2nd fl, Ave de l'Indépendance; mains Ar14,000-

30,000; ⊗ noon-3pm & 6-10pm) Perched on a 2nd floor above Ave de l'Indépendance, La Terrasse is a fantastic vantage point to admire the hustle and bustle of Tana's main thoroughfare. The delicious food is Malagasy with a hint of French, with dishes such as tilapia in ginger and spring onion and zebu *romazava* (traditional Malagasy beef-and-vegetable stew).

★ Lokanga   INTERNATIONAL €€€

(Map p42; ☑ 020 22 235 49; www.lokanga-hotel.mg; Haute Ville; mains Ar25,000-26,000; ⊗ noon-3pm & 7-9.30pm Wed-Sun) In a stunning setting whichever way you look – the 19th-century building or the city views from the terrace – Lokanga serves a mix of Malagasy and international dishes. Try the duck breast with pineapple reduction, seafood *romazava* or zebu chimichurri. Professional service rounds out a fine culinary experience.

★ La Varangue   INTERNATIONAL €€€

(Map p50; ☑ 020 22 273 97; www.hotel-restaurant-lavarangue-tananarive.com; 17 Rue Prince Ratsimamanga; mains Ar34,000-40,000, 2-/3-course lunch menu Ar65,000/85,000; ⊗ noon-2.30pm & 7-10pm; 🖘) One of the best addresses in the city for real gourmet cuisine, La Varangue serves an elaborate melange of French gastronomy and Malagasy flavours. Meals are served either in the beautiful dining room, with its low lighting and fabulous antique collection, or on the terrace, which overlooks a charming garden. Booking is advised.

Highlights from the menu include quail stuffed with mushrooms or seafood en papillote with lemongrass scent. Admire the antique saxophones and cars on your way in.

Kudéta   FUSION €€€

(Map p50; ☑ 032 07 611 40, 020 22 611 40; www.kudeta.mg; 16 Rue Réunion; mains Ar20,000-47,000, 2-course lunch menu Ar29,000; ⊗ noon-2pm & 7-10pm Mon-Sat, 7-10pm Sun; 🖘) Playing on the region's reputation for political instability may not be very PC, but it really would take a coup d'état to unseat this stylish bar-restaurant from its position among the top of Tana's eating scene. The menu makes imaginative use of local ingredients, creating a sophisticated fusion cuisine that suits the chic ethnic decor perfectly. Bookings are advisable. The zebu is a recurring theme – with foie gras, in carpaccio form, ribs – but the menu is always assured; try the chocolate *coulant* with lime sorbet for dessert. There's a kids menu, and a couple of vegetarian choices.

TANA'S CAFE CULTURE

Whether it's a remnant of French influence or a sign that Tananarivians have a sweet tooth, the Malagasy capital has a number of cafes, some in a league of their own when it comes to cakes and pastries.

Pâtisserie Colbert (Map p50; ☑ 020 22 219 52; www.patisseriecolbert.com; Rue Prince Ratsimamanga, Hôtel Colbert; pastries Ar3000-9000, sandwiches & quiches Ar5500-16,000; ☺ 7am-7pm; ☏) This excellent patisserie is a popular meeting place for local business-people and a great place for breakfast, a quick lunch or an afternoon treat – the cake selection is mouthwatering, and the ice creams are very popular too. It also sells gourmet chocolates, which make fantastic presents.

Bread Mafan' (Map p50; ☑ 032 05 668 57; www.facebook.com/breadmafan; Rue Andrianary Ratianarivo; breakfast Ar10,000; ☺ 6am-8.30pm; ☏) Part patisserie, part cafe, Bread Mafan' is a cool choice if you're stocking up for a picnic. It has great breads, a range of enticing pastries and sweets, and it does breakfast, good coffee and a selection of teas. There's a small but carefully chosen range of packaged gourmet delicacies as well.

La Potinière (Map p50; Ave de l'Indépendance; cakes from Ar1000; ☺ 7am-7pm Mon-Sat, to noon Sun) This Chinese-run bakery heaves at weekends, when locals come for a treat. As well as pastries, it has quiches and sandwiches for a light lunch. It's a more earthy choice than the upmarket patisseries, but the clientele is also more diverse.

Chez Mariette MALAGASY €€€
(Map p42; ☑ 020 22 216 02; Rue Rakotomalala; menu Ar60,000; ☺ 7-10pm) Superchef Mariette Andrianjaka has cooked for notables as diverse as Paloma Picasso and Prince Albert of Monaco during her long career. These days she entertains guests in her 19th-century villa, preparing elaborate multicourse set meals based on *haifi* cuisine – traditional royal banquets. Advance reservation is mandatory. Chez Mariette is up in the Haute-Ville – taxis know where to find it.

Drinking & Nightlife

Tana has a lively nightlife, with a number of good bars and busy nightclubs. Beer and rum are the tipples of choice and live music is a popular fixture in many establishments. Most nightclubs in Tana are packed with sex workers, so unaccompanied guys can expect a bit of unsolicited attention.

Kudéta Urban Club LOUNGE
(Map p42; ☑ 020 22 611 40; www.facebook.com/kudetamadagascar; off Rue Stibbe, Hôtel Carlton, Anosy; ☺ noon-late Mon-Sat) Tana's most exclusive (and expensive) bar turns from bar-lounge during the day to nightclub–DJ platform as the night draws in; there are regular parties and events.

Madagascar Underground BAR
(Map p50; ☑ 034 29 909 07, 034 20 019 83; 18 Lalana Rainitovo; ☺ 6am-midnight) This cool traveller hang-out is a fun bar to pass the night,

but keep an eye out for live music many nights at 7pm when local musicians take to the small stage. An intimate, fun venue and a good place to meet other travellers.

Le Club CLUB
(Map p42; ☑ 020 22 651 00; www.facebook.com/leclubantanimena; Ave Rainizanabolone; Ar5000; ☺ 10pm-5am Fri & Sat) Tana's biggest, flashiest club space, with modern design, has a DJ spinning recent tunes from the lofty winged booth above the dance floor.

Manson BAR
(Map p50; Rue Ramanantsoa; ☺ 7pm-late) The clientele in this trendy bar can be a little seedy. It's a shame because the graffiti decor is fun and the music will have you on your feet.

Buffet du Jardin BAR
(Map p50; ☑ 020 22 338 87; www.lebuffetdujardin-antananarivo.com; Pl de l'Indépendance; ☺ 7am-11pm Sun-Thu, 24hr Fri & Sat; ☏) This long-standing bar is a firm favourite among locals, expats and tourists alike for anything from a morning coffee to evening drinks or a night out (it serves good food). There is live music on Thursdays, Fridays and Saturdays, and happy hour is at 6pm Thursdays and Saturdays.

☆ Entertainment

Cinepax CINEMA
(Map p42; ☑ 034 05 735 01; www.cinepax.mg; Tana Water Front; adult/child weekdays Ar25,000/15,000, weekends Ar30,000/15,000)

Central Antananarivo

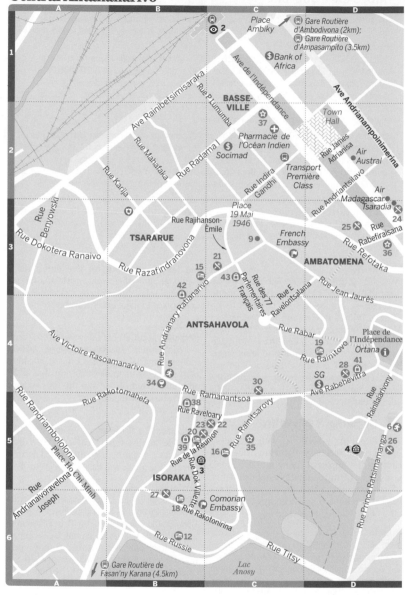

Madagascar's premier multiplex cinema shows new releases subtitled in French as soon as they're released internationally. Other films are dubbed in French. It's on the ground floor of the Tana Water Front (p53).

Institut Français Madagascar PERFORMING ARTS

(Map p50; 020 22 213 75; www.institutfrancais-madagascar.com; 14 Ave de l'Indépendance; tickets from Ar3000; office 8.30am-12.15pm & 2-6pm Mon-Fri) Antananarivo's foremost cultural

Central Antananarivo

◎ Sights

⊕ Activities, Courses & Tours

⊜ Sleeping

⊗ Eating

⊜ Drinking & Nightlife

✪ Entertainment

⊜ Shopping

venue hosts excellent concerts, theatre events, dance performances, art exhibitions and film screenings almost daily. Pop in to pick up the bimonthly schedule or check it online. Booking is recommended for most of the shows.

ℹ WHAT'S ON

To find out what's going on and where, buy any of the three national daily newspapers (*Midi Madagasikara, Madagascar Tribune* and *L'Express de Madagascar*); all have advertisements for upcoming events, particularly in the Friday issue. Posters around town also give notice of forthcoming concerts. Other resources include the free listings magazines *Sortir à Tana* (www.sortir atana.com) and *No Comment* (www. nocomment.mg) which you will find in many hotels and restaurants in town.

Hôtel Le Glacier LIVE MUSIC
(Map p50; www.hotel-glacier.com/calendar; Ave 26 Juin 1960; Ar5000; ⊘6pm-2am) This slightly disreputable bar has cabaret, bands and traditional music performances every night of the week; it's always full and the atmosphere is good.

Antsahamanitra CONCERT VENUE
(Théâtre de Verdure; Map p50; Ave Rainitsarovy) This amphitheatre has occasional shows featuring artists from the Malagasy charts, as well as regular gospel-music or church-choir concerts that set the crowd on fire. Tickets are generally very cheap, and the crowd predominantly local.

🛍 Shopping

The shopping in Tana is excellent (if spread out), with souvenirs from across the country as well as original boutiques. Croc Farm (p57) has an excellent shop too. The city has a couple of shopping malls, including Tana Water Front (p53). English books are hard to come by: your best bets are hotel libraries and swap shelves.

Marché Artisanal de La Digue GIFTS & SOUVENIRS
(La Digue; ⊘9am-5.30pm) A popular place to pick up souvenirs is this market located about 12km out of town on a bend in the Ivato airport road. There are products from all over the country, including embroidered tablecloths, raffia products, woodcarvings, spices, vanilla, gemstones etc. Bargaining is essential – divide the initial price by three or four and work from there. A taxi (around Ar20,000 return) is the easiest way to get here and back with your purchases. Otherwise, if you're going to the airport with a taxi, leave an hour early and stop on your way there. Cash only.

La Chocolaterie Robert CHOCOLATE
(Map p50; ☎032 11 205 83; www.chocolaterie robert.com; Ave Rabehevitra; ⊘9.30am-6pm Mon-Sat, 10am-2pm Sun) Madagascar's most celebrated chocolate maker has a lovely little boutique next to the Leader supermarket within sight of Pl de l'Indépendance. Some of the pieces can be bought individually, there are some already packaged, and the only problem is choosing what to buy. If only all of life's decisions were so pleasurable.

Épicerie Fine La Ferme de Morarano FOOD & DRINKS
(Map p50; ☎020 24 798 47; www.ladistillerie dumaido.com/madagascar.html; Rue Russie; ⊘8am-6pm Mon-Sat) This shop sells the products of an organic farm in the highlands. It specialises in essential oils, which its uses in a range of natural lotions and potions (moisturiser, shampoo, soap etc). You can also buy the oils themselves in small bottles, along with artisan jams, chutneys and spices.

Lisy Art Gallery GIFTS & SOUVENIRS
(Map p42; ☎033 14 085 00; Rte du Mausolée; ⊘8am-6pm Mon-Fri, to noon Sat) This huge shop stocks anything and everything you could possibly want to bring back from Madagascar, from bottles of *rhum arrangé* (rum with macerated fruit) to leather goods, raffia baskets, hats and spices. The only thing you won't find are gemstones. Prices are fixed but reasonable. It's a short taxi ride from the centre (Ar10,000 one way). Card payments accepted. It has recently expanded across the road.

La Boutique GIFTS & SOUVENIRS
(Map p50; ☎020 22 605 60; Rue Andriandahifotsy; ⊘8.30am-6pm Mon-Sat) This pleasing little shop sells a stylish array of gifts, from baskets and scarves to baobab-themed ornaments.

Pili Pili Dock FOOD & DRINKS
(Map p42; ☎020 22 327 96; cammercial@made-pices.mg; Tana Water Front; ⊘9am-6pm Mon-Sat, to 1pm Sun) If you'd like a gourmet souvenir from Madagascar, look no further than Pili Pili Dock. The boutique is stunning and everything is beautifully packaged – spices, condiments, soaps, essential oils and more. Prices are obviously higher than in a market, but you pay for the presentation and the convenience.

Kudeta Etnik Shop FASHION & ACCESSORIES
(Map p50; Rue Isoraka; ⊘9.30am-12.30pm & 1.30-5.30pm Mon-Sat) A gorgeous boutique stocking high-end, well-finished Malagasy products such as raffia baskets and purses, silk scarves,

jewellery, framed photographs and original clothes by Malagasy designers.

La Teeshirterie · CLOTHING

(Map p50; Rue Andrianary Ratianarivo; ⊙8am-6pm Mon-Sat, 9am-4pm Sun) By far the best place to come for Madagascar's funky T-shirts. You'll find all the main brands here (Baobab, Carambole, Maki etc), and a large choice of models and sizes. Credit cards accepted.

Roses & Baobab · ARTS & CRAFTS

(Map p50; ☑032 40 615 60; www.rosesetbaobab. com; Rue des 77 Parlementaires Français; ⊙9am-6pm Mon-Sat) A collective of 85 local artists showcasing sculptures, woodcarvings, paintings, metalwork and more. The quality varies, but it's worth poking your way around the warren of rooms in search of treasure.

CS Events · SPORTS & OUTDOORS

(☑034 01 234 53; www.csevents-madagascar.com; Rte du Mausolée, Andrainarivo; ⊙8am-12.30pm & 1.30-6pm Mon-Fri, 8am-1pm Sat) For hiking, camping gear and the like; there is a wide but expensive selection of international branded products.

Tana Water Front · MALL

(Map p42; www.tanawaterfront.mg; Ambodivona; ⊙9am 6.30pm Mon-Sat, to 1pm Sun) This modern shopping mall and office complex 2km north of the centre has a cinema (p49), boutiques, a food court, a Shoprite supermarket and ATMs.

ℹ Information

DANGERS & ANNOYANCES

➡ Insecurity has increased in Tana since the political events of 2009. It is not safe to walk after dark; you should always travel by taxi at night.

➡ Pickpocketing is rife around Ave de l'Indépendance and Analakely, so be very careful with your belongings.

➡ Touts posing as official guides prey on travellers who haven't arranged to be met at the airport; stick to the official taxi rank or book one through your hotel.

EMERGENCY

Ambulance	☑020 22 625 66
Fire	☑118
Police	☑117

INTERNET ACCESS

Every hotel in Tana offers free wi-fi (even if only in the reception area), as do an increasing number of bars and restaurants. The quality of the connection varies; it is usually good enough for emails and social media, but not necessarily for Skype or data-hungry downloads. You might find the occasional internet cafe around town (look for the @ symbol), but they're increasingly a thing of the past.

MEDICAL SERVICES

Clinique des Sœurs Franciscaines (Map p42; ☑020 22 235 54; Rue Dokotera Rajaonah, Ankadifotsy; ⊙24hr) Has X-ray equipment and is well run.

Dr Chapuis (☑032 07 154 19; Lalana Hydrocarbures; ⊙8am-12.30pm & 2 7pm Mon-Fri, 8am-1pm Sat) A reliable dentist.

Espace Médical (Map p42; ☑020 22 625 66, 24hr 034 02 009 11; www.espacemedical.mg; Ambodivona; ⊙8am-4pm Mon-Fri, 9.30am-3.30pm Sat, to 5pm Sun) A private clinic with 24-hour A&E, with laboratory and X-ray equipment; it organises medical repatriations.

Hôpital Militaire (Hospital Center De Soavinandriana; Map p42; ☑020 23 397 51; Rue Dokotera Moss, Soavinandriana; ⊙24hr) The best-equipped hospital in the country.

Pharmacie de l'Océan Indien (Map p50; ☑020 22 224 70; 18 Ave de l'Indépendance; ⊙8am-noon & 2-6pm Mon-Fri, 8am-noon Sat) Centrally located and well stocked.

Pharmacie du Roi (Map p42; ☑020 22 645 40, 033 15 695 40; Tana Water Front; ⊙9am 6.30pm Mon-Sat) Modern pharmacy at Tana Water Front.

Pharmacie Métropole (Map p50; ☑020 22 200 25; www.pharmacie-metropole.com; Rue Ratsimilaho; ⊙8am-12.30pm & 2-6.30pm Mon-Fri, 8am-noon Sat) One of Tana's best and most convenient pharmacies.

MONEY

All banks change foreign currencies, and most will change travellers cheques and offer cash advances on credit cards (both Visa and MasterCard). Virtually all have reliable ATMs although some aren't accessible outside banking hours.

ℹ SECURITY ESCORTS

Since 2013, some hotels, bars, restaurants and shops in the upmarket neighbourhoods of Isoraka and Antsahavola have hired private security firm COPS to improve safety in the area, and to keep clients coming. This is a boon for travellers staying in the area who want to get out of their hotel at night: COPS agents will simply escort you from your hotel to the bar/restaurant where you'd like to go (and escort you back at the end of the night).

Bank of Africa (BOA; Map p50; ☑ 020 22 277 09; www.boa.com; Ave de l'Indépendance; ⊙ 8am-4pm Mon-Fri) Visa-only ATM.

BNI Madagascar (Map p50; Ave 26 Juin 1960; ⊙ 8am-4pm) Has an ATM (Visa and Master-Card).

SG (Map p50; Rue Rabehevitra; ⊙ 8am-4pm Mon-Fri) Has an ATM for Visa and MasterCard.

Socimad (Map p50; Rue Radama I; ⊙ 8-11.45am & 2-4.45pm Mon-Fri, 8-11am Sat) Changes cash and travellers cheques. Also has a 24-hour office at the airport.

POST

Tana's two main post offices are in **Basse-Ville** (Map p50; www.paositramalagasy.mg; Ave 26 Juin 1960; ⊙ 8am-4pm Mon-Fri) and **Haute-Ville** (Map p50; Rue Ratsimilaho; ⊙ 8am-4pm Mon-Fri).

TOURIST INFORMATION

Ortana (Map p50; ☑ 034 20 270 51; www.tour-isme-antananarivo.com; Pl de l'Indépendance; ⊙ 9am-5pm) is an excellent and knowledgeable tourist office that can offer advice without any hard sells in French or English. This is also the place to go to if you would like a guide to visit historical sites around Tana. Most guides are knowledgeable and many speak English and/or Italian as well as French. Staff can also advise on other sights around the capital.

The office organises one- to three-hour group walks around the Haute-Ville at 9.30am, 10.30am and 2pm on Mondays, Wednesdays and Satur-

---

ⓘ IVATO AIRPORT

➡ The bureaux de change at Ivato airport offer similar rates to the banks in Tana; it also exchanges travellers cheques.

➡ BNI Madagascar at the terminal has an ATM that accepts both Visa and MasterCard.

➡ All three phone networks have booths in the arrivals area where you can buy a SIM card and credit.

➡ Ariary are not accepted in the departure area, even at the cafe (euros or US dollars only).

➡ To go to the airport, ask your hotel to book the shuttle (that way they can chase it if it's running late), and make sure you leave plenty of time as it's not possible to know how many pickups the shuttle will have to do before setting off or whether the traffic will be bad or terrible.

---

days (Ar5000 to Ar30,000 per person depending on the circuit and the number of people).

ⓘ Getting There & Away

AIR

You can get domestic and international flights to and from **Ivato Airport** (☑ 020 22 440 41). The following airlines have offices in Tana.

Air Austral (Map p50; ☑ 020 22 303 31; www.air-austral.com; 23 Ave de l'Indépendance) Serves France and Indian Ocean islands, including Madagascar, Réunion and Mauritius.

Air France (☑ 020 23 230 23; www.airfrance.mg; Tour Zital, Rte des Hydrocarbures, Ankorondrano; ⊙ 8.30am-5pm Mon-Fri) French carrier with five flights a week between Paris and Antananarivo.

Air Madagascar (Map p50; ☑ 020 22 510 00; www.airmadagascar.com; 31 Ave de l'Indépendance; ⊙ 7.30am-7pm Mon-Sat) Madagascar's national carrier.

Madagasikara Airways (☑ 032 05 970 07; www.madagasikaraairways.com; La City, Ivandry; ⊙ 8.30am-5pm Mon-Fri) Domestic and international flights.

Tsaradia (Map p50; ☑ 020 22 222 22; www.tsaradia.com; 31 Ave de l'Indépendance; ⊙ 7.30am-7pm Mon-Sat) Madagascar's largest network of domestic flights, most of which pass through Tana.

BUS

Cotisse (Map p42; ☑ 032 11 027 33; www.cotisse-transport.com; Ambodivona) Nice 16- or 19-seater Mercedes minibuses that link Antananarivo with Majunga (from Ar34,000, 11 hours, 7am, 8am, 8.30am and 6.30pm), Morondava (Ar45,000, 12 to 14 hours, 6.30am), Fianarantsoa (from Ar25,000, eight hours, 7am, 8am and 9am) and Toamasina (from Ar20,000, 10 hours, 8am, 9am and 8.30pm). Cotisse has its own terminal, with a modern waiting room. Departures are punctual.

Transport Première Class (Map p50; ☑ 034 22 588 88, 033 15 488 88; www.malagasycar.com; 3 Rue Indira Gandhi, Hôtel Le Grand Mellis) Runs comfortable, air-con vehicles only between Tana and Majunga (Ar78,000, 10 hours, 6.45am), Morondava (Ar118,000, 12 hours, 6am) or Ankify (Ar198,000, 14 hours, 6am). It sits just two people to a row and includes a packed lunch. Booking is essential. Departures are from the Hotel Le Grand Mellis for Majunga and Ankify, from the **Motel Anosy** (Map p42; Rue Dr Ravoahangy Andrianavalona) for Morondava.

Transpost (Map p50; Rue Ratsimilaho, Post Office; ⊙ 7.30am-5pm Mon-Fri, to noon Sat) More punctual than normal *taxis-brousses* (bush taxis), but similar in comfort and price, Transpost is run by Madagascar's postal service. It has minibuses between Majunga and Tana only

TAXIS-BROUSSES FROM ANTANANARIVO

DESTINATION	STATION	FARE (AR)	TIME (HR)	DEPARTURES
Ambanja	Ambodivona	60,000	19	Afternoon
Antsirabe	Fasan'ny Karana	10,000	4	All day
Diego Suarez (Antsiranana)	Ambodivona	74,000	28	Afternoon
Fianarantsoa	Fasan'ny Karana	26,000	10	Morning & afternoon
Fort Dauphin (Taolagnaro)	Fasan'ny Karana	100,000	60	Afternoon Tue & Thu, morning Sat
Majunga	Ambodivona	30,000	12	Morning & afternoon
Manakara	Fasan'ny Karana	30,000	15	Afternoon
Miandrivazo	Fasan'ny Karana	28,000	9	Afternoon
Moramanga	Ampasampito	7000	2¾	All day
Morondava	Fasan'ny Karana	48,000	18	Afternoon
Tamatave (Toamasina)	Ambodivona/ Ampasampito	20,000	7	Morning & afternoon
Tuléar (Toliara)	Fasan'ny Karana	from 40,000	18	Afternoon

(Ar35,000, 12 hours, 6am Tuesday, Thursday and Saturday); pickup and drop off is at the central post office in both cities. Booking required.

CAR

There are a number of reputable tour agencies (p294). Big international car-rental agencies are present in Tana, but they often come with a driver too. Prices quoted are for short journeys.

Budget (☑ 032 05 811 13; www.budget.com/en/locations/mg/antananarivo; Rue Dr Raseta; ☺7.45am-noon & 2-5.30pm Mon-Fri) Offers compact cars and 4WD with driver. Also has an office at the airport.

Europcar (☑ 020 23 336 47; www.europcar.com; Lalana Hydrocarbures; ☺7.30am-noon & 2-5pm Mon-Fri, 7.30am-noon Sat) From Ar150,000 a day for a short trip in a small city car (with driver); fuel is extra.

Joachin (Zo) Randriamahefa (☑ 034 66 782 97; joachinrmada@gmail.com) This excellent private driver can arrange a 4WD vehicle at cheaper than normal rates, and is experienced in driving throughout Madagascar. You'll need to arrange your own hotels etc.

Rajaona Mahery (☑ 034 12 294 87, 020 22 422 26; maheryt@gmail.com) Small private company offering well-priced 4WDs capable of going anywhere in Madagascar.

Ramartour (☑ 020 22 487 23; www.ramartour.com) One of few operators to offer self-drive vehicles, although it also offers vehicles with driver and a range of tours.

TAXI-BROUSSE

For morning departures, turn up early (6am); for afternoon departures, come around 2pm. It may take up to four hours for some vehicles to fill.

Gare Routière d'Ambodivona (Northern Taxi-brousse Station; Map p42; Ambodivona) About 2km northeast of the city centre. A taxi to/from the centre costs Ar10,000.

Gare Routière d'Ampasampito (Eastern Taxi-brousse Station; Map p42; Ampasampito) About 3.5km northeast of the centre. A taxi to/from the centre will cost Ar15,000.

Gare Routière de Fasan'ny Karana (Southern Taxi-brousse Station; Map p42; Anosibe) About 4km southwest of Lac Anosy. A taxi to/from the centre costs Ar20,000.

❶ Getting Around

TO/FROM THE AIRPORT

Ivato Airport is 12km from the city centre. A taxi to/from the city centre costs Ar60,000 during the day, up to Ar80,000 at night – you're better off arranging a transfer from your hotel.

TAXI

Tana's cream-coloured taxis are plentiful and cheap, even at night. Fares are negotiable: a journey in town should cost Ar5000 to Ar10,000 during the day, or Ar10,000 to Ar20,000 at night. Always agree on a price before leaving. You may pay a different rate for the same route depending on whether you are going downhill or uphill!

TAXI-BE

Large minibuses called taxi-be meander around Antananarivo and the outlying suburbs; the standard fare is Ar500. They are of limited use to travellers because of the difficulty in working out the route and where bus stops are. If you do take a taxi-be for a straightforward journey (to

THE MERINA

The region surrounding Antananarivo is known as Imerina (Land of the Merina Tribe). Historically, the Merina have been Madagascar's dominant tribe, reigning over the country for several centuries.

Merina hierarchy was based on a three-tier caste system, largely dependent on skin colour. The *andriana* (nobles; generally fairer-skinned and with pronounced Asiatic rather than African features, reflecting their Indonesian ancestry), comprised the upper echelon, while the *hova* (commoners) made up the middle class. The remainder – descendants of former slaves – were known as the *andevo* (workers).

The first Merina kingdoms were established around the 16th century, and by the late 19th century they were the dominant tribe in Madagascar. Ordinary Merina citizens customarily worked as administrators, shopkeepers, teachers and traders. Their position was enhanced by the choice of Antananarivo as the seat of the French colonial government, and by the establishment of an education system there.

Today, the Merina are still among the best-educated Malagasies and many remain at the forefront of public life: former presidents Hery Rajaonarimampianina and Marc Ravalomanana, and the current president Andry Rajoelina are all Merina.

Ivato or Ambohimanga for instance), be very careful with your belongings as pickpockets are a problem.

AROUND ANTANANARIVO

The highlands around Antananarivo are often ignored by travellers pushing on to other regions, but the whole area is perfect day-trip country. Two of Antananarivo's 12 sacred hills are easily accessible, offering great insight into the history and culture of the Merina people. There's also an excellent lemur park and a crocodile farm.

Lemurs' Park

You'll find nine species of lemur at this **private wildlife reserve** (☑ 033 11 252 59; www.lemurspark.com; RN1; adult/child Ar40,000/20,000; ⊘8.30am-4pm), 22km west of the capital. It's a good place to visit if you haven't yet seen lemurs elsewhere, or if you need one final lemur fix before you go! The lemurs are free-ranging (except for the two nocturnal species, which are confined to rather small cages) and well habituated, so you'll see them up close. There are about 50 individual lemurs including Coquerel *sifakas*, ring-tail lemurs and black-and-white ruffed lemurs.

Most of the animals are former pets or individuals that were threatened in their natural habitat, and the reserve has a breeding program together with other private sanctuaries.

Nestled on a bend of the River Katsaoka, the 5-hectare park is a beautiful and tranquil spot. The park can arrange transfers from Tana if you don't have your own vehicle: it costs Ar140,000 per person (minimum of two people) return for one/two people, including admission. Call ahead to arrange – they leave Tana at 9am and return at 2pm.

There's an on-site restaurant (three-course meal Ar48,000).

Ivato

About 13km from Antananarivo, the village-suburb of Ivato is where the international airport is located. If you just have one night or day to spend between flights, or on your way in or out of Tana, spend it here: you'll save yourself time (traffic between Tana and Ivato is perennially bad) and money. There are a couple of decent attractions here, including a crocodile farm and model-shipbuilding workshop, and the hotels out this way are excellent.

◉ Sights

Le Village   WORKSHOP
(☑ 032 07 129 50, 020 22 451 97; www.maquettes debateaux.com; off Rte de l'Aéroport, Talatamaty; ⊘showroom 8am-4.30pm Mon-Sat, workshops Mon-Fri only) Around 30 highly skilled artisans work here producing intricate scale models of historic ships, fishing boats and famous vessels. Everything is made by hand – from miniature cannons to the ships' sails. One model takes about six months to complete. You can view the artisans at work from Mon-

day to Friday. The showroom (models start at around €200) also opens on Saturday.

The workshop is about 6km south of the airport (p54) in the direction of Tana.

Croc Farm
FARM

(☑ 032 11 301 43; Ar25,000; ⊙9am-5pm) This is an unusual place: a commercial crocodile farm that breeds crocs, as well as a zoo where you can see the reptilian giants in all their basking glory, along with lemurs, chameleons and even the rare fossa (striped civet). There's been a recent shift away from the commercial aspect towards that of a zoo. The park is about 3km from the airport (p54). A taxi will cost around Ar25,000 return from Ivato, including an hour's wait.

🛏 Sleeping

Ivato has some excellent hotels, with an especially good selection in the top-end category. Although most are a few kilometres from the airport, that's nothing by Tana's standards and all offer airport shuttles.

Le Manoir Rouge
GUESTHOUSE €

(☑ 032 05 260 97; www.facebook.com/manoir. rouge.hotel.ivato.madagascar; Lalana Ambohijanahary Antehiroka; d/f €20/25, dm/s/d/f without bathroom €8/12/14/19; 🛜) This backpacker-friendly guesthouse is a scant 900m from the airport. It has real charm, with creaky floorboards and a lovely big garden. The varied rooms (most with shared bathroom) sleep up to four people. There is a good on-site restaurant too, offering fresh market cuisine (mains Ar12,000 to Ar17,000) and regular evening entertainment. Airport transfer included.

Meva Guesthouse
GUESTHOUSE €€

(☑ 033 50 896 62, 032 42 896 62; www.mevaguest house.com; Talatamaty; d/tr €25/35; 🛜) About 6km south of Ivato, off the road to Tana, this gorgeous guesthouse is a warm and authentic place to stay. The Dutch-Malagasy owners have thought about everything: the rooms are homely and spacious, guests have access to the kitchen, the garden is beautiful, and rooms on the upper floors have nice views of the neighbouring paddy fields. Airport transfers cost Ar30,000.

Gassy Country House
HOTEL €€

(☑ 034 07 144 64, 032 07 144 64; www.gassy countryhouse.mg; off Rte de l'Aéroport; r from €25; 🛜🏊) Lovely wood-floored rooms with mosquito nets and bright colours dominate things here. The warm welcome is a feature,

and the rooms are among the best value you'll find this close to the airport.

Relais des Plateaux
Hotel & Spa
HOTEL €€€

(☑ 032 05 678 93, 020 22 441 18; www.relais-des-plateaux.com; off Rte de l'Aéroport, Talatamaty; d from €109; P ❄ 🛜🏊) This four-star hotel is an excellent Ivato choice, offering enough add-ons – good restaurant, a well stocked bar, a gym and fitness centre, a spa – to mean you could easily stay here and not move for 24 hours if that's what you need. The rooms are large and comfortable, and it's a good option for the airport.

Hotel San Cristobal
HOTEL €€€

(☑ 034 05 024 90, 020 22 538 24; www.san cristobal.mg; Maibahoaka Talatamaty; d/tw/ste incl breakfast from €67/74/102; P ❄ 🛜) Just 4km from the airport and with free shuttles, this excellent place has large, stylish rooms with white and slate-grey colour schemes, a decent restaurant and bar, and professional service. As an airport hotel, it's an excellent mix of reasonable prices and high levels of comfort.

Savanna Cafe
GUESTHOUSE €€€

(☑ 032 04 760 29; savannacafe@yahoo.fr; Rte de l'Aéroport; s/d/tr Ar120,000/140,000/160,000; ❄🛜) Upstairs from the cafe of the same name, this fine place has reasonably priced, simply furnished rooms with balcony overlooking the valley. It's an excellent choice if you're not looking to pay high-end prices.

🍴 Eating

The hotel restaurants out here are usually pretty good, with the one at Relais des Plateaux especially good. There are at least two other good options away from the hotels.

⭐ Savanna Cafe
INTERNATIONAL €€

(☑ 032 04 760 29; Rte de l'Aéroport; mains Ar19,000-30,000; ⊙6.30am-10.30pm; 🛜) With lovely views from the terrace, a warm welcome from the Cameroonian owner Paul Roger, Savanna Cafe is a terrific choice at any time of day. The Malagasy and West African dishes are especially well executed but it also does snacks, burgers, pizza and good salads.

La Terrasse de Tydouce
FRENCH €€€

(☑ 033 11 336 99, 020 24 522 51; www.facebook. com/restaurantghesthouse; Rte de l'Aéroport; mains from Ar22,000; ⊙11.30am-2.30pm & 6.30-9pm; 🛜) This well-regarded French restaurant along the main road through Ivato has

Around Antananarivo

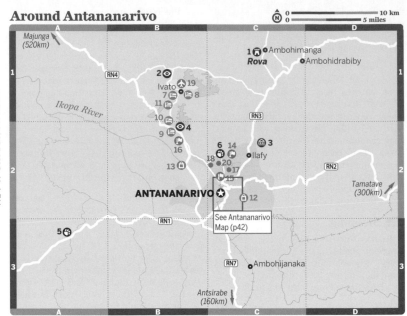

creative dishes such as profiteroles of wild mushrooms, local classics such as medallions of grilled zebu and French mainstays such as snail served in a ceramic pot. Dine on the pretty garden terrace.

🚊 Getting There & Away

A taxi between the airport and Ivato village will cost Ar10,000. A taxi from Ivato village to Antananarivo costs at least Ar40,000, probably more.

Taxi-be route D (Ar1000, one hour) links the taxi-brousse stand behind Gare Soarana (p41) in Tana to Ivato bus station, near the market.

Ilafy

Originally called Ambohitrahanga, Ilafy was founded around the turn of the 17th century on a sacred hilltop and was used as a country residence by the Merina royal family. The wooden residence was redesigned in the 1830s by Ranavalona I and used as a hunting lodge by Radama II, whose body was initially buried in a modest tomb on the grounds before being transferred to the rova (palace).

The hunting lodge was reconstructed in 1957, after the original had fallen into disrepair; it now houses the **Ethnographic Museum** (Ar5000; ⊙9am-5pm Tue-Sun). Ilafy

lies 12km from Antananarivo, just east of the road leading to Ambohimanga. You'll need your own transport to get here.

Ambohimanga

Ambohimanga ('blue hill' or 'beautiful hill') was the original capital of the Merina royal family. Even after the seat of government was shifted to Antananarivo for political reasons, Ambohimanga remained a sacred site, and was off limits to foreigners for many years. The entire hill was listed as a Unesco World Heritage Site in 2001 for being 'the most significant symbol of the cultural identity of the people of Madagascar'.

The entrance to Ambohimanga village is marked by a large traditional gateway, one of the seven gateways to the eyrie-like hilltop. To one side is a large, flat, round stone. At the first sign of threat to the village, the stone would be rolled by up to 40 slaves, sealing off the gate.

◉ Sights

★ **Rova**   PALACE
(Ambohimanga; Ar10,000; ⊙9am-5pm) Poised atop Ambohimanga hill is the Rova, the fortress-palace. The walls of the compounds were constructed using cement made from

Around Antananarivo

sand, shells and egg whites – 16 million eggs were required to build the outer wall alone. Inside, there are two palaces: the traditional palace (1788) of the all-powerful Merina king Andrianampoinimerina, and the European-styled summer palace of Queen Ranavalona I (r 1828–61), constructed by French engineer Jean Laborde in 1870 (he was thought to be Ranavalona's lover). The word 'palace' seems over the top to describe King Andrianampoinimerina's simple wooden hut (1788), but palace it was.

The original was thatched, but Jean Laborde replaced the grass roof with more durable wooden tiles in the 19th century. The central pole of the hut is made from a single trunk of sacred palisander (rosewood), which was reportedly carried from the east coast by 2000 slaves, 100 of whom died in the process. The top of the pole is carved to show a pair of women's breasts, a symbol of the king's polygamy. The king supposedly hid in the rafters when visitors arrived, signalling whether the guest was welcome by dropping pebbles onto his wife's head.

The royal bed is in the sacred northeast corner of the hut and is elevated to indicate the king's superior status. The simple furniture is aligned according to astrological rules.

Behind the hut are the open-air baths where the king performed his royal ablutions once a year, in the company of his 12 wives and diverse honoured guests. Afterwards his bathwater was considered sacred and was delivered to waiting supplicants.

Next door to King Andrianampoinimerina's hut, in a striking style contrast, is Queen Ranavalona I's elegant summer palace. It's been beautifully restored and has original European-style furniture inside. The dining room was lined with mirrors, which allowed the queen to check that no one was sneakily poisoning her food.

Ambohimanga is still revered by many Malagasies as a sacred site, and you will see offerings (zebu horns, blood, sweets and honey, as well as small change) at various shrines around the compound where individuals or families have come to invoke royal spirits for luck and fertility. Don't disturb these sacred locations and never point at them with your finger outstretched.

There are sensational views of the surrounding countryside from around the compound. Make sure you take a guide to go round the Rova to learn about the site's historical and cultural significance. Guides (French- and English-speaking) trained by OSCAR, the local tourist office, are available at the entrance where you pay your admission. A tip of around Ar5000 is appropriate.

ℹ Getting There & Away

Ambohimanga is 21km north of Antananarivo and easily visited as a day trip in combination with Ilafy. Taxis-bes (route H) leave throughout the day from Ambodivona (Ar2000, 1½ hours); from the village, you'll need to walk 1km up the hill to the Rova.

Central Madagascar

Best Places to Eat

➜ La Rizière (p81)

➜ Chez Jenny (p66)

➜ Sharon (p74)

➜ Résidence du Betsileo (p84)

➜ Hôtel Thermal (p71)

➜ Le Pousse-Pousse (p66)

Best Places to Stay

➜ Hôtel Anjara (p68)

➜ Betsileo Country Lodge (p84)

➜ Les Chambres du Voyageurs (p65)

➜ Hôtel Thermal (p70)

➜ Cristo (p70)

➜ Sous Le Soleil de Mada (p71)

Why Go?

With its smooth granite outcrop mountains, cool and damp climate, and intensive agriculture, the high plateau of Central Madagascar is a different world to the hot and wild lowlands that make up most of the rest of the country. The lifeline of this region is the RN7 road which winds all the way from Antananarivo to beyond Fianarantsoa.

Travelling along this road, you'll discover a potpourri of travellers' delights that together make for a perfect introduction to Madagascar. Wander around bustling market towns clogged with colourful pousse-pousse (rickshaws); snap photos of the distinctive village architecture of two-storey, fortress-like mud-brick homes; explore a mountain stronghold of lemurs; or stride through national parks with landscapes ranging from thick jungle to wide-open grandeur.

For many people this is their first taste of the country, and it's a good one, with almost all attractions accessible by paved road.

When to Go
Antsirabe

Jul–Sep *Famadihana* (exhumation and reburial) ceremonies take place across the region.

Apr & May Countryside is at its greenest following the end of the rainy season.

Sep & Oct Best weather of the year; animals are active, and lemurs have babies.

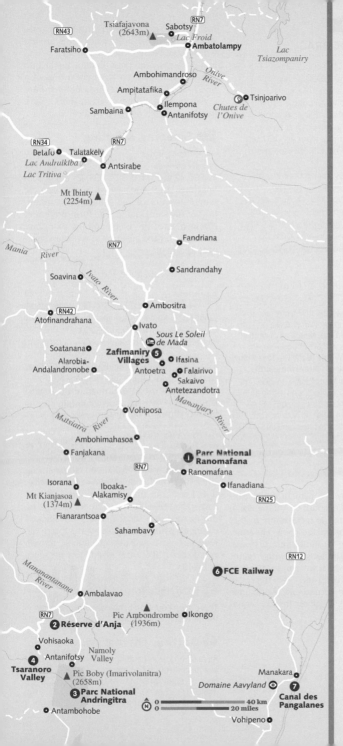

Central Madagascar Highlights

❶ Parc National Ranomafana (p71) Counting how many species of lemurs and chameleons you can tally up in this World Heritage forest park.

❷ Réserve d'Anja (p82) Communing with ring-tailed lemurs in this inspiring community-run private reserve.

❸ Parc National Andringitra (p85) Watching the sunrise from the summit of Madagascar's second-highest mountain, Pic Boby.

❹ Tsaranoro Valley (p86) Hiking, climbing, swimming or simply relaxing by the village well in this paradisaical valley.

❺ Zafimaniry Villages (p71) Learning the secret meanings behind the Zafimaniry wood carvings while trekking from village to village.

❻ FCE railway (p76) Embarking on the epic train journey from Fianarantsoa to Manakara.

❼ Canal des Pangalanes (p74) Paddling a pirogue down peaceful coastal canals.

WORTH A TRIP

COIN DU FOIE GRAS

This hillside **restaurant** (☑ 034 97 296 05; mains Ar10,000-15,000; ⊘ 6am-9pm) just south of the village of Behemjy gets busy at weekends with people coming for one thing and one thing only: foie gras (stuffed-goose liver). A simple entree of foie gras costs from Ar6000 and main courses consist of duck in various delicious forms.

You can also by packets of foie gras to take away (Ar5500 for 250g).

Due to the production technique, foie gras is considered a controversial food item in some Anglophone countries and some animal rights organisations oppose the production of foie gras.

ℹ Getting There & Around

Perhaps the most common itinerary in Madagascar is to head down the RN7 from Tana to Tuléar (Toliara), sampling everything along the way, then fly back to Tana. Nearly all of central Madagascar's towns and attractions lie near this two-lane highway, one of the few reasonably well-maintained sealed roads in the country.

This makes central Madagascar an easy destination for budget travellers, who will be able to go everywhere by *taxi-brousse* (bush taxi). For the few attractions that do require a private vehicle, enquire with local tour operators, ask at your hotel, or charter a taxi.

Ambatolampy

☑ 042 / POP 28,500

A small and attractive plateau town, Ambatolampy lies 68km south of Antananarivo on the RN7, among the picturesque forests and hills of the Ankaratra Massif. The town is best known for its aluminium artisans, who make the ubiquitous *marmites* (giant aluminium pots) which you can see in every household and hotel up and down the country. A visit to the furnace-like workshops is fascinating and shocking in near equal measure.

◉ Sights

**Aluminium Pot
Workshop**   WORKSHOP
(Ar5000; ⊘ 8am-6pm) The grimy and utterly fascinating aluminium pot workshops are all gathered in one small area behind the market. The area is filled with small workshops and superheated brick kilns around which soot-coated men bash and pound metal sheets and pour molten metal into moulds without even the merest hint of a nod to health- and safety-precautions. After a visit here, you'll never again think you've just had a tough day in the office!

🛌 Sleeping & Eating

**Au Rendez-Vous
des Pêcheurs**   HOTEL €€
(☑ 020 42 492 04, 032 05 098 43; d Ar51,000) Spacious, but very faded rooms can be found upstairs of the atmospheric restaurant of the same name. The furniture hasn't changed since the 1950s and the rooms are perhaps a bit too basic for most tastes. However, the manager is a mine of information on the area and can also organise tours between here, Antsirabe and Ambositra.

La Pineta   GUESTHOUSE €€
(☑ 034 74 265 40, 020 42 493 02; lapinetasarl@ yahoo.com; Route d'Antsirabe; tr Ar70,000, d/tr without bathroom Ar55,000/60,000; 🛜) With its vaguely Swiss-chalet feel, La Pineta is an unusual but enjoyable option in Ambatolampy. The four basic rooms have creaky, shiny wooden floors and bright colours. Staff give a big, warm, smiley welcome. Meals (mains from Ar14,000) are served either in the homely dining room or in the garden.

**Au Rendez-Vous
des Pêcheurs**   INTERNATIONAL €€
(☑ 020 42 492 04, 032 05 098 43; mains Ar10,000-16,000, lunch menu Ar25,000; 🛜) Going strong since 1951, the Rendez-Vous is a local institution. Every tour travelling between Tana and Antsirabe seems to stop here for lunch. The dining room has the feel of an old-fashioned canteen (with log fire in winter) and the food is hearty and decent enough, though you do pay a little over the odds for the sense of history.

ℹ Information

There are a couple of banks with ATMs around the central market area.

ℹ Getting There & Away

All *taxis-brousses* heading south towards Antsirabe pass through Ambatolampy (Ar7000, two hours). Heading north to Antananarivo costs Ar5000 (1½ hours). *Taxis-brousses* stop right by the small market in the very centre of the town.

Antsirabe

📍044 / POP 238,500

Antsirabe is best known for its thermal springs. The city emerged as a spa town in the late 1800s when Norwegian missionaries built a health retreat here (still in use to this day). French colonists then turned it into a chic getaway from nearby Tana, hence the numerous turn-of-the-century villas and the broad tree-lined avenues so typical of French cities.

Much of this colonial heritage is fading now, nowhere more so than at the famous Hôtel des Thermes, whose magnificent facade hides a seriously ageing interior. But the city itself is full of life: it is a beacon of industry in Madagascar (the town has large textile, food and drink factories) and many Tananariviens would move here at the drop of a hat if they could. Travellers will no doubt find the city's energy infectious and its wealth of sightseeing, activity and eating options appealing.

🔘 Sights

Antsirabe is famed for its skilled artisans and a popular activity is to visit a few workshops over the course of a morning or afternoon. Some people charter a pousse-pousse (rickshaw) for the occasion and let the driver take charge of the itinerary (make sure you discuss the number of stops, length and price beforehand; allow Ar20,000 to Ar40,000 for a circuit) but you could simply take a different pousse-pousse between each stop, if you know where you want to go.

★**Chez Mamy Miniatures** WORKSHOP
(📞034 05 693 00; mamyminature44@gmail.com; Parc de l'Est; ⊙8am-noon & 1.30-6pm Mon-Sat) For 30 years this family workshop has been creating miniature objects (cars, rickshaws, bicycles etc) made from recycled materials – anything from aluminium cans to (unused) intravenous tubes, textiles and old cables. Watch how parts of the models are made; it's an incredibly fiddly and inventive process. The results are works of art suitable for the most discerning of mantelpieces.

Hôtel des Thermes HISTORIC BUILDING
(📞020 44 487 62) Once the grand dame of Antsirabe, the exterior of this landmark hotel is still gorgeous and a sight in its own right. Sadly, the interiors have been allowed to decay which means we wouldn't suggest staying here, but do walk up to admire the outside of the building and take in the views over town from its gardens.

If you do get to look around the interior – or even choose to stay here – then take note that like all proper old manor houses, this one has the requisite ghost or two. We spoke to someone who stayed here who said that someone or something opened their bathroom door in the middle of the night!

Atelier Corne de Zébu WORKSHOP
(Parc de l'Est; ⊙8am-6pm) Zebu horn is a versatile – and beautiful – material, which artisans at this family-owned workshop turn into numerous objects, from jewellery to salad spoons, sculpted animals and accessories. You'll see the whole production process: from how to separate the bone from its keratin shell to polishing the final products with old denims.

Chez Marcel WORKSHOP
(📞032 50 874 92; Rue Danton; admission incl 6 packets sweets Ar10,000; ⊙7am-noon & 1-6pm) The technique used to make traditional sweets here hasn't changed in decades: a syrup is prepared, then rapidly cooled down and kneaded on a granite slab. Ingredients such as vanilla, orange peel, ground coffee or crystallised ginger are added to the mix for flavour; the preparation is then cut into individual sweets. *Voila* – done and dusted in 15 minutes! The enthusiastic family who run the business produce up to 50kg of sweets a day and they're sold countrywide.

Brasserie Star BREWERY
(📞020 44 480 39; www.star.mg; Rue Danton; ⊙tours 9am & 2pm Tue, Wed & Thu) 🆓 Wondering where all that Three Horses Beer comes from? Look no further. Madagascar's dominant and unmissable brand is made in this, the country's biggest brewery. Starting at the THB billboard on the corner of Ave Foch and Rue Danton, head west on Danton (toward Morondava) for 800m. If you've seen breweries elsewhere, though, this will be familiar. Bookings required. Visitors must wear long trousers and closed shoes.

Sabotsy Market MARKET
(⊙7am-4pm Sat) A Malagasy version of a Moroccan souk, this sprawling open-air market, with distinct areas of jewellery, clothing, food and more, will keep you occupied for hours either shopping or simply absorbing the spectacle. Located in a vast walled compound, it is a Pandora's box of unusual sights

Antsirabe

CENTRAL MADAGASCAR ANTSIRABE

and sounds, not to mention things for sale, with all of local society seemingly on display.

🏃 Activities

Thermal Baths SWIMMING
(Station Thermale; pool Ar5000; ⏰ 7.30-9.30am, 10.30am-12.30pm & 2-4pm Mon-Wed & Fri, 7-9am, 10am-noon & 2-4pm Sat, 7-9am & 10am-noon Sun) Antsirabe's thermal baths have been attracting those in need of cures – or just a splash about in the pool – for decades. Cures are by advance appointment only but the pool is open to all. It gets uncomfortably busy at weekends and you can expect to be the only foreigner there, so anticipate to be at the centre of considerable interest.

☞ Tours

★ Rando Raid
Madagascar MOUNTAIN BIKING
(📱 032 04 900 21; www.randoraidmadagascar. com; Rue Stavanger; half-/full day guided mountain-

biking excursion from €15/25, guided treks from €5, half-/full day guided horse riding from €25/50; ⏰ 8.30am-noon & 3-6pm Mon-Sat) The rollicking hills around Antsirabe are a paradise for outdoor sports and Bazoly and Jean-Marc have devised a plethora of activities (mountain biking, hiking, horse riding, canoeing, quad bikes and motorbikes, often in combination) and excursions (lakes, mountains, Betafo) to make the best of this amazing playground. Options range from a half-day to several days.

AGAVE TOURS
(Association des Guides Agréés Volontaires de l'Environnement; 📱 020 44 484 88; chezbilly@ moov.mg; Chez Billy, Rue la Myre de Villers) This local guides' association was created to encourage greater professionalism, collaboration and sustainable practice among guides. This is the most reliable organisation to contact to organise a guide, whatever your plans; it is based out of Chez Billy guesthouse.

Antsirabe

✦ Festivals & Events

Just when you thought you'd seen it all: June to September is the time for *famadihana* (literally, the 'turning of the bones'), the ritual exhumation and celebration of ancestors' bones by the Betsileo and Merina people. *Famadihana* are joyous and intense occasions, which occur in each family roughly every seven years.

Famadihana ceremonies take place in the *hauts plateaux* (highlands) region from Tana to Ambalavao every year. Hotels or guides can help you find one and arrange an invitation. If you receive an invite, it's polite to bring a bottle of rum or a monetary contribution as a gift for the host family, and to ask before taking pictures. Foreigners are generally warmly welcomed, and most people find that the experience, far from being morbid, is moving and fascinating.

🛏 Sleeping

★**Chez Billy**　　　　　　　　　GUESTHOUSE **€**
(☑032 45 740 71, 020 44 484 88; www.chez-billy.com; Rue la Myre de Villers; d/tr/q Ar55,000/70,000/85,000, without bathroom Ar35,000/50,000/65,000; 🛜) This eclectic melange of guesthouse, bar and restaurant, awash in loud art, inspires a hostel-like conviviality among the staff, backpackers, guides and in-the-know *vazaha* (foreigners) who form its crossroads clientele. The rooms are simple but well kept, the showers hot and powerful, and the jovial owner Billy, a former guide, is a mine of information.

It's always full, so book ahead.

Green Park　　　　　　　　　　BUNGALOW **€**
(☑020 44 051 90; greenparktsara@yahoo.fr; Rue Labourdonnais; camping per tent Ar7000, d/f Ar45,000/70,000; 🛜) The bungalows are simple but pretty at Green Park (do check a couple as some are a little damp), but it's the low prices, beautiful garden and interconnecting ponds and streams that seal the deal (and the proximity to Chez Jenny, the town's best restaurant). Camping is also available.

Lovasoa　　　　　　　　　　GUESTHOUSE **€€**
(☑020 44 486 85; www.lovasoa.mg; Rue Stavanger; dm Ar17,000, s/d Ar70,000/90,000, d without bathroom Ar47,000; 🛜) Run by the Lutheran Church and a Norwegian aid agency, this guesthouse in the centre of town is a little gem. The grounds are large and feel like an oasis. Inside, the dorms (sleeping eight) are immaculate and cheerful, with separate bathrooms for men and women. There are gorgeous double rooms too, which are surprisingly high end and therefore more expensive.

Trianon　　　　　　　　　　GUESTHOUSE **€€**
(☑020 44 051 40; Ave Foch; d/tr Ar92,000/107,000; 🛜) This charming throwback to the colonial era, a nicely renovated French chateau with grand embracing stairways, is just oozing with atmosphere, from its old airline posters to its uniformed staff. The classy restaurant and terrace strike just the right note, as do the attractively faded but comfortable rooms. The downside is the location: off a busy road. We love the old-world bar with its cocktails of the week and never-changing cast of old regulars.

★**Les Chambres
du Voyageurs**　　　　BOUTIQUE HOTEL **€€€**
(☑032 83 083 61; androdenis@yahoo.fr; d/tw/tr/f bungalows Ar150,00/160,000/170,000/300,000 ; 🛜) 🌱 This ecolodge is a rarity in Antsirabe, an island of nature on the edge of the city. The owner's passion is gardening and

WORTH A TRIP

LAC ANDRAIKIBA & LAC TRITRIVA

There are two attractive lakes outside of Antsirabe that are popular day trips from the city. Lac Andraikiba, the closest and largest of the two, is 7km west off the road to Betafo. Frequented by Malagasy tourists, it has craft booths with some annoying hawkers, but it's also easy to get away for a nice quiet walk or picnic. The turquoise Lac Tritriva, a further 12km away, also has a hawker problem, and there is a Ar5000 entry fee, but this crater lake is even prettier, and the path around it makes for an easy circumnavigation.

You'll find the lovely Case à Tritriva (p66) nearby, ideal if you fancy a hot meal rather than a sandwich. It's run by a Franco-Malagasy couple who serve simple, wholesome cuisine in the courtyard of their home, complete with panoramic views. There is also basic accommodation if you fancy a night away from the bustle of town (half board per person Ar25,000).

A great way to get to the lakes is to cycle – Rando Raid Madagascar (p64) in Antsirabe rents mountain bikes and provides an excellent map guaranteed to get you there and back; it also organises guided mountain biking and canoeing trips to the lakes. Green Park (p65) also rents bikes (Ar25,000 per day).

you'll find numerous species of plant in the themed gardens as well as all the chirpy birds they attract. The brick bungalows are pretty, spacious and very comfortable with splashes of subtle Malagasy art.

Couleur Café   BOUTIQUE HOTEL €€€
(☑032 02 200 65, 020 44 485 26; www.couleur-cafeantsirabe.com; Route d'Ambositra; s/d/tr €42/52/62; ☜) If you're after a romantic night, this exquisite 15-room boutique hotel is the place for you. The brick 'pavilions' are an elegant blend of eye-candy decor and Malagasy crafts (old Chanel posters alongside lampshades made of weaver bird nests), and each has its own fireplace. There is an excellent restaurant (menu Ar32,000) and massages are available (from Ar30,000).

✖ Eating

La Chocolatière   SWEETS €
(Rue Jean Ralaimongo; per kg from Ar75,000; ☺8.30am-5.30pm Mon-Sat, 10am-1pm Sun) Part of a small national chain, this enticing place produces its own fabulously rich and delicate handmade chocolate. Although prices are by the kilo, it sells them by the dainty little piece.

Café Mirana   MALAGASY €
(Rue Jean Ralaimongo; mains Ar4000-7000; ☺7am-6.30pm) This cafeteria is one of the busiest in town, with reason: reliably tasty, great-value Malagasy staples such as *vary' aminana* (rice soup served for breakfast), *mi sao* (noodle stir-fry) and zebu stews are served in the restaurant section, while the

bakery has reasonable croissants and cakes which make it ideal for a breakfast pause.

La Case à Tritriva   MALAGASY €
(☑034 67 159 56; Lac Tritriva; 2-/3-course menus Ar10,000/14,000; ☺noon-2.30pm & 7-9pm) You'll find the lovely Case de Tritriva near Lac Tritriva. It's run by a Franco-Malagasy couple, who serve simple, wholesome cuisine from the courtyard of their home, complete with panoramic views. Locals drive out from Antsirabe simply to eat here.

★Chez Jenny   INTERNATIONAL €€
(☑034 44 990 22; Rue Labourdonnais; mains Ar14,000-18,000; ☺7am-2.30pm & 6-10pm; ☜) Hands down the best restaurant in town, Chez Jenny is a winning combination of colourful decor (including some captivating Zafimaniry wood carvings), delicious food, warm service and atmosphere, complete with a well-stocked bar and a cosy fireplace for cold winter nights. Try the duck in three pepper sauce or opt for one of the lovely pizzas.

Le Pousse-Pousse   FUSION €€
(☑033 02 555 90; Antsenakely; mains Ar12,000-20,000; ☺11am-10pm Mon-Sat) This charming place, where you eat inside a pousse-pousse, is known for its cheeseburgers – rare hereabouts – and delicious fusion cuisine (such as stir-fried pork in pineapple, or duck in peppercorn and honey sauce). There is occasional live music.

Zandina   PIZZA €€
(☑032 67 633 31; 5 Ave Foch; mains Ar10,000-17,000; ☺11.30am-10pm; ☜) Zandina has

become something of an institution thanks to its all-day service, good wi-fi connection, satellite TV, and generally warm and relaxed atmosphere. The food is good too, a mixture of salads and grills, but it's best known for its wood-fired pizzas. Portions are huge.

ⓘ Information

INTERNET ACCESS
If your hotel connection isn't good enough, you can try Zandina.

MONEY
There are several banks with ATMs in town, including **BNI Madagascar** (Rue Jean Ralaimongo; ⊙ 8-11.30am & 2-4.30pm Mon-Fri), which has a reliable 24-hour ATM.

POST
Post office (Rue Jean Ralaimongo; ⊙ 8-11.30am & 2-4.30pm Mon-Fri)

ⓘ Getting There & Away

Antsirabe is 170km south of Antananarivo. For *taxi-brousses*, the gare routière is located about 2½ km north of town, behind the Jovenna petrol station. Services from Antsirabe include the following:

DESTINATION	FARE (AR)	DURATION (HR)
Ambositra	8000	3
Antananarivo	10,000	4
Fianarantsoa	18,000	6
Miandrivazo	18,000	7
Morondava	35,000	15
Tamatave	32,000	10

ⓘ Getting Around

Antsirabe can be easily negotiated on foot, but for longer trips, you'll have a wealth of options: pousse-pousse, *cyclo-pousse* or tuk-tuk. A trip around town should cost around Ar2000 for pousse-pousse or *cyclo-pousse* (Ar5000 between the *taxi-brousse* station and the centre). For tuk-tuks, it's a fixed Ar1000 per trip, but the route often is more circuitous because of other passengers on board.

Ambositra

🔊 047 / POP 38,000

Rising up like a fortress out of a cool, green and picturesque valley lined with rice paddies and ringed by verdant peaks, Ambositra (am-boo-str) is famous for the quality of its woodcarvings and marquetry (objects inlaid with coloured woods), which you'll find in dozens of shops, along with raffia products and other souvenirs.

The surrounding rural vistas are a lot more attractive than the town itself; this means that few people stop over for the night. However, many travellers pause here for lunch and a quick flurry through the town's many woodcarving shops. If you're looking to explore the interesting and seriously off-the-beaten-track Zafimaniry villages however, Ambositra is the best place from which to organise a trip.

⦿ Sights

Cathedral of the
Immaculate Heart of Mary   CHURCH
(Rue du Commerce) Jutting up above all other buildings in Ambositra, the cathedral, at the heart of the old town, is worth a quick look, although the doors are often locked outside of service times.

Benedictine Monastery   MONASTERY
(⊙ 6.30am-noon & 2-5pm Mon-Sat, from 7.30am Sun) At the western edge of town is a Benedictine monastery, where the nuns sell delicious cheese, honey and jam. The red-brick church warrants a look if it's open, there is beautiful choral singing every day between 11.50am and noon.

⦿ Tours

There are good walks from Ambositra to nearby villages, where you can see the artisans at work in their homes, carving wood with homemade tools or spreading brightly dyed raffia out in the sun to dry. Enquire in any of the more traveller-savvy hotels for a guide.

ORTAM   TOURS
(Office Régional de Tourisme d'Amoron'i Mania; 🖉 020 47 710 21; Rue du Commerce) Loosely based out of Hôtel Mania (the hotel manager is the tourist office's president), ORTAM is a good place to organise tours of local workshops or walks in the surrounding hills. It can also recommend and arrange guides for trips to the Zafimaniry villages.

⨼ Sleeping

Hotel du Centre   HOTEL €
(🖉 034 47 710 36, 032 86 658 39; hotelducentre. mada@yahoo.fr; Rue du Commerce; d/tr Ar40,000/50,000; 🛜) With beds that sag like

Ambositra

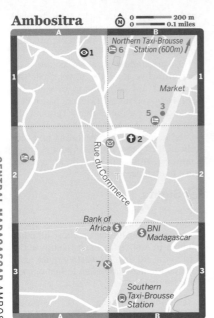

✖ Eating

Oasis   CHINESE €
(RN7; mains Ar5000-9000; ⏰11am-9pm; ✎)
This place near the southern *taxi-brousse*
station has an inexpensive and tasty menu
with lots of veggie and Chinese options, and
a popular outside terrace.

L'Artisan Hotel   INTERNATIONAL €€
(Manarintsoa; mains Ar9000-14,000; 🛜) This
hotel restaurant, which is full of old clocks,
serves a mix of Malagasy and French classics
and is the best place to eat in town. If there's
a tour group stopping by, folk bands sometimes come in to liven up mealtimes.

🛈 Information

MONEY

There are a couple of banks with ATMs in town.

Bank of Africa (Rue du Commerce; ⏰8-11.30am
& 2-4.30pm Mon-Fri)

BNI Madagascar (RN7; ⏰8-11.30am & 2-4pm
Mon-Fri)

POST

Post office (Rue du Commerce; ⏰8am-noon &
2-4.30pm Mon-Fri)

🛈 Getting There & Away

Transport to points north, including Antsirabe (Ar7000, two hours) and Antananarivo
(Ar15,000, five hours), departs from the northern *taxi-brousse* station at the far northern end
of town, about 600m north of the fork and down
a small staircase from Rue du Commerce. Departures for Fianarantsoa (Ar10,000, five hours)
and other points south are from the southern
taxi-brousse station.

a hammock, this concrete hotel right on the
ring road is nothing to write home about,
but it's fairly clean, very centrally located
and certainly cheap.

★Hôtel Anjara   GUESTHOUSE €€
(✐032 55 931 91; https://hotel-anjara.business.
site; Vohidahy; r from Ar55,000) You could spend
days in this lovely guesthouse, a beautiful
three-storey traditional Malagasy house set
in a rambling garden, with panoramic views
in every direction. To find it, take the stairs
heading downhill from the western part of
the ring road; cross the plain of paddy fields,
and the hotel will be signposted to your
right.

L'Artisan Hotel   BUNGALOW €€
(✐034 04 642 53; artisan_hotel@yahoo.fr; Manarintsoa; d Ar60,000, bungalows Ar60,000-90,000;
🛜) Thanks to its excellent customer service
and attention to detail, L'Artisan has gradually become top of its class. The Zafimaniry bungalows, which feature traditional
woodcarvings and construction methods,
are works of art (although they are a bit
cramped – rooms and brick bungalows are
more spacious).

The owners can arrange excursions in
the area.

SILK WEAVING IN SOATANANA

The village of Soatanana is famed for its silk weaving, and you can come and visit the artisans (mostly women) at work.

Borocera Madagascariensis, an endemic silkworm that feeds on tapia trees, is Madagascar's answer to *Bombyx Mori*, the originally Chinese silkworm that feeds on mulberry trees. They both produce silk in their cocoons, and although the fibres look slightly different (Malagasy silk, also called wild silk, is darker, coarser and less shiny), they have the same properties, incredibly insulating, light and soft.

Wild silk has been woven in Madagascar for centuries. Cocoons are harvested in the wild (there is no sericulture of *Borocera Madagascariensis*), then prepared in artisanal workshops – they need to be boiled for several days before drying. The fibre then needs to be threaded, dyed and woven.

Most women work on their loom at home, so workshop visits are an intimate experience. There are no signs indicating these workshops, so you'll need to ask a local to point you in the right direction (everyone will know why you're in town). You can of course buy scarves here: prices are low (Ar15,000 to Ar70,000 depending on the size) and the choice is bewildering. Some scarves are made exclusively of wild silk; others use a mix of wild and farmed silk (*Bombyx Mori*).

The village is also known for its 'white shepherds' who, dressed in bleached white shawls, herd livestock across the surrounding hills. If you're there on a Sunday morning, pop into the church and you might find the aisles packed with the white shepherds (minus their livestock!).

Simple accommodation (rooms Ar15,000) is available around the marketplace if you would like to spend the night in the village. Meals cost Ar8000.

The village of Soatanana is located about 40km southwest of Ambositra: 13km south on the RN7, then 15km west on the RN35 to the village of Anjoman' Akona, before taking a dirt road for the last 10km. The trip from Ambositra takes about 1¼ hours; if you don't have your own vehicle, you could charter a taxi, or contact ORTAM (p67) in Ambositra.

To get to Ranomafana by public transport, you generally need to go to Fianarantsoa first, but you could ask to get out at the Ranomafana junction about 30km north of Fiana and try and wave down a ride from there (expect to pay up to Ar10,000).

Ranomafana

POP 19,400

The village of Ranomafana (hot water) first evolved as a thermal bath centre popular with French colonials. The creation of the nearby Parc National Ranomafana in 1991 and its growing popularity have caused the town to expand; it is now a busy place, especially on Sunday (market day) when street stalls, football games and children's rides give the town a festive atmosphere.

As more and more tourists come to Ranomafana, the small town is developing the stirrings of a traveller centre, but for the moment it's all very low-key. Almost all the accommodation and restaurants serving the national park are based here in Ranomafana town.

Sights

Ranomafana Arboretum   GARDENS
(☑ 034 99 164 66; RN25; adult/child Ar10,000/5000; ⊙ 8am-5pm) This stunning arboretum, which is located about 2km east of Ranomafana, is worth visiting for its scenic location alone. There are around 250 species of plant here including 36 tree species, many of which are extremely rare. It's also a very good place to find chameleons, including the giant Parsons chameleon, which looks like something from a Disney movie. There's a self-guided walking trail in English, with lots of explanations, or you can take a guide (tip expected).

🏃 Activities

Kayaking   KAYAKING
(Varibolo Restaurant; 2hr per person Ar60,000) Kayaking along the chocolate-brown Namorona River is a new activity for Ranomafana. Organised by the Varibolo Restaurant up by the park entrance, the kayaking starts in Ranomafana town and runs for a gentle 8km through mixed-use agricultural land and patches of forest. There's time to stop

for birdwatching on the way and you might even see some of the artisanal gold panners searching the riverbed for their fortune.

Thermal Baths SWIMMING
(Ar5000; ⊙pool 6am-noon & 1-5.30pm, baths 7-11.30am & 2-4.30pm) The hot springs after which Ranomafana is named are located across the Namorona River. The setting is pretty, and the impressive outdoor swimming pool that is fed by the springs is very popular with locals. Best to swim here on Wednesday, as the pool is cleaned and re-filled on Tuesday. There are also hot baths which have a temperature of between 40°C and 50°C.

🛏 Sleeping

Forêt Austral BUNGALOW €
(☑ 034 16 391 74; RN 25; bungalows Ar45,000; ☜) There's an overriding sense of calm at this relaxed place which has 18 cozy, wooden bungalows which are tightly packed together in a pretty tropical flower garden. It's on the road between Ranomafana town and the park. There's a reasonable in-house restaurant.

Hôtel Manja HOTEL €€
(☑ 033 09 010 22; r Ar65,000, bungalows Ar65,000-75,000; ☜) Very popular with backpackers, this place has three types of accommodation: bedrooms, which are on the dingy side, and two kinds of bungalows, which are bigger and lighter. Bungalows at the top of the hill offer majestic views (if you don't mind the stairs). It's just to the east of the town centre, so is nice and quiet.

Le Grenat BUNGALOW €€
(☑ 034 12 780 84; legrenatran@gmail.com; s/d Ar60,000/70,000; ☜) Le Grenat's tidy little bungalows have a nice location by the banks of the river, but the decor is rather kitsch (those fluffy pink floor mats are just so you!). No matter, this is a well-run place with friendly management, and a decent restaurant.

★ Hôtel Thermal BOUTIQUE HOTEL €€€
(☑ 034 75 512 26; www.thermal-ranomafana.mg; d €52; ✳☜) For many years this was a broken relic of colonial days, but today the Hôtel Thermal has been given a new lease of life and is one of the best boutique hotels in all of central Madagascar. Set in manicured flower gardens, the hotel's 21 rooms are minimalist, modern and very cool. Service is excellent.

Various spa and massage treatments help sooth away the aches and scrapes of a forest walk.

★ Cristo LODGE €€€
(☑ 034 12 353 97; RN25; r Ar100,000; ☜) Perched on a gorgeous bend in the Namorona River, this charming, family-run hotel feels a lot like a classy homestay. The upper-floor rooms in the main building bask in a glorious panorama of rainforest and hills, while the riverside bungalows are more secluded.

Karibotel BUNGALOW €€€
(☑ 033 15 629 50; www.karibotel.com; RN25; d incl breakfast Ar115,000; ✳☜✳) The sharp, angular lines jar against the more organic curves of the surrounding forest, but otherwise this place is making a splash with its colourful bungalows, lovely bathrooms, stupendous views of Ranomafana and panoramic pool. It's located about halfway between the park and the village.

Centrest Sejour LODGE €€€
(☑ 034 16 524 33; centrestsejour@gmail.com; d r/bungalow Ar170,000-175,000, tr Ar200,000; ✳☜✳) This is more slick city hotel than Tarzan jungle hang-out. The rooms and bungalows here are some of the smartest in town and are decorated in bold, clashing whites and oranges. Bungalows offer more privacy than the rooms. It's popular with tour groups. The restaurant, which has a mostly French menu, is excellent but pricey (mains from Ar18,000).

🍴 Eating

Manja MALAGASY €
(☑ 033 09 010 22; mains Ar10,000; ⊙6.15-8am, noon-3pm & 6-9pm; ☜) A long-standing favourite, Manja serves big portions of traditional Malagasy food such as *romazava* (beef and vegetable stew), *ravitoto* (pork stew with manioc greens) and *hen'omby ritra* (zebu in tomato sauce). Its flambé bananas are the best around. Sit in the big, wooden dining room or grab one of the prized tables on the porch.

Le Grenat INTERNATIONAL €€
(☑ 034 12 780 84; mains Ar8000-16,000; ⊙noon-2pm & 6-9pm) Everything from the soups and pastas to the zebu kebabs or the *poulet coco* (chicken in coconut sauce) is cooked just right at the convivial Le Grenat. It also serves local crayfish in season (spring).

WORTH A TRIP

ZAFIMANIRY VILLAGES

This cluster of villages southeast of Ambositra is famous for its woodcarving, and is a Unesco World Heritage Site. The villages are a low-key, but fascinating homestay destination, where visitors can stay with a family (conditions are very basic) and experience life in this rural and remote part of the world. The Zafimaniry people, who number around 25,000 today, are descendants of the Betsimisaraka and Tanala ethnic groups. Formerly seminomadic peoples who lived in forested areas of the country, they migrated to the central regions of Madagascar in the 18th century due to deforestation in areas where they previously lived. The carvings and woodwork items they produce have great symbolic value with each design having a different and very specific meaning. Guides will explain the hidden meaning behind each motif to you.

Accommodation generally includes a bucket shower and composting toilet, a straw mattress, and traditional rice-based meals. There may be little or no English spoken. You may also get the chance to participate in traditional crafts, and to explore the region. The best villages to visit are Sakaivo, Falairivo and Antetezandotra.

ORTAM (p67) in Ambositra organises three- or four-day circuits in the area, including transfers from Ambositra and stays in two or three villages. Allow about Ar100,000 per person per day.

Another – and perhaps better – alternative is to stay at the delightful **Sous Le Soleil de Mada** (☑ 034 64 739 65; www.souslesoleildemada.com; s/d/tr/q half board Ar145,000/196,000/281,000/320,000) and explore the region from here. This remote and scenic lodge has 15 beautifully carved traditional-style Zafimaniry bungalows set in large grounds with airy views over fields, hills and rivers. Evening meals are served on one large table and are joyous occasions – thanks in part to the great collection of *rhum arrangé* (homemade rum with fruit inside). There is a massage room and a small book exchange.

Sous Le Soleil de Mada is located 12km down the dirt road leading to Antoetra, the biggest (but least interesting) Zafimaniry village. If you don't have your own vehicle, Sous Le Soleil can organise transfers from Ambositra. The lodge is the perfect base for the Zafimaniry villages. The closer ones can be visited as easy day trips, while overnight treks with expert local guides can be arranged to more distant villages.

Hôtel Thermal   FUSION €€€
(☑ 034 75 512 26; www.thermal-ranomafana.mg; mains Ar18,000-20,000) The restaurant at this classy hotel offers easily the most upmarket dining in town. There's a daily changing menu which has tropical takes on many classic French dishes. It's pricey but worth it. If you're not staying at the hotel, then you should reserve an hour or so in advance.

❶ Information

Be forewarned: there are currently no banks or ATMs in Ranomafana. The nearest banks are two hours away in Fianarantsoa.

❶ Getting There & Away

Taxis-brousses go daily from Ranomafana to Fianarantsoa (Ar6000, two hours), Manakara (Ar13,000, five hours), and Mananjary (Ar10,000, three hours). When arriving, let the *taxi-brousse* driver know if you want to get off in the village, at the park entrance, or at a hotel in between.

Parc National Ranomafana

The **Parc National Ranomafana** (www.parcs-madagascar.com; permits per day adult/child Ar55,000/25,000, community tax Ar5000) is a steamy hothouse of jungle biodiversity where the hum of insects is ever present and the wail and squeal of a dozen lemur species entices wildlife-watching tourists.

One of the six sites that make up the Unesco-listed Rainforests of Atsinanana World Heritage Site, the 41,600-hectare park was created in 1991 largely to protect two rare species of lemur (the golden bamboo lemur and the greater bamboo lemur, the former discovered only in 1986); for good reason, it has fast become a staple on almost every Madagascar itinerary.

The park is known for its diverse wildlife, although some of it is quite elusive. Including the lemurs, there are 29 mammal species present. The forest abounds with reptiles and amphibians, and the birdlife is exceptional (though the thick vegetation makes many of the birds hard to see).

Sights

Centre ValBio   CULTURAL CENTRE
(☑ 034 13 581 71; www.centrevalbio.org; tours Ar15,000, lectures Ar30,000; ☉ tours 9am, 10.30am & 3pm Mon-Fri, lectures 4pm) This international training centre for the study of biodiversity is housed in attractive buildings on the edge of the national park. If you have any interest in the scientific research going on in and around Ranomafana, you should make time to either visit the centre or to attend one of the regular evening lectures given by resident researchers. Tours and lectures must be reserved at least 24 hours in advance.

One of ValBio's main activities is outreach within the communities living on the park's borders. The centre has therefore developed good relationships with local associations and is able to organise activities such as basket making and silk weaving, or visits to artisan workshops. All activities and tours must be booked in advance.

🏃 Activities

Wildlife Watching

Seasons matter when it comes to wildlife in Ranomafana. Lemurs can be spotted pretty much year-round, and on a typical day's walk, you are likely to see between three and five species, including the famed golden bamboo lemur (Ranomafana is one of its two known habitats – a handful of individuals are now well accustomed to the presence of visitors) and the overly cute *sifaka* lemur.

Of the estimated 118 bird species here, an incredible 68 are endemic to Madagascar. The best season for birdwatching is spring, from September through to December, when migratory species return to the park.

Reptiles and amphibians are at their most active in summer, from December to March. The park has 13 species of chameleon (easily seen during a night walk), 14 species of snake (all harmless) and an amazing 106 species of frogs and toads. Summer is also the best time of year to admire the park's beautiful flora, including some 80 different species of orchid and nearly 200 ferns.

As with so many Malagasy parks, much of the wildlife is disarmingly nonplussed by humans and easy to approach. Binoculars though are a bonus for watching lemurs frolicking in the canopy.

Parc National Ranomafana

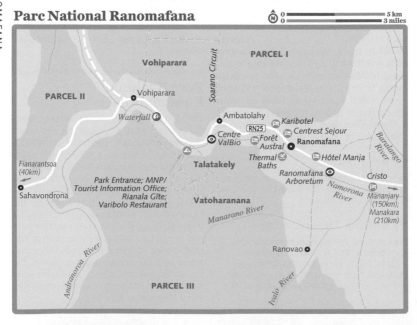

ℹ PARC NATIONAL RANOMAFANA

Best time to visit Between September and December, when the weather is warm and dry.

Key highlight Spotting a bamboo lemur.

Wildlife Lemurs, birds, frogs, chameleons.

Habitats Primary and secondary rainforest.

Gateway town Ranomafana.

Transport options *Taxi-brousse* (bush taxi) from Fianarantsoa (Ar6000).

Things you should know Be prepared for rain and temperature swings, particularly in winter, when a 25°C day becomes a 10°C night.

Night Walk   WILDLIFE WATCHING

(Ar30,000; ⊙ from 6pm) Night walks in search of chameleons, frogs and nocturnal lemurs are a popular activity. Walks last around an hour and don't take place within the forest proper but on the side of the road just above the national-park entrance. While this is hardly a wilderness experience, it's about the easiest way to find chameleons who, despite being fairly hard to find in daylight seem to virtually grow on trees after dark!

Hiking

The park is divided into three parcels of land containing both primary and secondary forest. The former is more impressive, with enormous trees, but takes more hiking to reach. The best thing to do is to discuss your options with your guide, depending on how much you want to walk and what you want to get out of the walk. Walking circuits vary in length from four hours to eight hours. Ranomafana is a very popular park but the vast majority of visitors only spend one night in the area and do a single morning tour of the forest. While this will give you some snapshots (albeit with several dozen other tourists all elbowing their way into frame!) of lemurs and a brief overview of the park, it's not the most rewarding way of seeing Ranomafana. Much better is to do one of the longer six- or eight-hour treks. This will allow you to see more of the forest and give

you a pretty decent chance of communing with lemurs all alone.

The Talatakely Trail system in Parcel III (secondary forest) is the most visited and also one of the best for spotting lemurs (walks will vary from three to four hours). There is a nice lookout (where striped mongooses are regular visitors) and a pretty waterfall popular for picnics. Guide fees per person: four hours (Ar75,000), six hours (Ar105,000) or eight hours (Ar120,000).

It can be very muddy in the park and heavy afternoon rain storms are common, so bring good boots and some waterproofs.

🛏 Sleeping & Eating

Although technically not part of the park, there are a couple of basic but very handy options right by the park entrance. Most people stay in or around the village of Ranomafana, which is around 6km downhill from the park entrance.

Rianala Gîte   HOSTEL €
(☑ 034 12 740 85; rianalagite@gmail.com; Ranomafana National Park entrance; dm Ar15,000) A rustic wooden cottage with two very basic eight-bed dorms. Its location right by the park entrance will save you to-ing and froing between the village and the park, but otherwise you'd only want to stay here if you are desperately short of cash.

Varibolo   MALAGASY €
(☑ 034 06 298 45; Ranomafana National Park entrance; mains Ar5000-10,000; ⊙ 7am-9pm) Perched on a hill overlooking the national park, Varibolo scores equally high on location and taste. The food is simple – grilled chicken, *romazava* (beef and vegetable stew), sandwiches – but always good. It's right by the start of the trails so come for a prewalk breakfast (crêpes, yum!) or a postwalk lunch. Alternatively, it can prepare picnic baskets (Ar15,000).

ℹ Information

The **Madagascar National Parks office** (MNP; ☑ 034 78 339 89; ⊙ 7am-4pm) is located right at the entrance of the park. Park visitors pay the entry fee here, part of which goes to the community. Several guides speak good English, but it's worth trying to reserve one in advance.

ℹ Getting There & Away

The gateway town for the park is Ranomafana, which is 6km east of the park entrance on the

RN25. If you don't have a private car, travelling between Ranomafana and the park will be tricky. *Taxis-brousses* heading in/out of the village may be happy to take you (Ar2000); some hotels arrange transfers for about Ar10,000. Alternatively, hitch a ride with other travellers.

Manakara

🖉 072 / POP 38,000

Well off the beaten tourist trail, Manakara, which is divided into two distinct parts by a canal, is innately interesting and a highly underrated destination. The steamy hot inland side, known as Tanambao, has a dynamic Caribbean vibe, with sandy streets, tin-roofed shacks and a buoyant daily market, while on the other side of the bridge lies the breezy seaside district of Manakara-Be.

For those not planning on visiting the Canal des Pangalanes elsewhere, this is your chance. It can make a welcome beach break from the highlands, particularly after hiking in the parks. While Manakara is geographically on the east coast, virtually all travellers visit on a round trip from Fianarantsoa, often by the infamous FCE railway (p76), making Manakara an important part of many a highlands itinerary.

◉ Sights

Domaine Aavyland PLANTATION
(🖉 032 44 653 25; RN12; guided tours Ar10,000; ☺ 9am-noon & 2.30-5pm) Some 18km south of Manakara on the road to Vohipeno, you'll find Domaine Aavyland, a 31-hectare organic plantation and distillery producing medicinal and fragrant essential oils such as *ravintsara*, *niaouly*, clove, cinnamon and ylang-ylang. With advance notice staff can offer fascinating two-hour guided tours of the plantation and distillery, explaining the virtues and production process of every essential oil.

⌒ Tours

★ **Canal des Pangalanes** BOATING
(full day incl lunch for 2 people around Ar100,000) The most popular excursion in Manakara is a pirogue day trip along the Canal des Pangalanes, which was dug out by the French in the 1890s to circumvent the capricious Indian Ocean. Tours usually make a couple of stops on the way (eg cultural monuments, a village, an artisanal distillery) and include a sumptuous lunch on the beach. Half-day tours are also possible.

🛏 Sleeping

Les Flamboyants HOTEL €
(🖉 020 72 216 77; lionelmanakara@dts.mg; Tanambao; d Ar20,000-40,000; ☎) This is a cheap if uninspiring hotel in the centre of Tanambao, with a shady patio, fans and a restaurant. The attentive owner has been living in Manakara for more than a decade and has plenty of local travel information.

Parthenay Club BUNGALOW €€
(🖉 034 29 803 14, 020 72 216 63; Manakara-Be; bungalows Ar75,000-100,000; ☎🏊) These tiki-hut bungalows, set in a well-landscaped compound on the beach, are a great way to enjoy the unique feeling of straddling both canal and sea. Each bungalow has been individually decorated, with special attention given to the bathrooms (a rarity in Madagascar). The restaurant is excellent too (mains Ar12,000 to Ar18,000), with meals presented with artistic touches.

Club Vanille BUNGALOW €€
(🖉 034 17 209 68, 020 72 210 23; hotellavanillemanakara@yahoo.fr; Manakara-Be; bungalows with/without air-con from Ar75,000/70,000; ☎) Located 8km south of Manakara, this popular place has thatched-roofed, canal-side bungalows that are comfortable without being overly fancy. The impressive restaurant offers catch of the day and cold beer. Best of all, you are caught between the absolute roar of the surf on one side, and the placid canal on the other. Shuttle service (Ar5000) available.

🍴 Eating

★ **Sharon** MALAGASY €
(Tanambao; mains Ar2500-4000; ☺ 11am-9pm Tue-Sun) This cheap and cheerful eatery heaves with young locals every night of the week. It serves the best *brochettes* (kebabs) in town, cooked on a street-side BBQ (don't miss the peanut dipping sauce). The huge *mi sao* (a traditional dish that combines noodles or pasta with meat, prawns and soya sauce) is the house's other signature dish.

Les Délices d'Orient INTERNATIONAL €€
(🖉 032 41 747 95; Tanambao; mains Ar10,000-18,000; ☺ 11.30am-2pm & 6-9pm) Les Délices is well known in Manakara for its excellent cuisine, particularly its seafood – grilled fish, prawns in coconut sauce, garlic *camarons* (a kind of king prawn). It's all delicious and great value, with friendly and efficient service to boot.

Manakara

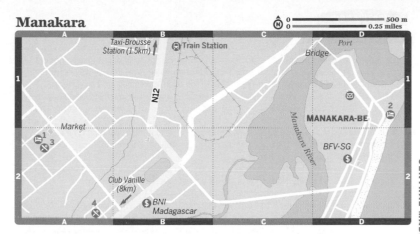

Manakara

🛌 Sleeping
1 Les Flamboyants.................................A2
2 Parthenay Club D1

🍴 Eating
3 Les Délices d'Orient...........................A2
4 Sharon..A2

❶ Information

MONEY

Manakara has several banks and ATMs to choose from

BFV-SG (Manakara-Be; ⊘ 8-11.30am & 2-4.30pm Mon-Fri)

BNI Madagascar (RN 12; ⊘ 8-11.30am & 2-4.30pm Mon-Fri)

POST

Post office (Manakara-Be; ⊘ 8-11.30am & 2-4.30pm Mon-Fri)

❶ Getting There & Away

Taxi-brousse There are usually two *taxis-brousses* per day between Manakara and Ranomafana (Ar13,000, five hours), continuing to Fianarantsoa (Ar6000, seven hours). These leave from the *taxi-brousse* station, which is a few minutes' walk north of the centre, at 9am and 3pm or 4pm. There is one service a day to Tana (Ar30,000, 15 hours). The *taxi-brousse* station is 2km north of town.

Train Most travellers prefer to travel at least one way by train between Fianarantsoa and Manakara. The train leaves Manakara on Wednesday and Sunday at 7am and takes anywhere between 12 and 24 hours to reach Fianarantsoa. Tickets cost Ar70,000 in 1st class. Tourists are not allowed to travel in 2nd class. The train station is right in the town centre.

❶ Getting Around

Take a pousse-pousse or tuk-tuk in town. Fares to Tanambao/Manakara-Be from the railway station are Ar1500/2000. These double at night.

Sahambavy

📙 075 / POP 17,000

Beautiful Sahambavy (sam-bav) is an idyllic place to put your bags down for a couple of days. The tender green of the tea bushes stretches for kilometres, there is a beautiful lake, a fantastic hotel-restaurant and a generally laid-back vibe.

Sahambavy is the second stop after Fianarantsoa on the FCE railway line, so it's an ideal place to get on or off the train: the stretch between here and Fianar isn't very interesting, and more importantly it means you save an hour's sleep in the morning on the way to Manakara (or arrive an hour earlier in the evening coming from Manakara).

◉ Sights

Sahambavy Tea Estate   FARM
(Sahambavy; Ar7500; ⊘ 7.30am-3.30pm Mon-Fri) Established in 1969 and specialising in green teas, this is Madagascar's only tea plantation. Visits take you from the fields to the processing plant and finish with a tasting. Tea is picked every day from October to April, and three days a week the rest of the year (visits cost Ar5000 when there is

WORTH A TRIP

THE FCE RAILWAY

For those with a flexible schedule, an abundance of time and a lot of patience, a popular thing to do in Madagascar is to take the FCE (Fianarantsoa–Côte Est) railway between Fianarantsoa and Manakara on the east coast. The train leaves around 7am (theoretically – in practice it is almost always late) on Tuesday and Saturday (from Manakara it leaves at 7am on Wednesday and Sunday) and chugs along at 20km per hour on tracks built in the 1930s, reaching its destination between 12 and 24 hours later. Sometimes 48 hours later (yes, it's that variable)! It all depends on the loading/unloading times along the way, the conditions of the tracks and the train, derailings (commonplace), how heavy the train is, and what the weather's like.

Along the way, you'll pass plantations, waterfalls and green hills, cross 67 bridges and four spectacular viaducts, and go through 48 tunnels. Despite its antiquity and unreliability, the train is still an economic lifeline for the people of the inland villages (where there are no roads), who use it to transport their cargoes of bananas and lychees to be sold and exported. Stopping at each tiny station is a colourful experience, with Malagasy passengers leaning out of the windows to haggle with hordes of vendors balancing baskets of bananas, crayfish or fresh bread on their heads.

For the best views of the cliffs, misty valleys and waterfalls en route, sit on the left side when going from Fianarantsoa to Manakara (and vice versa).

Because of the FCE's erratic schedule, taking the train requires a little planning and a good dose of pragmatism and flexibility should it all go wrong. The most scenic landscapes are between Sahambavy and Fenomby, so it is generally better to take the train from Fianar to Manakara to make sure you travel through this stretch in daylight (it's also downhill). However, the delays are often more severe from Fianar because this is where maintenance and repairs are done.

Bring enough water and food for 24 hours (street food is available along the way but comes with the usual precautionary warnings), and some warm clothes in winter.

For a more detailed history of the railway and the regions through which it passes, pick up a booklet called *Le Dernier Train du Corridor* by Maggie L Formentin (Ar5000) at Fianar's train station or in souvenir shops.

no picking as there is less to see). Tours are available in English, but it's sensible to reserve an English-speaking guide in advance.

Note that you should only pay for your visit at the processing plant where you will be issued a ticket, and not at the estate gate (visitors have been ripped off). The easiest way of organising a visit is through the Lac Hôtel.

🛏 Sleeping

⭐ **Lac Hôtel** BOUTIQUE HOTEL €€€

(🖰 020 75 959 06; www.lachotel.com; Sahambavy; bungalows €50-60, train carriages €70; ❄ 🛜) Beautifully located on the shores of Lake Sahambavy, this exquisite boutique hotel offers a variety of accommodation, including show-stopping bungalows on stilts. The local carvings and fabrics form a refined Malagasy style, and there are gorgeous views of the lake. Honeymooners and/or rail enthusiasts should plump for the vintage FCE wagon (€70), which has been lovingly renovated.

🛈 Getting There & Away

Sahambavy is located about 23km east of Fianarantsoa; the turn-off from the RN7 is clearly signposted, about 10km northeast of Fianar. The track is in pretty bad condition. There are daily *taxis-brousses* (Ar3000), or you could take the train.

Fianarantsoa

🗹 075 / POP 190,300

Fianarantsoa (fi-a-nar-ant-*soo*), or Fianar for short, has a lot going for it. There's an attractive, village-like old quarter, markets that hum and whirl with life, and some excellent places to stay and eat. However, more than all of this, Fianarantsoa is both a transit hub for central and southern Madagascar and a base from which to strike out to absorbing nearby national parks and reserves and luminous tea gardens.

Orientation

The city is divided into three parts. Basse-Ville (Lower Town), to the north, is a busy, chaotic area with the main post office and the train and *taxi-brousse* stations. Up from Basse-Ville is Nouvelle Ville (New Town), the business area, with banks and several hotels. Further southwest and uphill is Haute-Ville (Upper Town), which has cobbled streets, a more peaceful atmosphere, numerous church spires and wide views.

◉ Sights

★ Haute-Ville   AREA

The oldest and most attractive part of town is the pedestrian Haute-Ville (known as Tanana Ambony in Malagasy). Utterly removed from the hustle of the rest of the town, the Haute-Ville feels more like a quiet hilltop village. It's famed for its architecture – two-storey brick houses with steep roofs, balconies and tumbling plants – which dates back to the late 19th and early 20th centuries. A stroll around the cobbled streets here offers great views of the town and surrounding countryside.

There are six churches on this small hill alone, including the imposing Ambozontany Cathedral. Many of the buildings in the Haute-Ville are in a bad state of repair – local association Fondation Heritsialonina is working to restore and promote the area's heritage. You'll see an information board about its mission on the main cobbled stairway through the Haute-Ville. Many locals will tell you that the Haute-Ville is a Unesco World Heritage Site. This is not true.

Maromby   MONASTERY

(www.maromby.org; ⊘ 9.30-11.30am & 3-4.30pm) **FREE** The monks at this monastery continue to do what they have done for centuries: make wine (red and white, and flavoured aperitifs) and honey (which you can buy in the shop). The modern church, with its striking stained-glass windows, vaulted wooden ceiling and carved doors, is particularly interesting as it reflects the integration of Christianity and Malagasy culture.

The monastery is located 7km north of Fianarantsoa. To get here without a private vehicle, take *taxi-be* 29 or 34 (Ar400) from Place Zoma towards Andriamboasary and ask the driver to drop you off at the junction where the monastery is signposted – you'll have to walk the last 300m.

Zoma   MARKET

(⊘ 7am-6pm) Fianar is a market town, with at least one small market open every day. The largest is the Zoma, where you'll find everything under the sun. It's held every day along Ave de l'Indépendance and Rue de Verdun, although Tuesday and Friday are best.

☞ Tours

Most outfits propose day hikes in the surrounding Betsileo villages (sometimes with overnight stays). A popular option is a day trip combining a pirogue (canoe) river trip with a visit to the Sahambavy Tea Estate, handy for those without a vehicle. Fianarantsoa is also a good place to organise trips to Parc National Andringitra.

Mad Trekking   HIKING

(☑ 034 14 221 73; mad.trekking@moov.mg; Rue Philibert Tsiranana; ⊘ 8.30am-noon & 2-5.30pm Mon-Fri) A reliable operator specialising in multiday excursions around Fianarantsoa and hiking packages in hard-to-reach places such as Andringitra or the Makay (north of Isalo National Park). For two people, allow around €30 per person per day for local excursions, €60 to €70 for more adventurous hikes (prices include transport).

Maison des Guides   HIKING

(☑ 032 02 728 97, 034 03 123 01; coeurmalgache@hotmail.com; Route MDRM; ⊘ 8am-5.30pm Mon-Sat) Memorably located in an old railway car in front of the train station, this cooperative of local guides offers a variety of tours in the area. It specialises in hikes to the picturesque Betsileo villages nearby (per person from Ar30,000), as well as multiday hikes in Parc National Andringitra and other areas. English-speaking guides available.

🛏 Sleeping

Peniela   GUESTHOUSE €

(☑ 032 40 486 56; peniela.house@yahoo.fr; Haute-Ville; d Ar33,000) One of the few buildings in the Haute-Ville to have been entirely renovated, the beautiful Peniela is a boon for travellers keen to stay in a traditional Malagasy highland house in relative comfort. The rooms are homely and clean, and the Haute-Ville is quiet and a joy to explore. There is no vehicle access for the last 200m.

It's essential to phone in advance and let them know you're coming because there's often nobody present at the house.

GODDARD_PHOTOGRAPHY/GETTY IMAGES ©

1. *Marmites* (giant aluminium pots)
Aluminium pots are made in workshops in Ambatolampy (p62).

2. Parc National Ranomafana
This diverse jungle reserve is a Unesco-listed World Heritage Site (p71).

3. FCE railway
The FCE (Fianarantsoa–Côte Est) railway runs between Fianarantsoa and Manakara on the east coast (p76).

4. Fianarantsoa
Looking over Fianarantsoa's Haute-Ville, with its 19th- and early-20th-century buildings (p76).

Fianarantsoa

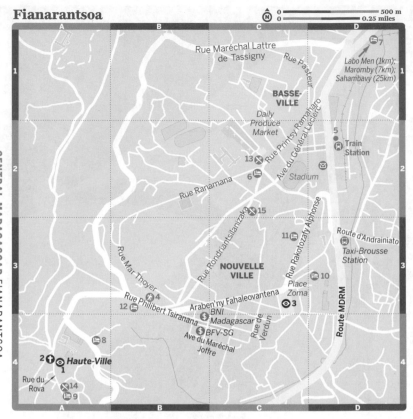

Raza-ôtel GUESTHOUSE €

(☑ 020 75 519 15, 034 14 221 73; d Ar40,000, without bathroom Ar35,000; 🛜) This is a charming family-run guesthouse with paint-flaking window shutters and a peaceful countryside vibe, even though it's just 100m from busy Place Zoma at the end of a bumpy dirt track. There are just four simple rooms with shared facilities (and one with private bathroom). Meals (mains Ar8000 to Ar10,000) are available on request.

La Case Madrigal GUESTHOUSE €€

(☑ 032 60 316 40; www.lacasemadrigal.wordpress. com; incl breakfast s €8-13, d €17-22, apt €45; 🛜) A lovely French-run guesthouse on the edge of town, with just three impeccably decorated and turned out rooms. The trump card is the convivial lounge-cum-dining-room and terrace where guests congregate in the evenings for an aperitif. Meals can be arranged (three-course menu Ar32,000).

Residence Matsiatra GUESTHOUSE €€

(☑ 034 65 598 18; www.hotelmatsiatra.com; Rue Rakotozafy Alphonse; d/tr from Ar50,000/70,000; 🛜) There are five spacious, well-equipped and comfortable rooms in this welcoming Malagasy-French-run guesthouse. It's a particularly good option for travelling families as some of the rooms are interconnecting, plus the owners have a little one of their own so there's an instant playmate available! The in-house restaurant makes good wood-fired pizzas, which can be eaten in the garden terrace.

La Rizière BOUTIQUE HOTEL €€

(☑ 020 75 502 15; www.lariziere.org; Haute-Ville; d Ar95,000-110,000; 🛜) This gorgeous hotel is the training ground of hospitality school La Rizière. Students here learn how to work in and run a hotel, and they're doing a pretty good job. The rooms are impeccable, with lovely wooden floors and bright green

Fianarantsoa

feature walls, and the atmosphere is warm and relaxed. There are sensational views of Fianarantsoa from the gardens.

Hôtel Cotsoyannis   HOTEL €€
(☏020 75 514 72; www.hotel.cotsoyannis.mg; 4 Rue Printsy Ramaharo; d Ar86,000; ☏) The exterior of this hotel might be uninspiring, but it is actually a very well cared for hotel centred around a garden courtyard crammed with banana plants. The elegant wood-floored rooms all have fans and mosquito nets over the beds and it's quieter than its town-centre location might lead you to expect.

There's a reasonable in-house restaurant and a tour company offering trekking and car transfers to nearby parks and sights.

Tsara Guest House   HERITAGE HOTEL €€€
(☏020 75 502 06, 032 05 516 12; www.tsaraguest. com; Rue Philibert Tsiranana; d Ar98,000-160,000, without bathroom Ar48,000; ☏) This classy plantation-style heritage guesthouse is perennially popular. The public spaces are excellent. The reception area has a roaring fire, the glass-walled restaurant serves delicious food and the beautiful outdoor terrace offers great views. There are four categories of room, all homely, cozy and with a historic feel.

✖ Eating

Chez Imanoela   CAFE €
(Haute-Ville; sandwiches & cakes Ar2000-8000; ☺9am-6.30pm Mon-Sat) What a great idea this was: a cafe in the picturesque and atmospheric Haute-Ville. The flower-decked terrace is a lovely spot to while away an hour or two, be it with a beer, coffee or light meal. Lunch options include freshly made soups or sandwiches. The cafe also bakes its own cakes.

Chez Dom   FAST FOOD €
(☏034 87 785 01; Rue Ranamana; mains Ar6000-10,000; ☺11am-2pm & 5-9.30pm Mon-Sat, ☏) A small, neighbourhood cafe-bar offering local rum and a quick menu (burgers, omelettes, zebu steaks, salads etc). It's frequented by backpackers, French expats and tourists and is painted in lurid colours which get more lurid with each extra mojito (Ar4000) you knock back. Some guides are based here; they offer the usual circuits around Fianar, but can be quite pushy.

Chez Ninie   MALAGASY €
(Rue Rondriantsilanizaka; mains Ar4500-7000; ☺8am-8.30pm Mon-Sat) Don't be fooled by the facade: lurking out the back is a rather chic multilevel, open-porch dining area with an extensive, inexpensive and very tasty Malagasy menu that keeps this place very popular. Supercheap beer (Ar2000).

★ **La Rizière**   INTERNATIONAL €€
(☏020 75 502 15; www.lariziere.org; Haute-Ville; mains from Ar12,000, 3-course menu Ar34,000; ☺noon-2.30pm & 6.30-9.30pm, closed Feb–mid-Mar) For gastronomic fare at average prices, make sure you book a table at La Rizière. The restaurant is a working culinary school and the chefs and waiters are all perfecting their trade. Service is charming (the chefs come and introduce themselves at the end of the meal) and the dining room phenomenal: a glasshouse with panoramic views of Fianarantsoa.

Tsara Guest House Restaurant   INTERNATIONAL €€
(☏020 75 502 06, 032 05 516 12; www.tsaraguest. com; Rue Philibert Tsiranana; mains Ar14,000-22,000; ☺6.30am-midnight) Expect well-presented French dishes with a Malagasy

twist in the classy glass-fronted dining room of this historic hotel. Classical music plays in the background while you eat.

🛍 Shopping

Labo Men ART

(www.pierrotmen.com; ⊙8am-noon & 2.30-6pm Mon-Sat) Madagascar's most famous photographer, Pierrot Men, is a native of Fianarantsoa, where he still lives and works. His shop is stocked full of his beautiful images in various formats: postcards (Ar2000), posters and framed photographs (from Ar60,000) and coffee-table books.

ℹ Information

INTERNET ACCESS

Every recommended hotel has wi-fi, but if you did need an internet cafe then there are still a couple hanging on down around the train station and stadium in the city centre.

MONEY

Fianar has many banks with ATMs that also change currency and do Visa card cash advances.

BFV-SG (Rue Philibert Tsiranana; ⊙8-11.30am & 2-4.30pm Mon-Fri)

BNI Madagascar (Rue Philibert Tsiranana; ⊙8-11.30am & 2-4.30pm Mon-Fri)

POST

Post office (Route MDRM; ⊙8-11.30am & 2-4.30pm Mon-Fri)

ℹ Getting There & Away

AIR

There is an airport in Fianar, but no regularly scheduled flights.

TAXI-BROUSSE & MINIBUS

The **taxis-brousse station** (Route MDRM) is in the centre of town and just a short walk from the train station. Frequent *taxis-brousses* connect Fianarantsoa with Ambositra (Ar15,000, five hours), Antsirabe (Ar18,000, seven hours) and Antananarivo (Ar26,000, 10 hours).

Minibuses also go daily to Ambalavao (Ar5000, two hours), Ranohira (Ar35,000, seven hours) and on to Tuléar (Ar52,000, 12 hours). Departures from Fianarantsoa to Tuléar are around 8am and 6pm. Heading east there are multiple vehicles daily between Fianarantsoa and Ranomafana (Ar6000, two hours) and Manakara (Ar15,000–AR18,000, eight hours).

TRAIN

Fianarantsoa is connected to Manakara on the eastern coast by the famous FCE railway (p76).

Departures from Fianarantsoa are scheduled for Tuesday and Saturday at 7am, and from Manakara on Sunday and Wednesday at 7am. There are frequent delays and cancellations, making it wise to visit the station the day before to confirm.

The trip can take anywhere from 12 to 24 hours – sometimes more – so you should pack enough food to keep you going (as well as warm clothes for the night). Tickets cost Ar70,000 in 1st class. Foreigners are not allowed to travel in 2nd nclass.

ℹ Getting Around

Taxis operate day and night. The daytime price anywhere in the city is usually Ar5000, and at night it's Ar6000 (note that taxis can be hard to find after 9pm).

Villages and destinations in the surrounding area are served by *taxi-bes* (minivans), which have route numbers marked in their front window. The fare to all destinations is Ar400; departures are from the *taxi-brousse* station.

Ambalavao

📋 075 / POP 28,030

Set amid beautiful mountainous countryside with numerous boulder-like peaks rearing up beyond it, Ambalavao is a charming market town centred on a Gothic cathedral which looks as if it's been parachuted in from the French Loire Valley. The small town is home to a number of interesting cottage industries which can be visited and it makes a handy base for up-close encounters with the ring-tailed lemurs of the nearby Reserve d'Anja.

◎ Sights

★ **Réserve d'Anja** WILDLIFE RESERVE

(Anja; Ar10,000; ⊙6am-6pm) This 370,000-sq-metre reserve encompasses three mountain-size granite boulders (the three sisters) ringed at the base by a forest full of ring-tailed lemurs. Anja's lemurs are famous for sunning themselves on the boulders (generally early in the morning); there are around 800 individuals in the reserve and surrounding hills and they're very well habituated so you'll get the chance to get relatively close. The reserve is a completely community-run initiative and has been extremely successful, generating revenues and jobs for the village.

Anja is not just one of the most enjoyable community reserves to visit, it's also one

THE BETSILEO

The Betsileo, Madagascar's third-largest tribe, inhabit the *hauts plateaux* (highlands) area around Fianarantsoa and Ambalavao. They only began viewing themselves as a nation after being invaded and conquered by the Merina in the early 19th century.

The Betsileo are renowned throughout Madagascar for their rice-cultivation techniques – they manage up to three harvests a year instead of the usual one or two, and their lands are marked by beautiful terracing and vivid shades of green in the rice paddy fields. Betsileo herders are famous for their trilby hats and the blankets they wear slung in a debonair fashion around their shoulders. Betsileo houses are distinctively tall and square, constructed from bricks as red as the earth of the roads.

As well as the *famadihana* exhumation and reburial, literally 'the turning of the bones'), which was adopted from the Merina after the unification of Madagascar, an important Betsileo belief centres on *hasina*, a force that is believed to flow from the land through the ancestors into the society of the living. Skilled traditional practitioners are thought to be able to manipulate *hasina* to achieve cures and other positive effects. The reverse of *hasina* is *hera*, which can result in illness and misfortune.

of the most successful in Madagascar. This means it sees around 14,000 tourists a year, so you are unlikely to be alone, particularly from April to November. Guiding fees cost a hefty Ar24,000/36,000/48,000 for 30 minutes/one hour/two hours. Some guides speak basic English (they know their script well but struggle with questions). Not only are you certain to see the ring-tailed lemurs up-close, but chances are you'll also find many different chameleons, including the thumb-nail-sized leaf chameleons (*Brookesia*) which, as the name suggests, spend their lives creeping through the leaf litter looking like oversized ants.

Anja is located about 12km south of Ambalavao on the RN7. There are regular *taxis-brousses* (Ar1000) from Ambalavao.

Parc Communautaire de Sakaviro Miray
WILDLIFE RESERVE

(☑ 033 71 793 57, 034 94 509 86; Laritsena; admission & guide Ar25,000) For the moment, the Parc Communautaire de Sakaviro Miray, a community conservation project preserving a small patch of forest that is home to three groups of semihabituated ring-tailed lemurs, is little known to international visitors. There are currently three different walking circuits, plus you can take a kayak out onto the river to look for crocodiles. Guides (some of whom speak English) are available. To reach the reserve, drive 7km west of Ambalavao to the village of Laritsena and then head 5km NW on a bumpy track. It's vital to phone in advance and let them know you're coming, otherwise there won't be any guides waiting.

Soalandy
WORKSHOP

(☑ 033 14 987 45; RN7; ☺ 7.30am-5.30pm Mon-Sat, to noon Sun) **FREE** Madagascar is home to an endemic species of silkworm, which feeds on tapia trees in the wild and whose cocoons are threaded and woven like 'conventional' silk. The labour intensive production process of this 'wild silk' is laid out in this workshop. You can buy beautiful scarves (Ar30,000 to Ar500,000) in the adjoining shop.

Fabrique de Papier Antaimoro
WORKSHOP

(☑ 020 75 340 01; ☺ 7.30-11.30am & 1-5pm Sat, 8.30am-noon Sun) **FREE** This workshop, at the back of the Aux Bougainvillées hotel compound, showcases the production of a unique kind of paper, made from the bark of a Malagasy bush, which has flowers pressed into it. Antaimoro cards, envelopes and picture frames are all for sale.

Zebu Market
MARKET

(RN7; ☺ Wed morning) Ambalavao hosts the largest zebu market in the country. Tough, wizened herders walk from as far away as Tuléar and Fort-Dauphin to sell their cattle. It is quite a spectacle, especially as the animals make their way up the bluff where the huge enclosure is located. The market reaches fever pitch around 10am or 11am.

It's located about 1km west of central Ambalavao.

Activities

Foudia
HIKING

(☑ 034 84 964 79; ☺ 8am-5pm Mon-Sat) This small tour operator has English-speaking guides and organises circuits in Parc National Andringitra and the Tsaranoro Valley, as well as overland hikes between Ambalavao and Manakara. It also rents out camping equipment and can organise paragliding in the Tsaranoro Valley (€75 per person including equipment and transport).

🛏 Sleeping

Résidence du Betsileo   HOTEL €

(☑ 034 10 665 45, 032 82 841 81; residencedu betsileo@gmail.com; s/d Ar35,000/45,000; 🛜) This charming bargain is the best place to stay – and eat – in the town centre. The owners are slowly renovating the building (the rooms do need updating), but the atmosphere is redolent of slow, lazy days. Choose the off-street rooms for a more peaceful night.

Espace Zongo   LODGE €

(☑ 033 83 724 59; espacezongo@gmail.com; RN7; d/tw/bungalows Ar50,000/60,000/80,000; 🛜) In a scenic spot 2km north of Ambalavao, Espace Zongo offers eight simple but impeccable rooms and a smattering of comfortable bungalows. It's all well maintained, but it lacks a little spirit, even the spacious restaurant and terrace. The grounds are spacious, however; perhaps it just needs a little time to grow into its ambitions.

Hot water in the rooms comes from solar panels and is reliable only in the afternoons and evenings. The bungalows have hot water at all hours.

Aux Bougainvillées   HOTEL €€

(☑ 034 20 737 85, 032 43 680 69; auxbougainvilles ambalavao@gmail.com; d/q Ar70,000/121,000; 🛜) Draped in its colourful namesake plant, this hotel has a bit of character. Rooms are spread across several buildings in a quiet compound; all are comfortable, clean and rather colourful. There's a decent but expensive restaurant (mains Ar14,000 to Ar16,000), which is popular with tour groups at lunch.

★ Betsileo Country Lodge   GUESTHOUSE €€€

(☑ 034 42 363 16; www.betsileocountrylodge.com; RN7; incl breakfast r from Ar200,000, bungalow s/d/ tr Ar209,000/247,000/285,000; 🛜🏊) Peaceful, and set in a beautiful rural location 8km south of Ambalavao on the RN7, the Betsileo Country Lodge basks among glorious landscapes and enormous skies. The pretty rooms and bungalows (all newly built) are incredibly homely and the friendly Dutch managers will bend over backwards to help their guests. The pool is a lovely bonus.

The delicious three-course dinner is a set menu (Ar38,000). The lodge has mountain bikes for guest use and an in-house guide.

🍴 Eating

Tsienimparihy   BAKERY €

(Ambalavao; pastries from Ar1000, mains Ar8000-10,000; ⊙ 7am-7pm) This bakery-cum-restaurant has made a name for itself for the quality of its cakes and bread. The food is good too: expect plenty of chicken/zebu in sauces, omelettes and noodles.

★ Résidence du Betsileo   FRENCH €€

(☑ 032 82 841 81, 034 10 665 45; residencedu betsileo@gmail.com; mains Ar17,000-20,000; ⊙ 6am-9pm) The owner of this gently old-fashioned, small-town bistro is a maestro in the kitchen as he sizzles, boils and fries delicious and authentic French countryside meals with just a pop of Madagascar about them. People come from far and wide to eat here and the foie gras is popular. The bar is an enjoyable spot for a predinner aperitif.

ℹ Getting There & Away

Ambalavao lies 56km south of Fianarantsoa. The town has direct taxi-brousse connections with Fianarantsoa (Ar4000, 1½ hours), Ihosy (Ar10,000, three hours) and Ranohira (Ar15,000, six hours). For destinations further north, you'll have to go to Fianarantsoa first. The taxi-brousse station is close to the cathedral.

Massif de l'Andringitra

Andringitra (An-*drintch*) is a majestic central mountain range with two gorgeous valleys on either side, the Namoly and the Tsaranoro (sometimes called the Sahanambo, for the river that runs through it), forming an epic playground for walkers and climbers.

One could easily spend a week hiking here. There are spectacular views in all directions, well-developed hiking trails, excellent accommodation, interesting villages, plus three extraordinary peaks: Pic Boby (Imarivolanitra), at 2658m the second-highest peak in the country; the Tsaranoro Massif, which reaches 1910m, including an 800m vertical column considered to be one of the most challenging rock-climbs in the world; and the great stump of Pic Dondy (2195m). The latter two form the Portes du Sud (Gates of the South) and separate the Betsileo and Bara regions.

Compared to some parks in Madagascar, Andringitra gets relatively few visitors, which means it's possible to have these soaring granite peaks largely to yourself.

ℹ️ Information

Bring all the money you might need with you.

ℹ️ Getting There & Away

The lack of visitors to Andringitra is mostly due to the difficulty of accessing the area, which can be both timely and costly. The dirt roads running here can become impassable after heavy rain. There is no public transport into the Namoly Valley and the national park, and even in dry weather you will need a sturdy 4WD. For the Tsaranoro Valley, there is infrequent public transport to the village of Vohitsoaka from Ambalavao (Ar5000), but from there to the camps (12km to 15km away) there's no public transport. If you don't have much baggage, then you could walk it in about six hours (the route is easy to follow, but it gets searingly hot). But almost all visitors come by private 4WD; you'll need a good one because even at the best of times the 'road' (such as it is) is terrible.

Parc National Andringitra

Parc National Andringitra is the pièce de résistance of the wider Massif de l'Andringitra. It encompasses a high-altitude granite plateau of epic beauty, small tracts of primary rainforest, scenic trails along mountain streams and waterfalls, and Pic Boby, the highest accessible mountain in Madagascar. The best time to visit the national park (www.parcs-madagascar.com; permits per day Ar45,000; ⏱ ticket office 6.30am-3.30pm) is from June to November, when the rains aren't relentless (between January and March heavy rains make access to the park very difficult). Afternoon mists are common year-round in these high altitudes and you should be prepared for bad weather at any time of year.

If you are climbing Pic Boby, you will need a torch (flashlight) with several hours of battery life as the summit attempt generally starts way before dawn so that you can be there for sunrise).

🏃 Activities

The huge majority of visitors to Andringitra come for the hiking, which is among the best in Madagascar. Only a very small minority of people come exclusively for wildlife.

Wildlife Watching

Andringitra is mainly about hiking in spectacular scenery; it is not primarily a wildlife destination. Thirteen lemur species have been identified here, but sightings by visitors are rare since most of their habitat is outside the tourism zone. Ring-tailed lemurs are the most commonly seen. The park's rich flora includes more than 30 species of orchid, which bloom mainly in October and November.

Hiking

The national park proper offers 100km of trails that traverse a variety of habitats and offer fantastic hiking. There are five main circuits catering to various abilities, but if you are going to come here, and are in good shape, take the Imarivolanitra Trail (p86) to the summit of Pic Boby to get the full Andringitra experience.

Other circuits include the easy **Asaramanitra** (6km, about four hours), which includes waterfalls and a cave, and the scenic **Diavolana** (12km, 10 hours), which is the next-best choice after Imarivolanitra, as it takes in much of the plateau beneath the mountains. The best route for lemur spotting is **Imaitso** (9km, four hours), which goes through the eastern primary forest. Details of the various routes are available at the park office.

Note that whichever trail you take, the heat bouncing back off the granite rock can

---

ℹ️ PARC NATIONAL ANDRINGITRA

Best time to visit October to November during orchid bloom.

Key highlight Sunrise from the summit of Pic Boby.

Wildlife Ring-tailed lemurs, multi-coloured grasshoppers.

Habitats High plateau, meadows, rocky peaks, some primary rainforest (Imaitso).

Gateway town Ambalavao.

Transport options Private car.

Things you should know Water freezes at night during winter. If you are climbing Pic Boby, you will need a torch (flashlight) with several hours of battery life.

be almost overpowering and can turn what should be a simple enough hike into something much more draining. Take plenty of water and sun protection.

Imarivolanitra Trail

The best way to see Andringitra is on the Imarivolanitra Trail. Enter through the Namoly Valley, summit Pic Boby and then descend into the Tsaranoro. The circuit usually takes three days but you could do it in two if you don't mind a long second day (12 hours).

On Day 1 you'll hike from the Namoly park entrance to the Pic Boby base camp. This entails hiking up 600m or so until you reach a high plateau that hugs the rocky skyline for kilometres. It's a generally gentle climb, with a few steep 50m ascents, that takes four hours. The camp is by a stream, so you can fall asleep while listening to a waterfall beneath the stars.

On Day 2 awake early, and depart by torch (flashlight) at 4am for a two-hour hike to the summit, which is not where you think. When you reach the top of the skyline, with the sky beginning to lighten, you finally see what looks like Gibraltar sitting on top. This strenuous last leg takes you to the (second) roof of Madagascar, just in time for sunrise. Here you stand astride the entire island, a sea of clouds on one side, and an unbroken vista on the other. Beneath a cairn lies a metal box with a guestbook.

Now it's back to camp for breakfast, and onwards to new territory. You walk along the flat plateau for hours, breathing in the finest scenery. The sky is huge, the ridgeline dramatic. After crossing over the mountains through a deep pass, the Tsaranoro Valley comes into view, a grand vista. You pass through an alluring desert landscape, with the unforgettable sight of the great massif's vertical drop ahead.

About a third of the way down to the Tsaranoro is the second MNP campsite where you can break off. If you're carrying on, it's another three hours of down, down, down until you reach the first few villages, and another hour to Morarano and your hotel for the night, with the Gates of the South towering above. The next day you can hike more of the valley, or head back to the RN7. Unforgettable.

🛏 Sleeping

In the winter temperatures fall into the cold-as-hell zone, reaching as low as -7°C at night.

You will need extrawarm clothing and a good sleeping bag. For camping equipment, try Foudia (p83) in Ambalavao. If you'd rather not have to worry about all the logistics, Foudia, Mad Trekking (p77) and Malagasy Tours (p294) all organise packages.

The park has five wilderness **MNP camping grounds** (per tent Ar6000) with roof-only sites, a cooking hut, running water and long-drop toilets.

Tranogasy   LODGE **€€**
(📞 033 14 306 78; www.tranogasy.com; Namoly Valley; bungalows Ar69,000, without bathroom Ar48,000) These chalets near the Namoly park entrance are very basic and none too clean, with erratic water supply. However, the food (advance notice needed) is good and it's the obvious place to stay if you want to arrive in the afternoon, arrange your hike, and start off the next morning. The mountain valley setting is incredible.

ℹ Information

Guide fees are Ar80,000 per day; porters (who will also cook for you) cost Ar30,000 per day and can carry up to 20kg. Note that only a couple of guides speak basic English.

MNP office (MNP; 📞 020 75 340 81; www. parcs-madagascar.com; ⊙ 6.30am-3.30pm) In Namoly; has all you need to hike into the park, including entry permits. Here you can hire guides, porters and cooking utensils (but not camping equipment – you'll need to organise this in Ambalavao).

ℹ Getting There & Away

The Namoly Valley is a nearly three-hour drive from Ambalavao, with some iffy bridges, but it is also a scenic trip through rocky hill country full of small villages, rice paddies and smiling children. The track is very rough and requires a hefty 4WD. There is no public transport. In the rainy season access can become very difficult.

Tsaranoro Valley

The hot and dry Tsaranoro Valley is hemmed in by massive, smooth-as-butter granite outcrops and dotted with mango trees, zebu pastures and unusually fertile paddy fields that can churn out two harvests a year. There's some very good hiking around the valley fringes and it's a wonderful place just to kick back and enjoy slow-paced village life.

Technically most of the Tsaranoro Valley lies outside the boundaries of Parc National Andringitra, but when people speak of the

Parc National Andringitra & the Tsaranoro Valley

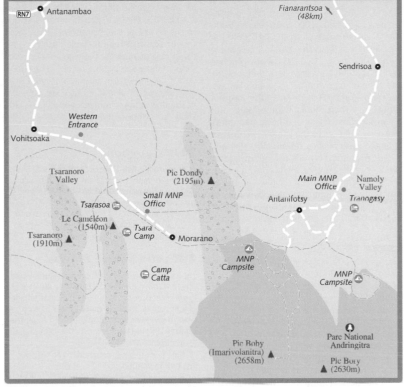

park, they tend to mean the entire Massif de l'Andringitra region and, probably on account of its better accommodation, this valley tends to be more popular with travellers than the park itself.

All visitors must pay a Ar10,000 entry fee. This is collected in the village of Morarano.

🏃 Activities

There are numerous walks to enjoy in Tsaranoro. Some tackle the Tsaranoro Massif, others simply take you to local villages, natural swimming pools and waterfalls. All hotels will be able to provide you with a guide, or you can go direct to the visitor centre in Andonaka village.

Hiking

There are around eight different established hiking routes which vary in difficulty. The classic route is the four- to five- hour ascent of Mt Caméléon (1540m) after which you descend back to your camp via a natural swimming pool (in contrast to the hot sun, the water here is frigid). This costs Ar70,000.

A shorter and more gentle three-hour hike (Ar50,000) takes you to the natural swimming pool via a couple of villages. Or, for those with legs of steel, there's a nine-hour 'Grand Tour' around the base of Tsaranoro (Ar100,000). The daunting vertical rock face of Tsaranoro is considered a world-class rock climb, but it's only for experts who are fully equipped.

Note that on most of the walks around the valley you will spend a lot of time walking across exposed granite with no shade. The sun and heat reflects off this rock and it can get painfully hot. Be prepared with adequate sun protection and lots of water.

🛏 Sleeping

Tsarasoa
LODGE €€

(☑034 60 193 26; www.tsarasoa.com; camping per person Ar10,000-20,000, safari tents Ar25,000-40,000, huts/bungalows Ar30,000-170,000) 🌴 The beauty of Tsarasoa is that it has something for every budget: penny-pinchers can camp; budget travellers will opt for the simple huts; whilst those who like their creature comforts will love the original bungalows (bathrooms with mosaics and coloured glass, suspended beds, panoramic views etc). All share the same beautiful setting and owner Gilles' inimitable welcome.

The restaurant is built around three giant boulders, but sadly the food is only average.

Tsarasoa is working hard to minimise its environmental footprint: it serves free filtered water to guests and has planted thousands of trees over the past decade.

Camp Catta
LODGE €€

(☑034 96 957 04; www.campcatta.com; camping per site Ar10,000, equipped tents Ar61,000, bungalows Ar91,000-200,000; ☒) With a breathtaking location at the foot of the Massif, habituated ring-tailed lemurs roaming through the camp and a gorgeous eco-swimming pool (the water is cleaned by a reed bed), this is a promising option. The bungalows are the best deal and the more expensive ones are decidedly plush. The safari tents are dank and avoidable.

Good meals are available and the bar is a cool place to hang out and talk.

Tsara Camp
LODGE €€€

(☑020 22 248 47, 034 12 657 99; www.boogie-pilgrim-madagascar.com; Tsaranoro Valley; d Ar135,000) 🌴 In a jaw-dropping location in the centre of the Tsaranoro Valley, Tsara Camp features comfortable safari tents complete with private bathrooms (the open-topped shower is a nice touch). The interiors of each tent are nicely decorated with old farming implements and are coloured in the deep reds of Malagasy soil. The camp lacks atmosphere however, and is rather overpriced.

ℹ Information

Tsaranoro Visitor Centre (☑034 59 226 26; Tsaranoro Valley; ⊘6.30am-5pm) In the small village of Morarano; you can organise a guide (the camps can also do this for you for no extra money). All visitors to the valley also have to pay Ar10,000, which will be collected here as you drive past.

ℹ Getting There & Away

The Tsaranoro Valley is 60km from Ambalavao. The first few kilometres of the route are in pretty good condition, but beyond the small village of Vohitsoaka the route deteriorates badly and it normally takes a couple of hours to cover the 12km to 15km to the camps. In the rainy season it can take longer. Much longer!

There is a road maintenance toll of Ar4000 just before Vohitsoaka.

There is no public transport deep into the Tsaranoro Valley and the tourist camps, but there are occasional *taxis-brousses* (Ar5000) from Ambalavao and Vohitsoaka. If you only have a light pack, you could walk the 12km to 15km to the camps (the route is easy to follow). Most people come in a private 4WD.

Southern Madagascar

Best Places to Eat

➡ Olo Be (p107)

➡ Bakuba (p99)

➡ Five Senses Lodge (p106)

➡ Auberge Peter Pan (p110)

➡ L'Estérel (p101)

➡ Isalo Rock Lodge (p94)

Best Places to Stay

➡ Olo Be (p107)

➡ Bakuba (p99)

➡ Five Senses Lodge (p106)

➡ Isalo Rock Lodge (p94)

➡ Auberge Peter Pan (p110)

Why Go?

Southern Madagascar is a wide-open adventure among some of nature's most dramatic forms. The stark desert canyons of Parc National Isalo rival those of Arizona. The west coast offers gorgeous coastal settlements that serve as gateways to the fifth-largest coral reef in the world. And vast kilometres of spiny forest contain the strangest and most formidable plants on earth. The cape is also the last stop before Antarctica. There are two scruffy cities, Tuléar (Toliara) and Fort Dauphin (Taolagnaro), but that's not why you come. The question is how to tackle a region of this size. For many, a lodge in Isalo and a slice of beach are enough. But for others, the south is the perfect recipe for off-road exploration, when the security situation permits. After all, away from the RN7 it's strictly 4WD country, ripe for the adventure of a lifetime.

When to Go
Tuléar (Toliara)

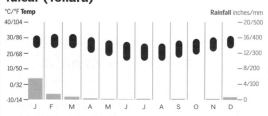

Jul–Sep Whale-watching season on the Great Reef.	**Sep–Nov** Good 4WDing season.
Dec–Mar or Apr Rainy season makes travel difficult away from the RN7; many dirt roads impassable.	

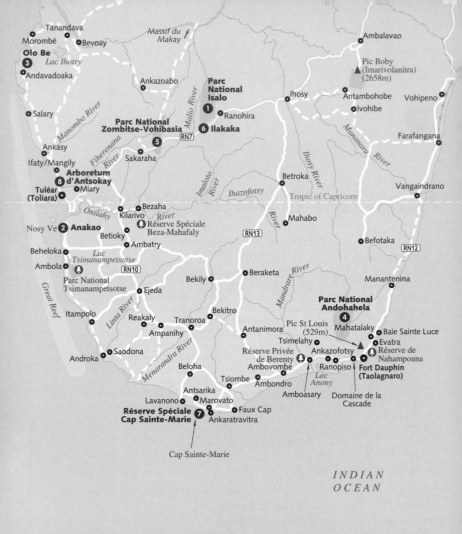

Southern Madagascar Highlights

① Parc National Isalo (p91)
Hiking canyons, swimming in rock pools and tracking down lemurs.

② Anakao (p109) Diving the Great Reef then whale watching off this languid fishing village.

③ Olo Be (p107) Contemplating a turquoise sea from

this stunning designer hotel in Andavadoaka.

④ Parc National Andohahela (p113) Exploring one of Madagascar's most diverse parks.

⑤ Parc National Zombitse-Vohibasia (p96) Tracking down rare birds and nocturnal lemurs in a last vestige of forest.

⑥ Ilakaka (p95) Visiting the intriguing sapphire mines in this rugged boom town.

⑦ Réserve Spéciale Cap Sainte-Marie (p112) Standing at the very tip of the 'eighth continent'.

⑧ Arboretum d'Antsokay (p99) Enjoying wonderful and weird plant life.

ℹ️ Getting There & Away

Fort Dauphin (Taolagnaro) and Tuléar (Toliara) are the two hubs of the south, both served by Air Madagascar/Tsaradia. Tuléar is the gateway to the Great Reef and is easily reached from Antananarivo (Tana) by *taxi-brousse* (bush taxi) or private car along the sealed, but deteriorating RN7. Fort Dauphin and the cape can only be reached by 4WD, although the tenuous security situation means it is preferable to fly to/from Tana.

THE DESERT

Two fine national parks and a sapphire boom town provide many reasons to linger in the desert, southern Madagascar's cauterised interior. Parc National Isalo is one of Madagascar's best, with good wildlife and even better landscapes. Parc National Zombitse-Vohibasia is a little-known jewel for birdwatchers. In between the two, Ilakaka feels like Madagascar's wild west.

Parc National Isalo

Parc National Isalo (www.parcs-madagascar. com; per day adult/child Ar65,000/25,000) is like a museum dedicated to the art of the desert canyon. Gorges here are filled with yellow savannah grasses, sculpted buttes, vertical rock walls and, best of all, deep canyon floors shot through with streams, lush vegetation and pools for swimming. All of this changes with the light, culminating in extraordinary sunsets beneath a big sky. Add all this to easy access off the RN7 and you understand why this is Madagascar's most visited park.

At more than 800 sq km, there's plenty of room for exploration, with everything from two-hour to week-long hikes. The park is served by the small town of Ranohira, which contains the park office and most of the cheap hotels and restaurants, while fabulous resorts extend all along the park's southern border. Friday is market day in Ranohira.

👁️ Sights

La Fenêtre de l'Isalo   VIEWPOINT
La Fenêtre de l'Isalo is a popular natural rock window that frames the setting sun, although we actually prefer it for the surrounding views of sweeping plains and weird-and-wonderful rock formations turned golden at sunset. At the time of writing, visitors were encouraged not to

visit alone due to the threat of robbery – if there are other vehicles in attendance, take the 800m track off the RN7; the turn-off is around 1.5km south of La Relais de la Reine.

La Reine de l'Isalo   MOUNTAIN
(Queen of Isalo) If you like finding figures in stone, La Reine de l'Isalo sits about 3km south of the museum, on the left side of the road. It's cool once you spot it, but you'll probably need someone to point it out.

Maison de l'Isalo   MUSEUM
(🕐 8am-5pm) **FREE** The buttons don't work at this once-interactive little museum, but it's still a good introduction to the history, culture and geology of the park. If you're staying in town, combine it with a trip to La Fenêtre, or pause on your journey to/from Tuléar.

🏃 Activities
Wildlife Watching

Although animal life isn't the park's most prominent feature, there's a good chance you'll spot two of the park's three diurnal lemur species: ring-tailed lemur and Verreaux's *sifaka*. Your best chance of spotting them is any time between 11am and 3pm from March to October at the campsite close to the start of the Namaza trail; there's a resident female Verreaux's *sifaka* at the campsite, which is an 800m walk in from the car park. The red-browed brown lemur is also possible, although hasn't frequented the campsite area in recent years. These three species can also be seen at **Canyon des Makis** (Canyon des Singes) and Canyon des Rats.

The park is also home to four nocturnal lemur species: grey mouse lemur, greater mouse lemur, red-tailed sportive lemur and Coquerel's giant mouse lemur, but as night walks inside the park are no longer allowed,

> ### WHAT'S IN A NAME: RANOHIRA
>
> According to local legend, one of the springs and the surrounding pool in the Canyon des Makis in what is now known as the Parc National Isalo were once accessible only to the local king. One day, while bathing in the pool, the king spied a lemur taking in the royal waters. The king told his people what he had seen, and the name for the town became Ranohira, which means 'Waters of the Lemur'.

Parc National Isalo

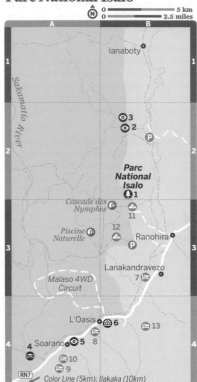

long way across hot, open country in most cases. Bring sunscreen, a hat and enough water for your visit. Picnic lunches can be arranged – ask your guide or hotel.

Piscine Naturelle Short hike to a beautiful natural pool. One of the easiest and most popular trails, although there is some steep walking. Start early as much of the trail leads across open country with no shade. It's 3km by car and 3km on foot.

Namaza A variety of possibilities but one of the more rewarding heads through deep gorges, taking in (at its lengthiest) the lemur-rich Namaza campsite, the pretty Cascade des Nymphs, a ridgetop lookout and two deep natural pools. The full trail trail runs 6km and takes three to four hours.

Circuit Crête (Crest Circuit) Begins at the Piscine Naturelle (combine the two hikes for a fine day walk) and then climbs up to follow the ridgeline with fine views en route. The hike covers 5km in 2½ hours and is of medium difficulty.

Canyons Takes in the Canyon des Makis (p91), with chances of seeing lemurs, and the Canyon des Rats burial area (p91). A 17km drive and easy 2km hike, taking around 2½ hours.

Falls of Anjofo Hike by the river's edge to two waterfalls. It's 29km by car, and a somewhat-difficult 3km hike that should take around five hours, including the drive.

Grand Tour An 80km, six- to seven-day hike that takes in as much as the park can

your only chance of seeing these is to camp overnight at Namaza or Canyon des Makis campsites. Even then, chances are slim.

At last count, 82 recorded bird species inhabit the park. Birders get particularly excited here if they track down the Benson's rock thrush, Madagascar sand grouse, Madagascar partridge or the hooded vanga.

Near streams and in the lush pockets of forest in the deeper canyons, there are ferns, pandanus and feathery palm trees. At ground level in drier areas, look for the yellow flowering *Pachypodium rosulatum* (especially beautiful in September and October), which resembles a miniature baobab tree and is often called 'elephant's foot'.

Hiking

The length of time the various circuits require depends on your level of fitness, and whether you take a car to the trailhead (which we strongly recommend). Otherwise you must walk in from Ranohira, which is a offer, including the Portuguese Grotto, a picturesque 30m-long cave in the park's north. The way to get away from it all.

4WD Circuit

The Malaso 4WD circuit is primarily intended to provide a window on the park for those of impaired mobility. It leaves the RN7 south of town, although you'll still need to pick up a guide from the park office in Ranohira. The route takes you across the plains and broad valleys and to the edge of some canyons, with stops at some short trails. It's a 42km, four-hour drive with some optional walking.

Via Ferrata

At two places, climbing aids have been bolted into the rock, scaling to the top for fine views. In both cases, you're provided with all of the equipment. The climbs are considered suitable for people who have never climbed before and those with basic fitness, but those with a fear of heights should give it a miss.

Via Ferrata A 750m circuit around 27km northwest of Ranohira. The starting point is the same as for the Falls of Anjofo hike.

Le Relais de la Reine This hotel (p94) offers a 1½-hour circuit up to the canyon summit for fine views. The climbing portion only lasts around 10 minutes, making it suitable for all fitness levels. It's open to nonguests and costs Ar70,000 per person.

Horse Riding

Le Relais de la Reine (p94) has a small equestrian centre that is open to nonguests and is a fine option for exploring the canyons beyond the park. One-hour/half-day rides cost Ar60,000/175,000 per person, while children's pony rides can also be arranged. Longer expeditions into the park are also possible.

Mountain Biking

The park's MNP office (p94) rents out OK mountain bikes for Ar25,000/40,000 per half-/full day. Le Relais de la Reine (p94) also rents bicycles to guests for Ar70,000 for 90 minutes.

🛏 Sleeping

There are **campsites** (camping Ar10,000) at Namaza, Piscine Naturelle and Canyon des Maki (p91).

Leader Lodge HOTEL €€
(☑ 034 25 489 53; leaderlodge@hotmail.fr; RN7; r Ar50,000-130,000, d/tr without bathroom Ar25,000/35,000; P 🛜) A real surprise packet near the eastern end of town, this engaging little hotel-guesthouse has simple rooms, but those with private bathroom, especially the two 'suites' on the left as you enter, represent outrageously good value. More rooms were being built when we visited and there is also a house that sleeps eight people for Ar200,000.

ITC Lodge BUNGALOW €€
(☑ 032 45 703 36, 034 17 850 44; www.itclodge-isalo.com; off RN7; camping Ar10,000, s/d bungalows Ar70,000/75,000, f Ar90,000-135,000; P 🛜) Just down the hill from the MTC Office, the ITC Lodge is a well-run place with Dutch-Malagasy owners. The rooms are tidy, rather than remarkable, but they're excellent mid-range value. Nice gardens, a good restaurant, and some reasonable campsites round out a good package that's close to town but far enough away to feel you're in the wild.

Chez Alice BUNGALOW €€
(☑ 033 07 134 44, 032 02 055 68; chezalice@yahoo.fr; off RN7; camping Ar8000, paillote Ar42,000, d/tr/f bungalows Ar48,000/62,000/76,000; 🛜) It's a rough drive in, and somewhat-bare surrounds hide this convivial backpacker's hang out and budget gem not far from the centre of Ranohira. Run by the irrepressible Alice, who would otherwise be running an Old West saloon, this place has bungalows of various types and prices, all of which are colourfully painted and excellent value.

ℹ HIKING ITINERARIES

To make the most of your time in Isalo requires careful planning.

Day One Combining Piscine Naturelle with Namaza gives you a good mix of landscapes and wildlife. If you're more interested in landscapes than lemurs, take the Circuit Crête instead of Namaza. Really fit hikers could cover all three in a day. And don't miss sunset at La Fenêtre de l'Isalo.

Day Two Do whichever hike you didn't take on day one and add in the Canyons trail. Another option is Falls of Anjofo. The Malaso 4WD Circuit takes you to places in the park you can't reach on foot, and is possible for the foot-weary.

★**Isalo Rock Lodge** LODGE €€€
(☎020 22 328 60; www.isalorocklodge.com; off
RN7; r €120; ❋🛜🏊) This stylish hotel has a
beautiful terrace overlooking sandstone formations as well as a spa and fitness room
and a lovely pool. The restaurant (set menu
Ar70,000) serves works of art, while the
rooms, bathed in soothing earth tones, are
triumphs of contemporary design. A sharp
manager ensures perfection.

Jardin du Roy BOUTIQUE HOTEL €€€
(☎034 02 351 66, 033 07 123 07; www.lejardin
duroy.com; off RN7; bungalows from €100;
P❋🛜🏊) This stunning property shares
amenities and owners with the adjacent Le
Relais de la Reine. On offer are unique stone
bungalows, including custom hand-crafted
furniture, and all rooms are air-conditioned.
Like its sister property, it's situated among
sandstone formations.

Satrana Lodge LODGE €€€
(☎034 14 260 87, 020 22 219 74; www.satrana
lodge-madagascar.com; d €60-95; P🛜🏊) This
wonderful lodge, beautifully situated beneath a range of sandstone outcrops, has a
majestic pool in the shape of Madagascar,
with endless desert views, a classy restaurant
and atmospheric wood-floored safari-tent
rooms with writing desks and stunning
bathrooms.

Le Relais de la Reine BOUTIQUE HOTEL €€€
(☎034 02 123 29, 020 22 336 23; www.lerelais
delareine.com; off RN7; d from €100; P❋🛜🏊)
Beautifully designed, this lovely property
sits among canyons with elegant stone-built
cottages. Service is impeccable (it's the sort

of place where you come back from dinner
to find your bed prepared), the restaurant
is outstanding (three-course set menu for
lunch/dinner Ar50,000/65,000) and there's
a real attention to detail that you just don't
find in many places in Madagascar's south.

The memorable rooms (tiled floors,
four-poster beds, exposed-stone walls and
soft lighting), refurbished in 2012, are merely the start. There's also a fine swimming
pool, a clay tennis court, a stunning garden
with frangipani and bougainvillea, a stylish
bar, a spa and massage centre, a via ferrata
in the neighbouring canyons and an equestrian centre for sunset gallops across the
savannah.

It's 14km beyond Ranohira, on the left if
coming from Tana.

Isalo Ranch BUNGALOW €€€
(☎034 20 319 02, 020 24 319 02; www.isalo-ranch.
com; RN7; camping Ar15,000, d/tr/f bungalows
from Ar160,000/180,000/200,000; 🛜🏊) 🌿
The sand pathways of this lodge tie its bungalows together into a welcoming little village, aided by a shady and cosy restaurant
with an international menu. It's solar energy
only here and the rooms are as pleasing as
the surroundings. It's an excellent choice
5km down the road from Ranohira.

✗ Eating

The top-end Isalo Rock Lodge, Le Relais de
la Reine, Satrana Lodge and Jardin du Roy
hotels all have stellar restaurants that are
open to nonguests – book ahead if you're not
staying overnight. Otherwise, there are two
good, well-priced options in town.

---

❶ PARK GUIDES & PARK PRACTICALITIES

After paying your park entrance fees at Parc National Isalo's **MNP office** (☎032 09 402
36, 033 49 402 36; www.parcs-madagascar.com; off RN7; ⊘6.30am-4pm), cross to the **Guides
Association Office** (agei.isalo@gmail.com; off RN7; ⊘6.30am-4pm), which has a list of
more than 80 accredited guides, along with the languages they speak and their phone
numbers. Guides cost Ar80,000/120,000 per half-/full day. Here you must also pay the
Ar5000 community tax.

Toussaint (☎033 71 029 66; raztouss02@yahoo.fr) Speaks English, French, Spanish, Italian
and German.

Roland (☎033 08 437 94; rolaljust@gmail.com) French and English.

Roxy (☎034 70 929 59; roxyisalo@gmail.com) French and English.

Xavier (☎034 98 094 84; louisxavierrakotonanahary@gmail.com) French and English.

Momo Trek (☎034 12 062 88, 032 44 187 90; www.madagascar-trek.com) Experienced
Ranohira operator with all-inclusive hiking packages, including multiday expeditions to
the remote Massif du Makay.

ℹ️ PARC NATIONAL ISALO

Best time to visit May to October.

Key highlight Piscine Naturelle.

Wildlife Seven lemur species (four of them nocturnal), 82 bird species, *Pachypodium* flower.

Habitats Dry desert rock, spring-fed oases.

Gateway town Ranohira.

Transport options *Taxi-brousse* (bush taxi) or car to Ranohira.

Things you should know While the luxury resorts are expensive for Madagascar, they're a bargain compared to other parts of the world.

⭐**Pizza Liberta** PIZZA €€

(☎ 034 76 699 63; l.mainini@libero.it; off RN7; pizzas Ar19,000-32,000; ⏰ noon-2.30pm & 6-8.30pm) Arguably the best pizza in Madagascar's south, this fine little place, run by the amiable Luigi, does real thin-crust Italian pizzas, with all the usual ingredients, as well as some local surprises like zebu sausage. If you want an early lunch and a quick getaway, ring ahead, and he'll fire up the oven early.

Restaurant Le Zébu Grillé MALAGASY €€

(☎ 032 44 676 89; www.orchidee-isalo.com; RN7; mains Ar10,000-19,000; 🍴) The best restaurant in Ranohira itself serves a good mix of Malagasy specials (such as pork with beans) and international dishes (such as roast chicken or zebu brochette), all in a pleasant setting in the heart of town. It's attached to Le Orchidée d'Isalo hotel.

ℹ️ Information

DANGERS & ANNOYANCES
Police (☎ 117; RN7)

INTERNET ACCESS
Most hotels have free wi-fi for guests. The **post office** (RN7; ⏰ 8-11.30am & 2-4.30pm Mon-Fri) has a few computer terminals and charges Ar50 per minute – just like in the old days.

MONEY
There are no banks or ATMs in Ranohira. The nearest bank is in Ihosy, 91km away.

ℹ️ Getting There & Away

For points north, you may be lucky enough to find a *taxi-brousse* travelling between Tuléar

and Tana with an empty seat. If you get lucky, destinations include Fianarantsoa (Ar20,000, six hours), Antsirabe (Ar45,000, 11 hours) and Antananarivo (Ar50,000, 14 hours). Each morning one or two *taxis-brousses* connect Ranohira directly with Ihosy (Ar10,000, two hours), from where there are more options. Public transport heading north generally arrives in Ranohira between 10am and 1pm.

Heading south, vehicles from the north usually arrive before 10am, continuing on to Tuléar (Ar20,000).

Ilakaka

POP 30,000

Ilakaka is the perfect setting for a James Bond movie. In the middle of nowhere, about half an hour west of Ranohira, this sapphire boom town spontaneously erupted astride the RN7 – it's only been here since the 1990s. The main street is lined with ramshackle structures selling provisions for the miners, from shovels to mobile phones. Side streets are lined with gem buyers in shaded huts and women with painted faces squatting on the footpath organising piles of stones by quality. The highlight is the nearby mining area, where hand-dug mines pockmark the earth. One can imagine 007 running across this landscape pursued by the henchmen of some evil gem lord.

In any case, you have to see this. By accident it has become one of the more fascinating sights in southern Madagascar, all the more so because it appears completely unconscious of the fact.

👉 Tours

Color Line TOURS

(☎ 033 17 720 17, 033 20 123 08; www.colorline gems.com; RN7; per person Ar12,000; ⏰ 8am-6pm) The gem dealer Color Line, at the southern end of the main street (on the left as you come from Ranohira), offers tours of the sapphire mines. Far from destroying the authenticity, it's fully part of it, taking you out to the rough-cut mines and explaining the whole process and intrigue. The guide, Mohammed, speaks French and a little English. Tours last 45 minutes to an hour.

Color Line also owns a gem showroom and workshop.

🍷 Drinking & Nightlife

Color Line Bar BAR

(RN7; ⏰ 1am-3am Sat) To really enter the local scene in all its shadiness, attend the gem

MINING THE OLD-FASHIONED WAY

The sapphire mining process begins with a borehole large enough to lower a person 30m into the earth. If round stones – the signs of an ancient riverbed – are found, sapphires might be found as well. This leads to the digging of a second hole by the mining equivalent of a bucket brigade, with one person shovelling to the next, and so on, for a very, very long time. If it rains, walls collapse and the digging begins anew. Some mines are dug by individual owners, while others are financed by groups of investors. Some yield valuable sapphires, others produce nothing. There have been enough of the former to create a sapphire rush in Ilakaka involving tens of thousands of people. In fact, Ilakaka sits on top of the biggest sapphire deposit in the world, all 40 sq km of it, even though you will not see a single piece of mining machinery beyond a spade. Just be careful if considering what you are offered in the street. As the saying goes, 'the closer you get to the mine, the more synthetic you find'.

dealers' party starting at 1am every Friday night at Color Line's adjacent bar, known as Al2O3 (the formula for sapphire, naturally). This is only for a particular kind of traveller and is a long way from respectability – think the bar scene in the first *Star Wars* movie, without the aliens.

ⓘ Information

Ilakaka has long had a reputation for being dangerous. The reputation was certainly warranted in the past when the boom was hot, but things have quietened down a little since then. You don't have anything to worry about here during the day, particularly during a tour, but we can't vouch for 3am, when the party ends.

ⓘ Getting There & Away

If you're in Isalo and want to take a tour of the mining fields, call Color Line (p95) to arrange transport, or any *taxi-brousse* heading west on the RN7 will get you here. Otherwise we recommend visiting from Ranohira or en route elsewhere along the RN7.

From Ilakaka, *taxis-brousses* leave every morning and afternoon for Tuléar and Fianarantsoa (Ar22,000, six hours).

Parc National Zombitse-Vohibasia

One of Madagascar's least known, yet most accessible parks, Parc National Zombitse-Vohibasia (www.parcs-madagascar.com; per day adult/child Ar45,000/25,000, guide Ar10,000) is a surprise packet; most visitors just drive on by and don't realise what they're missing. The park's dense dry forest is how all of Madagascar's arid south must once have appeared, and the park's 363 sq km are all

that remain – a forested island in what has become a denuded semidesert landscape.

The park's relict forest shelters an astounding 72 recorded bird species. Lemurs are also an attraction here with eight recorded species.

Pay your fees at the barely functioning park office, just set back from the RN7, and let a guide lead you along any of the circuits that range from 15 minutes to two hours in length.

🏃 Activities

Birdwatching

The park has quite a reputation among birders, not just for the number of species (72) on offer in a relatively small area, but for the endangered endemics you won't see elsewhere.

Commonly sighted here are the grand and Coquerel's coua, white-browed owl, black parrot and blue vanga. But the real prize is the Appert's greenbul – sometimes, quantifying the science of extinction is all too easy because if this forest were to disappear, so too would this species as it survives nowhere else on the planet.

The optimum time for birdwatching is 6am to 9am or 10am.

Wildlife Watching

Although they're less famous than the birds, Zombitse-Vohibasia has more than its share of lemurs. Five are nocturnal, but you're pretty likely to come across skittish bands of Verreaux's *sifaka* and the oh-so-cute (and endangered) Hubbard's sportive lemur. The latter is nocturnal but is commonly seen resting in tree hollows by day.

There are some real plant highlights here as well, including strangler figs and the occasional baobab.

🛏 Sleeping

Le Palace Hotel & Restaurant   HOTEL
(☑ 032 75 709 50, 033 71 772 37; lepalacehotel.
sakaraha@gmail.com; RN7, Sakaraha; r with cold-
water bathroom Ar28,000-35,000, d with hot-
water bathroom Ar35,000-59,000, tr with hot-water
bathroom Ar45,000-70,000) Although simple,
the rooms at this Indian-owned hotel are
the best you'll find close to Parc National Zombitse-Vohibasia, 20km away to the
northeast. They're nicely set back from
the busy road and there's a good restaurant (breakfast Ar2000 to Ar12,000, mains
Ar9000 to Ar15,000); mains range from duck
or zebu to chicken tandoori.

Zombitse Ecolodge   BUNGALOW €€
(☑ 033 12 325 64, 033 80 651 63; www.zombitse.de;
RN7; s/d/tw/tr bungalows incl breakfast Ar90,000
/130,000/150,000/170,000) Around 7km west
of the park entrance, the only accommodation close to the park is OK but could do
with some sprucing up. The bungalows have
poor mattresses but are otherwise fine; hot
water comes in a bucket from the kitchen.
The real reason to stay here is to enable you
to get to the park at dawn.

There's a simple restaurant (lunch/dinner
Ar20,000/35,000); they prefer advance notice if you plan to eat here.

ⓘ Getting There & Away
The park straddles the RN7, 90km southwest of
Isalo and 147km northeast of Tuléar. Any *taxi-
brousse* between the two can stop here. Trails
start right by the roadside.

GREAT REEF

A reef stretches over 450km along the southwestern coast of Madagascar, making it the
fifth-largest coral reef in the world. Running
from Andavadoaka in the north to Itampolo
in the south, it's the main attraction in the
region, with its own changing personality.

The Great Reef comes in three forms: a
fringing reef close in, a patch reef of coral
heads and an outer barrier reef. The last cre-
ates very broad and shallow inshore lagoons
and makes for dramatic scenery, with large
waves crashing in the distance, forming a vibrant line of white. The beaches range from
broken coral to spectacular white powder.
There are many activities to pursue here:
sunbathing, snorkelling, diving, fishing,

whale watching (mid-June or early July to
September), surfing and sailing among them.

Resort towns and ramshackle fishing
villages line the shoreline, while the city of
Tuléar is the gateway to both the Northern
and Southern Reef.

ⓘ Getting There & Away
Tuléar is the hub of the Great Reef. North of
Tuléar, there is little or no public transport after
Mangily. With the exception of private planes, the
northern hotels are all reached by private 4WD.
Transfers can be arranged, but are expensive.

South of Tuléar, there are boat transfers to
Anakao, which is a quick and wonderful way to
arrive, but south of Anakao you need a private
4WD again, and *lots* of time.

Tuléar (Toliara)

POP 156,710

Tuléar is where the sealed road (the RN7)
ends and many adventures begin – its main
appeal is as most travellers' gateway to the
Great Reef (found both north and south of
the city). Your most enduring memory here
is likely to be a sea of bicycle rickshaws
bouncing down dusty lanes – the city itself
has little to detain you beyond an outstanding out-of-town arboretum and some fine
hotels and restaurants. Add a somewhat-
raffish tropical ambience fuelled by local
French and Italian expats, and you have the
setting for your first novel. Do take taxis
after dark.

ⓘ SECURITY IN SOUTHERN MADAGASCAR
••••••••••••••••••••••••••••••••••••••

At the time of writing, a number of roads
in southern Madagascar were considered to be unsafe, due to the risk of
banditry. These included the following:

➡ *All* overland routes to/from Fort
Dauphin (Taolagnaro) south of the RN7
and from Tuléar (Toliara), except in the
vicinity of Fort Dauphin. Even when the
security situation improves along these
roads, they should never be driven at
night.

➡ The road between Anakao and Tuléar,
especially close to Betioky where a
tourist vehicle was robbed in broad
daylight in July 2019. If travelling to
Anakao, take the boat to/from Tuléar.

Great Reef

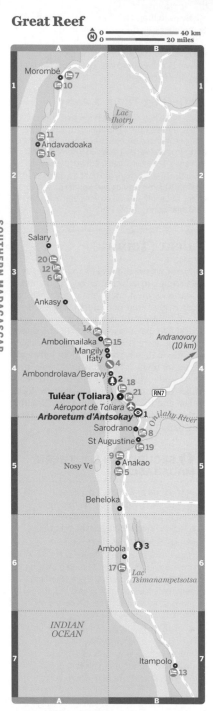

SOUTHERN MADAGASCAR

◉ Sights

★ Arboretum d'Antsokay GARDENS

(Map p98; ☑ 034 07 600 15; www.facebook.com/Antsokay; off RN7; adult/child Ar15,000/5000; ◷ 7.30am-5.30pm, closed Feb) This is the one must-see attraction in Tuléar. Essentially a 400,000-sq-metre distillation of the entire spiny forest in one place, it's a fantastic collection of 900 plant species; take a guide (tip expected) to learn more about the weird and wonderful plants on show here. It was established by a Swiss botanist and conservationist in 1980; his ancient Citroën that once used to gather the plants is now being consumed by them. Madagascar National Parks (MNP) take note: clone this place. Night tours (Ar10,000) leave at 5.45pm.

There's a small museum, a shop, a stylish restaurant and some excellent, inexpensive bungalows, Auberge de la Table (p100), with pool.

The arboretum lies about 12km southeast of town, just a few hundred metres from the RN7, so it's a good stop as you arrive by car. Otherwise take a taxi or ask any *taxi-brousse* heading toward Befety to drop you off at the junction (you'll have to walk in). Transfers to Tuléar or the airport cost Ar30,000.

La Table MOUNTAIN

(Map p98) This table mountain is unmissable as you approach Tuléar down the RN7, about 10km from town. There's a relatively easy trail to the top, which takes about 20 minutes to climb, and is a great place to watch the sunset. Go early or late in summer. For Ar40,000 you can hire a taxi in town to take you here and the nearby arboretum.

Musée Cedratom MUSEUM

(Map p100; ☑ 034 99 764 55; manambita.lahiratiman@gmail.com; Rue Flayelle; adult/child Ar10,000/5000; ◷ 7.30-11.30am & 2.30-5.30pm Mon-Fri) This small, three-room museum is run by the local university and features exhibits on local culture, an elephant-bird egg and other oddities, including an ancient mask with real human teeth. Interesting place that's worth half an hour of your time.

🛏 Sleeping

Chez Alain GUESTHOUSE €

(Map p100; ☑ 020 94 415 27; www.chez-alain.com; d with shared toilet & cold-water shower Ar35,000, with bathroom & hot water Ar65,000-70,000, with air-con Ar110,000; P ❄ 🛜) It may be close to the *taxi-brousse* station, but Chez Alain has a quiet garden area sheltered from the surrounding clamour. The simplest rooms are basic but well kept, while any of the rooms with private bathrooms are well priced. The most expensive are spacious and have air-con.

Chez Lala HOTEL €

(Map p100; ☑ 032 07 708 67; Ave de France; d with/without air-con Ar45,000/3045,000, d without bathroom Ar20,000; ❄ 🛜) This laid-back and genial guesthouse is your best budget option; most nights there are more Malagasy guests than foreigners. The simple rooms in the tropical courtyard are smaller than those in the parquet-tiled main block, but they're all decent value. A TV lounge, great espresso, loads of info and free wi-fi help clinch the deal.

Serena Hôtel HOTEL €€

(Map p100; ☑ 032 45 377 55, 020 94 411 73; www.serenatulear.com; Blvd Philibert Tsiranana; d Ar85,000-115,000, ste Ar225,000; ❄ 🛜) The rooms here are attractive and wonderfully central – the newer, more expensive doubles on the 2nd floor are worth the extra price and most have views over the centre of town. It's not quite the design hotel it once was, but for this price it's a steal.

Longo Hotel Arcobaleno BUNGALOW €€

(Map p98; ☑ 032 82 614 75; www.longohotelarcobaleno.com; off Blvd Branley; d with/without air-con Ar75,000/65,000; P ❄ 🛜) This simple Italian-run place feels like a small oasis of calm at the north end of town. Rooms are outstanding value for the price and those with air-con are a little larger. The bathrooms come with, wait for it, bidets. It's the best lower-midrange choice in the town itself, although it's quite a walk from the centre.

★ Bakuba GUESTHOUSE €€€

(Map p98; ☑ 032 51 528 97; www.bakuba-lodge.com; r/ste €125/170) It would be more accurate to describe this place as a work of art that you stay in rather than an arty guesthouse. The work of Bruno Decorte (a Frenchman who has spent much of his life in Africa), Bakuba has three unique rooms and three similarly stunning suites, with features such as a water wall, a dugout-canoe-turned-bath-tub and lamps made of gourds.

The house is anchored by large towers reminiscent of baobab trees. One serves as a hidden water tower, another as a hammam and conversation room. The interior contains a vast hall inspired by Mauritanian

Tuléar (Toliara)

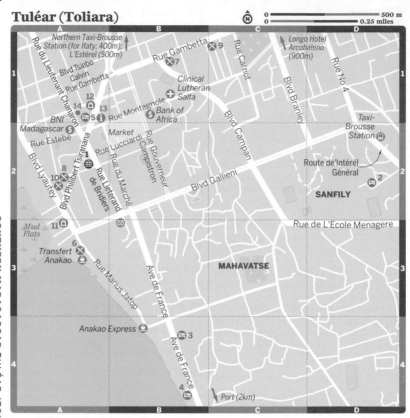

temples. Doorways are lined with real palm trunks and the decor includes a fetching statue of a West African chief – Bakuba himself. If any of this sounds kitsch, think again. Decorte has managed to integrate everything with a strong sense of naturalism in the manner of Gaudí. The hotel also has some more run-of-the-mill benefits, such as 100m of beachfront, catamarans and canoes and quads for hire.

There's also an exquisite attention to detail (you choose your soaps and shampoos upon arrival), and nothing is too much trouble for the staff.

It's located 14km southeast of the centre, signposted off the RN7.

★ Famata Lodge   LODGE €€€
(Map p98; ☑ 032 02 108 48, 020 94 937 83; www. famatalodge-tulear.com; d bungalow Ar122,000-380,000; ☒) Down the coast, 16km from town and 11km from the airport, lies this interesting ecolodge. Located in the mangroves, it has everything from budget bungalows to luxurious treetop villas, all with private bathroom, hot water and a large terrace. There's a restaurant and a great pool. The family bungalow is a steal, with an open wall facing the sea.

Auberge de la Table   BUNGALOW €€€
(Map p98; ☑ 034 07 600 15; off RN7; d/tr/f bungalows €40/52/64, d superior bungalows €60; ☐ � ☒) The bungalows at the Arboretum d'Antsokay, 12km east of the city, represent fabulous value as long you don't need to be in town. The superior bungalows are large, light-filled, and beautifully appointed with some original stone furnishings and they're lovely and quiet. The standard doubles are a little small and dark, but still decent value.

Breakfast or dinner (Ar15,000/40,000) at the restaurant is similarly excellent. Airport transfers cost Ar30,000.

Tuléar (Toliara)

Victory Hotel   HOTEL €€€

(Map p98; ☑034 14 440 63; www.hotel
tulear-victory.com; RN7; d Ar99,800-154,000, ste
from Ar248,000; P🖙🛇) This old Tuléar stalwart has rather attractive rooms arrayed
around a large garden and set back from the
road at the eastern entrance to town. The
rooms aren't that exciting, but it's a well-run
place that's worth every ariary.

Hotel Hyppocampo   HOTEL €€€

(Map p100; ☑032 42 866 83; www.hyppocampo.
net; Ave de France; d/ste €60/90; ✳@🛇) With
its oceanfront setting, pool, good restaurant
and well-appointed rooms, the Hyppocampo
is the high end of in-town accommodation,
although we reckon it's a touch overpriced.
The suites have huge tubs and queen beds
tucked away from a sitting room.

✕ Eating

Gelateria Italiana   ICE CREAM €

(Map p100; ☑020 94 439 08; Rue Gambetta; ice
cream per scoop Ar3000, mains from Ar15,000;
☺9am-12.30pm & 4-10pm Tue-Sun; 🛜) Have
confidence in this place: it's owned by an
Italian and he hasn't forgotten the mother-
land. Great ice cream, decent pizza, pasta
and sandwiches, along with a patisserie for
the early hours. Throw in free wi-fi and you
have the perfect snack stop.

Food Stalls   BARBECUE €

(Map p100; Blvd Philibert Tsiranana; brochettes
from Ar750; ☺from 8pm) Grab a stool – this is
where you down brochettes and beer for the
cheapest dinner in town and a real slice of
local life. Popular into the wee hours, but
take a taxi to and from here after dark.

★ L'Estérel   ITALIAN €€

(Map p98; ☑032 40 026 20, 032 40 618 66; Rue de
la Voirie; pizzas Ar12,000-20,000, mains Ar12,000-
18,000; ☺11am-2pm & 6-10pm Mon-Sat) Our
pick of the restaurants in Tuléar, Italian-
run L'Estérel has a tranquil garden setting
and a menu that includes some of the best
Italian cooking in southern Madagascar –
pasta, pizzas and salads you can trust – as
well as the occasional French dish. Service is
attentive without being in your face.

L'Etoile de Mer   INTERNATIONAL €€

(Map p100; ☑032 02 605 65; Blvd Lyautey; mains
Ar15,000-25,000; ☺10am-2.30pm & 5.30-11pm
Wed-Mon) A full range of meat and seafood
dishes, expertly executed, fill the menu at
this classy cafe-style restaurant close to the
centre. Although the culinary influences
span the globe, the Indian dishes are especially good. The service is also excellent.

Corto Maltese   INTERNATIONAL €€

(Map p100; ☑032 04 009 13; cnr Rue Gambetta
& Blvd Campan; mains Ar17,000-23,000; ☺noon-
2pm & 5-10pm Mon-Fri) One of the best restaurants in Tuléar, yet moderately priced,
this creative bistro offers an eclectic menu,
ranging from steaks that look and taste the
part to pasta, seafood brochettes and great
desserts. Nice outdoor seating, too. Shame it
doesn't open on weekends.

Oasis Cafe   CAFE €€

(Map p100; ☑032 07 100 33; Blvd Philibert Tsiranana; mains from Ar19,000; ☺7.30am-10pm) Much
loved by expats, tourists and well-to-do locals, this cafe has become one of Tuléar's
most popular meeting places. The menu is
small but carefully chosen, the garden setting lovely and quiet, and the service friendly. It's down an enclosed alleyway, behind La
Chocolaterie Robert.

Blu Bar   INTERNATIONAL €€

(Map p100; ☑033 52 002 30; Blvd Lyautey;
breakfast from Ar8000, mains Ar14,000-27,500;
☺7.30am-late; 🛜) This lively, beautifully
designed bar and expat hang-out with its
own private beach is *the* place to come for
breezy waterfront dining, with burgers,

SOUTHERN MADAGASCAR TULÉAR (TOLIARA)

SOUTHERN MADAGASCAR TULÉAR (TOLIARA)

MANGROVE INFORMATION CENTER

On the west side of the road, 12km north of Tuléar, a sign directs you to the **Mangrove Information Center** (Map p98; 032 54 042 76, 032 70 465 04; guided tour per person Ar15,000; ☺sunrise-sunset), a 2-sq-km wetland complex created by Honko, a Belgian NGO. The main attraction is a 1.5km wooden boardwalk. It's a nice place to stretch your legs on the way north, with a trail through the mangroves, educational placards and a lovely tower overlooking a river. Guided tours of between 2km and 4km, and one to three hours in duration, are excellent.

pizzas, sandwiches and kebabs to displace the memory of all that rice you've been eating. Quality can be patchy.

🛍 Shopping

★ La Chocolaterie Robert CHOCOLATE (Map p100; 032 03 100 20; www.chocolaterie robert.com; Blvd Philibert Tsiranana; ☺8am-12.30pm & 3-6pm Mon-Sat, 9am-noon Sun) The Tuléar outpost of this celebrated purveyor of fine Malagasy chocolates carries a small but exquisite range – buy by the piece or in prewrapped packs.

Handicrafts Market MARKET (Map p100; Blvd Lyautey; ☺8am-6pm) More than two dozen stalls of local handicrafts line the street at this recently opened handicrafts market. You'll find woodwork, basketry, textiles and other items, and what it lacks for the atmosphere of more traditional market spaces, it makes up for with quality and choice.

ℹ Information

DANGERS & ANNOYANCES

Tuléar is considered to be generally safe (although you should always take a taxi after dark), but there is one place to avoid: Batterie Beach. North of the city centre, Batterie Beach has been the scene of violent attacks on foreigners in recent years, and most foreign travel advisories and travel-insurance companies warn strongly against visiting. It lies beyond the city limits and there's little chance of wandering here by accident, but it's still worth knowing the name and steering clear of it.

MEDICAL SERVICES

Clinical Lutheran Salfa (Map p100; Rue Montagnole; ☺24hr) Tuléar's best hospital, but still not brilliant.

MONEY

There are plenty of banks and ATMs in Tuléar (Toliara).

Bank of Africa (Map p100; cnr Rue Gouverneur Campistron & Rue Raseta; ☺8am-4pm Mon-Fri, 8.30am-noon Sat)

BNI Madagascar (Map p100; 020 94 426 22; cnr Rue Estebe & Rue Lieutenant Chenaron; ☺8-11.30am & 2.30-5pm Mon-Fri)

POST

Post office (Map p100; Blvd Gallieni; ☺8-11.30am & 2-4.30pm Mon-Fri)

TOURIST INFORMATION

Office Regional du Tourisme (Map p100; 034 30 994 94; Blvd Tsiranana; ☺8am-noon & 2.30-5.30pm Mon-Fri, 8am-1pm Sat) There's a person here to answer questions and it has a few brochures, but that's about it.

ℹ Getting There & Away

AIR

Tsaradia (Map p100; 020 94 415 85, 034 11 222 15; www.tsaradia.com; Rue Henri Martin; ☺8-11.30am & 2.30-5pm Mon-Fri, 8-10am Sat) has an office in town but not at the **airport** (Map p98; 020 94 438 05). It flies between Tuléar (Toliara) and Antananarivo (from €207). Tsaradia claims between one and three services a week between Tuléar (Toliara) and Fort Dauphin (Taolagnaro) on its schedules, but it wasn't operating at the time of writing.

BOAT

Anakao Express (Map p100; 034 60 072 61/2; www.anakaoexpress.com; Rue Marius Jatop, Mahavatse; per person one way/return Ar60,000/120,000) This speedboat company leaves Tuléar (Toliara) around 9.30am and arrives in Anakao an hour later. It leaves Anakao at 7.30am, unless Tsaradia decides to push its Tana departure earlier, in which case the speedboats adjust.

Transfert Anakao (Map p100; 034 91 468 36; www.transfert-anakao.com; Restaurant Le Blu; per person one way/return Ar60,000/120,000) These speedboats connect Tuléar (Toliara) with Anakao, leaving the former every day at 9am. It leaves Anakao at 7.30am (or earlier to connect with Tsaradia's unpredictable timetable).

CAMION-BROUSSE

The mother of all *taxis-brousses*, the *camion-brousse* is a troop transport that plies the god-awful roads between Tuléar (Toliara) and Fort Dauphin (Taolagnaro; Ar50,000), with stops in Betioky (Ar18,000), Ampanihy (Ar30,000) and Ambovombe (Ar40,000). This takes a whopping 30 to 60 hours (more likely the latter), depending on breakdowns and road conditions. But beware: these amusement-park rides are packed beyond capacity. Passengers bounce around and are frequently ill. There are a limited number of breaks. You'll need a scarf and pullover for the dust and wind. And if you do the trip in stages, you could spend a lot of time waiting for a seat, as the vehicles that pass the towns en route are often full. Finally, provisions are sparse along the way, so you need to stock up ahead of time. All things considered, we challenge you to find a rougher form of public transport. Services leave from the main taxi-brousse station.

HITCHING

It's relatively easy to hitch a lift from Tuléar to Antananarivo with a tour company car as many tourist vehicles and supply trucks from Antananarivo return to the capital empty. Expect to pay a bit more than the *taxi-brousse* fare. The best places to ask are the major hotels, particularly Chez Alain (p99).

TAXI-BROUSSE

Taxis-brousses leave the main **station** (Map p100; Roue de l'Interieur Géneral/RN7) early every day for Antananarivo, arriving a day later. Vehicles to Antananarivo may fill up quickly, so get to the station early or book a seat the afternoon before. Destinations and fares along the way include the following – journey times vary greatly.

DESTINATION	FARE (AR)
Ambalavao	25,000
Ambositra	35,000
Antananarivo	from 40,000
Antsirabe	38,000
Fianarantsoa	30,000
Isalo/Ranohira	20,000

Transport along the sand road north to Ifaty/Mangily (Ar10,000, three hours) departs from the northern *taxi-brousse* station on Rte de Manombo. There are a few trucks daily, generally departing between 6am and early afternoon.

A *taxi-brousse* leaves for Morondava a few times weekly (Ar60,000, two to three days). The road is very rough and you'll need to overnight in Manja (Ar35,000) on the way.

Taxis-brousses also connect Tuléar with St Augustine (Ar5000, two hours) once a day, Tuesday to Saturday.

There's a *taxi-brousse* every Thursday to Beheloka and Itampolo (Ar30,000, 12 hours).

ℹ Getting Around

TO/FROM THE AIRPORT

A taxi between the airport and the city centre costs between Ar20,000 and Ar30,000 and many hotels in Tuléar and Ifaty do airport transfers; some charge around the same as a taxi.

CAR

Numerous companies hire 4WD vehicles. Your best bet is to ask for a recommendation from your hotel.

POSSE-POUSSE

Standard rates for pousse-pousse (cycle rickshaws, also called *cycle-opus*) rides start at about Ar2000.

TAXI

For rides within town, taxis charge a standard rate of Ar4000 per person, but can climb as high as Ar15,000 at night. Don't be afraid to bargain.

Northern Reef

The reef north of Tuléar is a gentle curve punctuated by a number of villages and resorts all the way to Andavadoaka, some 207km distant. We're not huge fans of Ifaty and Mangily, but they have a few worthwhile spots. On the coastal track between Ambolimailaka and Andavadoaka, you'll find yourself slithering along a difficult sandy track through a spiny forest full of huge baobab trees and wandering tribespeople. At Ankasy and Salary and many points in between, the ocean is a shade of turquoise that looks for all the world like paradise, villages are few and far between, and the resorts in this area are world-class retreats from the world and its noise.

Most travellers visit the area for its own sake from Tuléar or as part of the three-day 4WD expedition between Tuléar and Morondava.

Ifaty & Mangily

Ifaty and Mangily, around 25km north of Tuléar, are two separate villages 3km apart that share the same beach, confusingly known as Ifaty Beach (the Dunes d'Ifaty, for example, is in Mangily). Ifaty is by far the smaller tourist destination, even while its name continues to usurp the latter. The popularity of this area is largely due to its location close to Tuléar and the excellent paved road that connects them. The beaches are really quite poor relative to other

GETTING AROUND SOUTHERN MADAGASCAR

If you wish to go by road anywhere off the RN7, you'll need either a 4WD or, if there happens to be public transport, a very strong stomach. *Taxis-brousses* (bush taxis) can be brutal in the south.

At the time of research, the state of some major routes was as follows (many of these routes are impassable in rainy season):

RN7 to Tuléar (Toliara) Excellent sealed surface, but showing signs of deterioration; no 4WD necessary.

Tuléar to Ifaty/Mangily Excellent sealed road making the latter a viable base for the south.

Ifaty to Andavadoaka via coast road Sand track with rutted deep sand in spots; requires 4WD.

Ifaty to Andavadoaka via RN9 Usually quicker but potholed in patches; 4WD needed for second half.

Tuléar to Anakao via Betioky Terrible road but better closer to Anakao; security might be an issue; 4WD required.

Itampolo to Ampanihy via Androka Very bad, often rocky road, confusing tracks, maps not accurate. Use a local guide.

Ampanihy to Ambovombe Improved dirt road, particularly good on first half, but 4WD still needed.

Ambovombe to Ihosy Terrible road rutted by *camions-brousses* (large trucks) and not safe at time of writing, especially after dark.

Ambovombe to Fort Dauphin (Taolagnaro) Terrible road, a deteriorated sealed surface with craters worthy of the moon; 4WD required.

---

options: rocky at times, very shallow for much of the day and with seagrass beds rather than sandy bottoms. The unkempt villages, saturated by tourism, are not very attractive, either. Nevertheless, the snorkelling is good, the whales come past here and there are a lot of resorts to choose from, including some really good ones.

◉ Sights

If you visit Ifaty village around 1pm to 2pm, you can enjoy watching the local fishers beach around 50 pirogues full of catch. Ask around or at your hotel for the best place to witness the spectacle.

Reniala Nature Reserve   WILDLIFE RESERVE
(Map p98; ☑ 034 03 790 40, 032 02 513 49; www.reniala-ecotourisme.jimdo.com; Mangily; Ar22,000-28,000; ⊙ 7am-noon & 2-5pm) This is a 0.6-sq-km spiny forest full of baobab trees and some birds. There are two circuits, one of 45 minutes to an hour and the other of 1½ to two hours. The Arboretum (p99) in Tuléar is better, but this one's still worth supporting and worth a visit. There's also an on-site lemur rescue centre, with some in cages,

others in semiwild enclosures in readiness for their release into the wild.

Village des Tortues   WILDLIFE RESERVE
(Map p98; ☑ 032 02 072 75, 034 19 841 55; Mangily; adult/child Ar15,000/5000; ⊙ 9am-5pm) **FREE** Near Reniala Nature Reserve, this 70,000-sq-metre park protects over 1000 radiated and spider tortoises. A guided tour of the grounds (in English) tells you the full story of these endangered animals and how they are being conserved. It takes less than an hour, so it's a worthy break from the beach.

🏃 Activities

Diving possibilities include everything from shallow inshore 5m to 10m dives and up to 26m dives on the edge of the barrier reef. The latter focuses on two passes, north and south, with the former containing a famous network of rocky arches called the Cathedral. While most sections of the reef are damaged, there is a variety of fish.

★ Mangily Scuba   DIVING
(Map p98; ☑ 034 64 781 76; www.ifatyscuba.com; Mangily; dives from €45) Widely regarded as

one of the best dive operators along this stretch of coast, Mangily Scuba runs PADI courses as well as dive excursions. It also runs whale-watching trips in season.

★ **Atimoo** DIVING

(Map p98; 034 02 529 17; www.atimoo.com; Mangily; first dive from €45) This outfit takes a more adventurous approach than other operators, which tend to stick to their local section of the reef. Instead, Atimoo ranges from one end of the reef to the other in small dive parties that sometimes rough it ashore. Prices vary depending on the destination.

Nautilus Deep Sea Club DIVING

(Map p98; 032 07 418 74, 032 04 848 81; www.nautilusmada.mg; Ifaty; first dive from €50) Respected dive club catering to all levels of expertise and with its own OK bungalows and restaurant.

🛏 Sleeping

★ **Sur la Plage** BUNGALOW €€

(Chez Cecile; Map p98; 034 94 907 00; www.surlaplagechezcecil.com; Mangily; bungalows Ar70,000-120,000; 🛜) Easily the pick of Mangily's midrange options, Sur la Plage is tidy, colourful, if simple bungalows that are kept sparkling clean – they're actually just as good as many places where you'll pay double the price. The restaurant here is first rate. There are bicycles for borrowing as well.

★ **Bamboo Club** BUNGALOW €€

(Map p98; 020 94 902 13, 032 66 552 31; www.bamboo-club.com; Mangily; thatched d bungalows €18-50, apt €55; 🛜🌊) This place caters mostly to divers, but offers comfortable bungalows climbing up through the trees from the beach, a small swimming pool and an excellent terrace restaurant serving Indian Ocean specialities. If you can, opt for one of the new solid bungalows over the older thatched versions, although all of the rooms are excellent, the grounds are lovely and service is excellent.

Ifaty Beach Club BUNGALOW €€€

(Map p98; 034 29 709 99; www.ifaty.com; Mangily; d/tr/f incl half board Ar140,000/210,000/260,000; 🛜🌊) This classic Mangily bungalow village is more village than garden, but the whitewashed bungalows are tidy and tumble down the hill to an OK beach.

Dunes d'Ifaty LODGE €€€

(Map p98; 034 07 109 71, 032 07 109 16, 020 22 376 69; www.lesdunesdifaty.com; Ifaty; d bungalows €89-105, villas €125; P🛜🌊) This high-end property has a magnificent thatched-roof lodge for eating and pretty bungalows made of locally quarried stone. The villas get the beach views, but the bungalows are still pleasantly sited among the gardens. Some villas have brightly painted walls, Italian baths and thoughtful amenities. Beach security keeps away hawkers and ensures privacy, which is a problem further north.

Hôtel Le Paradisier LODGE €€€

(Map p98; 032 07 660 09; www.paradisier.net; Ifaty; d €70-105; 🛜🌊) 🍃 This luxury, but attractively priced Ifaty property has a tropical-jungle lobby that opens onto a sea-facing courtyard dining room and a shimmering infinity pool. The waterfront bungalows are nicely integrated into the beach (although some are set back in the trees) rather than manicured, and everything runs on solar. Be careful of pricey extensions.

🍴 Eating

★ **Sur la Plage** SEAFOOD €

(Chez Cecile; Map p98; 034 94 907 00; www.surlaplagechezcecile.com; Mangily; mains from Ar12,000; noon-2.30pm & 5-10pm) This sand-floor restaurant offers the best of this stretch of coast – feet in the sand, grilled fish fresh off the boat, expertly mixed punches and cocktails – bliss! It also does huge plates of pasta and seafood grills.

Chez Freddy MALAGASY €€

(Map p98; 034 19 842 76; Mangily; mains Ar14,000-18,000; 7.30am-3pm & 6-11pm Tue-Sat) This excellent roadside place along the main track through town between the paved road and the beach does well-executed grilled seafood and some surprises, such as zebu in a Creole sauce. On Saturday night from 7.30pm, there's live traditional music, as well as an ample buffet (per person Ar30,000).

ⓘ Getting There & Away

Ifaty village lies around 25km north of Tuléar. Several *taxis-brousses* leave daily from the northern *taxi-brousse* station in Tuléar, usually between 6am and early afternoon. The trip costs Ar10,000 and takes one hour. Transfers provided by the hotels to/from their clients to/from the airport cost Ar50,000 per person, while taxis in Tuléar charge around Ar60,000.

Ambolimailaka

If you really want to get away from it all on the Northern Reef, you might consider this a smart alternative to Mangily; it's also spelled Ambolimailaky. There are plenty of activities on offer, including zebu-cart trips, forest excursions, kitesurfing, diving, whale watching, fishing, quad biking and horse riding. Stay or not, it's definitely worth stopping by here around noon to watch the return of the fishing fleet, over 200 pirogues strong, just below Hôtel Belle Vue.

🛏 Sleeping

⭐ **La Mira de Madiorano**   HOTEL €€€
(Map p98; ☑ 032 02 621 44; www.lamira-hotel.com; Madiorano; s Ar110,500-194,000, d Ar125,000-209,000) This excellent place is filled with light and the bungalows are all dressed in white, and are spacious with subtle but discernible charm. The views are exceptional, there are two restaurants and a lovely pool, and it offers a general sense of quality that puts to shame many more expensive places along this coast. It's 3km south of Ambolimailaka and 36km north of Tuléar.

Hotel de la Plage   BUNGALOW €€€
(Map p98; ☑ 032 04 346 63, 032 04 362 76; www.hotelplage-tulear.com; s/d/tr/q bungalows €50/54/65/68) Located between two fishing villages, this resort offers some neat circular bungalows strung along an elegant arc of beach. The rooms are fine, if unspectacular, although you could almost dive off your terrace and into the water from the beachfront bungalows. The local dive centre is located here and whale watching and windsurfing are possible.

ⓘ Getting There & Away

Ambolimailaka is 40km north of Tuléar along a good paved road. *Taxis-brousses* between Tuléar and Morombé pass by, although they're usually full when they do.

Ankasy

With barely a village to speak of, Ankasy, 100km north of Tuléar, has an excellent upmarket lodge. The sea here is a wonderful shade of turquoise and there's a palpable sense of blissful isolation. It's the sort of place where you get the sand between your toes, without compromising on comfort. Plan to stay for as long as you can.

🛏 Sleeping

⭐ **Five Senses**
Lodge   DESIGN HOTEL €€€
(Map p98; ☑ 034 07 020 21, 032 98 447 39; www.fivesenseslodge.com; villas d €160-265, f €180-360) Perched high on sand dunes looking out over a turquoise sea along an otherwise-deserted stretch of coast around 10km north of Ankasy, Five Senses is a magnificent place. Horizons without end, spacious, stylish rooms with contemporary design features, and one of the best restaurants anywhere along Madagascar's coast – linger for as much time as you have. Activities are possible, including diving.

It's between Ankasy and Salary.

Ankasy Lodge   LODGE €€€
(Map p98; ☑ 032 05 400 42; www.ankasy.com; d €62-90; 🛜) With massive (100 sq metre) high-end bungalows, on a broad, beautiful 1.3km of private beach, the family-friendly Ankasy Lodge is terrific. Food is straight off the pirogue and activities range from pirogue excursions, zebu carriage rides, kitesurfing and waterskiing to a relaxing massage, just in case you were somehow stressed. All-inclusive packages are sometimes available.

ⓘ Getting There & Away

The 'road' in here is terrible for 60km in any direction – a 4WD is essential, unless you've arranged a transfer through the hotel.

Salary

The sandy village of Salary, 129km from Tuléar, sits just over the sand dunes from the shore. The beaches here are long and lovely and the Salary Bay resort, a few kilometres north of the village, is a wonderful place to stay.

🛏 Sleeping

Salary Bay   RESORT €€€
(Map p98; ☑ 032 49 120 16, 020 75 514 86; www.salarybay.com; d bungalows €100, 4-/8-person villas €220/300) 🏖 This resort sits high on a sandy headland, affording spectacular 270-degree views from the restaurant (mains Ar40,000), taking in a broad turquoise lagoon and the resort's own 7km of beach! It's a popular choice for honeymooners and divers (the local dive centre is here). It can also organise whale watching (€50 per person, minimum four people). Wood-floored rooms are lovely and white.

SNORKELLING THE GREAT REEF

The Great Reef is a prime snorkelling ground. However, human proximity has taken its toll, meaning that some sections of the reef are in better shape than others. Using information on coral health and fish populations supplied by local marine conservation NGO Blue Ventures, we've graded the quality of the reef from 1 (low) to 10 (high).

Andavadoaka (grade 7) Some nice small bommies (shallow, isolated patches of reef) can be reached from the shore. Slightly deeper reefs are a short pirogue (dugout canoe) trip from the village. Longer pirogue trips reach shallow sites off the island of Nosy Hao.

Salary (grade 6) Good sites are really too deep to snorkel, but there are some small bommies inshore.

Ifaty/Mangily (grade 6) Snorkelling can be done by pirogue in the Rose Garden Marine Reserve (for a fee).

Tuléar (grade 4) Reef can be shallow, but requires a short pirogue/boat trip.

Anakao/Nosy Ve (grade 5) Snorkelling in the marine reserve off the northern tip of the island (for a fee).

Beheloka (grade 6) Good sites are further offshore and need to be reached by a pirogue trip from the village.

Ambola (grade 6) Most sites can be reached by a pirogue trip from the village.

Itampolo (grade 8) One great site for snorkelling straight off the beach in the north; great coral cover, diverse fish and shallow depth.

Getting There & Away

It may not look far, but the 78km drive to Andavadoaka is epic: it takes at least three, possibly four hours by 4WD. The sand can be deep, the bumps are like a funfair ride, the baobab forest is dramatic and you may even pass through shallow mangroves en route. If you're coming from the south, things aren't much better – count on at least four hours in a 4WD from Tuléar.

Andavadoaka

POP 1500

Yes, it's a long 78km from Salary, and just as far in the other direction from Morombé, but this remote and laid-back outpost of 1500 people is one of the more interesting spots north of Tuléar, and a gorgeous spot to spend a few days. After passing through the tidy local village, you end up at the tip of a sandy peninsula spotted with ramshackle beach bungalows and a basic restaurant enlivened at night by the staff and volunteers of NGO Blue Ventures. A couple of excellent resorts are nearby.

Sleeping

Coco Beach BUNGALOW €€
(Map p98; ☑ 034 14 001 58; nassim.tahora@gmail.com; d/tw bungalows Ar55,000/75,000) These very basic bungalows that seem to lean into the wind support many Blue Ventures personnel and are the only near-budget ac-

commodation around. Coco Beach a friendly place and the restaurant does simple chicken or fish dishes and teases with a big sign advertising the rarely working pizza oven.

★ Olo Be DESIGN HOTEL €€€
(Map p98; ☑ 034 11 221 41, 034 64 927 82; www.olobe-lodge.com; r €125-180; P 🛜 ❄) Now here's something special. Designed in part by Bruno Decorte of Bakuka in Tuléar, and opened in earnest in 2019, Olo Be has stunning rooms, all lovely curves, earth tones and expansive views (even from some bathrooms) with exquisite attention to detail. The restaurant is among the best along the Northern Reef, and the public areas are as stunning as the rooms.

Laguna Blu RESORT €€€
(Map p98; ☑ 034 41 895 47; www.resortmadagascar.com; d bungalows from €100) Laguna Blu is an excellent Andavadoaka choice, blissfully isolated and with good if unexciting-for-the-price beachfront bungalows. For a long time, it traded on the absence of any real competition, but with the arrival of Olo Be, it just ups its game (or lowers its prices).

Getting There & Away

A *taxi-brousse* leaves from the central market in Morombé (Ar15,000) almost daily. It is also possible to take a pirogue from Morombé or Salary

SOUTHERN MADAGASCAR NORTHERN REEF

(Ar80,000, five to eight hours depending on wind) as long as you depart early in the morning.

Morombé

The northern end of the Great Reef peters out at Morombé, 280km north of Tuléar. Most travellers visit as part of the three-day epic road trip between Morondava and Tuléar. It's a decent place to break up the journey, with a pleasant enough beach and its handful of decent accommodation options.

🛏 Sleeping

⭐**Chez Katia**   GUESTHOUSE €€
(Map p98; ☑032 74 273 40, 033 01 769 30; rogeka_momo@yahoo.fr;   d/tr/f   A80,000/ 120,000/190,000) This charming beachside *maison d'hôte* (gueshouse) is warm and welcoming. The large, spotless rooms are outstanding and look like they've been freshly painted. The restaurant, on an elevated wooden platform so you can see the beach, serves up meals from Ar25,000.

Auberge Chez Laurette   GUESTHOUSE €€
(Map p98; ☑032 47 194 68; d/f Ar80,000/ 90,000; 🅿🛜) At the eastern end of town, Chez Laurette has excellent rooms, all arrayed around a pretty, shaded garden.

ℹ Getting There & Away

It's around 270km between Morombé and Tuléar; there's at least one daily *taxi-brousse* (Ar20,000, six hours) in either direction. The road is excellent for the closest 100km to Tuléar, mediocre for the rest. There are also occasional services to Manja (Ar25,000, eight hours) and Andavadoaka (Ar12,000, three to four hours).

Southern Reef

There are some interesting places to visit on the reef south of Tuléar, including its best overall tourist destination, Anakao. But after that, places of interest are fewer and rather far between. The area inland contains a massive spiny forest, which can be vast and monotonous, but it does house two excellent protected areas: Parc National Tsimanampetsotse and Réserve Spéciale Beza-Mahafaly. There are also some lovely stretches of deserted coastline.

How far you go along this coast depends on how much time you have. For those with limited time, a day trip to Sarodrano and St Augustine, or one or two days in Anakao, will suffice. For those wanting to unearth

an unknown gem in a more remote location, consider Ambola.

Sarodrano

Sarodrano, betwen Anakao and Tuléar, is a fishing village of grass huts on a sandy peninsula that extends into the ocean beneath some cliffs. It's a short distance from the city, on a good road, but worlds away in every other respect.

🏃 Activities

Grotte de Sarodrano   SWIMMING
(Map p98; Ar2500) The Grotte de Sarodrano, near La Mangrove, is worth a look (and swim). It's a bilevel natural pool jointly fed by tidal flow and freshwater springs, so it contains both freshwater and saltwater fish at different depths (and lots of them). From here you can take an interesting pirogue ride to Sarodrano. If one isn't waiting, call Auberge de Pecheur.

🛏 Sleeping

Auberge de Pecheur   BUNGALOW €
(Chez Manjaka; Map p98; ☑032 42 903 90; d Ar30,000, without bathroom Ar18,000) You can rent a very basic hut at this place right on the beach, and do nothing the rest of the day.

La Mangrove   BUNGALOW €€
(Map p98; ☑020 94 936 26; d Ar60,000) For the closest Sarodrano comes to midrange accommodation, try this place, which appears on the right side of the road just before the peninsula. Putting the wobbly dock and muddy swimming hole aside, the bungalows are good value and the grounds are well kept and shady.

ℹ Getting There & Away

From Sarodrano, you can go on to Anakao by sail pirogue for only Ar25,000 – far less than the Ar55,000 speedboat trip from Tuléar – or back to Tuléar for the same amount. Either way it's 45 minutes to two hours, wind depending. Daily *taxis-brousses* from Tuléar are Ar6000.

St Augustine

The little tropical town of St Augustine sits on a sandy former floodplain and is very scenic from above, with an alluring end-of-the-world feel down at street level. It lies at the mouth of the Onilahy River, on the other side of the cliffs from Sarodrano, along a good road. It's an excellent drive through see humpback whales from mid-June or early July to September.

★ Il Camaleonte

WATER SPORTS

(Map p98; ☏ 032 63 672 34; www.ilcamaleonte anakao.wordpress.com; 1/2 dives €55/90, snorkelling equipment rental from €10) Just a short walk along the sand from Auberge Peter Pan, this excellent Italian-run place organises diving, snorkelling, kitesurfing, stand-up paddleboarding, kayaking and numerous combinations of the same to fill your days. Andrea and Nicoletta are warm and welcoming and simply love what they do, which helps make it all the more enjoyable.

Longo Vezo

ADVENTURE SPORTS

(Map p98; ☏ 020 94 901 27, 032 02 695 12; www.longovezo.com) Longo Vezo, which has a CMAS-certified dive centre, also does numerous water sports, can organise whale watching and runs 4WD trips that go as far south as Parc National Tsimanampetsotse.

Anakao Club

ADVENTURE SPORTS

(Map p98; ☏ 020 94 919 57; www.anakaoocean lodge.com) One of the better activity centres, at the Anakao Ocean Lodge, Anakao Club arranges boat excursions to the islands, mangroves, and whales (in season), diving, kitesurfing, windsurfing and extensive quad excursions that are a great way to see the area.

Whale Watching

Anakao is one of the best places along the Great Reef to watch humpback whales from mid-June or early July to September. You'll spend around two hours on the water and the whales are regularly seen, sometimes not far beyond the reef. Check wind conditions – it's not really worth going if seas are choppy.

Most hotels offer whale watching, but the experience (and cost) vary. Expect prices to start at Ar80,000 for whale watching, and Ar130,000 if you include time for snorkelling at Nosy Ve. If you organise your trip through Auberge Peter Pan (p110), you'll go out with local fishers in a small, motorised pirogue. Some of the other operators use larger, more modern boats.

🛏 Sleeping

Mada Surf Lodge

BUNGALOW €

(Map p98; ☏ 032 26 126 23; dm/ste Ar29,000/164,000; 🛜) Choose from simple six-bed bunk dorms or an expansive suite with a shaded terrace overlooking the beach. There's something for everyone at this lodge

---

FITAMPOHA

Ask for directions to the house of the *tromba* (a local spirit), a small wooden building that houses sacred religious relics. Every 10 years (the next one in 2023), the relics are taken to the beach for a ritual bathing known as *fitampoha*. You can visit the house by seeking the permission of the local chief – go barefoot and take an offering of two bottles of rum.

---

switchbacks over the ridge and down into the lost valley – the site of the very first English settlement in Madagascar in 1645 – beyond. Only 12 of 140 people survived that brief stay. Later it became a safe harbour for pirates and, in the 19th century, Daniel Defoe, author of *Robinson Crusoe*, is said to have drawn inspiration from the location.

🛏 Sleeping

Longomamy

LODGE €

(Map p98; ☏ 020 94 444 56; d Ar40,000) Longomamy is perched at the end of the Onilahy River, where local fishers practice their timeless rhythm. It's a place where hours slip past unnoticed. The hotel offers great seafood straight from the sea, and can arrange a pleasant pirogue trip (Ar20,000) upriver to a crystal-clear natural pool.

ⓘ Getting There & Away

Daily *taxis-brousses* from Tuléar cost Ar5000.

Anakao

POP 3000

Strung out along a series of perfect semicircles of white-sand beaches and looking out over turquoise waters, Anakao is laidback in the finest tradition of small seaside Malagasy settlements. It's our pick of the options along the Southern Reef coastline. Excellent sleeping and eating options round out a fine all-round destination.

🏃 Activities

Activities here are mostly arranged through the hotels, with at least one excellent independent operator. In addition to the full range of water activities, most hotels can also arrange excursions to Parc National Tsimanampetsotse (p110), as well as **whale-watching trips** (per person from Ar80,000) to where surfers of the world converge and swap stories.

Chez Emile
BUNGALOW €

(Map p98; ☑ 032 04 023 76; chezemile.anakao@yahoo.fr; d bungalow with/without bathroom Ar60,000/40,000) These bungalows are set back from the beach near the local village, in a well-kept sandy garden. The beach restaurant serves fast and cheap seafood (mains from Ar8000).

Longo Vezo
BUNGALOW €€

(Map p98; ☑ 020 94 901 27; www.longovezo.com; d bungalows off/on beach €23/26; 🛜) A secluded location overlooking the spiny forest to Nosy Ve, a private stretch of beach, wooden bungalows discreetly hidden in the dunes with hammocks and bucket showers, and convivial family-style dining all combine to form a unique, casual beach-camp ambience.

★ Auberge Peter Pan
BUNGALOW €€€

(Map p98; ☑ 032 82 614 54, 034 94 437 21; www.peterpanhotel.com; d/f bungalows Ar120,000/200,000, d/f suites Ar240,000/400,000; 🛜) This creative burst of liberal personality is one of the best hotels south of Tana, and it just keeps getting better. Dario and Valerio, the young Italian owners who have made this place their life's work, have crafted a selection of warmly eclectic bungalows, set in a playful yard of political art contained by a fence of enormous crayons.

There's a stone tower with reading room and sweeping views, too, and the suites and bungalows are fabulous value. All of this on a beautiful beach and with strong ties to the local community.

The dynamic bar within is a fusion of revolutionary and hip, with Che Guevara looking on while you sip a deadly rum drink from an enormous green coconut. Apart from understanding the science of cool, these boys know how to cook. The spectacular ever-changing menu (mains Ar30,000), a mixture of Italian and Malagasy, is precisely what's missing in hotels three times the price, and there's a wood-fired pizza oven. The problem is that word has spread and people are staying for weeks if not months. So book ahead and be careful of that Molotov cocktail. English spoken.

★ Anakao Ocean Lodge
LODGE €€€

(Map p98; ☑ 020 94 919 57; www.anakaooceanlodge.com; d/f bungalows €171/198, ste €209; 🛜) This is the premier resort along the Southern Reef. It's not that any of the elements are unique, but each one is carried off to perfection. The bungalows, with enormous baths, are beautiful, the smiling uniformed staff members are always there when you need them and the food (set menu €20) is a work of art.

Lalandaka
BUNGALOW €€€

(Map p98; ☑ 032 05 622 80, 020 94 922 21; www.lalandaka.com; d/f bungalows from €40/60; 🛜) 'Upscale beach shack' sounds like a contradiction in terms, but this place manages to pull it off. The family versions are claustrophobic, but the doubles on the beach have a charming veranda where you can float in your hammock for hours, while the classy central lodge is just as attractive.

Safari Vezo
BUNGALOW €€€

(Map p98; ☑ 034 07 602 52, 020 94 413 81; www.safarivezo.com; s half board Ar190,000-305,000, d half board Ar265,000-380,000; 🛜) Lots of nice touches set these beach bungalows apart from the crowd, including stone steps, drapes, shady terraces and well-appointed bathrooms with seawater toilets. There's

---

WORTH A TRIP

PARC NATIONAL TSIMANAMPETSOTSE
....

This 432-sq-km park (Map p98; www.parcs-madagascar.com; adult/child Ar45,000/25,000, guide per person Ar15,000; ☺ 6am-6pm) and its large, ancient salt lake hosts some part-time resident flamingos (April to October). Amid the spiny forest, watch also for a large banyan tree full of parrots and ring-tailed lemurs. The park is home to four further lemur species. Verreaux's *sifaka* are commonly seen during daylight hours, and keep an eye out for sleeping nocturnal species such as the tiny grey-brown mouse lemur, fat-tailed dwarf lemur and white-footed sportive lemur.

The Madagascar National Parks (MNP) office is located in the town of Efoetse, 3km from Ambola. You can arrange a mandatory guide and itinerary here, and a map of all the current routes is on display. There are several circuits, from 30 minutes (1km) to 3½ hours (7km) in length. A good English-speaking guide is Laurent.

RÉSERVE SPÉCIALE BEZA-MAHAFALY

The **Réserve Spéciale Beza-Mahafaly** (www.parcs-madagascar.com; adult/child Ar45,000/25,000; ⊘8am-4pm) is better known as a scientific venture than a tourist destination, but travellers are welcome to explore six hiking circuits. The spiny and riverine forest here harbours four species of lemur (ring-tailed, white-footed and mouse lemur, as well as Verreaux's *sifaka*), four species of tenrec (including the large-eared tenrec), fossa and more than 100 bird species, making it one of the south's lesser-known yet rewarding wildlife destinations.

Be aware, however, that a tourist vehicle was attacked in July 2019 while travelling close to Betioky. Check the security situation before visiting.

Activities

There are six circuits through the park, though the following are our three favourites:

Circuit Ihazoara (4km, three hours) Natural botanical garden, canyons and good lemur viewing.

Circuit Parcelle 1 (2km, two hours) Gallery forest, excellent lemur viewing, a riverside bird hide and the chance to see radiated tortoises.

Circuit Parcelle 2 (12km, four hours) Spiny forest, diurnal lemurs and a sweeping viewpoint.

Getting There & Away

To get here and around you'll need a 4WD (the reserve is 35km east of Betioky on rough tracks; the turn-off is signposted at the southern end of Betioky). The roads between Andranovory and Betioky and south of Betioky are considered unsafe after dark.

also a lively beach bar with Bahamian shutters for a bit of Caribbean vibe.

ⓘ Getting There & Away

Almost everyone coming to Anakao arrives by speedboat. By 'road' (a relative term), it's a rough, bone-shaking seven- to eight-hour drive from Tuléar.

BOAT

Anakao Express (☏ 034 60 072 61/2; www.anakaoexpress.com; per person one-way/return Ar60,000/120,000) This speedboat company leaves Tuléar around 9.30am and arrives in Anakao an hour later. It leaves Anakao at 7.30am, unless Tsaradia decides to push its Tana departure earlier, in which case the speedboats adjust.

Transfert Anakao (☏ 034 91 468 36; www.transfert-anakao.com; per person one way/return Ar60,000/120,000) This enjoyable speedboat connects Tuléar with Anakao, leaving the former every day at 9am. It leaves Anakao at 7.30am (or earlier to connect with Tsaradia's unpredictable timetable).

Ambola

The tiny town of Ambola is found on a remote corner of the reef. While not on many maps, it is home to a charming boutique hotel and is wonderfully removed from all the world's noise. There are a couple of attractions – go diving from Le Domaine d'Ambola lodge or use it as a base to visit Parc National Tsimanampetsotse. But doing nothing here is also the point – come for a week simply to disconnect and soak up the sounds of waves lapping gently upon the shore.

🛏 Sleeping & Eating

★**Le Domaine d'Ambola**   LODGE €€€
(Map p98; ☏ 034 66 413 47; www.ambola-madagascar.com; small/large d from €55/60) Le Domaine d'Ambola is one of those special places that lingers in the mind for its serenity – you know you're somewhere special when a place lists its address as 'Beach'. The hotel sits up high on a bluff overlooking the reef, with pleasant breezes.

It's also set apart by its design, with its white walls and blue accents looking inspired by the Greek islands. The simply furnished rooms are brightly coloured, with tiled floors and distant views. The restaurant serves up great seafood fresh from the village. Perhaps most surprising is the resident dive operation, which gets high marks from customers who come a long way to use it.

There is no pampering here, but if you want a few days of low-key charm in pristine surroundings, this is worth the trip from Tuléar.

Chez Henriette et Richard MALAGASY €

(Map p98; Ambola Beach; mains from Ar8000; ☺8am-9pm) So close to the water you could almost cast a fishing line from your table, this simple little open-sided eatery at the northern end of Ambola serves up simple Malagasy coastal cooking – fish, octopus and the like served with rice, beans and cold beer. Nice. Opening hours vary, but there's no need to book.

ⓘ Getting There & Away

Ambola is 90km south of Tuléar. You could travel the whole distance by road, but you're far better off taking the Tuléar–Anakao boat and driving from there. There's no public transport.

Itampolo

The reef ends here, around 75km from Ambola, and the main attraction is a gorgeous beach and decent diving. It's far enough from Tuléar to feel remote, and the village is a quiet, rather ramshackle coastal settlement.

🛏 Sleeping

Gîte d'Etape Sud Sud BUNGALOW €

(Chez Alain; Map p98; ☑ 020 94 415 27; www.chez-alain.com; camping Ar10,000, bungalows Ar75,000-80,000, r without bathroom Ar30,000-45,000) There are some basic bungalows right alongside a long arc of sand. The restaurant is also decent, with set menus for Ar30,000 or à la carte dishes from Ar15,000. It's run by the same people as Chez Alain in Tuléar.

Villa Milahehe Mitongoa GUESTHOUSE €€

(Chez Neretse; Map p98; ☑ 034 77 732 36; www.milahehe.com; bungalows/d/f €20/30/40) The simple whitewashed rooms at this friendly *maison d'hôte* (guesthouse) have mosquito nets and private bathrooms; the bungalows have shared facilities. It's all very simple, but you're just back from the beach and staff can arrange excursions. Equally simple meals cost €8.

ⓘ Getting There & Away

From Tuléar, you could either drive for 347km by road via the inland route, which is a full day on rough roads, or take the Tuléar–Anakao boat, then drive south along the coast – Itampolo is 75 similarly rough kilometres south of Ambola.

THE CAPE

The south of Madagascar narrows to a wild cape and the sense of isolation here is palpable. This feeling only grows the further south you go, until you finally reach the cliff at Cap Sainte-Marie, where there's nothing between you and Antarctica. Then it's back to civilisation – sort of. After many hours driving through dense spiny forest and one-zebu towns, the trail ends on the doorstep of lonely Fort Dauphin (Taolagnaro), a city isolated by hundreds of kilometres of tortuous roadways in all directions. And a word of warning – in the absence of any meaningful government, bandits are known to operate across much of the south, so please check the security situation before travelling in the region. Even at such times, Fort Dauphin and the nearby parks are generally considered to be safe.

OFF THE BEATEN TRACK

RESERVÉ SPÉCIALE CAP SAINTE-MARIE & AROUND

Madagascar's southernmost tip, Cap Sainte-Marie is a thought-provoking climax to the 'eighth continent', a stark and windswept place that, like so many places down here, feels like the end of the earth. This 18-hectare **reserve** (☑ 032 40 934 03; www.parcs-madagascar.com; adult/child Ar45,000/25,000), partly created to protect radiated and spider tortoises, ends at the cliff's edge.

A small Madagascar National Parks (MNP) office lets you know that you have arrived. Here you'll need to pick up a park guide (Ar50,000). A further drive takes you to the edge of the cliffs, where there is a lighthouse complex, a religious statue and, if your timing is right, a memorable sunset beneath a huge sky. Whales are also often visible offshore between July and November. A longer circuit takes you to a beach strewn with the eggshell fragments of the extinct elephant bird, *Aepyornis*.

There are no hotels, but camping (sites Ar20,000) can be arranged at the park office. Otherwise, the nearest accommodation is in Lavanono, a two-hour journey by 4WD.

Parc National Andohahela

This 760-sq-km **park** (www.parcs-madagascar.com; adult/child per day Ar55,000/25,000, guides from Ar80,000) northwest of Fort Dauphin (Taolangnaro) protects some of the last remnants of mountainous rainforest in southern Madagascar, as well as spiny forest and a remarkable 12 species of lemur. It also boasts more than 120 species of bird, and a variety of amphibians and reptiles, including crocodiles. In short, this is one of Madagascar's most diverse parks when it comes to both landscapes and wildlife. Remoteness and questionable security are our only explanations for why the park remains so little known.

The rainforest section of the park offers the best lemur-viewing possibilities. Daytime species include the collared brown lemur, southern lesser bamboo lemur and possibly even the Milne-Edwards' *sifaka*. Among the occasionally seen nocturnal lemurs, there's the Fleurete's sportive lemur, and rumours persist that the park has a population of aye-ayes...see one and you've hit the jackpot.

⚡ Activities

The park currently maintains three main circuits for visitors and, with an early start, it's possible to visit the park on a day trip, but it is advisable to camp overnight. If you are interested in longer hikes across the rainforest mountains, visit the MNP office (p116) in Fort Dauphin (Taolagnaro).

Circuit Tsimelahy (3.7km, two to 2½ hours) The most popular route is an excellent trail in the bird-rich transition zone between the humid east-coast forest and the dry vegetation of the central region. There are campsites and some natural bathing pools. From Fort Dauphin (Taolagnaro), turn right at the signpost 48km along the RN13, then proceed 8km along a rough road. Check the security situation before setting out.

Circuit Malio (10km; four to five hours) A bird- and amphibian-rich loop through low-altitude humid forest with waterfalls and natural bathing pools that may be inaccessible during rainy season. From Fort Dauphin, turn right after 25km on the RN13, then proceed 13km on a dirt road (4WD advisable).

Circuit Mangatsiaka (4km; two hours) A gentle loop in bird-rich dry forest. From

---

❶ PARC NATIONAL ANDOHAHELA

Best time to visit April to December (ie outside cyclone season).

Key highlight Circuit Tsimelahy.

Wildlife Three-cornered palm (only found here), spiny iguanas, harrier hawks, lemurs.

Habitats Humid rainforest, spiny forest, transitional forest.

Gateway town Tsimelahy village.

Transport options Rental 4WD (Ar175,000); *taxi-brousse* (bush taxi) and hike in.

Things you should know Best to stay overnight at Tsimelahy to give yourself enough time.

Fort Dauphin, follow the RN13 for 54km, then turn right and proceed 4km on a dirt road.

🛏 Sleeping & Eating

There's a handful of cheap and extremely basic hotels and guesthouses in Tsimelahy village. None stand out, but most are fine for a night. Expect to pay around Ar20,000 per person.

Tsimelahy has a few basic restaurants, but you're better off bringing your own supplies from Fort Dauphin (Taolagnaro).

❶ Getting There & Away

Parc National Andohahela lies around 40km (a two-hour drive) northwest of Fort Dauphin (Taolagnaro). To get here, you'll either need to rent a 4WD (Ar175,000 to 200,000 per day), or take a *taxi-brousse* to Tsimelahy and hike into the park.

Fort Dauphin (Taolagnaro)

POP 58,000

Fort Dauphin (Taolagnaro) could be one of Madagascar's premier resort towns if it weren't so far from everywhere else. The setting is superb, like a gateway to some tropical paradise, strung out along a peninsula between sea and mountains. And, if you've driven for days through the spiny forest to get here, or even if you've flown out over the trackless highlands of Madagascar's interior, this prosperous mining centre, with its

Fort Dauphin (Taolagnaro)

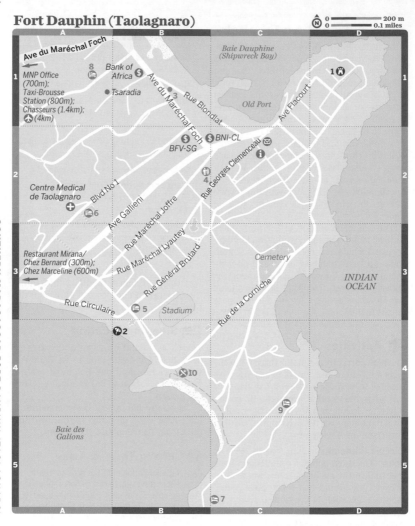

Fort Dauphin (Taolagnaro)

◎ Sights
1 Fort Flacourt.................................D1
2 Libanona Beach B4

⊕ Activities, Courses & Tours
3 Air Fort Services B1
4 Ankoba Watersports.....................B2
   Lavasoa...(see 7)

🛏 Sleeping
   Chez Georges................................(see 10)
5 Chez Jacqueline B3
6 La Croix du Sud A2
7 Lavasoa..C5
8 Népenthès....................................A1
9 Talinjoo..C4

✗ Eating
10 Chez Georges................................B4

sealed roads and street lights, looks for all the world like a mirage of civilisation.

Apart from some great beaches, the city proper has little to offer travellers and you need to keep your wits about you. But there's much to see in the surrounding area, so your best bet is to enjoy the decent in-town accommodation options and organise excursions or car hire through your hotel and get out to explore the dramatic hinterland.

⊙ Sights

Libanona Beach   BEACH
What luck for locals to have this fine beach right in the city! It's known for its surfing, both board and wind. Don't leave your belongings unattended on the sand or they may just disappear. And don't even think about wandering around here at night. But do come during the daytime for one of southern Madagascar's best beaches.

Fort Flacourt   FORTRESS
(Ave Flacourt; Ar10,000; ⊙8-11am & 2-5pm Mon-Sat, 2-6pm Sun) This fort is used as a military base and the soldiers at the entrance endlessly discuss whether or not to let you in, how much to charge and who should get the money. If they let you in, they'll insist on a guide. There's not much to see except for a few cannons, a small museum with some antique maps and some fine views, so consider these negotiations a highlight of your visit. The end-of-peninsula location is the other highlight.

If you're looking for a guide, try **Air Fort Services** (☑034 46 122 80; www.airfortservices. com; Ave du Maréchal Foch).

✦ Activities

Pic St Louis   HIKING
The summit of Pic St Louis (529m), which you can see around 3km north of Fort Dauphin (Taolagnaro), offers good views of the town and coast. From the base, allow 1½ to three hours for the ascent and 1½ hours for the descent. A dawn climb is ideal, before the going gets too hot or windy.

You'll need a guide to show you the way – ask in town, or contact an agency – and you should travel in a group as there is a security risk here.

Ankoba Watersports   SURFING
(☑020 92 215 15; www.ankoba.com; Rue du Maréchal Joffre; surfboard per hour Ar10,000, teacher per hour Ar10,000) If you've always longed to learn to surf, what better place to do so than here, where you can also organise windsurfing lessons and rental?

Most of the action takes place at in-town Ankoba Beach.

☞ Tours

Lavasoa   TOURS
(☑033 12 517 03; www.lavasoa.com) The Lavasoa hotel offers trips to Evatra and Lokaro, including stays at its sister property, Pirate Camp (p117). It can also organise surfing and kitesurfing.

🛏 Sleeping

Chez Jacqueline   BUNGALOW €
(☑033 12 839 15; Rue Gen Brulard; d Ar38,000) Jacqueline has cute little bungalows with high ceilings close by Libanona Beach. The rooms are small and breezy and have bucket hot water. There's a small on-site restaurant.

Népenthès   BUNGALOW €€
(☑034 60 832 54, 032 04 455 54; lenepenthes@ yahoo.fr; off Ave du Maréchal Foch, Ampasikabo; d Ar65,000) These charming chalet-style cottages in their own compound are clean, have hot water and are situated on spacious grounds.

Chez Georges   GUESTHOUSE €€
(☑032 48 097 38; georgesliban@yahoo.fr; Rue de la Corniche, Libanona Beach; d/tr Ar50,000/75,000) There are only two rooms here, but they are right on Libanona Beach. The triple, a studio, is the town steal. The adjacent bar and restaurant, which share a log-cabin ambience, make this a miniresort.

★**Talinjoo**   BOUTIQUE HOTEL €€€
(☑034 05 212 35, 032 05 212 35; www.talinjoo.com; Libanona; d incl breakfast €80; ☎⊠) This is the only stylish hotel in Fort Dauphin (Taolagnaro), with an attractive contemporary design and a classy infinity pool. Located high on a hill overlooking Libanona Beach, it has a postcard view, too. Rates include airport transfer and there's an on-site spa. We especially love the *Confort* Room with exposed-stone wall.

Lavasoa   BUNGALOW €€€
(☑0331251703; www.lavasoa.com; d/tr/f bungalows from €45/50/75; ☎) This friendly, well-run guesthouse has brightly painted bungalows in a superb location on the edge of a steep peninsula looking back over Libanona Beach and Pic St Louis – room 6 has one of the best views in Madagascar. The hotel also runs a tour company and owns Pirate Camp (p117) on the Lokaro Peninsula. Book in advance.

La Croix du Sud   HOTEL €€€
(☑032 05 416 98, 033 23 210 12; www.madagascar-resorts.com; Blvd No 1; d Ar140,000-190,000;

) The sister hotel to the adjacent Le Dauphin, and the better choice. It's like a large plantation house, with a big metal roof and porches. Painted in solid colours, the rooms manage to be cheery and the best have baths and balconies, while an attractive lobby ties it all together. A good and unpretentious all-round package.

✕ Eating

Chez Georges   SEAFOOD €
(Rue de la Corniche, Libanona Beach; mains Ar9000-14,000; ⊗8am-9pm) This popular local eatery and adjoining bar enjoys a laid-back surf atmosphere in cabins overlooking Libanona Beach. Catch of the day and crab farci are house specialities, but expect a wait. People swim after putting in an order and the sunset views are simply magical.

Chasseurs   MALAGASY €
(☎032 81 172 43, 033 14 368 61; Ave du Maréchal Foch; mains Ar7500-15,000; ⊗8am-10pm) Near the *taxi-brousse* station, this friendly neighbourhood institution offers traditional Malagasy fare, but is well above a *hotely* (small roadside place that serves basic meals).

★Chez Marceline   INTERNATIONAL €€
(☎034 12 606 43; www.facebook.com/chez marceline; Rue de la Corniche; mains from Ar15,000; ⊗11am-10pm) Many locals' pick for the town's best restaurant, Chez Marceline combines assured international cooking, local ingredients – the grilled fish or zebu steak are signature dishes here – and a fine location overlooking the ocean.

**Restaurant Mirana/
Chez Bernard**   EUROPEAN €€
(☎034 01 637 04; Rue de la Corniche; mains Ar18,000; ⊗11am-8pm Mon-Sat) This single room off a narrow side street is an insider spot known for its pizza, seafood and beef.

ℹ Information

INTERNET ACCESS
Some hotels have free wi-fi, but connections can be slow.

MEDICAL SERVICES
Centre Medical de Taolagnaro (☎034 20 009 12; www.cmdt.mg; Blvd No 1; ⊗24hr) The town's best medical care.

MONEY
There are plenty of banks and ATMs sprinkled around the city; some of the ATMs even work.

Bank of Africa (Ave du Maréchal Foch; ⊗8am-4pm Mon-Fri, 8.30am-noon Sat)

BFV-SG (off Ave du Maréchal Foch; ⊗8am-3.30pm Mon-Fri)

BNI-CL (Ave du Maréchal Foch; ⊗8-11.30am & 2-4.30pm Mon-Fri)

POST
Post office (www.mtpc.gov.mg; Rue Georges Clemenceau; ⊗8am-4pm Mon-Fri)

TOURIST INFORMATION
MNP office (☎020 92 904 85; Villa Dalia, Esokaka, off Ave du Maréchal Foch; ⊗9am-3pm Mon-Fri) Has information about Parc National Andohahela and other areas, but is hard to find; take a taxi.

AROUND FORT DAUPHIN (TAOLAGNARO)

Domaine de la Cascade (☎034 11 221 23; www.domainedelacascade.com; A20,000; ⊗8am-5pm Tue-Sun) This gorgeous park, about 9km from the Total station on the road to Ambovombe from Fort Dauphin (Taolagnaro), covers 136 hectares, and with a budding ecotourism project in play, it consists of a nursery set in a paradisiacal valley with several walking trails (from 30 minutes to two hours), including one to a pretty waterfall where you can take a dip. Most people come on a day trip, but there's a large bungalow with kitchen for rent (quads Ar160,000) – you'll probably have the whole place to yourself. Catering can also be arranged on weekends.

Réserve de Nahampoana (☎020 92 212 24, 033 02 212 34; www.nahampoana.com; admission incl guide Ar50,000; ⊗sunrise-sunset) This 0.67-sq-km forest reserve, 7km north of Fort Dauphin (Taolagnaro), deserves much greater recognition. Its exotic tropical setting, with mountains for a backdrop, is prettier than Berenty. Add to this a robust and varied lemur population, including ringtail, *sifaka*, brown, bamboo and mouse species (some with the habit of dropping from trees to say hello), more-humane crocodile pens, extraordinary bamboo groves, night walks and a cooling sea breeze, and you wonder why so many people are driving west. There are also bungalows (Ar120,000) and a restaurant, making this a peaceful alternative to staying in Fort Dauphin (Taolagnaro) itself. Just grab a taxi.

RESERVÉ PRIVÉE DE BERENTY

This well-known **private reserve** (☑ 033 23 210 08; Ar80,000) contains nearly one third of the remaining tamarind gallery forest in Madagascar, nestled between the arms of a former oxbow lake on the Mandrare River. It was one of Madagascar's first ecotourism destinations, its international reputation once drew nearly 8000 yearly visitors, helped by the friendly ring-tailed lemurs that greet you in the parking lot. Visitors can walk forest paths unguided in search of other lemurs. An excellent anthropological museum provides unique insights into local Antandroy culture.

The downside is that it's tough to get here thanks to worsening road conditions. Bungalows cost Ar120,000.

Trips here can be arranged by any Fort Dauphin (Taolagnaro) tour operator, or enquire at La Croix du Sud (p115).

Tourist office (☑ 032 02 846 34; Rue Realy Abel; ☺ 9am-3.30pm Mon-Fri) Useless except for a map.

❶ Getting There & Away

AIR

Tsaradia (☑ 020 92 211 22; off Ave du Maréchal Foch) flies from Fort Dauphin (Taolagnaro) to Antananarivo (from €90, two hours, daily). Between one and three services a week between Tuléar (Toliara) and Fort Dauphin (Taolagnaro) appear on Tsaradia's schedules, but they weren't operating at the time of writing.

TAXI-BROUSSE

Fort Dauphin's **taxi-brousse station** (Ave du Maréchal Foch, Tanambao) is in Tanambao, in the northwestern part of town, along the road leading to the airport.

Although *taxis-brousses* connect Fort Dauphin (Taolagnaro) with Ihosy (and beyond) along the RN7, we recommend against travelling this route for security reasons. Between Ambovombe and Ihosy, most *taxis-brousses* travel in convoy, but that doesn't eliminate the risk entirely and we recommend against overnight stops along this section. The roads are also appalling and facilities almost nonexistent.

Safer destinations include Ambovombe (Ar15,000, three to four hours) and the daily *camion-brousse* to Tuléar (Toliara; Ar50,000, two to three days).

❶ Getting Around

The airport is 4km west of town. Taxis to/from the centre cost around Ar15,000 per person. Taxis within town, including to the *taxi-brousse* station, cost Ar2500 per person.

Evatra & Lokaro Peninsula

Lokaro Peninsula is a spectacular and well-preserved area of inland waterways, green hills and barrier beaches. It lies about 15km northeast of Fort Dauphin (Taolagnaro) along the coast, or about 40km by road. Excursions from Fort Dauphin with Lavasoa (p115) begin with a 3km drive to the shore of Lac Lanirano then continue by boat to Lac Ambavarano and the tiny fishing village of Evatra. From here it is about 20 minutes on foot over the hills to a good beach. Once at Evatra, you can arrange a pirogue to visit nearby Lokaro Island, or just stay and explore the peninsula itself, which has numerous opportunities for canoeing and walking. Stay overnight, or return to Fort Dauphin to sleep.

If overnighting, try the rustic bungalows at **Pirate Camp** (☑ 033 12 517 03; www.lavasoa. com; Evatra; s/d €30/35) 🐾, run by Lavasoa in Fort Dauphin (Taolagnaro). It also has a campsite and hires equipment. The accommodation is made from local materials and there's solar electricity. The transfer here from Fort Dauphin costs €70 one way. If arriving under your own steam, call ahead. The open-air restaurant (mains from Ar12,000) serves up grilled seafood and steaks for dinner, and homemade bread and pancakes for breakfast.

❶ Getting There & Away

The easiest way to visit is on an organised excursion with Lavasoa (p115) – prices vary according to the number of people in your party and the length of the excursion.

Otherwise, to reach the Lokaro area by road under your own steam, you'll need a 4WD; allow about two hours from Fort Dauphin (Taolagnaro). If you go by foot, it will take a full day and require food and water. You should also walk with a group, as security can be a problem along this route.

Western Madagascar

Best Places to Eat

➜ Mad Zebu (p131)

➜ Bleu Soleil (p136)

➜ Chez Madame Chabaud (p124)

➜ Le Soleil des Tsingy (p132)

➜ Chez Maggie (p136)

Best Places to Stay

➜ Anjajavy (p130)

➜ Le Soleil des Tsingy (p132)

➜ La Maison de Marovasa-Be (p130)

➜ Chez Maggie (p135)

➜ PAP'S Chambres d'Hôtes (p123)

➜ Hôtel Entremer (p141)

Why Go?

Madagascar's western region – divided in two, with no roads linking the south and north – is filled with adventurous possibilities and it's from here that so many iconic Madagascar images originate. There are incredible highlights, from the *otherworldly* limestone spikes and crippled spires of the *tsingy* of the Parc National Bemaraha and the stomping ground of the fossa at the Réserve Forestière de Kirindy to the fabulous birdwatching of Parc National Ankarafantsika. Throw in the Allée des Baobabs, world-class resorts and so many opportunities to go out into the wilderness and you have a region that showcases all that's memorable about this remarkable country. Travel out here can be rough once you leave behind the paved national highways. Your rewards are priceless travelling epics you'll never forget.

When to Go
Majunga (Mahajanga)

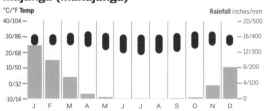

Apr–Oct The region's dry season and only time to see Parc National Bemaraha.

Nov Fossa mating season at Réserve Forestière de Kirindy.

Dec–Apr Despite the (relatively light) wet season, good for wildlife in Parc National Ankarafantsika.

ℹ Getting There & Around

With the exception of the well maintained RN4 between Antananarivo (Tana) and Majunga (Mahajanga), and the RN35 between Antsirabe and Morondava, there are no sealed roads in this region. All of these towns are connected to Antananarivo by *taxi-brousse* (bush taxi) and bus services. Both Morondava and Majunga are connected to Tana by daily flights.

A 4WD is imperative to explore sights off the RN network. The only way to get from Morondava in the south to Majunga in the north is to backtrack through Antananarivo.

BOENY REGION

The area around the regional centre of Majunga allows you to tick some of western Madagascar's most important boxes, from the finest cave system in the country at the Grottes d'Anjohibe to the much-photographed Cirque Rouge. Other reasons to explore include the sedate charms of Katsepy and the bird-rich destinations of easily accessible Parc National Ankarafantsika, or the far-more-difficult-to-reach Mahavy-Kinkony Wetland Complex. For real adventurers there's the off-the map allure of Parcs Nationaux Baie de Baly et Tsingy de Namoroka.

Majunga (Mahajanga)

POP 238,000

Majunga is a sprawling and somnolent port town with one of the prettier waterfronts of Madagascar's seaside cities – a palm-lined seaside promenade, as well as shady arcades and walls draped with gorgeous bougainvillea. With its large Comoran and Indian populations, and historical connections with Africa, it is one of the most colourful and ethnically diverse places in Madagascar. It is also the gateway to one of western Madagascar's more diverse regions, from stunning caves and rock formations to sacred lakes and bird-rich wetlands.

History

Arab traders established a number of trading posts along the coast in the 13th and 14th centuries, and the area became a thriving commercial crossroads between the Malagasy highlands, East Africa and the Middle East. Swahili and Gujarati traders settled in Majunga and the nearby town of Marovoay in the 19th century, and these communities were known for the exquisitely carved wooden doors that adorned their houses. A few can still be admired in Majunga and Marovoay.

◉ Sights

★ Cirque Rouge   NATURAL FEATURE
Dramatic Cirque Rouge is one of western Madagascar's most famous sights. This amphitheatre of eroded rock is tinted in a rainbow hue of colours, including red, pink, ochre and white – for the full effect, arrive late afternoon and stay until sunset. A stream runs along the bottom of the valley and through a small ravine down to the sea (a lovely 10-minute walk).

WORTH A TRIP

GROTTES D'ANJOHIBE
••

This series of subterranean rooms and galleries, some of them the size of buildings, are among Madagascar's most impressive. Stretching over 5km, and adorned with stalactites and stalagmites, the caves are penetrated by shafts of light from passageways and holes in the ceiling, giving an eerie feel. However, the stunning **natural swimming pools** (Ar20,000) of deep emerald green are the main attraction. Each is framed by luxuriant vegetation and ravinala palm trees fanning their leaves like parading ostriches.

The first pool you come to is shallow, while the second pool, at the foot of a spectacular waterfall, is deep and wonderful for swimming.

It takes a good 3½ hours to get to Anjohibe from Majunga and to do it as a day trip you'll need to leave at first light to be back by sunset. Local guide Rivo (p122), who speaks basic English, can organise two-day visits, with a night of camping by the pool (Ar10,000 per person). The facilities are basic (tent, bush toilet, no shower) and the meals (Ar20,000 each for lunch and dinner, Ar12,000 for breakfast), prepared by locals, are simple. The campsite is a favourite of local lemurs. At night, Rivo will get the campfire going. The track to the Grottes d'Anjohibe is passable only between April and October and requires a 4WD.

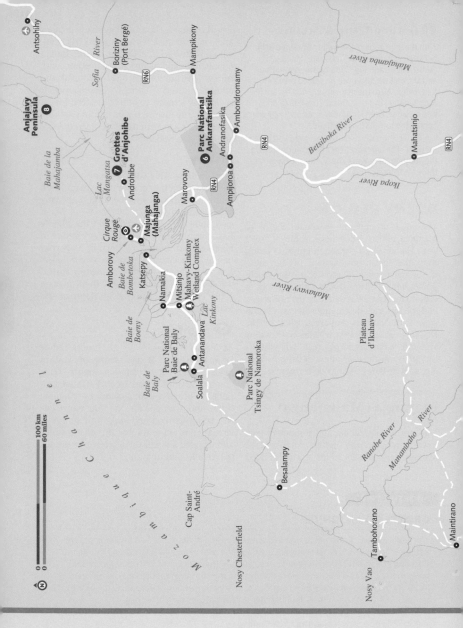

Western Madagascar Highlights

1 Parc National Bemaraha (p131)
Following the sensational via ferrata mountain route in the Grands Tsingy.

2 Allée des Baobabs (p138)
Admiring the sunset or sunrise at the photogenic baobabs close to Morondava.

3 Belo-sur-Mer (p140) Spending a couple of days in this remote seaside village.

4 Réserve Forestière de Kirindy (p139) Seeing the elusive fossa then night-spotting nocturnal lemurs.

5 Mad Zebu (p131) Enjoying Madagascar's most incongruous culinary experience in Belo-sur-Tsiribihina.

6 Parc National Ankarafantsika (p126) Nurturing your inner birder at this easily accessible park.

7 Grottes d'Anjohibe (p119) Splashing about in the emerald-green water of the natural swimming pools.

8 Anjajavy Peninsula (p130) Kicking back for a few days of remote, luxurious rest.

9 Morondava to Tuléar (p133) Driving one of Madagascar's most remote stretches of road with villages, river crossings and palpable isolation.

Majunga (Mahajanga)

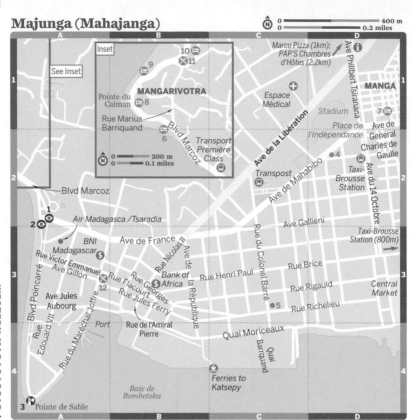

Cirque Rouge is just 12km north of Majunga. A charter taxi will cost around Ar60,000 for the return trip, including waiting time.

La Corniche
WATERFRONT

Majunga is all about the Corniche, the palm-lined promenade bordering the sea made up of Blvd Poincarré and Blvd Marcoz. In the evening residents come here to enjoy a stroll under the setting sun, sip a soft drink or nibble kebabs from numerous street carts. During school holidays (July to September) it has a fair-like atmosphere, with makeshift (and slightly scary-looking) Ferris wheels, horses to ride and families at play. At the T-junction with Ave de France, there is an enormous baobab tree (circumference 21m!) thought to be well over 700 years old. It is considered *fady* (taboo) to touch it.

Lighthouse
LIGHTHOUSE

Guides ships in from Pointe de Sable. It's an icon of Majunga's coastal skyline.

☞ Tours

Rivo
TOURS

(☎032 45 839 28) Local guide Rivo, who speaks basic English, can organise a two-day visit to Grottes d'Anjohibe (p119), with a night of camping by the pool (Ar10,000 per person). The facilities are basic (tent, bush toilet, no shower) and the meals (Ar20,000 each for lunch and dinner, Ar12,000 for breakfast), prepared by locals, are simple.

The campsite is right by the pools, so you'll have plenty of time to swim. It's also a favourite of local lemurs, who come here in the hope of food. At night, Rivo will get the campfire going.

Aventure & Découverte
ADVENTURE

(☎020 62 934 75, 034 08 521 96; www.aventure-decouverte.com; 401 Rue Ampasika) Specialises in quad-bike excursions to nearby attractions. Also organises 4WD and pirogue (traditional dugout canoe) trips, including to

Majunga (Mahajanga)

Parcs Nationaux Baie de Baly et Tsingy de Namoroka (p124).

La Ruche des Aventuriers   ADVENTURE
(☏ 032 47 488 98, 033 07 631 27; www.laruchedes aventuriers.com; Rue Richelieu; 8am-5pm) Affordable excursions to all the main sights around Majunga, including three-day camping trips to hard-to-reach Lac Kinkony.

🛏 Sleeping

Hôtel Chez Chabaud   HOTEL €
(☏ 032 40 530 05, 020 62 233 27; off Ave du Général de Gaulle; r Ar25,000-50,000; ❉) With neon light and white-and-blue walls, rooms at Chez Chabaud have the charm of prison cells. That said, the hotel is immaculate, the staff are friendly and you won't find better value anywhere else. The cheaper rooms have fans and shared facilities.

Hôtel du Phare   HOTEL €€
(☏ 033 37 000 20, 020 62 235 00; www.hoteldu pharemajunga.com; Blvd Marcoz; d/f with fan Ar60,000/90,000, with air-con Ar90,000/110,000; ❉ 🛜) Overlooking the Corniche, this friendly establishment has simple but spacious and spotless rooms, with tiled floors and colourful feature walls. Rooms at the back have fans, those at the front (with sea views) have air-con. There is a nice garden where breakfast can be served.

★PAP'S Chambres d'Hôtes   GUESTHOUSE €€€
(☏ 032 45 613 16; www.facebook.com/pap. smajunga; Rte de Mahavoky; r from €69; P ❉ 🛜 ≋) There are just three rooms here, but they're smart and stylish, with wood floors, colourful rugs, whitewashed walls and cool bathrooms, and public areas are just as delightful. It's all designed to catch the breeze and the views.

★Karibu Lodge   LUXURY HOTEL €€€
(☏ 020 62 247 05, 020 62 247 10; www.karibulodge. net; Blvd Marcoz; ste from €73; ❉ 🛜 ≋) The rather lovely Karibu offers 15 duplex suites with sea views, TV lounge and terrace/balcony. The rooms have been furnished to very high standards and the pool and bar-restaurant overlooking the sea are prime spots to enjoy the sunset.

Baobab Tree Hotel & Spa   HOTEL €€€
(☏ 020 62 241 72, 034 44 200 10; www.baobab-tree-hotel.mg; Blvd Marcoz; r/ste from €107/161; P ❉ 🛜 ≋) This large spa hotel is Majunga's most luxurious option with stylish rooms, an understated contemporary look and muted colour schemes. There's an excellent restaurant, a well-stocked bar, a well-run spa and priceless views from the more expensive rooms.

WESTERN MADAGASCAR MAJUNGA (MAHAJANGA)

WORTH A TRIP

MAHAVY-KINKONY WETLAND COMPLEX

The Mahavy-Kinkony Wetland Complex incorporates a diverse and fragile ecosystem consisting of marine bays, river, delta and 22 lakes, including Madagascar's second largest, Lac Kinkony. The reserve is home to dry deciduous and gallery forest, savannah, marshland, mangroves, caves and lots of wildlife. It gained temporary protection status in 2007.

The primary reason to come to Lac Kinkony, however, is the 143 species of bird. And it's the only place where all of western Madagascar's waterfowl species can be seen.

Getting to Lac Kinkony is virtually impossible under your own steam and there is no tourism infrastructure. Travel agencies in Majunga organise all-inclusive camping trips, but you'll need at least three days (the roads are very rough) and a minimum of Ar600,000 for the 4WD, fuel and guide (for two to four people).

GETTING AWAY FROM IT ALL

West of Majunga, Madagascar's western bulge is one of the island's least trampled corners, only accessible in dry season, from May to October.

Parc National Baie de Baly (www.parcs-madagascar.com; adult/child Ar45,000/25,000; ☺ May-Oct) Best known as the home of the critically endangered ploughshare tortoise, this remote park has dense dry, bamboo and mangrove forests, sand dunes and beaches, lakes and rivers. In addition to eight lemur species (Decken's *sifaka* and brown lemurs are most commonly sighted), the beaches are nesting grounds for green, hawksbill, Madagascar big-headed and loggerhead turtles. The four circuits through the park take from one to six hours; the longer circuits usually include a pirogue (traditional dugout canoe) ride. More than 120 bird species have also been recorded here.

Access to the park is only possible May to October and is from Soalala, 150km southwest of Katsepy. It's a two-day 4WD expedition from Majunga.

Parcs Nationaux Baie de Baly et Tsingy de Namoroka (www.parcs-madagascar.com; adult/child per day Ar45,000/25,000) This isolated park is home to that peculiarly Malagasy landform, the *tsingy*, a dense forest of jagged rocky pinnacles interwoven with deep canyons filled with streams and trees. It's a bit like visiting the more famous Parc National Bemaraha (p131), but without the crowds. Trails weave among the rocks, and rope bridges cross the canyons. There are three circuits through the park. The 70km Circuit Ambovonomy combines walking with 4WDing and there are fine panoramic views and a good chance of seeing Decken's *sifaka* or red lemurs. Circuit Mandevy (70km) is similar, with good baobab views, while the Circuit Antsifotra (60km) is also similar, if slightly shorter and with less chance of spotting lemurs. Most circuits take four to six hours.

Other lemur species include eastern lesser bamboo lemur, fork-crowned lemur, grey mouse lemur, Milne-Edwards' sportive lemur, fat-tailed dwarf lemur and the oh-so-elusive aye-aye. More than 80 bird species have also been recorded here.

It's a rough 150km, eight-hour 4WD expedition from Katsepy to Soalala, from where it's a further 50km south. Count on four days round trip from Majunga, plus time spent here. Aventure & Découverte (p122) is a Majunga operator that can organise trips.

Les Roches Rouges   HOTEL €€€
(☑ 032 05 875 80, 020 62 020 01; www.roches rouges.mg; off Blvd Marcoz; d Ar125,000-175,000, ste Ar250,000; 🅿 ❋ 🛜 🎬) This place gets the thumbs up from readers who enjoy the large rooms and friendly staff. The suite, really a villa, is stunning – you'll feel like royalty without the unreasonable price tag.

🍴 Eating

Parad'Ice   CAFE €
(Rue du Maréchal Joffre; mains Ar8000-15,000; ☺ 8am-9pm Tue-Sun) This cheerful cafe-restaurant serves simple but well-prepared meals, including salads you can tuck into without hesitation and rotating plats du jour such as *ravitoto* (pork stew with manioc greens) or zebu stew. It also does burgers and croque-monsieurs (ham-and-cheese grilled sandwiches), excellent homemade ice creams and breakfasts.

★ Chez Madame Chabaud   FUSION €€
(☑ 032 40 530 05; off Ave du Général de Gaulle; mains Ar12,000-18,000; ☺ 11am-3pm & 6-9pm Wed-Mon) Small, intimate and oh-so-delicious, Chez Madame Chabaud is a Majunga institution. Christiane (the original Madame Chabaud's daughter) prepares a divine fusion cuisine mixing Malagasy, Creole and European influences that befit the city's heritage. Try the *camaron* (large freshwater prawn) or the *ouassous* (a huge crayfish) and the mean cocktails.

Marco Pizza   PIZZA €€
(☑ 032 11 110 32; Ave d'Amborovy; pizzas from Ar12,000; ☺ 11am-9pm) This friendly joint with street seating churns out excellent – and absolutely huge – pizzas with a variety of meat, fish and vegetarian toppings. It's a couple of kilometres from the centre, but every taxi knows where it is so you won't have trouble finding it.

Fishing Residence   SEAFOOD €€
(☑ 032 05 160 93; www.fishingresidence.com; Blvd Marcoz; mains Ar12,000-19,000) This hotel and restaurant is well known for its exquisite seafood, such as calamari and prawns in *combava* (wild lemon) sauce or grilled swordfish.

ⓘ Information

MEDICAL SERVICES

Espace Médical (☎ 034 02 172 26, 020 62 248 21; www.espacemedical.mg; off Ave de la Libération, Magarivotra; ☺24hr) The best place for medical treatment.

MONEY

Bank of Africa (BOA; post office, cnr Rues Georges V & Nicolas II; ☺8am-4pm Mon-Fri, 8.30am-noon Sat) Changes money; Visa ATM.

BNI Madagascar (Rue du Maréchal Joffre; ☺8-11.30am & 2-4.30pm Mon-Fri) Changes money; ATM for Visa and MasterCard.

POST

Post office (Rue du Colonel Darré; ☺8-11.30am & 2-4.30pm Mon-Fri) Central post office.

TOURIST INFORMATION

Tourist office (☎ 034 08 088 80; www.majunga.org; 14 Ave Philibert Tsiranana; ☺8am-noon & 2.30-5.30pm Mon-Fri, 8am-1pm Sat) Can recommend excursions, arrange guides and help with all manner of bookings. Also sells city maps.

ⓘ Getting There & Away

AIR

Air Madagascar/Tsaradia (☎ 032 05 222 06, 020 62 224 61; www.tsaradia.com; Rue Girard; ☺8-11.30am & 2.30-5pm Mon-Fri, 8-10am Sat) Flies five times weekly to/from Antananarivo (one hour, from €112).

BOAT

Ferries to Katsepy (passenger/car Ar4000/40,000, one hour) leave from the port at 7.30am daily, then return from Katsepy around 9am. If there's demand, it sometimes does a second trip back from Katsepy in the afternoon. Private motorboats (Ar4500, 30 minutes) cross in both directions a few times a day until about 3pm.

BUS

To travel in luxury, **Transport Première Class** (☎ 032 43 588 88, 034 14 588 88; www.malagasycar.com/transport-premiere-classe; Blvd Marcoz) runs comfortable, air-con vehicles between Tana and Majunga (Ar96,000, 10 hours, daily). They sit just two people to a row and include a packed lunch. Departure is at 6.45am from Restaurant Chez Thi-Lan; drop-off is at Hôtel Le Grand Mellis in Tana. Bookings essential.

Another good alternative to a standard taxi-brousse (bush taxi) is **Transpost** (Rue du Colonel Barré, Post Office), run by Madagascar's postal service. It has minibuses between Majunga and Tana (Ar35,000; 12 hrs; ☺Tue, Thu & Sat); pickup and drop-off is at the central post office in both cities. Departure is at 7am. Bookings required.

Cotisse (☎ 032 11 027 33; www.cotisse-transport.com), in Ambodivona, runs nice 16- or 19-seater Mercedes minibuses that link Antananarivo with Majunga (from Ar34,000, 11 hours, four departures daily).

TAXI-BROUSSE

There are two taxi-brousse stations in Majunga: one on Ave du 14 Octobre near the town hall and the other, much bigger, one on **Rue George Ranaivoson** (Ave Barday), close to the Jovenna petrol station. For Nosy Be, change at Ambanja for Ankify (Ar4000, one hour), where you'll find boats for Nosy Be.

DESTINATION	FARE (AR)	DURATION (HR)	DEPARTURE
Ambanja	50,000	14	Afternoon
Antananarivo	30,000	12	Morning & afternoon
Diego Suarez (Antsiranana)	63,000	22	Morning & afternoon

ⓘ Getting Around

TO/FROM THE AIRPORT

The airport is 6km northeast of town. A taxi to/from town costs around Ar25,000. Taxis-brousses (Ar2000) stop about 300m from the airport.

CAR

Upmarket hotels and tour companies in Majunga can arrange car or 4WD rental. Expect to pay Ar200,000 to Ar250,000 per day for a 4WD and around Ar100,000 for a regular car. Petrol costs extra.

TAXI

The standard rate for a taxi ride in town is Ar5000, but they can ask as much as Ar10,000.

Katsepy

POP 12,000

Katsepy (kah-tsep) is a small, sleepy fishing village across Bombetoka Bay from Majunga with a couple of swimmable beaches. Most visitors are likely to go through Katsepy on their way to Kinkony, but there's an appealing lighthouse and an excellent hotel-restaurant that make a nice alternative to Majunga.

◉ Sights

Katsepy's Lighthouse   LIGHTHOUSE
(Ar5000) About 8km southwest of Katsepy, this lighthouse has sweeping views of Bombetoka Bay and Mozambique Channel. It's a hot, two-hour walk from Katsepy. Otherwise charter a taxi-brousse to take you there and back (Ar50,000, with 30 minutes at the site).

🛏 Sleeping

Chez Mme Chabaud BUNGALOW €€
(☑ 020 62 233 27; bungalows Ar45,000) The seven pretty bungalows have been built and decorated with local materials and are right by the beach, in a lovely garden. Run by the same family as the eponymous restaurant in Majunga (p124), Chez Mme Chabaud serves the same delicious blend of Malagasy and French cuisine with fresh, local ingredients (mains Ar12,000 to Ar18,000).

The hotel has eschewed generators in favour of wind and solar energy.

❶ Getting There & Away

The Majunga–Katsepy ferry (passenger/car Ar4000/40,000, one hour) leaves Majunga at 7.30am daily, then sets out for the return journey from Katsepy around 9am. If there are many cars and/or trucks waiting in Katsepy, it sometimes does a second trip in the afternoon. If the ferry doesn't come back, private motorboats (Ar4500, 30 minutes) ply the crossing in both directions between Majunga and Katsepy several times a day until about 3pm.

Parc National Ankarafantsika

Ankarafantsika (www.parcs-madagascar.com; adult/child per day Ar55,000/25,000, guide from Ar50,000) is the last strand of dry western deciduous forest in Madagascar, and the need for its protection is obvious – as you drive to Ankarafantsika, whether from Tana or the north, there isn't a tree in sight for hundreds of kilometres. The combination of accessibility (the park straddles the RN4 and is accessible even by public transport) and excellent wildlife viewing makes it one of western Madagascar's most popular and rewarding parks.

🏃 Activities

Wildlife Watching

Ankarafantsika is home to eight lemur species, many easily seen, including Coquerel's *sifaka* and the recently discovered golden-brown mouse lemur. You're also likely to see brown lemurs and four nocturnal species: sportive, woolly, grey mouse and fat-tailed dwarf lemur. More elusive is the rare mongoose lemur, which is observed almost exclusively here.

Ankarafantsika is one of Madagascar's finest birdwatching venues, with 129 species recorded, including the critically endangered

❶ PARC NATIONAL ANKARAFANTSIKA

Best time to visit Year-round.

Key highlight The profusion of birdlife and scenic landscape.

Wildlife Birds, birds, lemurs, more birds!

Habitat Dry deciduous forest.

Gateway town Ampijoroa.

Transport options *Taxis-brousses* (bush taxis) or private vehicle.

Things you should know Ankarafantsika makes an ideal stopover to break the journey between Tana and Majunga; check the security situation before travelling between Ankarafantsika and Majunga.

Madagascar fish eagle and the raucous sickle-bill vanga. There are also more than 70 species of reptile, including small iguanas, a rare species of leaf-tailed gecko and the rhinoceros chameleon (the male sports a large, curious-looking, bulb-like proboscis).

The Durrell Wildlife Conservation Trust (www.durrell.org) has been operating a very successful captive-breeding program for the critically endangered ploughshare tortoise in Parc National Ankarafantsika for 25 years. Because poaching is a problem, you'll only be able to watch the tortoises through a chain-link fence.

Hiking

Hiking is the name of the game here. There are eight short circuits in the park, some of which can be combined into a half-day hike. Circuits in the western half of the park go through dense forests on a sandy plateau and are great for lemur spotting (*sifakas* and brown lemurs in particular) and birdwatching. There's also a breathtaking canyon that is well worth the hike in baking heat across the grassland plateau.

The northern half of the park is all about the lake and the baobabs. The birdwatching is excellent here (and completely different from the south) and there are more reptiles, including crocodiles. If you have time, try to see both sides.

🛏 Sleeping

Gîte d'Ampijoroa BUNGALOW €€
(☑ 020 62 780 00; akf.parks@gmail.com; camping Ar8000, r without bathroom Ar40,000, bungalows Ar90,000) The national park's privately run

accommodation is adequate, if uninspiring – reasonable but exposed camping facilities, basic rooms with poor shared facilities and large, simple bungalows. The redeeming feature is the restaurant, which serves delicious three-course meals for a bargain Ar15,000.

Blue Vanga Lodge   BUNGALOW €€€
(☑034 08 522 22; d Ar105,000) Around 5km south of the park entrance, friendly Blue Vanga Lodge has large, spotless bungalows set around a sandy garden. There's no hot water, and electricity appears in the evenings only. If you want dinner, you'll need to phone ahead to give it notice to prepare. The brick bungalows can get *really* hot.

ℹ Getting There & Away

The entrance to the park is just off the RN4, about 114km southeast of Majunga and 455km from Antananarivo, close to the village of Ampijoroa. If you don't have your own vehicle, catch a *taxi-brousse* to Majunga from Tana (Ar40,000, eight hours) or a *taxi-brousse* towards Andranofasika from Majunga (Ar7000, three hours) and ask to be dropped off at the park. You'll have no problem flagging a *taxi-brousse* to go to Majunga whatever the time of day, but you may have to go to Majunga to find a *taxi-brousse* to Tana as many are likely to be full by the time they pass the park.

At the time of research, a number of attacks on vehicles had taken place along the road (RN4) between Parc National Ankarafantsika and Majunga. Please check the security situation before travelling this route, try and travel with other vehicles, and never travel this route after dark

TSIRIBIHINA RIVER REGION

One of Madagascar's top wilderness destinations, the region between Antsirabe and Morondava is home to the beautiful Tsiribihina and Manambolo Rivers, the spectacular Unesco World Heritage–listed Parc National Bemaraha and the Réserve Forestière de Kirindy with its population of fossa (Madagascar's largest predator).

Miandrivazo

Miandrivazo (mee-an-dree-vaaz), which lies along the main RN34 road around halfway between Antsirabe and Morondava, is the starting point for boat trips down the Tsiribihina River to Belo-sur-Tsiribihina. If you're coming from Antsirabe, there are fine views over the town and surrounding river plains on the final approach into town.

Riverboat guides will generally find you not long after you arrive in town. Be aware, however, that security was a major issue for river trips at the time of research – check the prevailing situation before travelling.

🛏 Sleeping

La Pirogue   BUNGALOW €€
(☑032 07 508 37; r Ar55,000, d bungalows Ar60,000-85,000) Simple but clean bungalow rooms, with good views from the restaurant. It's the best Miandrivazo choice for those on a tight budget, although the rooms are a little cell-like.

★**Princesse Tsiribihina**   HOTEL €€€
(☑033 11 301 72; www.madagascar-circuits.com; s/d/f Ar108,000/108,000/174,000; ⊙Mar-Nov; 🅿🛜🏊) Easily the best place to stay in Miandrivazo, Princesse Tsiribihina is run by one of the better river-trip operators. Rooms are attractively painted, spacious and come with terrific bathrooms. The location takes advantage of the hillside position with sweeping views and there's a decent restaurant (mains from Ar12,000) and swimming pool. It's 1km south of town, so nice and quiet.

ℹ Getting There & Away

There are daily *taxis-brousses* to Antananarivo (Ar28,000, nine hours), Antsirabe (Ar19,000, seven hours) and Morondava (Ar32,000, six hours) *Taxis-brousses* from Antananarivo leave the capital around 5pm or 6pm and reach Miandrivazo in the middle of the night.

ℹ RIVER TRIPS

At the time of writing, security was a major concern in this area. Armed groups were known to be operating, especially around the Tsiribihina River and while most of the fighting doesn't affect travellers, there have been attacks and robberies perpetrated against river-going tourist groups. Even at the height of the concerns, many operators continued to run trips in the area. Before signing up, however, please check local and international travel advisories for the current safety situation. Any information covered here must be viewed within this context, and applies only to those times where it is safe to travel downriver.

YANN GUICHAOUA-PHOTOS/GETTY IMAGES ©

DAVID HAVEL/SHUTTERSTOCK ©

1. Wooden carvings, Sakalava tomb
The area's dominant indigenous tribe, the Sakalava, cover the tombs of the dead with elaborate, often erotic carvings (p142).

2. Cirque Rouge
This amphitheatre of eroded red rocks (p119) not far from the sea and one of Madagascar's most famous sights, is located just north of Majunga.

3. Fossas
The Réserve Forestière de Kirindy (p139) is one of the most likely places in Madagascar to view the carnivorous fossa.

4. Baobabs
The RN8 road (p138) between Morondava and Belo-sur-Tsiribihina is flanked with this iconic tree, nicknamed 'roots of the sky'.

Belo-sur-Tsiribihina

POP 32,000

Belo-sur-Tsiribihina, lost in the marshes and mangroves of the Tsiribihina Delta, is a dusty collection of two-storey buildings. It's halfway between Morondava and Parc National Bemaraha and has that incongruous combination of utter remoteness and tourist hub. It's often referred to as 'Belo' and is not to be confused with the coastal village of Belo-sur-Mer, which lies further south. It's also the end point of trips down the Tsiribihina River, and has, somewhat incongruously, what could be rural Madagascar's best restaurant.

🛏 Sleeping

Hôtel-Restaurant du Menabe   HOTEL **€**
(📲 034 75 252 58, 032 42 635 35; hoteldumenabe@gmail.com; d/tw/tr from Ar40,000/60,000/70,000; 📶) In an old, colourful colonial building, Hôtel du Menabe offers some simple, airy rooms with huge double beds. Most have

bathrooms and all are kept clean. The hotel is run by a friendly Frenchman, Bruno, and there's a great atmosphere, notably in the evenings when the dining room fills with travellers swapping stories.

There's a 1940s-era film projector in the restaurant, where you can get sandwiches (Ar12,000 to Ar17,000), pizza (from Ar15,000) as well as a range of international and Malagasy dishes (mains Ar13,000 to Ar25,000).

Hôtel Ravinala   HOTEL **€**
(📲 033 51 085 70; r Ar30,000-40,000) Dirt cheap in the truest sense of the word, the Ravinala is only for those counting their ariary. The rooms are large, but only marginally cleaner than the grimy corridors. No mosquito nets.

Hotel Karibo   HOTEL **€€**
(📲 032 51 872 13, 034 20 872 13; hotelrestaurant karibo@gmail.com; d Ar26,000-61,000, f Ar101,000; 📶) The pick of the places to stay in town, the Karibo has cell-like rooms in the main building, but pricier ones out the back that

---

WORTH A TRIP

ANJAJAVY'S FLY-IN RESORTS

For those looking for something truly off the radar, the remote resorts on the Anjajavy Peninsula are the answer. Getting there alone costs an eye-watering €200 to €650.

Anjajavy (📲 France +33 1 44 69 15 03; www.anjajavy.com; s/d incl meals €653/1064; 🕙 Apr–mid-Jan; ❄🏠🏊) Part of the prestigious Relais & Châteaux network, Anjajavy is the quintessential desert-island idyll. The guest villas are luxurious, with polished wood, fine linen and their own private terrace. There are myriad activities – snorkelling, swimming, guided walks through the forest and to local villages – many of them free. Massages, fishing and boat excursions are also available. The hotel leases 4.5 sq km of native dry deciduous forest and protects it as a nature reserve. A three-day minimum stay is required; transfer is by private plane from Antananarivo.

La Maison de Marovasa-Be (📲 032 07 418 14, France +33 6 22 85 71 54; www.marovasabe.com; per person all-inclusive from €200; 🕙 Mar-Jan; 🏊) The exquisite Marovasa villa offers beautiful suites and bedrooms, each with balcony. The house has a 1930s colonial retro feel about it. The surrounding environment is more arid than at other Anjajavy resorts, but Marovasa is involved in local reforestation projects. The hotel is also powered by wind and solar energy rather than generator. Access is by private plane from Antananarivo, Majunga or Nosy Be.

Antsanitia Beach Resort (📲 020 62 023 34, 020 62 911 00; www.antsanitia.com; r/bungalows/ste from €67/70/123; 🏠🏊) Found on an isolated stretch of coast, some 40 minutes' drive north of Majunga, Antsanitia (pronounced 'An-tsan-tee') is a fantastic resort. As well as lovely bungalows with wood and raffia furniture, a gorgeous pool, open-air bar, fabulous restaurant and a wonderful setting, guests enjoy numerous activities, from sailing to hiking, snorkelling, pirogue (traditional dugout canoe) trips and cultural excursions. The hotel has put sustainability at the heart of everything it does, so many of the activities on offer involve trips to local villages or outings with local fishers. The resort also employs and trains a number of people from the area, and it donates part of the fees from activities to the local community's fund. Antsanitia is also doing its bit for the environment: hot water comes courtesy of the sun, 'air-con' courtesy of the sea breeze.

are really rather pleasant and worth the extra ariary. A good restaurant, too.

Eating

Karibo Restaurant   INTERNATIONAL €€
(☑034 20 872 13; mains Ar20,000-30,000; ☺8am-9pm; ☜) If for reasons we can't quite fathom you can't eat at Mad Zebu, this place, run by the same people, is a good fall-back option and worth a mention in its own right. Zebu steak or brochette, tagliatelle with prawns, or simply grilled prawns – they're all cooked expertly.

★Mad Zebu   INTERNATIONAL €€€
(☑032 40 387 15, 032 07 589 55; www.madzebu debelo.com; mains Ar25,000-35,000, 2-/3-course menu Ar45,000/60,000; ☺10am-3pm & 7-10pm Apr-Oct or Nov) The 'crazy zebu' is the most incongruous find in dusty Belo, possibly in all Madagascar. Dishes seem to come straight out of a Michelin-starred restaurant (the chef trained in prestigious kitchens in Madagascar and Europe), with exquisite creations such as pan-fried shin of zebu, prawn medallions, or snapper fillet with peanuts, risotto and coconut sauce, all elaborately presented.

Vegetarian options are available too. Save room for dessert. Everyone travelling between Morondava and the Parc National Bemaraha stops here and many companies reserve tables in advance – we suggest you do likewise or be prepared to wait. Around 11.30am is the lunchtime peak.

❶ Information

There is no bank or internet access in Belo. The nearest facilities are in Morondava.

❶ Getting There & Away

BOAT

Belo is on the northern side of Tsiribihina River so vehicles (and passengers) coming from Morondava need to use the ferry (passenger/vehicle Ar1000/50,000, 45 minutes, 6am to 5pm).

CAMIONS-BROUSSES

These huge, 4WD army-style trucks go to Bekopaka (for Parc National Bemaraha) every few days in the dry season (May to October). The trip (Ar30,000) takes anything from eight to 12 hours and is pretty rough.

TAXI-BROUSSE

There are daily taxis-brousses between Belo-sur-Tsiribihina and Morondava (Ar17,000, three to four hours). Departures are from the Morondava side of the river. The road is unsealed but in reasonable condition.

WORTH A TRIP

LODGE DE LA SALINE

This **lodge** (☑034 14 599 21; www.lodgedelasaline.com; s/d incl half board bungalows Ar225,000/255,000, cottages Ar255,000/285,000), well signposted 10km off the Belo-sur-Tsiribihina–Kirindy road, is blissfully quiet. There's a range of fascinating activities (including visits to local fishing villages, local salt pans, mangrove excursions and bird-watching at the nearby Ramsar-listed wetlands). The cottages are excellent value (the bungalows less so). It sees fewer tourists than it deserves out here, so come before word gets out.

Parc National Bemaraha

If you visit one place in western Madagascar, make it the **Parc National Bemaraha** (www.parcs-madagascar.com; adult/child per day Ar55,000/25,000). A Unesco World Heritage Site, its highlights are the jagged, limestone pinnacles known as *tsingy* and the impressive infrastructure – via ferrata (mountain route equipped with fixed cables, stemples, ladders and bridges, and organised through your guide), rope bridges, walkways – the park has put in place to explore them. Formed over centuries by the movement of wind and water, and often towering several hundred metres into the air, the serrated peaks would definitely look at home in a Salvador Dalí painting.

☆ Activities

Although there are a few 4WD circuits, you'll miss the best bits if you don't explore the park on foot. As a bare minimum, we recommend at least a day in the Petits Tsingy and a day in the Grands Tsingy – more, of course, if time allows.

Wildlife Watching

Although better known for its landscapes, the park's wildlife is exceptional. There are 11 lemur species in residence, with the most commonly sighted species being the Decken's *sifaka* and the red-fronted brown lemur; your best chances come while hiking in the Petits Tsingy. Even by day, you might chance upon fat-tailed dwarf lemurs and grey mouse lemurs catching up on sleep in tree hollows. If you're really lucky, you'll happen upon the Cleese's woolly lemur (also known as the Western woolly lemur) and the Sambirano lesser bamboo lemur, both of which are only found in this park.

Over 100 bird species are also present in the park, including the critically endangered Madagascar fish eagle. Other important raptors include Henst's goshawk, Madagascar sparrowhawk and Madagascar harrier, while sightings of the crested ibis and Madagascar grey-throated rail are also greatly prized among birders.

Some 45 reptiles and amphibians round out an impressive portfolio – watch in particular for the Antsingy leaf chameleon and Madagascar iguana.

🛏 Sleeping

Tanankoay BUNGALOW €

(☑ 034 18 251 93; www.tanankoay.com; camping per person Ar5000, igloo tent Ar10,000, d Ar15,000-75,000, f Ar120,000; ⊘ May-Nov) This super-friendly hotel offers everything from camping to spacious en suite bungalows. There is an expansive privately run botanical garden and the restaurant serves decent food. Rooms come in a rather bewildering range of shapes and sizes, but all are simple, tidy

---

ℹ PARC NATIONAL BEMARAHA

Best time to visit April to October.

Key highlight The dramatic, dark-grey, serrated pinnacles of the *tsingy* (limestone pinnacle formations).

Wildlife The park's main draw is its geology rather than wildlife, although you're bound to come across some of the park's 11 species of lemur.

Habitats Humid and dry forests, grassland, limestone rock formations.

Gateway towns Bekopaka.

Transport options Access to Bekopaka is possible by 4WD between April or May and October from Morondava.

Things you should know It is *fady* (taboo) to smoke, go to the toilet outside designated areas, or point at the *tsingy* with your finger outstretched.

Top tip During peak season (July and August), there aren't enough guides and harnesses, so arrange everything the day before. This also allows you to depart around 5am and avoid the human traffic jams along the via ferrata.

---

and well kept. Tanankoay is 900m north of Bekopaka, on the road to the Grands Tsingy.

Camp Croco CAMPGROUND €€

(☑ 034 79 293 80; www.madcameleon.com; s/d Ar75,000/90,000) This shaded tented camp, run by tour operator **Mad Caméléon** (☑ 020 22 206 91; www.madcameleon.com), has an atmospheric location with epic sunsets on the southern banks of the Manambolo River. The large canvas tents are quite bare and a touch overpriced considering you have to share bathrooms and toilets. They were due to add some tents with private toilets not long after we were there.

Travellers rave about the food (Ar18,000/30,000/45,000 for breakfast/lunch/dinner).

★ **Le Soleil des Tsingy** LODGE €€€

(☑ 034 14 719 68, 033 15 719 68; www.soleildes tsingy.com; d/f €99/139; P ❄ 🛜 🏊) 🏊 Set in a 200,000-sq-metre garden, with views out over the surrounding wilderness from the restaurant and gorgeous infinity pool, Le Soleil des Tsingy is easily the best base for visiting the national park. The beautifully appointed bungalows with flagstone floors are spacious and have expansive terraces. There's a good bar-restaurant and even a small children's playground. Service is attentive.

Olympe du Bemaraha BUNGALOW €€€

(☑ 032 03 210 52, 034 49 205 03; www.tsingy-olympedubemaraha.com; r Ar60,000-214,000, d/tr/f bungalows Ar239,000/289,000/500,000) Set in leafy grounds, this well-run place has nicely spaced bungalows and a few rooms, as well as a good restaurant and pool. The bungalows are the best choice, all swathed in wood with mosquito nets and a certain rustic appeal.

Le Grand Hôtel du Tsingy du Bemaraha BUNGALOW €€€

(☑ 032 02 488 13, 034 99 389 99; www.legrand hotel-du-tsingy.com; r/d/tr Ar80,000/194,400/244,800; ⊘ mid-Apr–Nov; P 🛜 🏊) Set amid expansive grounds, this three-star lodge has circular brick rondavel-style bungalows with good bathrooms, a shaded entrance terrace and 24-hour electricity. It's a good option with a reasonable price tag and a decent restaurant. It's after the village on the road to the Grand Tsingy.

Orchidée du Bemaraha HOTEL €€€

(☑ 032 50 898 79; www.orchideedubemaraha.com; Bekopaka; d Ar70,000-180,000, f from Ar300,000; 🏊) With beautiful grounds, two pools and a lovely bar, this is a fantastic place to return to after scaling the *tsingy*. Both tents and rooms are good value and well appointed, with numerous different varieties spread across this sprawling place. The latter have tiled floors, mosquito nets and plenty of space, the cheapest rooms are smaller and don't have fans.

❶ Information

ELECTRICITY
Bekopaka lacks mains electricity, and hotels generally switch on their generators between 5pm and 10pm, and early in the morning.

INTERNET ACCESS
Most hotels have functioning wi-fi, although usually only in the reception area and restaurants. Connections can be tenuous, and sometimes work only when the hotel turns on its generator.

MONEY
There are no banks so make sure you have enough cash before setting off from Morondava.

TELEPHONE
Most Malagasy networks operate here, including Telma and Airtel Madagascar.

TOURIST INFORMATION
Madagascar National Parks office (☏ 033 49 401 32, 033 49 403 31; www.parcs madagascar. com; ⊗ 6.30-11.30am & 1.30-4pm) At the entrance to Bekopaka, it arranges guides, payment of park fees (possible with Visa or MasterCard) and climbing harnesses if required. Most guides speak French, English and Italian.

❶ Getting There & Away

You need a 4WD to access the *tsingy* and Bekopaka is a seven-hour drive from Morondava. Bekopaka and the national park are on the north side of the **Manambolo River ferry crossing** (passenger/vehicle free/Ar10,000; ⊗ 6.30am-noon & 2-6pm). The crossing is about 80km of very rough track north of Belo-sur-Tsiribihina (four hours) and passable only from April or May to October. Bekopaka is about 3km from the ferry crossing. A car and driver from Morondava will set you back around €75 per day, including fuel.

In the dry season, there are infrequent *camions-brousses* between Bekopaka and Belo-sur-Tsiribihina (Ar30,000, eight to 12 hours). There's no public transport from Morondava.

MORONDAVA DISTRICT

Out here it's all about what lies beyond the end of the sealed road, and the area that

DON'T MISS

WALKING THE TSINGY

Much of the walking in the *tsingy* area of the park can be strenuous and requires careful conversations with your guides before setting out. Gaps between the rocks are sometimes narrow and bridges are high. Anyone with a low level of fitness or vertigo might find exploring the *tsingy* challenging, particularly the Grands Tsingy, where hauling, squeezing, crawling and pulling are all part of the fun and guides have developed an arsenal of tricks to coax even the most vertigo-struck hikers across the rope bridges.

There are at least 10 different routes, so take time to sit down with your guide, preferably the day before you plan to set out, to discuss the pros and cons of each – some are better for wildlife, others the views, some are strenuous, others an easy stroll and so on.

surrounds the remote western town of Morondava is at once worth visiting in its own right and the starting point for so many adventures into the wild. Close to town, the Allée des Baobabs (p138) is the sunrise or sunset photo that defines a nation. Away to the south is the wonderfully sleepy Belo-sur-Mer (p140) and the rarely visited Parc National Kirindy-Mite (p141) – this combination of wild isolation and somnolent seaside living is a beguiling mix. It's from the Morondava region, too, that the gruelling three-day, off-road 4WD adventure (p140) that connects western Madagascar to Tuléar in the country's south begins and ends. And wildlife nuts will want to track down the fossa at the Réserve Forestière de Kirindy (p139).

Morondava

POP 42,000

Morondava is a terminally laid-back seaside town with sandy streets and gently decaying clapboard houses. There is not much to do or see in the town itself, and most people come here on their way to and from Parc National Bemaraha, Belo-sur-Mer or Réserve Forestière de Kirindy. It's also the starting point for the gruelling three-day, off-road 4WD adventure that connects western Madagascar to Tuléar in the country's south. Closer-to-town attractions include the iconic Allée des Baobabs.

Morondava

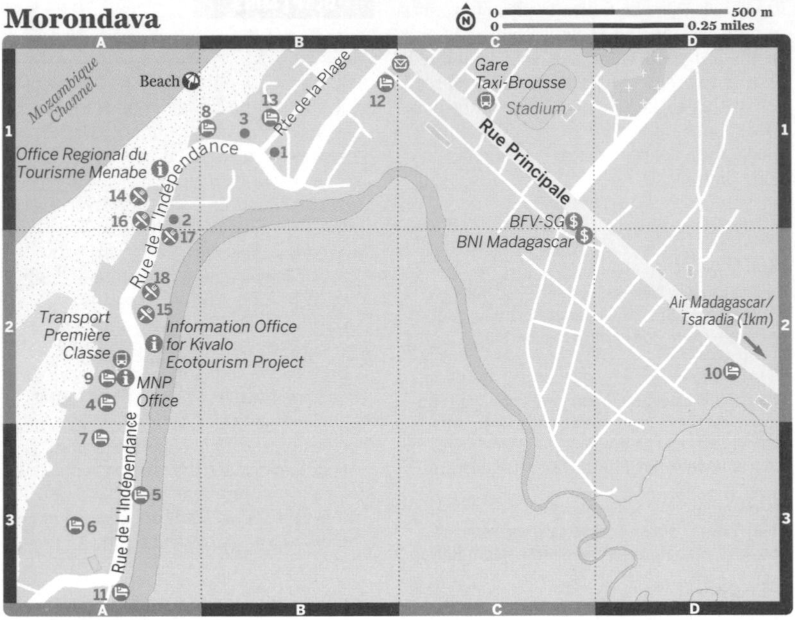

Tours

Local agents can help you organise trips to Belo-sur-Mer, Parc National Bemaraha and Réserve Forestière de Kirindy, as well as deep-sea fishing trips and sailing excursions.

Remote River Expeditions ADVENTURE
(032 47 326 70; www.remoterivers.com; Rue de l'Independance) Remote River Expeditions runs sustainable-travel-focused trips down the little-explored Mangoky, Mahavavy and Manambolo Rivers, as well as trips to all the usual attractions around Morondava and further afield. Find them at Chez Maggie (p135).

Loic Tours ADVENTURE
(032 20 009 89; www.facebook.com/loic.tours.services.agence.voyage; Rue de l'Indépendance; hours vary) A full portfolio of activities from 4WD rental to national-park trips.

François Vahiako ADVENTURE
(034 04 703 54, 032 04 703 54; visk_fr@yahoo.fr; Rue de l'Indépendance) Vahiako is the head of the Morondava Guides Association and is a good person to go to for affordable vehicles (4WD with driver) for trips to the Parc National Bemaraha, Belo-sur-Mer, or pirogue trips anywhere along the coast. Your best bet for finding him is at Les Bougainvilliers (p135).

Jean le Rasta ADVENTURE
(032 04 931 60, 020 95 527 81; L'Oasis, Rte de la Plage) Charismatic Jean le Rasta, or Rasta Jean, speaks English, is reliable and owns a 4WD. He runs a range of tours in the region and across southern Madagascar. Look for him at L'Oasis.

Rent 501 Madagascar MOUNTAIN BIKING
(032 11 110 86; Rue de l'Independance; hours vary) Multiday tours by quad bike across the west, including as far as to the Parc National Bemaraha. Ask also about shorter-term rentals.

Sleeping

Zoom Hôtel HOTEL €
(032 46 298 35; Rte de la Plage; r Ar30,000, without bathroom Ar22,000) If you can tear the receptionist away from his mobile phone, he might just rouse himself (then again, he might not) to show you the basic, clean rooms with fan but no mosquito nets (a concern in Morondava). No frills at all, but at this price did you really expect otherwise?

Vezo Hotel HOTEL €€
(032 11 220 00; www.vezohotel.com; Rue de l'Indépendance; r Ar100,000) This place could be so much more. The lovely large, whitewashed rooms have high ceilings and a

Morondava

colonial air, but are a little bare, with no nets. The downstairs bar-restaurant has a whiff of urban cool, but service veers between absent and borderline civil. Still, the price is about right and you won't mind coming back here at day's end.

Trecicogne GUESTHOUSE €€
(☑034 51 636 66, 020 95 924 25; www.hotel trecicogne.mg; Rue de l'Indépendance; d/tr with fan from Ar95,000/107,000, without bathroom Ar46,000/58,200, with air-con Ar119,000/131,000; ❄🌐) This Italian-run guesthouse, right at the end of Nosy Kely peninsula, is a lovely place and was renovated in 2017. Some rooms have polished wooden floors, white-washed walls, and all are absolutely spotless. The cheaper ones share bathrooms and only have fans. The restaurant is on a veranda overlooking the mangrove canal at the back; room 18 does likewise.

The hotel can organise trips to most regional attractions, including pirogue trips to Belo-sur-Mer.

Les Bougainvilliers HOTEL €€
(☑034 49 521 63; bol_nd@yahoo.fr; Rue de l'Indépendance; d/f bungalows Ar70,000/80,000, r without bathroom Ar35,000) The bungalows are right on the beach, but they're ageing and not particularly gracefully. However, at this price they remain among the best lower-midrange value in town. The cell-like cheap rooms are only for those who are really saving their ariary. There's an atmospheric restaurant.

★ Chez Maggie BUNGALOW €€€
(☑020 95 523 47, 032 47 326 70; www.chezmaggie. com; Rue de l'Indépendance; d with fan Ar131,000, with air-con Ar156,000-223,000; 🌐🏊) Whether you sleep in the atmospheric captain's cab-in with its marine-themed decor, the well-

appointed bungalows or the superb mezzanine 'chalets', Chez Maggie is a delight and fabulous value. You could spend many hours reading in the garden, lounging by the pool or admiring the ocean. Chez Maggie is an agent for Remote River Expeditions, which runs excellent excursions.

★ Hôtel Palissandre Côte Ouest LODGE €€€
(☑020 95 520 26, 033 15 349 74; www.hotel-restaurant-palissandrecoteouest.com; Rue de l'Indépendance; s/d/tr incl breakfast €155/170/205; P❄@🌐🏊) Morondava's premier address has supremely comfortable wood-floored bungalows away from the town's clamour. There are ample terraces from which to watch the setting sun, a stylish boutique, restaurant and swimming pool, and excursions can be arranged. We feel the food lets things down a little and the water's edge is a long way across the sand.

Laguna Beach RESORT €€€
(☑032 03 210 55; www.morondava-lagunabeach. com; off Rue de l'Independance; d/tr €69/82; P❄🌐) With brightly painted villas and bungalows by the sea, Laguna Beach follows a fairly standard formula but does so rather well. The rooms are large and well appointed, although some are a little cavernous and most look onto the garden rather than the sea. Great location.

Cap Kimony BUNGALOW €€€
(☑032 03 210 50, 034 07 205 50; www.morondava-capkimony.com; Kimony Rd; d/tr bungalows Ar262,000/310,000; P❄🌐🏊) This place has tidy bungalows and an appealing restaurant shaped like a ship. Despite what it promises, you're more than 1km from the beach and the trees need time to grow. But it's a

good choice, and a little removed from town, which means it's either quiet or inconvenient, depending on your perspective.

On weekends, well-to-do local families often visit the pool and restaurant.

Hotel Baobab
HOTEL €€€

(☑034 14 761 96; www.baobabcafe-hotel.net; Rue de l'Indépendance; r Ar135,000-320,000; P ✻ 🛜 ❄) Not all rooms are created equal here – take one of the more expensive 2nd-floor rooms with balcony overlooking the pool and the mangroves and you'll love this place. Service is friendly, and there's a good restaurant.

Kimony Resort
BUNGALOW €€€

(☑034 07 890 05; www.morondava-kimonyresort.com; Kimony Rd; d/tr/q Ar262,000/310,000/356,000, villas Ar500,000; P ✻ 🛜 ❄) The bungalows here are a little disappointing after the lovely pool-restaurant-reception area, but they're tidy enough with wood floors and are set in a mature garden. It's a long way into town but lovely and quiet.

Select Hotel
HOTEL €€€

(☑034 07 035 98; www.facebook.com/select hotelmorondava; Rue Principale; s/d/f with air-con Ar126,000/140,000/260,000, without air-con Ar108,000/120,000/220,000; P ✻ 🛜) It's a long way from anywhere, and the roadside setting is not Morondava's most appealing, but the rooms are large and supremely comfortable – ideal if you've had enough of bungalows.

Renala Au Sable D'Or
BUNGALOW €€€

(☑032 04 976 88; Rue de l'Indépendance; d Ar260,000; ✻ @ 🛜) Renala's pretty wood-lined rooms and clapboard bungalows are excellent Morondava value. The whole place lacks a little atmosphere, but the rooms are terrific and the beach is just over the back wall.

🍴 Eating

Small Supermarket
SUPERMARKET €

(Rue Principale; ⊗7am-7pm) There's a small, unnamed supermarket next to the Select Hotel along the main road into town. It's the best in town, and sells drinks and other basic supplies.

La Gargote Valisoa
MALAGASY €

(Rue de l'Indépendance; mains from Ar4000; ⊗7am-9pm) This place is simplicity itself, with prim tablecloths, a view of the sea out the door and tasty local specialities for

knock-down prices. Dishes change with market availability, but usually include fish, zebu and a few soup and noodle dishes.

★ Bleu Soleil
INTERNATIONAL €€

(Chez Patricia; ☑033 06 010 07; off Rue de l'Indépendance; mains Ar7000-18,000; ⊗8am-10.30pm Wed-Mon) Winning the prize for the best beach views of any restaurant in Morondava, this breezy place serves everything from tagliatelle to zebu brochettes, grilled fish and a mean smoked-fish salad. Step down the stairs to recline with a drink.

★ Chez Maggie
EUROPEAN €€

(☑032 47 326 70; www.chezmaggie.com; Rue de l'Indépendance; mains Ar10,000-18,000; ⊗7.30am-10pm) At Chez Maggies's thatch-roof restaurant, you can't fault the service, or the food. House specialities revolve around the grill: be it steak, jumbo shrimp or the catch of the day, everything comes out cooked to perfection. There's a sprinkling of Malagasy specialities as well. The bar has a wide selection of Scotch, whiskey and delicious homemade coconut rum.

Restaurant Le Corail
MALAGASY €€

(Chez Alain; ☑032 83 409 96; Rue de l'Indépendance; mains Ar15,000-30,000; ⊗8am-10pm) One of the best places in town for Malagasy cuisine, this place draws more locals than tourists - always a good sign. The menu runs into pages, with international dishes and fresh seafood alongside excellent *romazava* (stew) in all its varieties.

Baobab Cafe
INTERNATIONAL €€

(☑034 14 761 96; www.baobabcafe-hotel.net; Rue de l'Indépendance; mains Ar22,000-27,000; ⊗11.30am-2pm & 7-9pm) Assured cooking served on a pleasant deck overlooking the mangroves – Baobab is a good choice for its zebu steak, grilled prawns, spaghetti and all manner of seafood.

L'Etoile
INTERNATIONAL €€

(☑032 27 288 14; Rue de l'Indépendance; mains Ar15,000-19,000; ⊗8am-10.30pm Wed-Mon) This bright, French-owned place has a good mix of dishes, from sandwiches to grilled fish, spaghetti with prawns, or zebu hamburger.

La Capannina
ITALIAN €€

(☑020 95 527 49; Rue de l'Indépendance; mains Ar12,000-30,000, pizzas from Ar13,000; ⊗9am-11pm Wed-Mon) Run by an Italian-Malagasy couple, this place serves consistently yummy Italian food – think lots of pastas and

KIVALO ECOTOURISM PROJECT

If you're going to be in Morondava, plan to spend a day visiting the excellent new eco-tourism project at **Kivalo** (034 91 820 27; tsingynaina@yahoo.com; per person US$100; year-round).

At one level, the appeal is natural – here you'll encounter two very different ecosystems, the baobab and the mangrove. But the main reason to come here is to immerse yourself in the life of a local mangrove fishing village. A visit here includes the following.

➡ A traditional welcome ceremony with local songs and dance.

➡ Exploring the mangroves with a local guide, watching for grey mouse lemurs and more than 50 bird species along the way.

➡ A visit to the local boat-making area.

➡ Tree-planting in the mangroves.

➡ Crab fishing.

➡ Boating in a traditional pirogue (traditional dugout canoe).

➡ Eating a specially prepared local meal.

➡ Learning about local Sakalava Vezo culture.

To make the arrangements, contact the information office in Morondava. The cost for a one-day visit, including transfers to and from Morondava, is US$100 per person and it may just be the best money you spend in Madagascar.

To get here, take a motorised pirogue from Morondava, or drive past the Allée des Baobabs (p138) and take the Kivalo signpost heading west. It should take just under an hour to drive here from Morondava.

different sauces, and pizzas straight out of the wood-fired oven. Other good choices include crab spaghetti or the seafood brochette. It's all served in a thatched dining room overlooking the river.

Les Bougainvilliers MALAGASY €€
(Rue de l'Indépendance; mains Ar12,000-17,000, set menu Ar30,000; 7.30am-10pm) The Bougainvilliers has made a name for itself by serving Malagasy dishes and therefore attracting travellers as well as locals. You'll find traditional dishes such as *ravitoto* (pork stew with manioc greens), *romazava de la mer* (seafood stew) and coconut crab. The three-course *menu du jour* is excellent value. The sea breeze costs no extra.

ℹ Information

MONEY
BFV-SG (Rue Principale; 8-11.30am & 2.30-5pm Mon-Fri) Changes money; ATM.
BNI Madagascar (Rue Principale; 8-11.30am & 2.30-5pm Mon-Fri) ATM for Visa and MasterCard.

POST
Post office (Rue Principale; 8-11.30am & 2-4.30pm Mon-Fri)

TOURIST INFORMATION
Information Office for Kivalo Ecotourism Project (034 91 820 27; tsingynaina@yahoo.com; Rue de l'Independance; 8am-12.30pm & 2.30-7.30pm) This small shopfront information office provides information for booking tours to Kivalo.

MNP office (020 95 921 28, 033 19 117 06; www.parcs-madagascar.com; Rue de l'Independance; 7.30am-noon & 2.30-6pm Mon-Fri) National-park office with information on Parc National Kirindy-Mite (p141). It's at the reception of Renala au Sable D'Or. If no one is in residence, head to the tourist office for help in finding them.

Office Regional du Tourisme Menabe (032 99 466 19, 034 31 713 39; www.region-menabe.mg; Rue de l'Indépendance; 8am-noon & 2.30-5.30pm Mon-Fri, 8am-1pm Sat) Friendly tourist office that's good for high-level information.

ℹ Getting There & Away

AIR
Air Madagascar/Tsaradia (020 95 920 22, 032 07 222 14; www.tsaradia.com; Rue Principale, Amahora; 8-11.30am & 2.30-5pm Mon-Fri, 8-10am Sat) flies most days between the **Aéroport de Morondava** (032 40 766 82;

ALLÉE DES BAOBABS & BAOBAB AMOUREUX

One of Madagascar's most recognisable images, this small stretch of the RN8 between Morondava and Belo-sur-Tsiribihina is flanked on both sides by majestic *Adansonia grandidieri* baobabs. Some of the trees here may be 1000 years old, with huge, gnarled branches fanning out at the top of their trunks – it's easy to see why they've been nicknamed 'roots of the sky'.

The actual stretch of road is shorter than many visitors expect, but even this brief concentration in honour-guard formation is without parallel anywhere else in the country.

The best times to visit Allée des Baobabs are at sunset and sunrise, when the colours of the trees and surrounding earth deepen and the long shadows are most pronounced. That said, every vehicle driving down from Parc National Bemaraha aims to get here around sunset and it can therefore be very busy, particularly during the park's high season (July to September).

With popularity has arisen a small-scale local industry, with an excellent facility set up by the local community at the southern entrance to the Allée. It includes a gorgeous gift shop selling local handicrafts, lemur field guides and baobab jam or oils, as well as a coffee shop/bar, superclean toilets and a small breakfast restaurant. The whole complex opens at 5am and closes after the last sunset visitors leave. The handicraft shops across the road are part of the same setup. It's a worthy project that deserves your support. Parking costs Ar2000 per vehicle.

If you don't plan to see the Allée on your way to/from attractions north of Morondava (Parc National Bemaraha , Tsiribihina or Réserve Forestière de Kirindy), a taxi from Morondava town costs at least Ar60,000 return. All tour operators in Morondava can also help you out.

Providing inspiration for many a Malagasy wood sculptor, Baobab Amoureux are two *A grandidieri* baobabs that have twisted themselves into a perfect embrace, earning them the sobriquet of 'Baobabs in Love'. The entwined lovers are around 3km off the Morondava–Kirindy road, just north of the Allée des Baobabs – look for the Kivalo signpost. It's worth visiting before a sunset visit to Allée des Baobabs, or as a detour on your way between Morondava and Réserve Forestière de Kirindy or Belo-sur-Tsiribihina (p130).

off Rue Principale) and Antananarivo (from €154, one hour).

BOAT

Morondava is connected with the villages to the south, including Belo-sur-Mer, by pirogue and *boutre* (single-masted dhow used for cargo) – ask your guide to help with the arrangements and remember that safety is a concern on these boats, there are no facilities and you'll need to carry your own supplies.

BUS

For far more luxury than a *taxi-brousse* can muster, **Transport Première Class** (☑ 034 12 288 88, 032 03 788 88; www.malagasycar.com/transport-premiere-classe; Ave de l'Independance) runs comfortable, air-con vehicles between Tana and Majunga (Ar118,000, 12 hours, daily). They sit just two people a row and include a packed lunch. Departure is at 6am from outside Renala Au Sable D'Or (p136) and

drop-off is at Motel Anosy in Tana. Bookings essential.

Try also Cotisse (p54), with nicer 16- to 19-seater buses to Antananarivo (Ar45,000, 6.30am, 12 to 14 hours).

TAXI-BROUSSE

Most *taxis-brousses* leave from the **Gare Taxi-Brousse** (Rue Principale) in the town centre.

The road between Morondava and Tuléar (Toliara) is a very rough track that is only passable in dry season (April or May to October); the *taxis-brousses* that do the route are 4WD *bâchés* (small, converted pickup trucks) or *camions-brousses* – even worse in comfort than normal *taxis-brousses*. *Taxis-brousses* leave in the morning when they fill up.

ⓘ Getting Around

Taxis within town cost Ar5000., while taxis between town and the airport cost Ar25,000.

Réserve Forestière de Kirindy

The **Réserve Forestière de Kirindy** (☑ 032 40 165 89, 020 95 938 11; www.kirindyforest.com; adult/child Ar50,000/20,000, day/night guide per 2hr per person Ar10,000/20,000) is popular with scientists and travellers for its amazing wildlife. Night walks are a particular highlight, and it's one of very few places in Madagascar where seeing a fossa, Madagascar's most celebrated and largest carnivore, is highly likely. Located 60km northeast of Morondava, it covers about 125 sq km and was established in the late 1970s as an experiment in sustainable logging and forest management. It's now a protected area. One look at the cleared land either side of the reserve and area is. A guide is compulsory.

🏃 Activities

Walking through the forest looking for fossa, lemurs and birds with a knowledgeable guide is the main attraction here.

Wildlife Walks

Everyone comes here for the wildlife, with both day and night, guided two-hour circuits possible. Mornings (7am to 9am) are best for day walks, while night walks set out just after sunset.

Kirindy is one of few places in Madagascar where you are very likely to see the fossa (*Cryptoprocta felix*), the country's largest predator, a doglike creature with oversized ears and a strangely elongated body. The best time to see them is in mating season (September to November), although your chances are good year-round since they tend to hang around the Ecolodge in the hope of stealing goodies from the kitchen and rubbish dump.

Kirindy also has eight lemur species and you're likely to see three or four of the following nocturnal species on a night walk: grey mouse lemur, red-tailed sportive lemur, fork-marked lemur, fat-tailed dwarf lemur, Coquerel's giant dwarf lemur and the Madame Berthe's mouse lemur, which is considered the world's smallest primate and weighs around 30g.

The highlights of day walks are less likely to be lemurs – the reserve's Verreaux's *sifaka* and red-fronted brown lemur are commonly seen in other parks – but instead the

45 recorded bird species. Birding highlights include the rare crested ibis, the nocturnal white-breasted mesite and the Madagascar pygmy kingfisher. There are also 32 reptile species. Watch out also for tenrecs and the giant jumping rat.

🛏 Sleeping

Relais du Kirindy BUNGALOW €€€
(☑ 034 07 205 53, 032 03 210 53; www.relaisdukirindy.com; d/tr bungalows Ar200,000/290,000; P🗑😎) Certainly among the most pleasant places to stay in the Kirindy area, the Relais du Kirindy has tidy, elevated wooden bungalows with mosquito nets. There's a good restaurant and swimming pool, and it can organise excursions to nearby Réserve Forestière de Kirindy.

Le Camp Amoureux BUNGALOW €€€
(☑ 032 02 120 08; tourisme@sahala.net; d safari tents from Ar150,000) 🌿 Run by the local community, Le Camp Amoureux is, despite being an hour's drive south of Kirindy, many people's preferred base for visiting the reserve. It was closed for refurbishment at the time of research, but should have opened by the time you read this. Comfortable, African-style safari tents are planned. Night walks in the surrounding forest are possible.

If you're staying here, you'll need to drive to Ecolodge de Kirindy to arrange guided walks and see the fossa.

Ecolodge de Kirindy LODGE €€€
(☑ 033 16 303 78, 032 40 165 89; dm/bungalows incl breakfast Ar35,000/130,000) Friendly Ecolodge de Kirindy has oh-so-basic, overpriced wooden bungalows with mosquito nets, uncomfortable mattresses and questionable

---

ℹ RÉSERVE FORESTIÈRE DE KIRINDY

Best time to visit Year-round.

Key highlight The profusion of wildlife, including some of Madagascar's rarest mammals; night walks.

Wildlife Fossa, eight lemur species, tortoises and many birds.

Habitat Deciduous dry forest.

Gateway town Morondava.

Transport options Private vehicle or *taxi-brousse* (bush taxi), plus a 5km walk.

OFF THE BEATEN TRACK

MORONDAVA OR BELO-SUR-MER TO TULÉAR

The road from Morondava or Belo-sur-Mer to Tuléar cuts inland via Manja and rejoins the coast at Morombé. This road is only passable in dry season (usually May to October) and it takes three bone-shaking days – more if you linger along the towns of the Northern Reef. The *taxis-brousses* (bush taxis) that do the route are 4WD *bâchés* (small, converted pickup trucks) or *camions-brousses* – even more uncomfortable than normal *taxis-brousses*, and they're irregular at best. Whichever way you travel, the reward is an adventure that'll be worth telling the grandkids, with beautiful landscapes, remote villages, makeshift ferries and heavenly beaches.

One unfortunate recent development is the impromptu checkpoints at seemingly every village, with a makeshift barrier across the road. They will ask for payment of anything from Ar5000 to Ar10,000 but most will settle for Ar1000 or a little more. On our last journey here, we counted at least 20 such checkpoints between Morondava and Morombé. Although the amounts aren't much, they can add up, and the checkpoints slow you down.

Day 1: Morondava to Manja (six to eight hours) The tracks here are not as rough as those further south, but there are five wide, shallow rivers to cross and numerous streams to ford. Your prize at the end is Manja (around four hours if you're coming from Belo-sur-Mer), a lively provincial town with a pretty church. The only place to stay is **Kanto Hotel** (☎034 08 103 93, 032 55 627 92; mikanto91@gmail.com; Main St; d/tw/f Ar51,000/61,000/81,000), a friendly spot with a surprisingly good restaurant, but basic rooms with shower water that barely trickles from the wall. More rooms were under construction when we last visited. Try to avoid weekends when the downstairs bar bumps and grinds until the wee small hours. At around 2am, we gave up trying to sleep and went down to join them...

Day 2: Manja to Morombé or Andavadoaka (10 hours) This is a long, punishing day of off-road driving with a rickety vehicle ferry crossing at Bejoavy (per vehicle starting from Ar40,000 if you need to be pulled across by a team of locals...). You'll have to set off at first light and carry a picnic lunch.

Day 3: Morombé or Andavadoaka to Tuléar (eight to 10 hours) This splendid stretch of coastline hugs Madagascar's Great Reef, with the toughest section of road a 30km, baobab-lined stretch of sand south of Andavadoaka. There are numerous gorgeous hotels and lots of good snorkelling and diving, so you may want to split this into two days.

plumbing. Camping is no longer possible due to the rather brazen fossa, but you still may find one sleeping under your bungalow...lullabies are courtesy of the forest residents. There's a small, slow on-site restaurant serving ample meals (mains Ar20,000) and cold beer.

Bring a good torch.

Getting There & Away

Kirindy is about 60km northeast of Morondava, signposted off the Belo-sur-Tsiribihina road. If you're travelling by *taxi-brousse* (Ar15,000, two hours), this is as far as it will take you. The forest camp and office are 5km into the reserve – you'll have to walk to it if you don't have your own vehicle.

Belo-sur-Mer

Few places will make you feel so far away from anywhere as Belo-sur-Mer. The village, sitting on the edge of a small lagoon, appears to have been swallowed up by the dunes and in the heat of the midday sun, time literally seems to stand still.

This is a regional shipbuilding centre and huge cargo vessels are still constructed on the beach just as they were four centuries ago. It's also one of the country's main salt-producing areas, with vast salt marshes a few kilometres inland.

Sights & Activities

As the name of the village suggests, life in Belo is all about the sea, so spend a morning or an afternoon wandering along the beach. Watch fishers prepare their gear or bring their catch, admire the artisanship of pirogue and *boutre* (single-masted dhow used for cargo in) builders, or look for beautiful shells on the beach.

★ **Nosy Andrahovo**   SNORKELLING

Belo-sur-Mer's star attraction is this string of coral-fringed islands, some semi-submerged. The islands are uninhabited and offer fabulous snorkelling. All hotels in Belo can organise trips to Nosy Andrahovo with local pirogues. Allow around Ar40,000 per person for a half-day, or Ar70,000 for a full day with picnic lunch.

🛏 Sleeping

★ **Ecolodge du Menabe**   LODGE €€

(✉ 033 09 436 32; www.menabelo.com; s/d/tw/tr Ar80,000/90,000/95,000/100,000, fixed-menu breakfast/lunch/dinner Ar15,000/33,000/35,000) 🌿 Remote, scenic and peaceful, the Ecolodge is Belo's best accommodation option. The 12 bungalows are simple but comfortable and right on the beach. Meals are served under a large canopy and the food is good, with plenty of fresh fish. Everything is made from local building materials, it uses locally sourced ingredients and everything is recycled. Diving, snorkelling and sportfishing are all possible.

Tsara Belo   BUNGALOW €€

(✉ 033 02 911 64; s/d/tr from Ar75,000/90,000/110,000; ☺ Mar-Dec) Simple thatch bungalows, just back from the water's edge, are a good choice and will be even better once the lemon-and-baobab garden has time to mature. The bungalows sleep three to five people and are great for families.

Corail   BUNGALOW €€

(✉ 033 20 326 87; r Ar75,000) A handful of haphazard but coquettish bungalows, the Corail is a family-run outfit right by the beach just south of town. There are some nice touches throughout, such as the hammocks on the porch, open-roof (cold-water) showers and raffia-decorated mirrors, and the home-cooked food is delicious.

★ **Hôtel Entremer**   HOTEL €€€

(✉ 032 11 472 45; www.beloentremer.com; d/f bungalows €32/40; ☎) Watched over by amiable Frenchman Laurence, the Entremer is an excellent choice, with great food, nice bungalows right by the sea along a quiet stretch of coastline and deep roots in the local community. It's all powered by solar energy, and

it can arrange kayaking, snorkelling and other excursions. Rooms are lovely, with wood floors and plenty of space.

❶ Information

There are no banking facilities in Belo – the nearest bank is in Morondava – nor is there electricity, apart from that generated by the hotels.

❶ Getting There & Away

BOAT

From November to May, the only way to access Belo-sur-Mer is by sea. Local pirogues ply the route, but journey times are entirely dependent on winds. Prices vary widely depending on the season. It's much faster (2½ hours), but also more expensive, to arrange a motorboat transfer (from Ar350,000) with one of the tour operators in Morondava or Ecolodge du Menabe in Belo.

CAR

Access to Belo-sur-Mer by road is only possible by 4WD from April or May to October or November. There are irregular *taxis-brousses* (Ar42,000, four hours) between Belo-sur-Mer and Morondava in 4WD *bâchés* (small, converted pickups).

Parc National Kirindy-Mite

Not to be confused with the Réserve Forestière de Kirindy, the deliciously remote 722-sq-km **Parc National Kirindy-Mite** (www.parcs-madagascar.com; adult/child per day Ar45,000/25,000, guide per circuit from

---

❶ PARC NATIONAL KIRINDY-MITE

Best time to visit May to November.

Key highlight Brackish lakes and sand dunes.

Wildlife Birdlife, including flamingos; nine lemur species.

Habitats Dry deciduous forest.

Gateway town Belo-sur-Mer.

Transport options By boat year-round; by 4WD from May to October.

Things you should know It is easier to arrange a visit to the park from Morondava, where the Madagascar National Parks (MNP) office has admin staff, and any Morondava tour operators can take you there. In Belo, ask at Dorohotel.

SAKALAVA EROTICA

The western part of Madagascar has traditionally been the area with the strongest African influence. The language of the dark-skinned western peoples contains many words taken from mainland African languages. The area's dominant tribe is the Sakalava, who venerate the relics not of their own ancestors, but of their ancient royal families. This belief, plus the use of spirit mediums to communicate with dead royalty, also has an African base (Bantu).

The Sakalava are perhaps best known for covering the tombs of their dead with elaborate, erotic carvings, often depicting oral sex or other acts considered *fady* (taboo). Although Sakalava tombs were once visible throughout the entire western region, many were pillaged for their valuable carvings. Following this desecration, the Sakalava now understandably keep the location of those burial grounds still containing intact tombs top secret. It's important to respect their privacy. If you are lucky enough to see these erotic artworks, please take only photos.

Ar80,000), which surrounds Belo-sur-Mer, is one of Madagascar's newest parks and it's well worth the effort to get here. It's isolated and beautiful, with little infrastructure, and for that reason, seldom visited. What this means for visitors is that those making the effort to get here will be rewarded with a more personal experience in an environment rarely disturbed by visitors. Out here it's all about sand dunes, mangroves and untouched coastline, with some fine wildlife viewing thrown in.

🏃 Activities

Besides wildlife watching and hiking, you can also take a pirogue trip (Ar45,000) along the estuary and the mangrove; the park staff in Morondava can help you arrange it, as should any Morondava tour operator or guide.

Wildlife Watching

The main draw at Kirindy Mite is the birdlife – 58 recorded species in total, 18 of which are endemic to the region – although there are lemurs and reptiles, too. Of the park's nine lemur species, only three are easily seen by day: Verreaux's *sifaka*, the red-fronted brown lemur and the ring-tailed lemur. The nocturnal species are Madame Berthe's mouse lemur, fork-marked lemur, grey mouse lemur, Coquerel's dwarf lemur, fat-tailed dwarf lemur and red-tailed sportive lemur. Also present, if rarely seen, is the fossa.

Hiking

There are three hiking circuits through the park.

Circuit Agnolignoly (2km, one hour) Easy walk through mangroves and coastal estuaries with an emphasis on waterbirds.

Circuit Ambondro-Sirave (3km, two hours) With sand dunes, spiny forest, baobabs, the beach and plenty of waterbirds, this is our pick if you only have time for one walk.

Circuit Maetsakaloe (4km, two hours) Baobabs, birds, dry forest and lemurs are the highlights on this relatively new walk.

ℹ️ Information

In addition to the MNP office (p137) in Morondava, there's a small park office in Belo-sur-Mer, near the church: the building is unmarked, so ask people to point it out. Staff are often out and about; if that's the case, the hotels are generally well informed as to their whereabouts.

ℹ️ Getting There & Away

You'll need your own transport to access Kirindy Mite. The park can be reached by road between May and October or November (it's just off the rough Morondava–Belo-sur-Mer or Morondava–Manja roads). Access is by boat, which must be arranged with the park, for the rest of the year.

Northern Madagascar

Best Places to Eat

➡ La Table d'Alexandre (p156)

➡ Tsara Be Restaurant (p165)

➡ Côté Jardin (p152)

➡ Karibo (p155)

Best Places to Stay

➡ Sakatia Lodge (p158)

➡ Hôtel Carrefour (p176)

➡ Hôtel Gérard et Francine (p154)

➡ Tamana Hostel (p151)

➡ Nature Lodge (p170)

Why Go?

It's as if Madagascar had conspired to provide a microcosm of its myriad travel experiences all in one place: here you'll find the isolated Sava region with its wild coastline and vanilla-scented air, the relatively sophisticated city of Diego Suarez (Antsiranana) and the country's premier beach destination, Nosy Be. Travellers will revel in the region's diverse national parks while activity junkies will be spoilt for choice with everything from diving to kitesurfing.

You'll find more sea-based activities than you'll have time to try in Nosy Be, excellent seafood and idyllic scenery. It couldn't be more different from the mainland – here arid plains are fringed with lush ylang-ylang, vanilla and coconut plantations, while parks large and small feature strange geological formations, rainforests and rare species.

The region also hosts some of Madagascar's flagship cultural events, the Donia (p150), Zegny'Zo (p163) and the Nosy Be Jazz Festival (p149) – unique chances to discover Malagasy artists.

When to Go
Hell-Ville (Andoany)

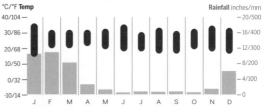

Apr–Jun Festivals bring together artists from across Madagascar and the Indian Ocean.	**Oct–Dec** Humpback whales make their annual visit to Madagascar and can be seen around Nosy Be.
May–Nov Best access to the Tsingy Rouges and the western part of Réserve Spéciale Ankarana.	

Northern Madagascar Highlights

1 Parc National Marin de Nosy Tanikely (p156) Snorkelling off this tiny, palm-fringed island to spy turtles, clownfish and rays.

2 Parc National Marojejy (p178) Spotting the silky *sifaka* (a type of lemur) – or even one of the world's smallest frogs.

3 Parc National Lokobe (p154) Watching black lemurs, boa constrictors, owls and more in Nosy Be's remarkable reserve.

4 Diego Suarez (p160) Taking a self-guided walk through the history-filled streets of this vibrant city.

5 Domaine d'Ambohimanitra (p177) Enjoying the heady aromas of vanilla and spices on this Sava plantation.

6 Les Trois Baies (p168) Learning to kitesurf over these remote beaches and bays.

7 Nosy Be (p146) Sailing between small, picture-postcard islands.

8 Tsingy Rouges (p161) Marvelling at the geological wonder of these limestone pinnacles as the setting sun casts its reddish light.

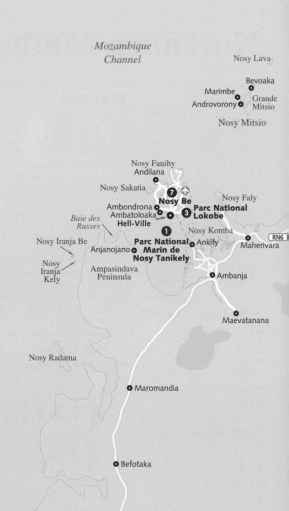

NOSY BE

POP 75,000

Madagascar's number-one beach destination, the island of Nosy Be has all the ingredients you'd expect: soft white sand, turquoise waters and wonderful seafood. A paradise for water-based activities with its sunny climate most of the year, its top draw is diving and there is plenty of swimming, snorkelling, sailing and fishing. Operators offer excursions to the surrounding islands with their beautiful beaches and great diving opportunities.

Once you've had enough of seascapes, head for the rolling landscapes of the little-explored hinterland: as well as the brilliant Parc National Lokobe, there are ylang-ylang and vanilla plantations, crater lakes and waterfalls, and kilometres of dirt tracks accessible only by foot or quad bike.

Nosy Be is the most expensive destination in Madagascar but compared to elsewhere in the world, prices are competitive, and many visitors find the lack of major development and relaxed, *mora mora* (slowly, slowly) lifestyle worth the extra money.

History

Nosy Be's first inhabitants are believed to have been 15th-century Swahili and Indian traders. Later, the island served as a magnet for refugees, merchants and settlers of all descriptions.

In 1839 the Sakalava queen Tsiomeko fled to Nosy Be and turned to the French for help in resisting her Merina enemies. In 1841 the Sakalava ceded both Nosy Be and neighbouring Nosy Komba to France.

In recent years, with increasing tourism development and local environmental pressures, deforestation has become a problem on the island, as has destruction and damage of offshore coral reefs.

Activities

Nosy Be has a plethora of activities. Most are sea-based (diving, snorkelling, fishing, day trips to islands etc), but operators also offer activities exploring the island's beautiful hinterland including Parc National Lokobe (p154).

Diving

Nosy Be and the surrounding islands are home to a rich diversity of marine life and offer world-class diving. Boxfish, surgeonfish, triggerfish, damselfish, clownfish, yellowfin, barracuda, eagle rays, manta rays and humpback whales (July to September) can all be spotted. Around Nosy Sakatia you will see turtles in the marine protected zone as well as clownfish, barracuda and perhaps dolphins and whale sharks.

On average, visibility on dives is about 15m year-round – much more on good days. The best months are April to December. July and August can be windy, especially to the north around Nosy Mitsio. The best months for seeing whale sharks are October and November, while manta rays are more prevalent from April to June and October to November.

Most operators run daily morning trips long enough for two dives, with boats leaving around 8am and getting back in time for lunch. Prices are about €50 for a *baptême* (first dive), €38/70 for one/two dives, and €50 for a night dive. Many operators also run all-inclusive, catamaran sailing trips (two to five days) to surrounding archipelagos such as Nosy Iranja, Nosy Mitsio and Nosy Radama, with two dives a day (€400 to €850, depending on the number of people on the boat, the length of the trip and the number of dives).

Courses are conducted in French or English, with many staff also speaking Italian. A Professional Association of Diving Instructors (PADI) course costs around €400; it's best to book certification courses in advance.

Nosy Be has a recompression chamber at the hospital, Centro Sanitario Santa Maria della Grazia (p153).

Océane's Dream   DIVING
(Map p148; ☎ 032 07 127 82; www.oceanesdream. com; 10 dives incl equipment €320; ⊗ 7.30am-7.30pm Mar-Dec) One of the most well-established and recommended operators on the island, Océane's Dream offers single and introductory dives (using Aqualung equipment) along with diving cruises to neighbouring islands and land-based excursions. It also offers PADI dive courses. It's involved in sustainable development and environmental protection.

A six-day diving cruise to Nosy Mitsio aboard the catamaran costs €1600 for two.

Madaplouf   DIVING
(Map p148; ☎ 033 14 248 33; www.divingin madagascar.com; Bemoko; incl equipment 2 dives on 1 day €95, 10 dives in 5 days €425) Madaplouf is a long-established outfit that runs PADI and Confédération Mondiale des Activités Subaquatiques (CMAS) courses in Spanish, German and Italian, as well as in French and English, using Aqualung equipment. It also

MONT PASSOT

Nosy Be's loftiest point, **Mont Passot** (329m; Map p148; ☑ 034 61 053 06, 032 02 930 68; www.madagascar-tourisme.com/fr/nosy-be-un-nouvel-itineraire-pour-acceder-au-mont-passot; Ar10,000; ☺8am-7pm), lies northwest of Hell-Ville. It's a wonderful spot for admiring sunsets and the sweeping panorama. It's also one of the best places to see Nosy Be's crater lakes. Unfortunately, the viewing area is now packed with souvenir stalls, which somewhat detracts from the experience.

If you have your own wheels, the summit is easily accessible by car or motorbike, although the road is badly degraded; it's about a two-hour drive from Hell-Ville. Otherwise, you could charter a taxi from Hell-Ville or Ambatoloaka (allow Ar120,000 for the return trip, including time at the top).

There have been muggings in the area so if you're on your own or on a motorbike, ensure that you drive back before it gets dark.

The tourist authority has launched a hiking circuit on Mont Passot called Amparihibe (for two Ar10,000). The 6km circuit walk (four to five hours, medium difficulty) takes in the sacred lake of the same name, and the lookout point on Mont Passot. You'll see orchids, ylang-ylang, cocoa and vanilla as well as lemurs. Paths are marked and have information boards, but a guide is obligatory (for two Ar10,000).

---

offers excursions to various other islands such as Nosy Tanikely by sailboat (per person including lunch €80) or whale watching by speedboat (€65).

Tropical Diving   DIVING
(Map p148; ☑ 032 49 462 51; www.tropical-diving.com; Hôtel Coco Plage; 2/10 dives incl equipment €72/300; ☺7am-7pm) Tropical Diving is a well-established outfit offering PADI courses and a variety of diving excursions to nearby islands, including a one-day trip to Nosy Iranja with two dives and lunch (per person with equipment €120).

Forever Dive   DIVING
(Map p148; ☑ 032 84 913 81; www.forever dive.com; Madirokely; 1/10 dives incl equipment €48/315; ☺ office 4.30-7pm) Forever Dive is run by the friendly Rolland and Sylvia, who've been living in Nosy Be since 1999. They speak French, English and Italian. They deliver National Association of Underwater Instructors (NAUI) courses as well as four- to six-day diving cruises to Nosy Mitsio and Nosy Radama. They take children from age eight.

Sakalav' Diving   DIVING
(Map p148; ☑ 032 07 437 21; www.sakalav-diving.com; Bemoko; 1/10 dives €42/294) Sakalav' Diving is operated by Alain and Natalie, who speak French, English and German. They offer three- to eight-day diving cruises to surrounding islands, as well as PADI courses, including for children aged eight and over.

They also offer day trips such as snorkelling on Nosy Tanikely (€42 per person).

Staying at Alain and Natalie's ecolodge, La Case Sakalava (p156) in Ambaro, gives you 10% off dive prices.

Snorkelling
Snorkelling is best at Nosy Tanikely, Nosy Mitsio and Nosy Sakatia. All tour operators on Nosy Be run trips to Nosy Tanikely, generally combined with a visit to Nosy Komba.

Whale Watching
Nosy Be is visited by humpback whales, Omura whales and whale sharks at various times of year, plus there are populations of green turtles, dolphins and rays that live permanently in the region. **Mada Megafauna Association** (Map p148; ☑ 032 26 527 64; www.madamegafauna.org; Hotel Senga, Madirokely; ☺8am-5pm Mon-Fri) has established codes of conduct when approaching these animals and organises educational programs, research projects and observations largely funded by visitors taking part in excursions organised by **Les Baleines Rand'Eau** (Map p148; ☑ 032 54 577 41, 032 24 509 87; www.baleinesrandeau.com; Madirokely; excursions €60-130; ☺8am-5pm) 🐾.

Fishing
If you've ever dreamed of a tussle with a giant trevally, these are the waters for you. The best time for fishing is March to June and October to December. Fishing excursions aren't cheap – expect to pay at least €600 per day per boat, including equipment, for up to four people. Sakatia Lodge (p158) and operators such as **Tropical Fishing**

NORTHERN MADAGASCAR NOSY BE

Nosy Be & Surrounding Islands

(📋 Alain 032 69 504 66; www.tropical-fishing.com; Nosy Mitsio; per boat per day from €450; ⊗8am-5pm Mon-Sat) specialise in sport fishing.

Quad Biking

Quad bikes are a great way to explore Nosy Be. Popular routes include a circuit around the crater lakes and Mont Passot, remote beaches in the north, and cocoa plantations to the south. Nosy Be Original (p149) hires out quad bikes. Some hotels also have their own quads and offer excursions to their guests.

Nosy Be & Surrounding Islands

Tours

MadaVoile   BOATING
(Map p148, ☑ 032 04 223 55, 032 22 266 27; www.
madavoile.com; ⊙ 8am noon & 3-5pm Mon-Fri, 8am-
noon Sat) One of the best sailing operators on
Nosy Be, with a superb fleet of sailing boats,
offering highly recommended cruises – from
day trips to Nosy Sakatia or Nosy Komba (per
person €60) to five-day trips to Nosy Mitsio
or Nosy Radama, including diving and fishing. Find it at the top of the hill, opposite Le
Coucher du Soleil (p154) bungalows.

Nosy Be Original   TOURS
(Map p148; ☑ 032 05 524 90; www.nosybe-original.
com; Bemoko; day trip incl lunch to Nosy Komba &
Nosy Tanikely per person €45, 5-day catamaran cruise
incl full board €120 per day; ⊙ office 5-7pm) A tip-
top operator organising a range of excursions
on and around Nosy Be, including lovely
sailing trips on an 18m catamaran, and quad
biking. It also offers whale-watching trips
during the humpback-whale migration (July
to September) and whale-shark trips (October to December). There is another branch at
Vanila Hôtel (p156), Ambaro.

Ulysse Explorer   BOATING
(☑ 032 04 802 80; www.ulyssexplorer.com; per day
2-3 people from €480) Max Felici operates three
catamarans (Ulysse carries six passengers,
Calypso and Coyote up to eight). You can design your own cruise and pick which islands
you'd like to visit for a day excursion or for as
many days as you like, living on board or on
land. Fishing, snorkelling and diving are all
available at an extra cost.

Evasion Sans Frontière   TOURS
(Map p152; ☑ 032 11 005 96; www.mada-evasion.
com; Rue Passot) This tour operator, one of
the biggest in Madagascar, specialises in the
north; it's a well-oiled machine, and its Diego–
Nosy Be circuits take in all the highlights. It
also organises excursions on Nosy Be, including a day trip around the island and excursions to Lokobe (p154).

Festivals & Events

Nosy Be Jazz Festival   MUSIC
(☑ 034 07 162 04; www.nosybejazzfestival.com;
⊙ Apr) Started in 2017, the Nosy Be Jazz Festival is hugely popular, attracting artists both

NORTHERN MADAGASCAR NOSY BE

local and international. Concerts are held all over the island.

Donia

MUSIC

(⊙ late May-early Jun) Every year Nosy Be holds a four- or five-day music festival known as the Donia. Groups from Madagascar, neighbouring islands such as the Comoros, Réunion and Mauritius, and France perform a wonderful mix of rock, reggae, Creole and pop. Fringe events include a carnival, sporting events and seminars. The main venue is Hell-Ville, although there are events across the island.

❶ Getting There & Away

Be aware that offers of 'direct' transfer from Nosy Be to Diego Suarez (Antsiranana) are often a scam. Resist all offers on Nosy Be, take the boat to Ankify (Ar15,000) and then choose your *taxi-brousse* (bush taxi; Ar30,000) as you would anywhere (the one in best condition and/or the fullest).

AIR

Nosy Be Airport (Fascene; Map p148) is on the island's east side, about 12km from Hell-Ville. A taxi fare from the airport to Hell-Ville is around Ar35,000. It is about Ar60,000 to Ambatoloaka or Andilana.

The airport is served by Air Austral (p153), which flies four times a week to Saint Denis (Réunion; €405, 1½ hours). Tsaradia has at least one flight per day to Antananarivo (Ar405,700, 1½ hours) and three flights per week to Diego Suarez (Ar380,800, 35 minutes); book through Air Madagascar (p153). Madagasikara Airways (p166) has a twice-weekly flight to Antananarivo (Ar660,820) via Diego Suarez. **Airlink** (Map p148; ☑ 032 67 251 17; www.flyairlink.com; Sambatra; ⊙ 8am-6pm) has two flights a week between Johannesburg and Nosy Be.

BOAT

➡ Sailing yachts regularly come into Nosy Be and many are prepared to take passengers. Their principal destinations are Mayotte, Mozambique and South Africa. If you're hiring a sailing boat or catamaran, you'll board at **La Marina Crater** (Nosy Be Yacht Club; Map p148; Crater Bay) near Ambataloaka.

➡ Small speedboats shuttle between the mainland port of Ankify and the main ferry port (p153) in Hell-Ville on Nosy Be (Ar15,000, 40 minutes, 5.30am to 4pm). Like *taxis-brousses* they leave when full. Winds pick up in the afternoon, so the crossing is smoother, and therefore more popular, in the morning – you'll never have to wait long for your boat to depart. Life jackets are provided.

➡ If you're travelling with a vehicle, ferries sail between Ankify and the car-ferry port (p153) in Hell-Ville in Nosy Be (from Ar160,000 each way, two hours, from 6am to 4pm).

➡ Pirogues (dugout canoes) to Nosy Komba leave from the petit port (p153) in Hell-Ville in Nosy Be (Ar5000, 20 minutes). If you're staying at a hotel on Nosy Komba, it will send its own boat for transfers for a fee.

➡ Pirogues to Nosy Sakatia (p158) leave from the beach next to Hotel Chanty Beach on the west coast.

➡ On arrival in Hell-Ville by boat from Ankify, a porter will want to take your luggage off the boat; a tip of Ar1000 is appropriate.

❶ Getting Around

BOAT

For the ultimate freedom to explore Nosy Be's shores and the surrounding islands, you can charter a boat from around €480 a day for two to three people from Ulysse Explorer (p149) or MadaVoile (p149).

CAR & MOTORCYCLE

The best way to get around Nosy Be is by motorcycle (helmets are compulsory): roads are not bad, traffic is light, distances are short and the weather is lovely – perfect conditions to ditch the car, which rules on the mainland. If you'd rather have a vehicle, a sedan (saloon) car is perfectly adequate.

Nosy Easy Rent (p157) rents Dacia Logan/Mitsubishi/Pajero vehicles for €35/52/65 per day, with a 100km mileage, and motorbikes from €20 per day. It's 3km from Hell-Ville in the direction of Ambatoloaka.

TAXI

➡ Collective taxis (Ar4000) travel between Hell-Ville and Ambatoloaka (15 minutes) and between Hell-Ville and Djamandjary (25 minutes), from 6am to 7pm. Pick them up near the market in Hell-Ville, and flag them down on the main road of Ambatoloaka as they cruise (and beep) for customers.

➡ A chartered taxi between Hell-Ville and Ambatoloaka costs Ar35,000, between Hell-Ville and Andilana Ar50,000. From Hell-Ville's centre to the jetty costs Ar4000.

➡ Tuk-tuks whizz around the towns of Hell-Ville and Ambatoloaka and are a cheap alternative to taxis. They cost Ar500 during the day, and Ar1000 after 8pm. A longer journey (from Hell-Ville to Ambatoloaka, for example) will cost more.

➡ A taxi from inside the main ferry port (p153) into Hell-Ville costs Ar4000. However, if you walk to the port boundary (100m), you can hire a tuk-tuk for Ar500.

ℹ NOSY BE ON A BUDGET

Nosy Be is expensive compared to the rest of Madagascar. Accommodation is particularly pricey, with most hotels falling squarely in the top-end category. There are, however, a number of ways to visit Nosy Be on a budget and still enjoy the very best of the island.

Accommodation Look carefully and you'll spot a few midrange options and one budget hostel in Hell-Ville. Ambatoloaka sports one midrange place, and there's even one on Nosy Komba.

Eating Food is generally good value in Madagascar, and Nosy Be has a couple of excellent budget eating options. The market in Hell-Ville is a good place to pick up picnic supplies.

Transport Use tuk-tuks between Hell-Ville and Ambatoloaka. For touring the rest of the island, rent a motorbike rather than a car: they're supercheap (Ar20,000 per day plus about Ar3000 of petrol for a day's riding) and ideal for exploring Nosy Be.

Hell-Ville (Andoany)

POP 22,680

Despite the off-putting moniker (named for Admiral de Hell, a French governor of Réunion), Nosy Be's main town is anything but hellish. Rather, it's an upbeat, comparatively smart place where frangipani and bougainvillea frame crumbling ruins of old colonial buildings, pavement cafes bustle with tourists and expats sip strong espresso.

⊙ Sights

Sacred Banyan Tree   HISTORIC SITE
(Map p148; Mahatsinjo village; Ar10,000) On the coast beyond tiny Mahatsinjo village, there's an enormous sacred banyan tree planted by the Queen of the Sakalava tribe in 1836. Nowadays, the Queen of Nosy Be makes an annual pilgrimage to sacrifice a zebu and gain benediction. Shoes must be removed before approaching the tree, and if you have bare legs, a wrap will be provided. The tree is signposted from Rte de l'Ouest just north of Hell-Ville, and is easily reached by quad- or motorbike.

Black lemurs play in the branches, making great photo opportunities.

🛏 Sleeping

★ Tamana Hostel   HOSTEL €
(Map p152; ☑ 034 61 418 36, 032 53 671 25; www.tamanahostel.com; Rue Fortin; dm incl breakfast Ar25,000-30,000; r Ar80,000-100,000; ☜) ✐
From the bright mural in reception to the cool, blond wood, rope and white cotton of the rooms, this place is a winner. The huge house has two dorms (one with 15 beds, one with six) and some private rooms with bathroom and sea views, a kitchen for guests, a bar and restaurant and a roof terrace with knockout views.

Hôtel Belle Vue   HOTEL €€
(Map p152; ☑ 032 04 798 94, 020 86 613 84; bellevue hotel_nosybe@yahoo.fr; Rue Reine Tsiomeko; d Ar55,000-100,000, without bathroom Ar32,000; ❄☜) Belle Vue is an excellent midrange option in Hell-Ville's centre. Cheaper rooms have fans and share a toilet, but all are immaculate and cheerful. The ones at the back of the building are the best – brighter, airier and with nice views. Galmache restaurant serves breakfast (6am to 11am), lunch (noon to 2.30pm) and dinner (6pm to 10pm, three-course menu Ar15,000).

Les Bungalows d'Ambonara   BUNGALOW €€€
(Map p148; ☑ 032 02 611 12, 020 86 613 67; off Rte de l'Ouest; bungalows d Ar60,000-90,000, family Ar90,000-110,000; ☜≋) Bungalows nestle in a luxuriant garden just outside Hell-Ville, off the road to Ambatoloaka. They are beautifully decorated using local materials but are dark and showing their age. Nets and fans are provided. It's a pity there's nowhere to sit in the garden. The restaurant is excellent (mains from Ar20,000).

🍴 Eating

Casa Mofo   CAFE €
(Map p152; ☑ 032 66 204 13; Rue Fortin; sandwiches from Ar8000; ⊙ 6.30am-5pm; ☜) A modern, hip place with seating inside and out, Casa Mofo is a bakery with great snacks (samosas Ar700, quiche Ar5000, scoop of ice cream Ar4000). It's one of the best places in town for breakfast (coffee and croissant Ar6000). Vegetarians are catered for, too. There's no alcohol served here.

Restaurant Manava   MALAGASY €€
(Map p152; Rue Reine Tsiomeko; mains from Ar18,000; ⊙ 10am-2.30pm & 5.30pm-midnight Tue-Sun; ☜) On the top floor, Restaurant

Hell-Ville (Andoany)

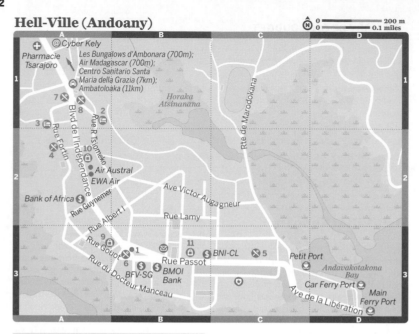

Manava is an unexpected gem. The fare is simple but incredibly tasty, including grilled meat or fish with seasonal vegetables, and rice or chips. The balcony terrace provides atmospheric people-watching, there's always a good vibe at the bar, with people playing pool, and live music several times a week in smart Le Club next door.

⭐ **Le Papillon**   EUROPEAN €€€
(Map p152; ☎ 032 84 791 56, 020 86 610 08; palma.nosybe@gmail.com; Rue Gallieni; mains Ar16,000-

25,000; ⏰8am-3pm Mon-Sat, 7-10pm Fri & Sat) Highly recommended by locals, Le Papillon is *the* place to eat (and be seen) in town. It is set in a beautiful, old, art-filled colonial house with a veranda in the heart of Hell-Ville. The Italian owner changes the menu according to the season and the fresh pasta and fish dishes are particularly good. Breakfast is also served.

Côté Jardin   MALAGASY €€€
(Map p152; ☎ 032 84 149 88; Rue Passot; mains Ar25,000-34,000;   ⏰8am-4pm Mon-Sat; 🛜) There's a charming colonial air to this old house with its veranda at the front overlooking the town gardens, cool interior and more seating in its own garden at the back. It's as fine dining as you'll get in Hell-Ville, but unfortunately not open for dinner. Breakfast includes fruit juice, coffee and a croissant for Ar13,100.

🔒 Shopping

Le Jardin des Sens   COSMETICS
(Map p152; ☎ 034 02 223 23; Villa Locullus, 37 La Batterie; ⏰10am-5pm Mon-Sat) Local essential oils of ylang-ylang, black pepper, *katrafay* (Malagasy bush tree) and more scent the air here, where you can also stock up on honey, spices, soaps and skin products. Set in a beautiful old house, Le Jardin des Sens has

knowledgeable staff who offer massage (50 minutes, Ar40,000) and reflexology (20 minutes, Ar20,000).

Souvenir Stalls ARTS & CRAFTS
(Map p152; Rue Passot; ⊙8am-noon & 2-7pm) On the northern side of Rue Passot between the post office and the BNI-CL bank are a number of souvenir stalls. They sell precious stones, crystals, batiks, jewellery, metalwork and T-shirts. You can try bargaining here, which you can't do in shops.

Société de Rhum Arrangé DRINKS
(Map p152; Blvd de l'Indépendance; ⊙8am-noon & 2.30-5.30pm Mon-Sat) If you'd like to take a taste of Madagascar home with you, why not plump for a bottle of *rhum arrangé* (homemade rum with fruit inside)? There are more than 20 flavours to choose from at this little place, from vanilla to cinnamon, liquorice to coconut. The 180ml plastic bottles (Ar10,000) make perfect presents.

ℹ️ Information

EMERGENCY
Police station (Map p152; ☑ Chef d'immigration 032 04 884 27, Chef du commissariat - station chief 034 05 998 63; Rue du Jardin; ⊙24hr) Has a Chef d'Immigration who deals with tourists.

INTERNET ACCESS
Most hotels and restaurants have wi-fi. **Cyber Kely** (Map p152; ☑ 032 47 779 90; kelyservices@gmail.com; Galerie Ankoay, Blvd du Général de Gaulle; per 1min Ar80; ⊙7am-10pm; 🕾) is in the Galerie Ankaoy shopping centre. The post office also has internet access.

MEDICAL SERVICES
Centro Sanitario Santa Maria della Grazia (Map p148; ☑ 034 86 925 55; Rte de l'Ouest; ⊙24hr) Run by an Italian NGO, this modern hospital features a recompression chamber. It's about halfway between Hell-Ville and Ambatoloaka.

Pharmacie Tsarajoro (Map p152; Blvd du Général de Gaulle; ⊙24hr Sun-Fri) This well-stocked pharmacy is open all the time except on Saturdays when it rotates with other pharmacies. The name and address of the *pharmacie de garde*, the one that is open, is posted in the window when Tsarajoro is closed.

MONEY
There are a number of banks along Rue Passot and Blvd de l'Independence: **Bank of Africa** (BOA; Map p152; Blvd de l'Indépendance; ⊙7.30-11.30am & 2.30-4.30pm Mon-Fri), **BFV-SG** (Map p152; Rue Passot; ⊙7.30-11.30am & 2.30-

4.30pm Mon-Fri), **BMOI Bank** (Map p152; Rue Passot; ⊙7.30-11.30am & 2-4pm Mon-Fri) and **BNI-CL** (Map p152; Rue Passot; ⊙7.30-11.30am & 2-4pm Mon-Fri). All have ATMs and money-changing facilities.

POST
Post office (Map p152; Blvd de l'Indé-pendance; ⊙8am-noon & 2.30-6.30pm Mon-Sat) On Blvd de l'Independence.

ℹ️ Getting There & Away

AIR
The following airlines have offices in Hell-Ville: **Air Austral** (Map p152; ☑ 020 86 612 32; www.air-austral.com; Blvd de l'Indépendance; ⊙8am-noon & 2.30 6pm Mon-Sat) and its subsidiary **EWA Air** (Map p152; ☑ 020 86 612 32/33; www.ewa-air.com; Air Austral, Blvd de l'Independence; ⊙8am-noon & 2.30-6pm), serving the Indian Ocean Islands, and **Air Madagascar** (Map p148; ☑ 020 86 613 60; www.airmadagascar.com; Rte de l'Ouest) and its internal-flight operator Tsaradia. Nosy Be airport (p150) is 13km north of Hell-Ville.

BOAT
➡ Small speedboats shuttle between the mainland port of Ankify and the **main ferry port** (Map p152; Ar15,000, 40 minutes, 5.30am to 4pm). They work like *taxis-brousses* and leave when full. Winds pick up in the afternoon, so the crossing is smoother, and therefore more popular in the morning – you'll never have to wait long for your boat to depart. Life jackets are provided.

➡ On arrival by boat from Ankify, a porter will want to take your luggage off the boat; a tip of Ar1000 is appropriate.

➡ If you're travelling with a vehicle, ferries sail between Ankify and the **car ferry port** (Map p152; from Ar160,000 each way, two hours, from 6am to 4pm).

➡ Pirogues to Nosy Komba leave from the **petit port** (Pirogues to Nosy Komba; Map p152; Ar5000; ⊙5am-4pm) (small port, Ar5000, 20 minutes). If you're staying at a hotel on Komba it will send its own boat for transfers for a fee.

ℹ️ Getting Around
You can hail a taxi anywhere in Hell-Ville, but the main **taxi rank** (Map p152; Blvd de l'Independance) is around the **market** (Map p152; Pl du Marché; ⊙6am-5pm). Tuk-tuks are the most popular form of transport at Ar500 per trip around town.

A taxi from inside the main ferry port into Hell-Ville costs Ar4000. However, if you walk to the port boundary (100m), you can hire a tuk-tuk for Ar500.

WORTH A TRIP

PARC NATIONAL LOKOBE

Parc National Lokobe (www.parcs-madagascar.com/aire-protegee/parc-national-lokobe; entry permits per day Ar55,000; ⊘ 8am-4pm Nov-Jan) protects most of Nosy Be's remaining endemic vegetation. The reserve is home to the black lemur (the male is dark brown, almost black, while the female is a lovely chestnut colour with white tufts around her ears and cheeks) and several other lemur species. You're also likely to spot boa constrictors, owls, chameleons and many wonderful plants, from ylang-ylang trees to vanilla orchids, travellers' palms and more. The best time to visit is November to January.

You will need a guide to visit Parc National Lokobe and one of the best is **Jean Robert** (☑ 032 02 513 85; jean.robertlokobeapphy@yahoo.fr; from Hell-Ville/Andilana Ar110,000/150,000). Jean organises excellent day trips. This includes a taxi between your hotel and Ambatozavavy, transfer in pirogue (dugout canoe) from Ambatozavavy to Ampasipohy (the starting point for walks), a two-hour walk in the forest, lunch, drinks and admission fees to the park.

As well as knowing the area intimately and being a mine of information on all things fauna and flora, Jean is a real character, who will have you singing a Malagasy version of 'Old McDonald's Farm' before you set off but then insist on silence during the visit to minimise disruption to Lokobe's wildlife (he'll just whisper the names of the animals as you go).

You'll need shorts and slip-slops (thongs) on the boat but long pants and closed shoes for walking in the forest. Sun cream, a hat and insect repellent are essential, too.

Ambatoloaka

Nosy Be's southernmost beach is the island's most touristy, although not its best. Ambatoloaka is a buzzy small town, stretched along one long street with most of the hotels, bars and restaurants clustered at the beach end. The beach itself is pretty, but the constant flow of touts, diving boats coming in and out, and noise from seafront establishment, mean it's not that relaxing; head north if that's what you're after. The nightlife is good by Malagasy standards, and the village comes into its own on Sundays when locals come en masse to enjoy a day at the beach.

Its popularity with foreign men of a certain age in search of young Malagasy love is what gives Nosy Be a bad name. Many travellers will feel uneasy about the sleazy atmosphere, particularly in bars and restaurants. That said, a number of hotels have taken a very firm stand against sex tourism.

🛏 Sleeping

Le Coucher du Soleil BUNGALOW €€
(Map p148; ☑ 032 02 087 21; www.coucherdu soleil-nosybe.com; bungalows €20-25; 🛜) This is the best budget option in Ambatoloaka. The bungalows all have hot water. There are also three very well-appointed apartments (€70 for four people). It's signposted from the main street in Ambatoloaka, and there's a shortcut down to the beach.

⭐ **Hôtel Gérard et Francine** GUESTHOUSE €€€
(Map p148; ☑ 032 07 127 93; www.gerard-et-francine.com; d €46-50; 🛜) 🍃 A tranquil, beautifully decorated family guesthouse with wooden floors and a veranda overlooking the beach. The rooms come in all shapes and sizes – some are in the main house and some in the garden. The hotel uses solar power and the owners are very involved in environmental initiatives in Nosy Be. They also lobby actively against sex tourism.

L'Heure Bleue BOUTIQUE HOTEL €€€
(Map p148; ☑ 020 86 060 20, 032 02 203 61; www.heurebleue.com; Madirokely; bungalows d/duplex €95/120, deluxe lodges €120; P🌸🛜🏊) 🍃 On a hill overlooking the beach of Madirokely, this gorgeous hotel has a terrace with great views and a sensational saltwater pool just above the sea (there's a second pool with fresh water). The bungalows have giant sliding-glass doors, which open on to balconies with distant ocean views and armchairs for private sunbathing.

🍴 Eating

⭐ **Chez Mama** MALAGASY €
(Map p148; mains Ar8000-10,000; ⊘11.30am-2pm & 5.30-8.30pm) For a true Malagasy eating experience, try Chez Mama, located on Ambatoloaka's main street. Mama buys her ingredients at Hell-Ville's market every morning and everything she cooks is fresh, tasty and incredibly cheap. Try some of the local staples such as *romazava* (beef and

vegetable stew) or *poulet sauce* (chicken in tomato sauce).

Karibo EUROPEAN €€€
(Map p148; ☑ 032 94 632 92; karibonosybe@gmail.com; mains Ar26,000-38,000; ☺ 6.30-10.30pm Mon-Sat) Sister to the excellent Le Papillon (p152) restaurant in Hell-Ville, the menu here is the same: very good pastas (Ar22,000 to Ar24,000) and a tasty range of meat and fish.

Baobab French Cuisine FRENCH €€€
(Map p148; ☑ 032 89 620 39; mains Ar29,500; ☺ noon-2pm & 7-10pm; ☏) This well-regarded place offers a traditional French menu upstairs on an open roof terrace.

Drinking & Nightlife

Djembe Disco CLUB
(Map p148; for men on Sat Ar5000; ☺ from noon Mon, Wed & Sat) This is Nosy Be's favourite nightclub, located at the end of the village on the road to Madirokely. It's the place to be seen in the evenings – popular with local couples, expats and foreign men on the prowl. Besides having a dance floor, Djembe regularly hosts live-music events (big stars attract a higher price). There are pool tables, too.

ℹ Information

MEDICAL SERVICES
Pharmacie Toko (Map p148; ☑ 032 55 682 06; ☺ 8.30am-12.30pm & 3-8pm Mon-Sat, 9am-12.30pm & 4-8pm Sun) On the main street.

MONEY
BNI-CA (Map p148; ☺ 24hr) ATM only, that takes MasterCard and Visa. There are no other banks in town.

ℹ Getting There & Away

Take a taxi (Ar10,000) or a tuk-tuk (Ar5000) from Hell-Ville to Ambatoloaka. **Location Jeunesse** (Map p148; ☑ 032 04 663 87; ☺ 8am-6pm) rents out motorscooters (per day Ar35,000) for exploring the rest of the island.

The West Coast

With its lovely beaches and postcard sunset views, it's no surprise most hotels on Nosy Be have decided to set up shop on this part of the island. It stretches from Madirokely just north of Ambatoloaka to Andilana, the northernmost tip of the island. The further north you go, the more isolated and quiet it

gets, so you'll need to eat where you sleep (or take a taxi to go out) if you stay up there. If you yearn for company, you'll be happier in Ambatoloaka or Hell-Ville.

Beaches

Andilana BEACH
(Map p148) Far and away Nosy Be's best beach, Andilana, at the island's northwest tip, is a long stretch of pearly white sand, with water that's true azure and clear as gin. It's ideal for swimming and chilling for an afternoon, with gorgeous sunsets.

Andilana ignites on Sundays, when French expats and Malagasy from around Nosy Be come for a lazy day in the sun. Families lay out picnics on a shaded bit of sand, tuck into a crate of beers, turn on their stereo, and swim and dance until the sun goes down.

Ambondrona BEACH
(Map p148) On a small bay just north of Madirokely, Ambondrona is more tranquil than its southern neighbours, with lovely views of the mainland hills across the sea.

🛏 Sleeping

Chez Eugénie GUESTHOUSE €€
(Map p148; ☑ 032 40 634 48; www.chez-eugenie.com; Andilana; incl breakfast r €30-40, without bathroom €20, bungalows €50; ☏) There are just five rooms at this little hotel and restaurant owned by a French and Malagasy couple. It has two separate wings joined under one big thatched roof to form a dining room (plat du jour Ar19,000). Abodes are small, but pretty, with firm mattresses and high-quality linens. There are no sea views, but it's 200m from Andilana beach.

> **DON'T MISS**
>
> **EDEN LODGE**
>
> Eight luxury tents are equipped with beautiful mahogany beds, colourful fabrics and private massage cabins at **Eden Lodge** (☑ 032 02 203 61, 034 86 93 119; www.edenlodge.net; Anjanojano; d per person full board €264; ☏) 🍃. Meals are served in the atmospheric thatched dining room–lounge (complete with fairy lights); the menu changes daily and makes the best of the hotel's vegetable garden and the abundant seafood.
>
> Eden Lodge is accessible only by boat transfer (30 minutes) from Nosy Be.

WORTH A TRIP

PARC NATIONAL MARIN DE NOSY TANIKELY

Nosy Tanikely is a protected **marine reserve** (Map p148; www.tanikely.com; Ar20,000; ⊙8am-5pm) 10km south of Nosy Be. It's one of the best snorkelling sites in the area, with coral, numerous fish and sea turtles.

Snorkelling is best in the morning, before the wind picks up. Although the reserve officially opens at 8am, you are allowed to come earlier – just stick around until the reserve officials arrive so that you can pay your admission fees. Snorkelling equipment is available from the reserve's cabin for Ar10,000.

★**Vanila Hôtel**   RESORT €€€

(Map p148; ☑ 032 03 921 01; www.vanila-hotel.com; Ambaro; d garden/sea view €99/129, ste €295; ❋ 🛜 ☂) One of the top beach hotels on this stretch of the coast, Vanila's design – small buildings with thatched roofs, and lots of local art – gives the hotel a boutique feel. Rooms are charming, with salmon-coloured walls and wooden furniture. As well as the two pools and beach, there is a sensational spa. There are two restaurants open to the public.

★**La Case Sakalava**   BUNGALOW €€€

(Map p148; ☑ 032 05 437 21, 032 07 437 21; www.case-sakalava.com; Ambaro; d €42) ✐ This ecolodge was built by the owners of Sakalav' Diving (p147) and is just 700m from the dive school, in a lush landscape on a hill over the sea. Plain but comfortable bungalows are brick and wood, all built by locals, and each has a private veranda with magnificent views. Excursions can be arranged. It's solar-powered and there's no internet. Half board €12 per person.

Nosy Be Hôtel & Spa   RESORT €€€

(Map p148; ☑ 034 06 771 86; www.nosybehotel.com; Ampasy; d €120-300; ❋ 🛜 ☂) ✐ Top-notch Nosy Be Hôtel stands out from the competition thanks to its highly original decor – stunning wooden furniture made on Nosy Be and lots of local artwork – and lush garden on the edge of the beach. All rooms are different, each offering European mattresses and pillows and beautiful bathrooms. Various plans are available, from half board to all inclusive.

Andilana Beach Resort   RESORT €€€

(Map p148; ☑ 034 65 000 10/11/12; www.andilanaresort.com; Andilana; garden/ocean view per person all inclusive €196/237, ste €309; P ❋ 🛜 ☂) This large resort of 210 rooms is in a stupendous location and caters for young and old. As it has everything you need, you never really have to venture out, although it does offer excursions. It's Italian-owned and they fly visitors in twice a week from Milan in chartered planes. You might feel left out if you don't speak Italian.

Le Grand Bleu   BUNGALOW €€€

(Map p148; ☑ 032 02 194 84; www.legrandbleunosybe.com; Antanamitarana village, near Andilana; bungalows €45-104; ❋ 🛜 ☂) ✐ On a hill overlooking the sea, Le Grand Bleu has spectacular views from its terrace restaurant. The star attraction is the dazzling infinity pool; the hotel is also a three-minute walk from a lovely beach. Each of the pretty bungalows has wood floors, four-poster beds, mosquito nets, terrace and hammock. A spa with massage rooms looks over the sea.

✕ Eating

★**La Table d'Alexandre**   FRENCH €€€

(Map p148; ☑ 033 14 247 22; Ambaro; mains Ar28,000-46,000; ⊙noon-2pm & 6-9pm by reservation only) For a decadent lunch on a day trip around the island, stop at Alexandre's. The debonair French chef here serves exquisite cuisine in a dining room that wouldn't have looked out of place on the set of *Out of Africa*: a gazebo perched on a low hill overlooking mangroves and Nosy Sakatia, decorated with traditional china and 19th-century paintings. Splendid.

Chez Loulou   SEAFOOD €€€

(Map p148; ☑ 034 25 939 93; Andilana; mains Ar25,000-40,000; ⊙11am-9pm Tue-Sat, to 3pm Sun) Right on the beach, this casual restaurant and bar is best known for its gargantuan Sunday seafood-buffet lunch (Ar65,000). Seafood also gets pride of place in the daily three-course meal. If you want to linger after dessert at lunch, grab a sunlounger and an ice-cold THB, and relax with a good book. Bookings are essential for the Sunday buffet.

ℹ Getting There & Away

The road around Nosy Be is sealed, but not in good condition. If you're staying at one of the hotels, it will organise a transfer for you from the airport or Hell-Ville.

To explore the region independently, hire a taxi for the day (Ar120,000), a motorbike from **Nosy Easy Rent** (Map p148; ☑ 032 05 399 59, 033 11 611 00; www.nosyeasyrent.com; Rte de l'Ouest; per day car €35-65, motorbike €20; ⊙7am-6pm Mon-Sat) or quad bike from Nosy Be Original (p149).

ISLANDS AROUND NOSY BE

If money is no object, the islands surrounding Nosy Be are all home to some idyllic resorts, ideal for a few days of remote tranquillity, diving and fishing. If you're on a tighter budget, take a day trip to check out the palm-fringed white beaches and do some excellent snorkelling.

Nosy Komba

This island rises off the ocean floor midway between the mainland and Nosy Be in an almost perfect cone shape; its summit reaches a mighty 622m (much higher than that of Nosy Be). There is one main village and several smaller ones, a lemur park and some wonderful crafts to browse. Beaches are idyllic and snorkelling is good.

Cruise liners stop here, and there are a large number of day trippers to Nosy Komba from Nosy Be. This has made a big impact on the island: the people have more disposable income and are building houses of concrete blocks rather than traditional grass; but it sometimes means that Ampangorinana (Nosy Komba's main village) is overcrowded.

◉ Sights

Lemur Park   NATURE RESERVE
(Map p148; Ampangorinana; Ar8000) In this small park, the black lemurs are wild, but locals feed them bananas so that the animals will eat off your hand or jump on your shoulder for that perfect photo op. The practice is detrimental to the animals but generates substantial revenue for the village, which has helped protect the forest. So if you'd like to support the village, pay the admission fee to admire the lemurs, but decline the offer to feed them.

🏃 Activities

Nosy Komba's interior is remarkably well preserved and is prime hiking territory. It takes about five sweaty hours to walk up to the summit from Ampangorinana and back

down. Ask for a guide in the village (Ar30,000 including lunch in a village near the top).

🛏 Sleeping

There is no electricity on the island. Hotels operate on solar power backed up by generators.

If you'd like to stay, the choice of accommodation is between relatively isolated top-end resorts, and less expensive options along the beach at Ampangorinana village.

Chez Yolande   BUNGALOW €€
(Map p148; ☑ 032 87 093 79, 032 04 787 29; www.hotel-nosykomba.com/contact-chez-yolande; Ampangorinana; s/d/tr from Ar52,000/60,000/100,000; ☞) The simple yet comfortable rooms at Chez Yolande offer very good value for Nosy Komba. More expensive ones have a terrace and sea view (Ar108,000 to Ar128,000). All have mosquito nets and fan.

They are attached to the restaurant (mains Ar21,000 to Ar26,000) and bar. Yolande speaks English, French and Italian.

★293 On Komba   GUESTHOUSE €€€
(Map p148; ☑ 032 93 825 59◌; www.293onkomba.com; Ampangorinana; per person half board €68-90; ☞◌≋) ⦿ Set among mango trees at the end of Ampangorinana's beach, this delightful guesthouse offers four stylish rooms, each with a veranda. For extra privacy, there are two more rooms next door. Local wood carvings grace the lounge and lush garden and there's a spring-fed infinity pool. South African owner Marcine is a mine of local information and serves superb food.

Tsara Komba   LODGE €€€
(Map p148; ☑ 032 07 440 40, 020 86 921 10; www.tsarakomba.com; d/ste full board per person €320/365; ☞) ⦿ With just eight bungalows, this superb lodge is about as exclusive and secluded as you can get. The polished wooden rooms have king-size beds and a porch looking out to the sea. The garden is a work of art, as is the food served in the dining room with panoramic views.

Jardin Vanille   LODGE €€€
(Map p148; ☑ 032 07 127 97; www.jardinvanille.com; d with half/full board €149/179; ☞) ⦿ This lovely ecolodge offers eight comfortable Malagasy-style bungalows and a large suite, all overlooking the beach near the village of Anjiabe. The restaurant serves a very fine menu and overlooks the sea. Numerous excursions can be arranged (Nosy Tanikely for two €85), along with Nosy Be transfers.

🍴 Eating

Gargote Vanille   MALAGASY €€
(Map p148; mains Ar21,000; ⊘11am-10pm) Timo
and Stéphanie have a miniscule veranda with
just four tables on which to serve their delicious food. Fish, prawns and lobster come
with garlic butter or coconut-citrus sauce
and chips. It's excellent value. The menu also
has zebu, pasta and lighter options like sandwiches and omelettes. Sadly, there's no sea
view as it's in the middle of the village.

Chez Madio   MALAGASY €€
(Map p148; Ampangorinana; mains Ar20,000-
26,000) Madio makes the most of local ingredients to produce excellent dishes. Seafood is
a speciality – order the fish of the day with
a platter of delicious chips. Eat upstairs to
catch the breeze.

Gargote La Marée   MALAGASY €€
(Map p148; ☑032 48 404 75; mains Ar15,000;
⊘6am-10pm) Vlad and Stella serve whatever
is freshest today in their open-air restaurant
overlooking the sea. Check out what they
have and then wander the market for half
an hour or so. It will be ready when you get
back. A good plate of fish and chips will set
you back Ar15,000.

🛍 Shopping

Ampangorinana Craft Market   ARTS & CRAFTS
(Map p148; Ampangorinana; ⊘8am-noon & 2-7pm)
Ampangorinana has an interesting craft
market with beautiful cut-work embroidered tablecloths and curtains, excellent
wood carvings and paintings spilling out of
almost every house. There are also spices,
vanilla and massage oils on sale.

❶ Information

MEDICAL SERVICES
Todi Pharmacie (Map p148; ☑032 04 013 93;
⊘8am-noon & 2-6pm Mon-Sat) In Ampangorinana; tiny but fairly well stocked.

MONEY
There are no banks on Nosy Komba, so make sure
you bring enough cash from Hell-Ville.

❶ Getting There & Away

There are no roads, so no vehicles on Nosy
Komba.

Organised tours to the island are available
from most tour operators in Nosy Be and cost
around Ar120,000 in combination with Nosy
Tanikely. Motorised pirogues (Ar5000, 20

minutes) leave the petit port (p153) in Hell-Ville
when full. Pay on the boat, not the touts on the
quay. Ask to be dropped off at your hotel, or at
the **pirogue port** (Map p148) near the village of
Ampangorinana.

Nosy Sakatia

Quiet and tiny, Nosy Sakatia is part of a
protected ecosystem and is famous for its
orchids. It's an easy place to wander around
and has several beautiful beaches. Snorkelling here is superb, and there are a couple of
excellent diving sites off the island, including a green-turtle protected zone. The island
sits just off the west coast of Nosy Be.

Family-run **Sakatia Lodge** (Map p148;
☑032 05 307 48; www.sakatia.com; d bungalows
Ar260,000-600,000; ⊛🖾) 🌿 offers garden
bungalows on a slope above the stylish open
restaurant and bar. There are also beachside
three-bedroom villas suitable for families
(Ar1,000,000/1,100,000). The lodge specialises in diving and fishing. Its dive school is
well equipped and recommended by readers, even for beginners, with highly experienced instructors. Snorkelling in the nearby
green-turtle sanctuary is blissful. Food is
excellent.

❶ Getting There & Away

To get to Sakatia, make your way to the Nosy Be
beach of Ambaro (next to Chanty Beach Hotel),
where you'll find motorised **pirogues** (Map p148)
to Sakatia (Ar5000, 10 minutes). Negotiate
a price for a tour of the island (depending on
the length of the excursion). This is also where
pirogues from Sakatia Lodge put in.

Nosy Mitsio

Nosy Mitsio is a beautiful, small archipelago
about 55km northeast of Nosy Be, close to
Cap St Sebastien on the mainland, where the
main attractions are the still relatively virgin
dive sites, the superb game fishing and the
picture-perfect beaches.

Waters are deep (on average 40m to
50m) and the archipelago is sheltered by
the northern tip of Madagascar, making the
area rich in diversity and density of flora
and fauna, and free of pollution.

🛏 Sleeping

Mitsio Tropical Lodge   BUNGALOW €€€
(☑ Alain Soulet 032 69 504 66; www.tropical-fishing.
com/notre-lodge; Nosy Mitsio; 6 days all inclusive
1 person €3920, per person in a group of 4 €1745,

without fishing €750; 🖥) 🏄 Owned by Tropical Fishing (p147), this ecolodge is a base for game-fishing expeditions. Seven comfortable, spacious wooden bungalows overlook the glorious beach and bright blue sea, and there is also a three-bedroom private villa. There are games such as pétanque, a massage room, and a friendly bar and restaurant with excellent food.

Constance Tsarabanjina LODGE €€€
(📞 032 02 152 29; www.constancehotels.com/en/hotels-resorts/madagascar/tsarabanjina; bungalows for 2 full board from €845; 🖥) 🏄 Tsarabanjina is a tiny island in the Mitsio archipelago where you'll find this exquisite lodge of 25 beach villas. There are no TVs or phones here (the only concession to modern living is wi-fi in the communal areas) – just the sea, the beach and the hills. Most people come here to dive. Tsarabanjina has a PADI-certified club.

ⓘ Getting There & Away

Most diving and tour operators in Nosy Be organise multiday diving or fishing trips and cruises to Nosy Mitsio (€500 to €1000, depending on the number of people on board, the number of dives and number of days). If staying at one of the lodges, the boat transfer from Nosy Be or Ankify takes two hours.

AMBANJA REGION

This lush region produces mangoes, cashew nuts, ylang-ylang, vanilla, cocoa and spices. You will pass through this area if you are travelling along the RN6 from Diego Suarez (Antsiranana) to Ankify and heading to Nosy Be by boat. You can visit a couple of plantations en route to find out about the farms and their products.

Ambanja

POP 30,620

Ambanja is a small, tree-lined town on the Sambirano River, and the junction for overland travel to and from Nosy Be. It is known for its large cocoa, spice and vanilla plantations, some of which can be visited.

⊙ Sights

Millot Plantations PLANTATION
(www.cananga.fr; per person 4hr tour Ar40,000; farmhouse 3-course lunch incl drinks Ar60,000; ⊙8am-5pm Mon-Sat) This beautiful plantation, established in 1904, is a leading producer of organic cocoa, spices and essential

---

NOSY IRANJA

The gorgeous Nosy Iranja, southwest of Nosy Be, consists of two islands: larger, inhabited Nosy Iranja Be (about 2 sq km) and tiny Nosy Iranja Kely (0.13 sq km). The islands are connected by a 1.5km-long sand bar, negotiable on foot at low tide. Sea turtles regularly lay eggs on the beaches.

Nosy Iranja is a popular sailing day trip from Nosy Be (for two Ar624,000). The excursion generally includes snorkelling, swimming and a good lunch on board the boat.

---

oils, and a visit to this little slice of paradise is not only highly informative but a true festival of the senses. The tour can be topped off with lunch in the beautiful old farmhouse. However, some readers report that the welcome here is less than gracious.

🛏 Sleeping

Palma Nova BUNGALOW €€
(📞 032 04 611 21; www.palmanova-ambanja.com; d/tr/q Ar60,000/70,000/85,000; 🅿🖥) Basic but clean hotel with 10 rooms set around a lovely, small garden with ylang-ylang trees. There's just one double with air-conditioning (Ar75,000) but it overlooks the car park and main road, so is noisy. Some rooms have a shower but share a toilet. Electricity between 9am and 3am. The huge dining room offers reasonable food (mains Ar18,000 to Ar25,000).

ⓘ Information

Bank of Africa (RN6; ⊙24hr) Has an ATM on the main road. Be warned: there are no banks in Ankify so withdraw here if necessary.

ⓘ Getting There & Away

From Ambanja there are regular *taxis-brousses* to Ankify (Ar4000, one hour), where you'll find the ferry to Nosy Be. *Taxis-brousses* also go to Diego Suarez (Antsiranana; Ar25,000, nine hours), Majunga (Ar50,000, 14 hours) and Antananarivo (Ar60,000, 19 hours).

Ankify

Ankify is the main port for boats and ferries between the mainland coast and Nosy Be. If you think you'll arrive too late for the crossing to Nosy Be (after 4pm) or the last *taxi-brousse* to Diego Suarez (Antsiranana; noon), it's better to overnight in Ambanja.

If you get stuck here **Les Baobabs** (☑033 07 208 87; baobab.ankify@gmail.com; garden bungalows Ar150,000, sea-facing rondavels Ar185,000; **P** 🛜) has modern round bungalows on a gorgeous beach with superb views across to Nosy Komba, or ordinary bungalows in the pretty garden. They are comfortable but lack charm and are not well maintained – there have been reports of roof leaks. The restaurant (mains Ar20,000 to Ar40,000) is on an enormous veranda. A taxi to the port costs Ar15,000.

❶ Information

There are no banks here so be sure to draw cash before you arrive.

❶ Getting There & Away

BOAT

Small speedboats shuttle between Ankify and Hell-Ville on Nosy Be (Ar15,000, 40 minutes, 5.30am to 4pm). They work like *taxis-brousses* and leave when full. Wind picks up in the afternoon, so the crossing is smoother, and therefore more popular, in the morning – you'll never have to wait long for your boat to depart. Life jackets are provided.

If you're travelling with a vehicle, ferries sail between Ankify and Hell-Ville on Nosy Be (from Ar160,000 each way, two hours, from 9am).

When heading to the port by private vehicle or by taxi from local accommodation, allow your driver to accompany you to offset the touts at the port.

TAXIS-BROUSSES FROM ANKIFY

DESTINATION	PRICE (AR)	DURATION (HR)	DEPARTURE
Ambanja	4000	1	All day
Ambilobe	15,000	4	Morning
Diego Suarez (Antsiranana)	30,000	10	Morning

4WD FROM ANKIFY TO DIEGO SUAREZ (ANTSIRANANA)

The popular northern circuit from Diego Suarez (Antsiranana) to Nosy Be offered by travel agents means that some 4WD drop their clients in Ankify for the final leg of their trip and head back to Diego Suarez empty. As a result, Evasion Sans Frontière (p149) accepts passengers on the way back for Ar50,000 per person (Ar20,000 more than the *taxi-brousse* and so much more comfortable). Ring ahead to find out when a vehicle might be available.

Drivers from other hire companies hang about the port after they've dropped their clients, so look out for an empty 4WD at the port and negotiate with the driver. The journey to Diego Suarez by private vehicle is 6½ hours.

ANTSIRANANA REGION

Madagascar's northernmost region is an alluring place: it's remote, it's host to weird and wonderful geological sights, and it has a fun city to explore.

Diego Suarez (Antsiranana), the main gateway town, sparkles with a great shopping and restaurant scene. There are glorious beaches within easy reach of the town with a growing array of adventure sports to try, such as quad biking and kitesurfing. The two major national parks of Montagne d'Ambre and Ankarana offer plenty of excellent hiking and the bizarre Tsingy Rouges beckon.

Diego is not the only place to base yourself when exploring the region. Some travellers stay in Joffreville (Ambohitra) and do day trips from there; others prefer to do a couple of days in Diego and then work their way along the RN6, sleeping in Joffreville for Montagne d'Ambre, and at Réserve Spéciale Ankarana, to minimise travelling time.

❶ Dangers & Annoyances

There have been a number of muggings in isolated areas popular with travellers such as Montagne des Français and Les Trois Baies. To minimise chances of things going wrong, never go alone. Even if you're part of a couple or small group, take a guide, tell your hotel where you're going and don't take valuables with you.

Diego Suarez (Antsiranana)

POP 82,940

With its wide streets, old colonial-era buildings, and buzzy atmosphere, Diego Suarez (Antsiranana) is an appealing base from which to explore Madagascar's northern region. While the city has a slow-moving pace (nearly everything shuts between noon and 3pm while residents indulge in long afternoon naps), there's a plethora of good restaurants, places to stay and plenty of shopping.

Diego is an important port in Madagascar; the town notably exports tinned fish, and soft and alcoholic drinks – there is an important Star (THB) bottling plant on the outskirts of town. Thanks to its deep-water anchorage, Diego has also become a firm

TSINGY ROUGES

One of Madagascar's most awesome natural wonders, these scraggly **pinnacles** (Red Tsingy; Ar10,000) – erosion's work of art – are made of laterite, an iron-oxide-rich soil with an intense red-brick colour. These surreal formations stand on the edge of beautiful canyons some 65km southeast of Diego. It's a fragile environment, and local authorities have thankfully stepped in to protect the site. There are three areas you can access, including a breathtaking viewpoint.

The most stunning site is at the bottom of a small ravine, where *tsingy* (pinnacle formations) line an entire bank like an army of sentinels. If you're here with a guide, ask him or her to show you the three natural pigments found in the soil – ochre, vermilion and magenta – which northern Malagasies use for face paints and natural dyes.

Because of their colour, the *tsingy* are best admired early in the morning (around 7am or 8am) or late in the afternoon (around 4pm), when the light is low and warm.

You will need a 4WD to access the Red Tsingy: the turn-off on the RN6 is 45km south of Diego Suarez (Antsiranana) and signposted. It's then 20km eastwards along a dirt track that's pretty good in some places, dismal in others. En route, you'll cross a number of eucalyptus plantations destined for charcoal production. (The majority of Malagasies use charcoal for cooking and its production is a leading cause of deforestation, so these plantations help preserve primary forests.) You'll also be treated to sweeping views of the Indian Ocean. The dirt track can be impassable during rainy season (December to April).

favourite of cruise ships, which visit between December and March. The ships are a magnificent sight as they cross the bay.

There are no beaches in Diego itself, but plenty of amazing views of the bay, and those glorious beaches with all their activities are but a short drive along the coast.

◎ Sights

A number of historic buildings have blue information boards in Malagasy, French and English, such as the house belonging to **Cassam Chenaï** (52 Rue Colbert), an Indian trader who settled in Diego Suarez (Antsiranana) around 1895. It's a pleasant walk along Rue Colbert towards the sea and then along Rue Richelieu to discover more, such as the imposing **Hôtel des Mines** (Rue de Richelieu), the **Japanese Monument** (Pointe du Corail), **La Résidence** (Rue de Richelieu) and the **Tribunal** (Rue de Richelieu).

The **Jardin Tropical** (☑032 83 296 21, 032 04 456 52; jardintropicaldiego@gmail.com; 11 Rue George de Villebois-Mareuil; adult/child Ar10,000/2000; ☺8.30am-12.30pm & 2.30-5pm) ✐ is a delightful 10,000-sq-metre garden in a quiet residential area. Children will enjoy exploring the three growing areas of primary forest, a rock garden and full sun to search for crocodiles, chameleons and porcupines.

If you're planning to visit the Camp Andrafiamena Andavakoera (p164) south of Diego Suarez or the Loky Manambato Protected Area (p175) in Daraina near Vohémar,

the Fanamby (p165) NGO has an office in Diego Suarez for information and bookings.

🏃 Activities

Le Grand Hôtel   SWIMMING
(☑20 82 230 64, 020 82 230 63; www.grand-hotel-diego.com; 46 Rue Colbert; per person with lunch weekdays Ar15,000, weekend Ar37,500-55,000) The hotel's pool has been beautifully landscaped, with tropical plants all around and an attractive deck for loungers. Towels are provided

The poolside restaurant has main dishes from Ar28,000 and pizzas from Ar13,000.

☞ Tours

Diego Suarez (Antsiranana) tour companies offer a variety of activities and excursions to Ankarana, Montagne d'Ambre, Les Trois Baies, Tsingy Rouges and Mer d'Emeraude. They're also the best place to go to if you'd like to hire a 4WD to explore the region under your own steam, notably between Diego and Nosy Be, and also the vanilla coast (Vohémar, Sambava and Antalaha). Allow Ar135,000 to Ar175,000 per day for a 4WD with driver plus fuel, depending on the distance.

Evasion Sans Frontière   TOURS
(☑020 82 217 23, Grand Hotel branch 020 82 255 61; www.evasionsansfrontiere.com; 62 Rue Colbert; Les Trois Baies full day for 2 Ar148,000, Montagne d'Ambre National Park 5hr for 2 Ar210,000; ☺8am-noon & 2-5pm Mon-Sat) This well-respected company with branches in various cities runs day

Diego Suarez (Antsiranana)

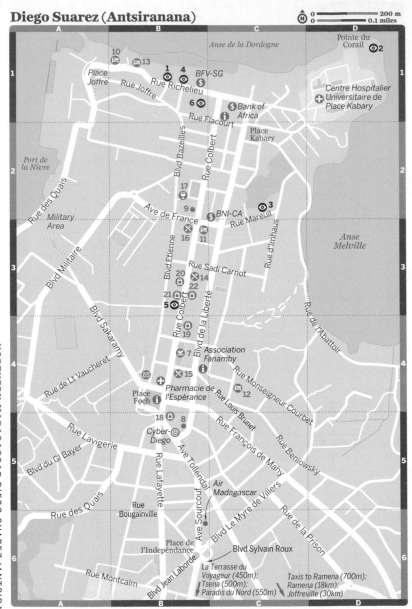

trips to the main regional sights, including Mer d'Emeraude, and further afield. A 4WD vehicle for four from Diego Suarez to Ankify costs Ar535,000. There's a second branch of the company inside the Grand Hotel (p164) on Rue Colbert.

Diego Raid TOURS
(☎ 032 05 890 77, 032 58 890 77; www.diegoraid. com; Rue Colbert; quad bike incl picnic lunch & guide per half-/full day from €90/120, 2-day quad-bike trips for 2 incl accommodation €640; ⊙ 7.30am-noon & 2-6pm Mon-Sat) This well-established operator

Diego Suarez (Antsiranana)

organises highly recommended quad-bike excursions to areas such as Les Trois Baies, Windsor Castle and Montagne d'Ambre. As well as taking in the main sights, the trips often leave the tarmac well behind and take the scenic route. Mountain bikes are also available at €15 per day including equipment.

Madabest TOURS
(☑ 034 28 325 14, 032 05 127 11; madabestrip@ gmail.com; 43 Rue de la Marne; per day with driver Ar125,000-165,000 plus fuel; ⊙ 8am-noon & 2-6pm Mon-Fri, 8am-noon Sat) Excellent 4WD hire with knowledgeable drivers for trips to Trois Baies, Ramena, Tsingy Rouge, Montagne d'Ambre and beyond.

New Sea Roc ADVENTURE
(☑ 020 82 218 54, 032 04 724 46; www.newsearoc. com; 26 Rue Colbert; ⊙ 8am-noon & 2.30-5pm Mon-Sat) 🔱 New Sea Roc specialises in adventure and climbing activities. It represents Jungle Park (p167) with its treehouses and eco-domes on the Montagne des Français. Other tours such as kite- and windsurfing, kayaking, paddleboarding, hiking and mountain biking are on offer. The company supports village development, environmental education and tree planting.

Paradis du Nord TOURS
(☑ 032 04 859 64, 020 82 214 05; www.leparadis- dunord-diego.com; Ave Princesse Fatima Achimo; per day with driver Ar120,000 plus fuel; ⊙ 8am-noon & 2.30-6pm) Run by affable Eric, this agency has a large fleet of quality vehicles at good rates. Find it behind the Tsena (covered market).

✯ Festivals & Events

Zegny'Zo Festival PERFORMING ARTS
(☑ 032 04 931 81, 032 02 358 15; www.zolobe. com; 6 Rue Imhaus; ⊙ May) In the third week of May, street theatre and traditional music are showcased in the streets of Diego Suarez.

🛏 Sleeping

Hôtel Valiha HOTEL €
(☑ 032 07 789 95, 020 82 251 06; valiha@moov.mg; 33 Rue Colbert; d Ar40,000-75,000) Well-located, this hotel is one of the cheapest in town. It is older but clean and well kept and has hot water. Opt for a room upstairs, as the cheapest rooms on the ground floor have no windows. The most expensive look out over Rue Colbert, which could be noisy. There's a bar and restaurant.

Perle de la Baie GUESTHOUSE €€
(☑ 032 95 964 37, 032 02 273 60; perledelabaie@ gmail.com; Rue Richelieu; d Ar100,000, without bathroom Ar80,000; ☜) This guesthouse probably has the most jaw-dropping view of the bay in Diego: breakfast or a sundowner on the balcony really takes some beating. The lounge and balcony are homely and cluttered, complete with large dog. The rooms are sparsely furnished but spacious and light (opt for one upstairs). Some share bathrooms.

La Belle Aventure GUESTHOUSE €€
(☑ 032 44 153 83; www.labellaventure-diego. com; 13 Rue Freppel; d Ar60,000-80,000, with balcony Ar100,000; ✳☜) Gilles and Elisabeth built their Beautiful Adventure in a great

WORTH A TRIP

CAMP ANDRFIAMENA ANDAVAKOERA

Located 60km south of Diego Suarez (Antsiranana), then 20km east, this **camp** (Black Lemur Camp; ☑ 034 02 351 66, 032 07 843 44, 020 22 336 23; www.friendlycamp.org/en/black-lemur-camp; camping/bungalows Ar20,000/150,000; ⊘ closed wet season Dec-late Mar) **FREE** is perched on a ridge overlooking the rainforest. This is the last refuge of the black *sifakas* (*Propithecus perrieri*) and guides lead walks to see them (2½ hours, Ar15,000), to a natural pool (five hours, Ar25,000) and other circuits to the *tsingy* (limestone pinnacle formations) and caves. The nearby village of Anjakahely is famous for its perfumed rice. Bungalows are very comfortable, with nets and bathrooms, and meals are available (menu Ar35,000).

Turn off the RN6 at the village of Marotaolana, 80km south of Diego Suarez and 64km northeast of Ambilobe. The badly rutted road from Marotaolana to Anjakahely will take about 30 minutes in a 4WD in dry season (April to November).

Bookings can be made at the Association Fanamby (p165) in Diego Suarez.

neighbourhood of Diego: quiet, yet close to the centre and with good views of the bay. Everything is bright, fresh and impeccable, with colourful sheets and lemur and baobab friezes on the walls. Rooms upstairs have a balcony and sea view. There's a friendly bar and restaurant at street level.

★ Allamanda Hôtel   BOUTIQUE HOTEL €€€
(☑ 032 07 666 15; www.allamanda-hotel.com; Rue Richelieu; d from Ar240,000-300,000; ❄ 🛜 🏊) The swish Allamanda is just steps from the sea and has all the luxuries you would expect from a top-end hotel. The exterior of the building is a bit bland and boxy, but the rooms are spacious and elegantly decked out in nautical-themed decor. It has stupendous views over the bay.

Grand Hotel   HOTEL €€€
(☑ 020 82 230 64, 020 82 230 63; www.grand-hotel-diego.com; 46 Rue Colbert; d/ste Ar375,000/575,000; ❄ 🛜 🏊) Diego's premier hotel sits proudly on the main thoroughfare. There's a coffee shop and bar on the front veranda, while the pool is in a lovely garden at the back. It's expensive by Malagasy standards but good value, given that the rooms have all you'd expect and there's a restaurant, bank, tour operator and spa on-site.

✖ Eating

Pâtisserie Le Grand Hôtel   BAKERY €
(Rue Colbert; pastries & sandwiches Ar2500-13,500; ⊘ 5am-9.30pm) This excellent bakery doubles as a cafe that's popular with tourists. It's a great choice for an economical and light breakfast, or a cheap lunch of salad or a sandwich. There are some lovely pastries too, which you can devour with real espresso

(Ar4500). Ice cream is Ar3500 per scoop. It's on the street-side veranda of this smart hotel.

La Rosticceria   ITALIAN €€
(☑ 032 67 637 03; 47 Rue Colbert; menu Ar17,000, mains Ar13,000-24,000) An old favourite, this Italian restaurant has a an interesting menu featuring freshly made pasta with pesto, cream, meat or seafood sauces. The fish is good: we loved the prawn and fish duo with ginger sauce. The restaurant decor follows a nautical theme, with intricately carved wooden vessels and old maps for decoration. Outside tables sit on a veranda.

La Cambusa   MALAGASY €€
(Rue Colbert; mains Ar16,000-20,000; ⊘ 10.30am-2pm & 5-10pm Mon-Sat) Full of Johnny Depp–inspired piratical wall art and ships' accoutrements such as greasy poles and muskets, oh, and a noose hanging from a beam, this restaurant is meat-oriented. Tables spill onto the street and have jaunty red-checked cloths.

L'Amiral IV Restaurant & Bar   SEAFOOD €€
(☑ 032 63 464 37; mains Ar18,000-22,000; ⊘ 8.45am-2pm & 3.45-10pm Mon-Sat) Seafood stars at this place where you can eat inside or out on the enclosed terrace. A seafood platter will set you back Ar46,000. The quality is good and the service friendly.

La Terrasse du Voyageur   MALAGASY €€
(☑ 034 20 061 04, 034 20 061 06; www.terrassedu voyageur-hotel.com; cnr Rues Justin Bezara & du Mozambique; mains Ar14,000-19,000; ⊘ 5-9pm) 🍽 The 4th-floor restaurant at hotel **La Terrasse du Voyageur** (d Ar20,000, s/d with fan Ar38,000/50,000, d/tr with air-con Ar75,000/82,000; ❄🛜) 🍽 has sweeping views of Diego. It's a cosy and convivial

space, with a TV lounge, library and bar. The Malagasy dishes are good value: portions are gargantuan and the food delicious. The restaurant is only open for dinner.

★ Tsara Be Restaurant · MALAGASY €€€

(📱 032 04 940 97; penverneric@gmail.com; 36 Rue Colbert; mains from Ar26,000; ☺9am-2pm & 6-10pm Mon-Sat, 6 10pm Sun) French cuisine with a touch of Madagascar, set off with a twist of Thai, make this restaurant a crowd-pleaser. It's the sort of place where locals dress up and go to celebrate. There are dark-red walls, white tablecloths, good service and a wide range of cocktails and wines. The large interior has tables spilling out onto the street.

Le Melville · FRENCH €€€

(📱 032 05 606 99; Rue Richelieu, Allamanda Hôtel; mains Ar21,500-30,000; ☺noon-2pm & 7-10pm; 🛜) Right by the sea, with a fabulous deck that's particularly alluring at sunset, the atmosphere at Melville is romantic and sophisticated without being stuffy. The food is delicious, featuring zebu and seafood: fish lovers will be spoilt for choice. Try the skewers of fish, prawn and calamari served with rice (Ar23,500). Service is also top-class. Booking is recommended for weekends.

🍺 Drinking & Nightlife

Taxi Be Nightclub · CLUB

(📱 032 40 794 15; Blvd Bazeilles; ☺5pm-2am) Taxi Be is *the* place to be in Diego Suarez (Antsiranana) – there's live music every night and everybody's here, locals and visitors. Try shaking your booty to the hot *salegy* (Kenyan-influenced music of the Sakalava tribe) dance music. The stage sports a Citroen 2CV taxi and the dance hall is enormous. Wear your best.

🛍 Shopping

Couleur du Monde · GIFTS & SOUVENIRS

(Rue Colbert; ☺8.30am-noon & 3-7pm Mon-Sat) You'll go in here for the chocolate, but then be tempted by the zebu-horn and shell jewellery, raffia bags, vanilla, shells and all sorts of gifts. It's difficult to tear yourself away from this gem.

Le Village · ARTS & CRAFTS

(Rue Colbert; ☺8.30am-6.30pm Mon-Sat) A nautical air pervades this shop, with pictures of fish, brass instruments and very impressive models of ships made of wood. They'll pack and post anywhere in the world.

Jewelers By Bleu Nuit · JEWELLERY

(Rue Colbert; ☺8am-noon & 3-6pm Mon-Sat) Dark-blue walls and good lighting set off the stylish silver jewellery here, some with gemstones, some plain. There is also a range of rather classy handbags.

La Natura · HEALTH & WELLNESS

(Rue Colbert; ☺8am-noon & 2-6pm Mon-Sat) Indigenous essential oils and health-related products such as noni juice and aromatherapy goodies fill the shelves here, along with local spices. The staff are helpful and knowledgeable.

Boutique Chocolat · CHOCOLATE

(📱 034 01 040 68; Ave Lally Tollendal; ☺8am-noon & 3-7pm Mon-Sat) Madagascar produces superb chocolate and here's a wonderful place to buy it. The exquisite creations cost around Ar10,000 for 100g.

ℹ Information

INTERNET ACCESS

Cyber-Diego (Ave Lally Tollendal, Hotel Les Arcades; 15min Ar1000; ☺8am-10pm Mon-Sat) An internet cafe in the Hotel Les Arcades complex.

MEDICAL SERVICES

Centre Hospitalier Universitaire de Place Kabary (📱 032 40 794 15; Rue Richelieu, Kabary; ☺24hr) The main hospital is located off Rue Richlieu near Pl Kabary, in the northeastern corner of town.

Pharmacie de l'Espérance (Rue Colbert; ☺7.30-noon & 2.30-6pm Mon-Sat) This prominent pharmacy is located close to Pl Foch.

MONEY

There are several banks along Rue Colbert, including **Bank of Africa** (BOA; Rue Colbert; ☺7.30-11.30am & 2.30-4.30pm Mon-Fri) and **BNI-CA** (cnr Ave de France & Rue Colbert; ☺8-11.30am & 2-4.30pm Mon-Fri), as well as a branch of **BFV-SG** (Rue Richelieu; ☺7.30-11.30am & 2-5pm Mon-Fri) on Rue Richelieu. All banks have ATMs and moneychanging facilities.

POST

The main **post office** (Pl Foch; ☺7am-3pm Mon-Sat) is on Place Foch.

TOURIST INFORMATION

Association Fanamby (📱 032 11 421 94; www.association-fanamby.org; Blvd de la Liberté; ☺8am-noon & 2.30-5.30pm Mon-Fri) Fanamby is the NGO that runs the Loky Manambato Protected Area (p175) and its Tattersalli Camp in Daraina, as well as the Camp Andrafiamena Andavakoera south of Diego Suarez. You can

NORTHERN MADAGASCAR DIEGO SUAREZ (ANTSIRANANA)

make bookings here for a visit to either of these (or book by email).

Main Tourist Office (☑ 032 04 332 20; www. office-tourisme-diego-suarez.com; Pl Foch; ⊗ 8am-noon & 3-6pm Mon-Fri) Friendly staff have booklets on what's available in Diego Suarez (Antsiranana), and maps of the city. A list of guides is on offer, too. There is a second **branch** (⊗ 8am-noon & 3-6pm Mon-Fri) at the corner of Rue Colbert and Rue Flacourt.

ℹ Getting There & Away

AIR

Diego Suarez Airport (Arrachart; N6) is served by Tsaradia – book at **Air Madagascar** (☑ 020 82 214 74; Ave Sourcouf; ⊗ 7.30-11.30am & 2-5pm Mon-Sat). It has one or two flights per day to Antananarivo (Ar451,000, two hours), two flights per week to Sambava (Ar329,000, 45 minutes) and three flights per week to Nosy Be (Ar298,300, 35 minutes). **Madagasikara Airways** (☑ 034 05 970 23, 032 05 970 04; www.madagasikaraa-irways.com; Diego Suarez airport) flies on Fridays to Antananarivo (Ar660,820).

TAXI-BROUSSE

DESTINATION	PRICE (AR)	DURATION (HR)	DEPARTURE
Ambilobe	15,000	5	All day
Ankify	25,000	9	1am
Antananarivo	74,000	28	Morning & afternoon
Joffreville	5000	1½	All day
Majunga	63,000	22	Morning & afternoon
Ramena	4000	1	All day
Sambava, dry/wet season	120,000/ 200,000	24/36	Afternoon

Costs and journey time from Diego Suarez to Sambava will change from 2021 once the new road is open from Ambilobe to Vohémar.

ℹ Getting Around

TO/FROM THE AIRPORT

Diego Suarez Airport is 6km south of the town centre. Taxis charge Ar30,000 to get from there to town.

TAXI

Taxi journeys in Diego cost a flat Ar1000 or Ar1500 at night. Tuk-tuks are Ar500, or Ar1000 at night.

Baie des Français

The road between Diego Suarez (Antsiranana) and Ramena hugs the coastline of this bay, part of the immense Baie de Diego Suarez. The sea is an ethereal aquamarine colour that contrasts beautifully with the ochres and browns of the towering Montagne des Français. Hiking on this mountain is rewarding with both stupendous views and a range of animals and birds to discover. The bay and mountain were named so in memory of the Malagasy and French forces killed in 1942 in Allied resistance to the pro-German Vichy French forces.

◉ Sights

Nosy Lonja   ISLAND

The small island of Nosy Lonja, in the middle of the Baie des Français, is known in French as Pain de Sucre (Sugar Loaf), as it resembles the much larger Sugar Loaf Mountain in Rio de Janeiro harbour in Brazil. It's off limits to foreigners and considered sacred by the Malagasy, who use it for *fijoroana* (ceremonies invoking the ancestors).

🏃 Activities

Anosiravo (☑ 034 06 739 71, 032 96 829 18; mdfanosiravo@gmail.com; Blvd Duplex, Montagne des Français; route per person Ar15,000-30,000, guide Ar15,000-20,000; ⊗ 7am-4.30pm) offers three trails so everyone can enjoy the history, plants, wide array of birds, including the drongo, and magnificent views of the bay. You can also see lemurs, chameleons and snakes. Note that it's *fady* (taboo) to answer the call of nature in the higher reaches of the mountain. A guide is obligatory and takes up to four people.

Valley of the Baobabs (1km, 35 minutes, Ar15,000, guide Ar15,000) Concentrates on these intriguing trees and aloes, and has excellent views of the bay.

Tours 360° (5.5km, 3½ hours, Ar20,000, guide Ar15,000) Medium difficulty. You'll enter the Ambohitr'Antsingy protected area to explore the vestiges of the colonial era and the French Foreign Legion. End with a climb of 650 steps to a 360-degree viewpoint.

Valley of the Parrots (8km, five hours, Ar30,000, guide Ar20,000) A more difficult but exciting trail that includes the *tsingy* (limestone pinnacle formations),

Baie de Diego Suarez

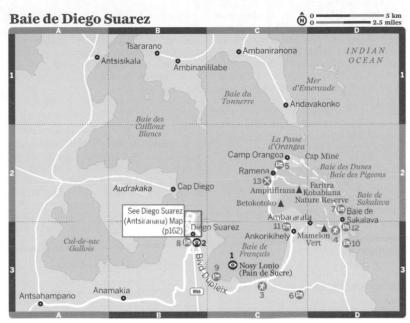

baobabs and pachypodium on the other side of the Montagne des Français. You need to be fit for this one.

🛏 Sleeping

⭐ Le Suarez ⁣ ⁣ ⁣ ⁣ ⁣ ⁣ ⁣ ⁣ ⁣ ⁣ ⁣ ⁣ ⁣ ⁣ ⁣ BOUTIQUE HOTEL €€€
(☏ 032 07 416 21/22; www.suarez-hotel.com; Blvd Duplex, Rte de Ramena; bungalows Ar236,000; ❄ 🛜 🏊) In serene countryside with fantastic views of the bay and Nosy Lonja, this boutique hotel has a gorgeous pool. The 12 bungalows have thatched roofs and red-brick-and-stone walls. Inside you'll find a breezy space with whitewashed walls and lots of local wood in the dark polished floors and four-poster beds. The children's playground is sensitively located out of the way.

Jungle Park ⁣ LODGE €€€
(☏ 032 04 724 46; www.jungle-park-nature.com/en; off Rte de Ramena; eco-dome/treehouse full board Ar360,000/280,000; ⊙ Apr-Nov; 🏊) 🌿 Built around a natural pool in the middle of a forest, the sustainable, brightly painted eco-domes are very comfortable, with their own bathroom. The wooden treehouses are more rustic and share a somewhat-smelly toilet. There's an open-air dining area and it's all solar-powered. It's a children's paradise but adults will enjoy the activities (and the massage), too.

Baie de Diego Suarez

The turn-off is 9km from Diego Suarez (Antsiranana) on the road to Ramena, and then it's a further 6km on a very rough track. A huge range of activities and excursions are on offer from kitesurfing to birdwatching, a fun activity park, cycling and archery.

Meva Plage
BUNGALOW €€€

(☑ 032 59 423 49, 034 82 073 46; www.meva plage-hotel-diego.com; Ankorikihely; d/family bungalows incl breakfast Ar280,000/400,000; [P] [❋] [🛜] [🏊]) Meva means beautiful in Malagasy, and this place certainly lives up to its name. It's right on the beach with mangroves on both sides. The bungalows are comfortably furnished with lots of local wood, and there's a pool. The restaurant has mains from Ar18,500 to Ar28,000. Should you need a new beach wrap or sunhat, there's a shop, too.

ⓘ Getting There & Away

A *taxi-brousse* from Diego Suarez (Antsiranana) will drop you at the hotel or the Anosiravo office (30 minutes, Ar2000). For Jungle Park, arrange transport with New Sea Roc (p163).

Ramena
POP 4000

Ramena, 18km northeast of Diego, has a truly beautiful beach: the sand is pale and soft, the limpid sea warm and good for swimming, and fisherfolk tinker with their boats, nets and catch.

A sleepy fishing village for most of the week, Ramena wakes up on Sundays, when seemingly half the population of Diego Suarez (Antsiranana) comes here for a knees-up on the beach: restaurants fill up for the traditional Sunday buffet and the beach at the northern end of the village becomes picnic central (complete with stereos, crates of beer and some quality dancing!).

Visiting on a Sunday is a great opportunity to partake in Malagasy fun. But staying in Ramena is also a good alternative to staying in Diego, particularly if you're after some beach time.

⭢ Sleeping & Eating

La Case en Falafy
BUNGALOW €€

(☑ 032 02 674 33; www.case-en-falafy.com; Chez Bruno; bungalows Ar70,000, mains Ar15,000-23,000; [🛜] [🏊]) One of the best-value options in the Diego Suarez area, La Case en Falafy is about 200m up the hill from the beach. It has a great bar, pool and restaurant. The thatched-roof bungalows sit in a lovely garden but have no sea views. Try for one at the back of the property – they are a bit quieter.

Badamera Park
GUESTHOUSE €€

(☑ 032 07 733 50; www.badamera.com; r Ar60,000, d/q bungalows Ar75,000/82,500; [🛜]) A few hundred metres up a hill from the beach, this popular and laid-back budget place has a stylish terrace, and a restaurant that gets good reviews for its food (the musical Sunday buffet, Ar33,000, is particularly popular). Rooms and bungalows are spread out in the exotic garden; though basic, they're clean and come with nets.

Wi-fi costs Ar3000 for 30 minutes.

Le 5 Trop Près
SEAFOOD €€

(☑ 032 07 740 60; www.normada.com/5trop; mains Ar16,000-20,000; ⊘ 8am-8.30pm Tue-Sun) Ramena is a fishing village so it's hardly surprising that seafood is plentiful. Right on the beach at Le 5 Trop Près (pronounced like St Tropez, a wink to the glitzy French Riviera town), it comes in many guises and everything is delicious. There's a buzzy, friendly vibe. It is especially popular on Sundays, when booking is recommended.

ⓘ Getting There & Away

Taxis-brousses run between Diego Suarez (Antsiranana) and Ramena (one hour, Ar4000) each day – although you sometimes have to wait a while for the vehicle to fill. Chartering a taxi is an easier option, but will cost about Ar90,000 return.

Les Trois Baies

On the eastern side of a peninsula jutting into the bay east of Diego, is a series of beautiful bays with stupendous beaches. There are many coves and inlets along this stretch of the coast, but the area is named after three majestic bays: Baie de Sakalava (Sakalava Bay), Baie des Pigeons (Pigeon Bay) and Baie des Dunes (Dune Bay). It's a wild, harsh and starkly beautiful environment, with few villages; expect strong winds from April to November and baking heat from December to March. You will need a 4WD for the sandy tracks. Hiking Les Trois Baies Circuit, which connects Baie de Sakalava (the southernmost of the three bays) to Ramena, is a rewarding excursion, with many tour operators in Diego offering it as a package. The whole peninsula is now a protected park, Faritra Kobabiana (p169), offering various trails.

🏃 Activities
Water Sports

Between December and March, when the wind has died down, swimming in the three bays is blissful: beaches are deserted and the sea is calm, with a translucent, pale turquoise colour that contrasts with the dark blue of the depths. Snorkelling is good, too. Baie des Dunes is the most sheltered of the three main bays. At the time of our visit, Baie des Pigeons was only accessible on foot or by quad.

From April to November, when the winds blow so strongly you'll struggle to retain ownership of your hat, the Baie de Sakalava is a prime kitesurfing spot. The hotels based in the bay offer equipment rental and courses and there are a few schools in the bay, too.

Readers rave about **North Mada Kite** (☑ 032 44 985 54, 034 11 225 45; www.madagascarkitesurf.com; Sakalava Bay; beginners per 1/10hr €40/340; ⊗ 8am-5.30pm) kitesurf school and its IKO-registered instructors. If you're not staying in Sakalava Bay, it will pick you up in Diego for the day. Equipment is available to hire (per day/week €60/300). Once you've learned the basics, you can have an assistant keep an eye on you (per hour/half-day €35/50). Freestyle kitesurfing is €30 per hour.

Hiking

Most of the peninsula is now incorporated into **Faritra Kobablana** (Oronjia Park; https://diegosuarez-tourisme.com/fr/la-destination/circuit-oranjia; per person Ar10,000) or Oronjia Park (or sometimes, Oranjia), for which you'll need to pay admission (Ar10,000 per person) at the gate manned by soldiers from the nearby military installation. There are various hikes you can do here. It's recommended that you either engage a guide from Sakalava village or Diego Suarez (Antsiranana; per day Ar60,000) or just hire a security guard (per day Ar40,000), as the route is not always obvious and there have been muggings in the area.

Les Trois Baies Circuit takes roughly half a day to walk from one end to the other, more if you include stops for swimming and/or a picnic. Tour operators in Diego will transfer you from Diego in a 4WD vehicle with a drop-off at Baie de Sakalava and pick-up at Ramena (or vice versa), and provide a guide and a picnic on the way.

Around the lighthouse at Cap Miné, you'll come across rusting military installations (cannons, bunkers, building ruins) dating to WWII. The cape dominates La Grande Passe, the entrance to the bay of Diego Suarez, and waves crash below the cliffs with thunderous might.

The Circuit Mamelon Vert is 3km and takes about 2½ hours. There are endemic lemurs to look out for, a number of birds and endangered trees in the forest, some of which are only found here.

Courses

Kite Alizé   KITESURFING
(☑ 032 58 216 99; www.kitealize.com; Sakalava Bay; beginner 1/10hr €45/400; ⊗ 8am-5.30pm) This kite- and windsurfing school has an IKO-affiliated instructor and four assistant instructors. They'll even train you to become an assistant instructor. As you progress, they can video your progress, and always keep in touch by radio. There's a free transfer from your hotel in Diego Suarez (Antsiranana) or Ramena.

🛏 Sleeping

**Kite Paradise
Madagascar**   LODGE €€
(☑ 032 93 781 54, 032 40 516 48; www.kiteparadise-madagascar.com; Sakalava Bay; incl breakfast yurts d/family €30/35, d with/without bathroom €40/25, bungalows €50; ⊗ mid-Mar–Nov; 🛜) 🏝 African safari-style tents, rooms with or without bathrooms and more luxurious bungalows are available in this lodge with a modern touch. Kitesurfing and windsurfing instruction and equipment are available. There's a communal dining room and lounge with musical instruments for a jam session after a windswept day.

**★ Sakalava
Lodge**   BUNGALOW €€€
(☑ 032 42 384 36; www.sakalava.com; bungalows with half board garden for 2 €66-90, seaside for 2/3/4 €110/135/160; 🛜) 🏝 The cheaper, brick garden bungalows have whitewashed walls and colourful soft furnishings. The seaside bungalows, however, are made of local materials. Both have bags of charm, and the whole place has a languid beach feel to it. It's all solar-powered and food is excellent. Kitesurfing and windsurfing rule (equipment and lessons are available), and there's a dedicated massage tent.

**Mantasaly
Resort**   RESORT €€€
(☑ 034 04 166 02, 032 03 166 02; www.mantasaly.com; Andovokonko Bay; d/tr ste incl breakfast Ar320,000/412,000, ste with sea view Ar512,000-592,000; 🅿✳🛜🏊) 🏝 South of Sakalava Bay, this beautiful resort has everything: a large pool, children's play area, good restaurant, gym, spa and sports centre offering lots of activities. Each bungalow comprises two rooms, some with air-con and some with fan. Set in the Oranjia Natural Reserve, it's on a remote beach. Solar energy powers the place and all cooking is over charcoal.

ℹ Getting There & Away

A private 4WD from Diego Suarez will cost around Ar135,000 return. The hotels will organise a transfer for you. There are no *taxi-brousses* serving Les Trois Baies.

Joffreville (Ambohitra)

POP 5000

Joffreville (Ambohitra), established in 1902, was once a pleasure resort for the French military. Today it's a sleepy but incredibly atmospheric place, with crumbling colonial buildings, ever-changing weather and gorgeous views of the valleys and mountains.

Most people use the town as a jumping-off point to visit the fabulous adjacent Parc National Montagne d'Ambre, but Joffreville also makes a brilliant base from which to explore northern highlights such as the Tsingy Rouges, Camp Andrafiamena Andavakoera, Diego, Ankarana and Les Trois Baies.

🛏 Sleeping

Monastère Saint Jean Baptiste des Benedictines de Joffreville MONASTERY €
(📞 032 04 795 24; benedictines@moov.ma; half board per person Ar90,000 for 1-3 people, Ar80,000 for 4) The eight rooms in this block have showers but share toilets, all set in a glorious garden. It's spartan and rooms are small, but it's all very clean. There are wonderful views over the mountains and bay.

The 10 sisters run a shop selling well-priced artisanal crafts that they teach the locals to make. Profits go to the community.

★Nature Lodge LODGE €€€
(📞 034 20 123 06; www.naturelodge-ambre.com; d bungalows Ar342,000; 🛜) 🍴 A couple of kilometres north of Joffreville, this ecolodge boasts magnificent views of the valley and lovely wooden safari-lodge-style cottages. The interiors are chic, with colourful batiks, original sculptures and raffia matting on the walls, and have great bathrooms. Meals are served in the large thatched dining room and bar (menu Ar60,000). It's solar-powered and they grow their own vegetables. The lodge is a 20-minute drive from the entrance to Parc National Montagne d'Ambre.

★Litchi Tree BOUTIQUE HOTEL €€€
(📞 033 03 422 72; www.thelitchitree.com; d €89; ☼May-Dec; 🛜) 🍴 Built in 1902 and once home to Marshall Joffre, this exquisite house was painstakingly restored by French owner Hervé Dumel. Its elevated position provides breathtaking views over the Suarez bay. The furniture was made locally using sustainable wood, and complements the rough-hewn walls and muted colours. Hervé produces excellent food and arranges excursions into the Montagne d'Ambre park (4km away).

ℹ Information

ELECTRICITY
There is no electricity in Joffreville; hotels generally turn on their generators from 5pm to 10pm.

MONEY
The nearest bank is in Diego Suarez (Antsiranana).

ℹ Getting There & Away

The road from Diego Suarez (Antsiranana) is in bad condition. It is easy to catch a *taxi-brousse* to Joffreville (Ar5000, two hours) from Diego. Vehicles depart from the Gare Routière behind the Jovenna petrol station. It is unlikely you'll find a vehicle back to Diego after 4pm. You can also take a tuk-tuk from Diego (Ar80,000). A private taxi will set you back Ar100,000.

Parc National Montagne d'Ambre

This wonderful **national park** (www.parcs-madagascar.com/aire-protegee/parc-national-montagne-dambre; permits per day Ar55,000, guides Ar50,000-100,000; ☉ticket office 8am-4pm Mon-Fri, to noon Sat) is literally a breath of fresh air from the arid northern plains: at 1000m, it is generally 10°C cooler than in Diego Suarez (Antsiranana) or Ankarana, even more in winter, and its luxuriant forests could not contrast more with the mineral beauty of the lower grounds.

For visitors, the park provides lovely walks in gorgeous forests, with plenty of waterfalls and lakes to rest by. The summer season (December to April) is best for seeing reptiles and amphibians, but birdwatching and views from the summit are better in winter. One day is enough to get a good sense of what the park and the wildlife are like, and two days will give you time to trek to the summit and discover many of the lakes and waterfalls which dot the park.

🏃 Activities

Hiking

There are six hiking trails in Montagne d'Ambre, ranging from easy one-hour walks to more strenuous eight-hour treks. Many can be combined to tailor your own circuit: ask your guide to recommend the best itinerary.

Highlights include the Voie des Mille Arbres (Path of a Thousand Trees), a majestic alley planted with tall exotic species (Montagne d'Ambre was an important research centre for forestry and tree plantations during the 20th century); the Petit Lac, a small crater lake also known as Lac de la Coupe Verte; and Cascade Antankarana, a beautiful waterfall flowing into a tranquil pool surrounded by fern-covered cliffs. Nearby is the path known as Jardin Botanique, a forest track lined by orchids, palms, lianas and bromeliads. Not far away, another trail leads to the small Cascade Sacrée, a sacred waterfall where locals often make offerings.

A longer track leads to the viewpoint over Cascade Antomboka (or Grande Cascade), a narrow waterfall that plunges 80m into a forest grotto.

The summit of Montagne d'Ambre (Amber Mountain; 1475m) is reached via an 11km trail heading south from the park entrance. From the campsite at Grand Lac, it's a relatively easy three- to four-hour hike, and it's less than an hour from the base to the summit. On clear days (sadly, a rare event), there are wonderful views of the lush forests. Just below the summit is Lac Maudit, where local fady (taboo) prohibits swimming, and to the southeast is the larger Grand Lac, where you are allowed to camp.

Wildlife Watching

Of the seven species of lemur found in the park, the most notable are the crowned lemur and Sanford's lemur. Others include the rufous mouse lemur, the dwarf and northern sportive lemurs, the aye-aye (rarely seen) and the local Montagne d'Ambre fork-marked lemur. Among other mammals, the ring-tailed mongoose is probably the most frequently observed.

Reptile and amphibian life thrives in the park's humid conditions, and Montagne d'Ambre is where you'll find the diminutive Brookesia chameleon, the world's smallest. It lives in leaf litter and you'll need your guide's well-trained eyes to find it.

🛏 Sleeping

Gîte d'Etape & Campsite   CAMPSITE €
(☑ 032 49 925 54, 032 41 646 06; www.parcs-madagascar.com; Station des Roussettes; cabins per person Ar10,000, camping per tent with/without cover Ar4000/2000) Run by the park, this cabin has a kitchen and a sitting area. It's located at the Station des Roussettes near the Cascade Sacrée, in a beautiful clearing.

The campsite is also here if you'd prefer to pitch a tent. Bring all your own provisions. Bookings are via the national park headquarters.

ℹ Information

The park's **headquarters** (☑ 032 41 646 06, 032 49 925 54; www.parcs-madagascar.com; ⊘ 8am-4pm Mon-Fri, to noon Sat), at the park entrance, 4km southwest of Joffreville, can help with information, permits and compulsory guides. Most guides speak French and English, and some German and Italian.

ℹ Getting There & Away

The park entrance is about 4km southwest of Joffreville. There are no taxis-brousses from Joffreville to the entrance so if you don't have a private vehicle, you'll have to walk. A chartered taxi for the day from Diego Suarez (Antsiranana) costs Ar160,000 and drivers prefer to take only two people as there's a sharp incline that's a tough climb.

Réserve Spéciale Ankarana

Réserve Spéciale Ankarana (www.parcs-madagascar.com/aire-protegee/reserve-speciale-ankarana; entry permit per day Ar65,000; compulsory guides Ar50,000-90,000) is a striking and

ℹ RÉSERVE SPÉCIALE ANKARANA

Best time to visit June to December, when both the eastern and western parts of the park are accessible (the west is cut off in the wet season).

Key highlights Dark-grey tsingy (limestone pinnacle formations) and magnificent caves.

Wildlife Bats, birds and lemurs.

Habitats Dry deciduous forest.

Gateway town Mahamasina.

Transport options Taxi-brousse (bush taxi) to Mahamasina (between Ambilobe and Diego), or private vehicle.

Things you should know Most lakes and rivers are sacred in Ankarana, so bathing and swimming are not permitted. Bring a torch for visiting the caves. Guides are compulsory.

undeveloped fantasy land that's home to uniquely Malagasy sights: astonishing fields of spiky *tsingy* (limestone pinnacle formations) sitting next to dry forests. Running through and under the *tsingy* are hidden forest-filled canyons, caves and subterranean rivers.

The park is famed for its bat-filled grottoes and mysterious caves steeped in legend and history, where the Antakarana (the predominant tribe in northern Madagascar) took refuge from the Merina (the traditional ruling elite from the highlands) during the 18th-century tribal wars.

◉ Sights

Ambohimalaza   VIEWPOINT
This plateau has surprising views: you can see Ambilobe in the west, and even the islands of Nosy Be and Nosy Mitsio in the Mozambique Channel. From the highest point, the whole of the northern region of the Ankarana park can be seen as well as Montagne d'Ambre itself. The hike takes four to five hours and is fairly easy except for a steep ascent. Birds of prey including the harrier hawk and the peregrine falcon hunt over the plateau.

Tourelles   LANDMARK
(Turret Tsingy) Reaching this turret-shaped *tsingy* will take about three to four hours and is an easy walk. You will need to cross a small river during the wet season. Walking through the turret-shaped *tsingy* allows you to study its formation and the plants that live here. Along the trail is an enormous baobab tree. Look out for the rare-crested coua bird as well as the northern sportive lemur.

Boucle Benavony   LANDMARK
(Big Tsingy of Benavony) Getting here will take about seven hours of quite difficult hiking over the *tsingy* (limestone pinnacle formations) itself. But the landscape is the reward, as is the underground cave of Benavony which has impressive stalactites and stalagmites. Suspension bridges here joining two canyons provide good views over the area. Lemurs inhabit the region as well as fossa.

Tsingy Meva   LANDMARK
(Beautiful Tsingy) This *tsingy* extends from the northern part of Ankarana and into the southern part of the Parc National de Montagne d'Ambre. It's a two to three hour hike. Here you can actually touch the *tsingy* and get a good idea of the plants that grow here, such as pachypodiums and euphorbias.

Tsingy Rary   LANDMARK
The hike here takes three to four hours and is not difficult. Here you notice the difference between the limestone and volcanic rocks. Birds to look out for include the crested ibis and the ground-dwelling, white-breasted mesite.

Perte des Rivières   LANDMARK
(Lost Rivers) A massive rock chasm into which three of the park's rivers plunge during the rainy season (they emerge 20km later in the Mozambique Channel). It's an easy one to two hours' walk and suitable for combining with other landmarks. There are remarkable views over the landscape from the Ampasambazaha viewpoint. You will also see baobab trees along the trail.

Grotte d'Andrafiabe   CAVE
Andrafiabe takes about five hours to reach from the western entrance to the park and is moderately difficult. Both the underground cave and the 'cathedral' have interesting stalactites and stalagmites. There is an opening in the ceiling of the cathedral where the sun shines through. Eleven species of bat live here as well as lemurs, birds and reptiles.

Grotte Squelette   CAVE
(Skeleton Cave) This cave can be reached in about two to three hours of hiking. It gets its name from the skeleton of a local warrior that was found in the cave. There are impressive dripstone formations, and lots of vegetation in the canyon. You can spot lemurs, parrots, guinea fowl and geckos.

Grotte des Chauves-Souris   CAVE
(Bat Cave) The impressive Grotte des Chauves-Souris (bat) cave has superb stalactites and stalagmites, and thousands of bats (eight species, including Commerson's leaf-nosed bat, or *Hipposideros commersoni*). The cave is fairly easy to reach from the park's main entrance in two to three hours.

🏃 Activities

Ankarana is best known for its serrated, dark-grey *tsingy* (the word means 'walking on tiptoes') and its caves, and there are a variety of circuits taking in the highlights. The *tsingy* is home to various lemurs, including Sanford's brown, crowned and northern sportive lemurs, as well as at least 50 species of mollusc including enormous snails, plus frogs, birds and lots of scorpions. Bats inhabit the caves, as well as Nile crocodiles hiding from hunters.

NORTHERN MADAGASCAR RÉSERVE SPÉCIALE ANKARANA

Réserve Spéciale Ankarana

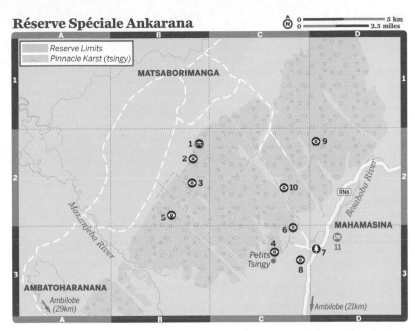

The park is split in two halves, which are distinct and not easily linked, so plan on a minimum of two days to visit both sides. There are several circuits that start at the park entrance in Mahamasina.

Eastern Half

Petit (small) circuits (two to three hours, guide Ar50,000) One circuit covers the Perte des Rivières, the Tsingy Rary and Tourelles. The other circuit includes the Grotte des Chauves-Souris and the Tsingy Meva.

Moyen (medium) circuits (five to six hours, guide Ar70,000) You can choose either to cross the rope bridge and visit the Perte des Rivières and the Tsingy Rary, or visit Ambohimalaza, the Grotte des Chauves-Souris and the Tsingy Meva.

Grand (long) circuits (up to nine hours, guide Ar90,000) include the following: Boucle Benavony, Tsingy Rary and the Perte des Rivières; and Rope bridge, Grotte des Chauves-Souris, Perte des Rivières and the Tsingy Rary.

Western circuit

Note that at the time of our visit, the Lac Vert circuit was closed to reconstruct pathways.

Réserve Spécial Ankarana

Western Half

The western half of Ankarana is different and only accessible from June to December. Here the focus is on three sets of caves, Grotte Squelette and Grotte d'Andrafiabe, which includes Grotte Cathédrale (Cathedral Cave), that you can visit through a subterranean circuit (if this doesn't appeal, another circuit links two of the caves via an above-ground path). There are beautiful canyons along the way teeming with vegetation, birds and animals.

🛏 Sleeping

Chez Aurélien
BUNGALOW €

(📞 032 40 630 14, 034 68 589 71; aurelien_ank@
yahoo.fr; Mahamasina; bungalows Ar40,000-
80,000) A brilliant option for independent
budget travellers, Chez Aurélien is located
right next to the park entrance on the RN6 –
perfect for those travelling by *taxi-brousse*.
Bungalows are basic and clean, and the
restaurant is excellent, with a lovely dining
room in a small thatched shelter. The *menu*
(a three-course meal with a choice of mains,
Ar25,000) is good value.

Park Headquarters Campsite
CAMPGROUND €

(camping per tent Ar5000; ⊘ office 7.30am-4pm)
With the closure of Campement du Prince,
you are allowed to camp around the Park
Headquarters where there are toilets. You
will need to bring all food and water from
Diego Suarez (Antsiranana).

★ Iharana Bush Camp
BUNGALOW €€€

(📞 032 11 062 96, Antananarivo 020 22 312 10;
www.iharanabushcamp.com; d half board per person €111, with lake view €121; ⊘ Apr-Nov; 🛜🖥)
🍃 Although not far from Ambilobe, this
gorgeous lodge is perfect for exploring Réserve Spéciale Ankarana. Wattle and daub
bungalows are widely spaced for privacy
and are beautifully appointed; each has its
own deck and some have views over a lake
and the *tsingy*.

Turn west 7.5m north of Ambilobe and
follow the (sparse) signposts along the
sandy track for 17km.

Ankaranana Lodge
BUNGALOW €€€

(📞 032 04 908 10; www.yorkpareik.wixsite.com/
ankarana-lodge-en; Mahamasina; d €94; ❄🖥)
The pool and garden are attractive, the restaurant is good (menu Ar60,000) and the
lodge is well located close to the park entrance. However, the staff are indifferent and
accommodation needs TLC. Doors don't lock
and the bedding is very poor quality. Air-con
is on from 6pm to 10pm only but there are
fans. There's no phone coverage or wi-fi.

ℹ Information

The park's headquarters is located at the
eastern entrance of the park in the village of
Mahamasina on the RN6. Entry permits and
compulsory guides must be arranged here.

There are no park offices at the western entrance of Ankarana, so make all arrangements in
Mahamasina. The western entrance is unreacha-
ble during the rainy season.

ℹ Getting There & Away

Mahamasina village is approximately 100km
southwest of Diego Suarez (Antsiranana) and
about 40km north of Ambilobe along the RN6.
The main park entrance at Mahamasina is accessible year-round and easily reached by *taxi-
brousse*; drivers can drop you off at your hotel or
at the park entrance, and you won't have problems flagging a vehicle for your onward journey.
Be aware that you'll likely have to pay the whole
Diego–Ambilobe fare (Ar15,000).

To reach the western half of the park (via the
western entrance), you'll need your own vehicle.
All tour operators in Diego Suarez (Antsiranana)
can arrange 4WD hire to Ankarana, as well as
multiday excursions or day trips from Diego.

SAVA REGION

Known for its four principal towns, Sambava,
Antalaha, Vohémar and Andapa, the isolated
Sava region sees few travellers. If you do venture east, you'll experience an unvarnished
version of Madagascar. It's certainly worth
it, with one of the country's flagship national
parks, Marojejy, and the adjacent Anjanhar-
ibe-Sud reserve that is rarely visited. Smaller
but no less interesting parks can be explored,
and village tourism takes you to the heart of
the country and its people. The coastline is
wild and untamed with little infrastructure,
but the area is economically better off than
most, thanks to the highly lucrative vanilla
bean. Visit in vanilla season (May to February) when this bean, along with spices, coffee
and coconut trees, scents the air. But come
soon: a new, improved road linking Vohémar
to the west coast could bring more tourists.

Vohémar
POP 30,000

The small town of Vohémar (Iharana) lies on
the coast and has beautiful, if wild, beaches. The town marks the start of the region
producing vanilla that stretches all the way
to Antalaha. Vohémar is a good place to stay
if you want to visit the Loky Manambato
Protected Area (p175) near Daraina, 56km
northwest. Swimming is not usually possible
along this coast because of strong currents,
but Vohémar is protected by a reef. Ask locals where it's safe to swim.

The name means 'many villages' and
you'll notice there certainly are many villages
along the coast. This area was one of the first
to be settled in Madagascar, mostly by Arabs
who traded from port to port in their dhows.

🛏 Sleeping & Eating

Le Lagon Bleu HOTEL €
(📞 032 04 396 46; Rue des Dames de France; d/bungalows Ar30,000/35,000; 🌐) Le Lagon Bleu is multifunctional: there are four rooms and one bungalow, a snack bar and a good restaurant serving Malagasy dishes (mains from Ar2400). The rooms are basic but clean and it's set in a central location. It costs an extra Ar5000 per night for air con in a couple of the rooms.

Hôtel Le Paradisia HOTEL €€
(Residence La Maison Blanche; 📞 032 50 219 57; attoumani.aboudou@orange.fr; d Ar55,000-80,000; 🅿️🛜) This large white house has four rooms in the main building all named after American cities, and modern bungalows in the grounds. Rooms are modern and white with black accents and are good value. There's a shady veranda in the garden for a cold beer, a good restaurant and it is set one block back from the beach. The dinner menu ranges from Ar16,000 to Ar20,000.

Baie d'Iharana Hôtel HOTEL €€€
(📞 032 43 806 35; www.iharana.normada.com; d Ar109,500-133,500; 🌐🛜) This hotel has a lot going for it: a stupendous location on a beautiful beach, a stylish colonial-type building set in a lush garden, and a good (if pricey) restaurant with great sea views. But rooms are drab and only ground-floor rooms have (holey) nets. And beware – sanitary-ware in the bathrooms is not actually fixed to the floor.

ℹ Information

BNI Bank (RN5A; ⊘7.30-11.30am & 2.30-4.30pm Mon-Fri) and **Société Générale BFV** (RN5A; ⊘8-11.30am & 2-4.30pm Mon-Fri) have branches with ATMs in the town.

ℹ Getting There & Away

The nearest airport is in Sambava (p177), 150km south. *Taxis-brousses* to Sambava (four hours, Ar10,000) run frequently.

Sambava

POP 31,520
Sambava is a pleasant town on the coast that makes a good base for exploring the whole Sava region. It's within easy reach of the Parc Nacional Marojejy (p178) and the Réserve Spéciale Anjanaharibe-Sud (p179), so is a good place to stay prior to a park visit or to recharge your batteries after a tough trek.

WORTH A TRIP

LOKY MANAMBATO PROTECTED AREA

Founded to protect flora and fauna and to support local villages, the forests of the **Loky Manambato Protected Area** (📞 Diego Suarez 032 11 421 94; www.friendlycamp.org/en/camp-tattersalli; near Daraina) **FREE** spectacularly host around 1000 critically endangered golden-crowned Tattersalli *sifakas*. This reserve is managed by the Malagasy NGO Fanamby (p165). Hire an official guide through the Friendly Camp website (www.friendlycamp) or the Fanamby office in Diego Suarez and note that they take a maximum of five people. Set out early, as the lemurs sleep during the heat of the day. Best of all, stay overnight at **Camp Tattersalli** (📞 034 02 351 66, 032 07 843 44; www.friendlycamp.org/en/camp-tattersalli; near Daraina; d incl breakfast Ar120,000, full menu Ar30,000) 🍴.

Capital of the vanilla industry, Sambava also produces cocoa, cloves, coconuts and coffee. The coastal road between Sambava and Antalaha is not only beautiful, but the air is redolent with the scent of vanilla. There is little tourism, but there are plantations to visit and some good places to stay, particularly at the beach. The beach itself is very long, and almost unoccupied, with enormous crashing waves. Take care with currents (and, some say, sharks).

⊙ Sights

Maison de la Vanille SHOWROOM
(📞 032 07 145 30; josephine.h.mac@gmail.com; RN5A, Antanifotsy I; ⊘7am-noon & 2-5pm) **FREE** In peak vanilla season (June to January), this is an interesting place to learn about processing vanilla in the large workroom at the back of the shop. It's free, but a purchase is appreciated: choose from heavenly scented vanilla beans and pretty wooden, raffia or tin boxes to store them, cloves, coffee and pepper, as well as vanilla-flavoured rum.

Soavoanio Coconut Plantation PLANTATION
(📞 020 88 966 35, 032 04 871 40; contact@soavoanio.mg; RN5A, 5km south of Sambava; Ar10,000, guide Ar5000; ⊘9am-1pm Mon-Fri) This enormous coconut plantation extends across 50 sq km, where the trees march away into

NORTHERN MADAGASCAR SAMBAVA

the distance in strict lines. On the two-hour visit you will see germination, seedlings and processing of the nuts into copra and coconut oil. Beehives produce coconut-flavoured honey. Tours are in French only, so hire a guide from the Office Régional du Tourisme de la SAVA (p177) and go with your own vehicle.

 Activities

The helpful staff at the Office Régional du Tourisme de la SAVA (p177) can organise trips to Parc National Marojejy (p178), Anjanaharibe-Sud (p179) and various other reserves, to vanilla and coconut plantations, as well as visits to village tourism projects in the Andapa region.

Sleeping

Victoria Hôtel HOTEL €
(☑ 032 21 906 19; RN5A, Ambodisatrana I; d with fan Ar40,000, with air-con Ar60,000-80,000; ❋) A no-frills hotel in town with plain, spotless rooms. Those on the street side are noisy but it's all very good value.

Mimi Hôtel HOTEL €€
(☑ 032 07 610 28; www.mimi-hotel.marojejy.com; RN5A, Analamandrorofo; r Ar45,000-50,000, bungalows Ar60,000; ☎) This is a pleasant hotel in a pretty garden setting. Rooms have fans and nets. It might not be on the beach, but the added bonus is the tearoom: Patisserie Mimi is the best place for breakfast and cakes. The owner's son, Bruno Lee, is involved with tourism in the region and can arrange all sorts of excursions.

Hôtel Las Palmas BUNGALOW €€
(☑ 032 40 073 72, 032 05 145 76; laspalmas.hotel@gmail.com; Plage des Cocotiers; bungalows/r Ar80,000/95,000; ❋☎) Las Palmas is not signposted, but is the most southerly of the beach hotels. It is a well-manicured property in a great location across from the beach, offering two rooms with great bathrooms, and some bungalows. The accommodation is spacious and comfortable. Staff rustle up some good food (mains from Ar25,000), served on the wide terrace.

★**Hôtel Carrefour** HOTEL €€€
(☑ 020 88 920 60; hotelcarrefour@yahoo.fr; Plage des Cocotiers; d with fan Ar70,000, with air-con Ar140,000, ste Ar170,000-250,000; ❋☎) Set in magnificent gardens, this hotel is the town's best. It has a colonial air with wide verandas back and front. Rooms are spacious and well appointed with great bathrooms, and face the gardens and beach. The bar serves really cold beer and the restaurant overlooks the sea (mains from Ar26,000). It will take credit cards (MasterCard or Visa) for a surcharge.

Hôtel Orchidea Beach II HOTEL €€€
(☑ 032 04 383 77; www.orchideabeach.marojejy.com; Plage des Cocotiers; d/bungalows Ar108,000/70,000; ❋☎) This charming, quiet, leafy hotel, tucked away on a pleasant side street across from the beach, has whitewashed buildings and a manicured courtyard. The brightly painted rooms have nice tiled baths (but no nets), and the amiable staff serves up excellent food (mains from Ar26,000). The two beachfront bungalows are a steal, with crashing surf right outside your door.

 Eating

Bolo Bolo Restaurant MALAGASY €
(Rue de Commerce; mains from Ar12,000; ☉10am-9pm) Cheap, cheerful, filling food that's heavy on the noodles and light on vegetables and meat. Wood-fired pizzas are on the menu too (from Ar15,000), if the oven is working. It's all quite pleasant on a wide veranda in a shady garden. Get there at 11.30am for lunch and expect an hour's wait.

Boule d'Or Restaurant & Bar PIZZA €€
(Rue de Commerce; pizzas from Ar16,000; ☉4-9pm Tue-Sun) This place does a roaring trade in tasty pizzas. But what draws the kids is the killer popcorn machine that churns out the toothsome stuff at Ar1000 a bag.

ℹ **Information**

INTERNET ACCESS
Internet access is available at **BIC** (RN5A; 15min Ar1000; ☉7.30-noon & 2-8pm): 15 minutes Ar1000.

MONEY
The following banks all have branches with ATMs at the northern end of town:
Bank of Africa (RN5A; ☉7.30-11.30am & 2.30-4.30pm Mon-Fri)
BMOI (52 Rue de Commerce; ☉8-11.30am & 2-4.30pm Mon-Fri)
Société Générale BFV (Rue de Commerce; ☉8-11.30am & 2-4.30pm Mon-Fri)

ℹ **Getting There & Away**

AIR
Tsaradia flies from Sambava daily to Antananarivo (Ar517,100, 1½ hours). There are also weekly

WORTH A TRIP

DOMAINE D'AMBOHIMANITRA

Meaning 'hill of perfumes', the **Domaine d'Ambohimanitra** (☎032 07 411 07; RN5A; tour incl lunch Ar90,000) produces various types of vanilla on its 60 hectares along with cinnamon, *ravintsara*, allspice and cloves. On a 2½-hour visit you will learn about production and processing and get to plant a vanilla vine. Lunch at the gracious colonial farmhouse is included. Tours are in English. Book two or three days in advance. Minimum of two participants.

flights to Diego Suarez (Antsiranana; Ar320,000, 45 minutes). Book at the **Air Madagascar** (☎020 88 920 37; RN5A; ⊙8am-noon & 2-6pm Mon-Sat) office. **Madagasikara Airways** (☎034 05 970 24, 032 05 970 15; www.madagasikara airways.com; Sambava airport; ⊙8am-noon & 2-6pm Mon-Sat) has one flight per week to Antananarivo (Ar660,820).

Sambava Airport (RN5A) is about 2km south of town. A taxi into town is Ar10,000.

TAXI-BROUSSE

- *Taxis-brousses* to Antalaha (Ar5,000, one hour) depart from the southern taxi-brousse station in the market.
- The northern taxi-brousse station handles transport (Ar7000, two hours) to Parc National Marojejy (p178); Andapa (Ar10,000, three hours); Vohémar (Ar10,000, three hours); Ambilobe (Ar100,000, 13 hours) and Diego Suarez (Antsiranana; Ar120,000, 24 hours).
- A private car to Andapa will cost you Ar90,000; buying the two front seats in a *brousse* is a far less expensive while still a comfortable proposition.

Getting Around

A taxi or tuk-tuk around town costs Ar1000. The fare doubles if you ask to be taken anywhere off the main road, such as to the beachside hotels.

To explore the region, visit plantations or the Loky Manambato Protected Area (p175), there are a couple of car-hire companies in town such as **Nord-Est Location** (☎032 07 145 36, 034 07 145 36; voromailala208@gmail.com; Ambodisatrana II; 4WD with driver per day excl fuel Ar200,000). It's best to hire a guide from the **Office Régional du Tourisme de la SAVA** (☎034 63 747 30, 032 67 487 76; www.tourisme-sava.com; RN5A, Analamandrorofo, Kiosque Artisanal chez, Mimi Hotel; ⊙8am-noon & 2.30-5.30pm Mon-Fri, in season 8-11am Sat), too, as tours are mostly in French, and drivers usually don't speak English. Drivers also become less informative as the day wears on and they start to chew *khat* (leaf chewed as a stimulant).

Andapa

POP 20,800

The small town of Andapa lies in a beautiful valley surrounded by lush rice paddies, fields of coffee beans and the high peaks of the Marojejy massif. It is the nearest base for exploring both the Parc National Marojejy (p178) and the Réserve Spéciale Anjanaharibe-Sud (p179). Between these two major parks lies the smaller Réserve National d'Antanetiambo. But you don't have to be planning a serious expedition into the parks: around the town are cool, shady forest walks and there are bicycles to hire to explore the villages.

Sights

Réserve National d'Antanetiambo NATURE RESERVE
(☎Désiré Rabary 032 89 959 65, Julien Bedimasy 032 54 513 23; www.antanetiambo.marojejy.com; Matsobe Sud; entry per person Ar30,000, guide Ar40,000; ⊙8am-4pm) Just 6km north of Andapa, this reserve is supported by the Lemur Conservation Foundation and run by Désiré Rabary. You can spot northern bamboo lemurs and mouse lemurs in the forest and a multitude of birds in the wetlands, ride a pirogue on the river or hire a bike (Ar5000) for riding through the rice fields. A taxi from Andapa costs around Ar15,000.

Village Tourism VILLAGE
(☎034 63 747 30, 032 67 487 76; www.tourisme-sava.com; Ambodimanga; 2 people for 1/2/3 days Ar760,000/1,290,000/1,630,000) Ambodimanga village, 10.5km south of Andapa, is one of several villages participating in this project. Help with agricultural chores, watch dancing, learn to cook rice Malagasy-style and generally take part in village life. You can also stay in a traditional house. Contact the Office Régional du Tourisme de la SAVA in Sambava to book a stay.

Sleeping

Hôtel Riziky BUNGALOW €
(☎032 40 214 22; http://riziky.marojejy.com/Riziky_e.htm; bungalows Ar30,000-40,000; P ᯤ) The six bungalows here are clean and bright and come with bathroom and TV. Two of the bungalows sleep four people. Breakfast (Ar9000) includes honey from their own hives, and there are meals on request. The

owner can arrange excursions to local villages and has bikes for hire (per day Ar20,000 to Ar25,000).

Hotel Beanana HOTEL €€

(☏ 032 07 161 13, 020 88 070 47; www.beanana. marojejy.com; d Ar52,000; P 🖥) An excellent choice in Andapa is this surprising bright-white drive-in hotel; it's clean and inexpensive. The 10 bungalows have hot water, mosquito nets and fans, and it's a very friendly place. There's a flowery garden and a pleasant courtyard. Breakfast is Ar9000 and meals are provided on request.

❶ Information

Bank of Africa (⏰ 7.30-11.30am & 2.30-4.30pm Mon-Fri) Branch with an ATM in town.

❶ Getting There & Away

The regional airport is at Sambava (p177). Tsaradia flies daily from Antananarivo (Ar517,100, 1½ hours). There are also weekly flights to Diego Suarez (Antsiranana; (Ar320,000, 45 minutes). Book at Air Madagascar (p177). Madagasikara Airways (p177) flies from Antananarivo weekly (Ar660,820).

A *taxi-brousse* from the northern taxi-brousse station (p177) in Sambava to Andapa takes three hours (Ar10,000). A private taxi from Sambava to Andapa costs Ar90,000.

Parc National Marojejy

Parc National Marojejy (www.marojejy.com; entry permit per day Ar45,000) is one of Madagas-

> ### ❶ PARC NATIONAL MAROJEJY
> ....
> **Best time to visit** April and May, September to December: it's dry season, and birding is best.
>
> **Key highlight** Silky *sifaka*.
>
> **Wildlife** Massive millipedes, paradise flycatcher, mantella frog.
>
> **Habitats** Four levels of forest: low altitude, dense montane, high montane, high altitude.
>
> **Gateway towns** Sambava and Andapa.
>
> **Transport options** Taxi from Sambava (Ar10,000) or Andapa (Ar7,000).
>
> **Things you should know** A minimum four-day trek to scale the summit.

car's great undiscovered parks, a fact all the more astonishing because it is one of the best managed and easiest to get to. Consisting of over 550 sq km of pristine mountainous rainforest – an often thick, steep and root-filled jungle with numerous streams and waterfalls – it is a primordial place where the astonishing 'angel of the forest' (aka the silky *sifaka*) resides. Hiking its misty mountains offers spectacular views of the Marojejy Massif, as well as a chance to gawk at its extraordinary biodiversity, including 2000 types of plants, 147 species of reptile and amphibian, 118 species of bird, and 11 species of lemur. Hiking up Mt Marojejy will take you through four levels of forest, which further enhances the variety of experience. In 2007 the park was designated a Unesco World Heritage Site.

◉ Sights

Besides the natural wonders of the park itself, there is an excellent interpretation centre at the MNP office (p179; with signs in English), a model for parks elsewhere.

🏃 Activities

The park has a single trail ascending through three camps to the summit. The expedition is in two parts: the first a fairly gentle nature ramble and the second a rigorous climb. For the former, there is no need to go past Camp Marojejia (p179), which anyone in decent shape can reach. Beyond it you must be very fit, and prepared for cold weather.

Hiking to Camp Mantella & Camp Marojejia

While you could arrange for a ride to the park entrance, it is a beautiful walk there from the MNP office (p179) in the village of Manantenina, along a dirt road through lush mountains, small villages and rice paddies. It is 5.6km and rises from 80m to 180m.

From the park entrance, you will climb to 450m over 3.5km to Camp Mantella (p179), the first camp. You can continue for 800m to Cascade de Humbert to see the impressive waterfall.

Overnight at Camp Mantella, or go on for 2km, which will take another one to two hours, to the second camp, Camp Marojejia (p179), at an elevation of 750m. This is the best place to see wildlife, including colourful millipedes the length of your hand (a lot more enjoyable than it sounds), leaf-tailed geckos and paradise flycatchers. It is also a wonderful place to hang out, surrounded by the sounds of the forest and the rush of a nearby stream.

Climbing Mt Marojejy

From Camp Marojejia, it's just 2.1km to the third camp, Simpona, at an elevation of 1250m. This climb will take around three to four hours. Camp Simpona is the base camp for ascents to the summit. It is a very steep and strenuous climb, requiring both hands and feet as you surmount one root after another, a challenge magnified when it's wet.

The final leg to the summit, 2132m high, stretches 2km and can take four or five hours to traverse.

Expedition Costs

As well as park fees of Ar45,000 per person per day, you will need facilitators who can be hired at the MNP office. All provide an excellent service and the revenue is distributed to local communities, helping turn conservation into a winning enterprise.

➡ Guide per day Ar60,000 if you provide their food; Ar70,000 if they bring their own.

➡ Specialist tracker per day for a minimum of two to three days to make sure you see the silky *sifaka*, Ar55,000.

➡ Cook per day Ar25,000 if you provide their food; Ar35,000 otherwise.

➡ Porters per day to Camp Mantella Ar10,000; from Camp Mantella to Camp Marojejia Ar8000; from Camp Marojejia to Camp Simpona Ar10,000.

➡ Accommodation costs Ar15,000 per person per night in cabins, or Ar4000 per night per tent.

🛏 Sleeping

Camp Mantella   CABIN €
(Camp One; cabins per bed Ar15,000, camping per tent Ar4000) Located at 450m elevation in lowland forest, Camp Mantella has six well-maintained cabins for two people (wooden frames with canvas sides) and a campground. All cabins are equipped with beds and bedding, and there is a covered cooking and dining area. Cooking utensils are provided.

Camp Marojejia   CABIN €
(Camp Two; cabins per bed Ar15,000, camping per tent Ar4000) The second camp, Marojejia is found at 775m elevation at the junction between lowland and montane rainforest. It has wonderful views over the mountains and lush vegetation. There are four cabins for

two, and six camping spots. A covered cooking and dining area is provided.

Camp Simpona   CABIN €
(Camp Three; cabins per bed Ar15,000, camping per tent Ar4000) Camp Simpona is at 1250m elevation. It has two cabins for two, three camping spots and a covered cooking and dining area.

❶ Information

The **MNP office** (📋 032 58 390 96; www.marojejy.com; Manantenina; ⊘ 7am-4pm) is located 60km from Sambava, and 40km from Andapa, in the village of Manantenina, and arranges entry permits as well as guides, trackers, porters and cooks.

❶ Getting There & Away

You can fly from Antananarivo or Diego Suarez (Antsiranana) to Sambava, jump in a *taxi-brousse*, and within an hour or two you are off on a world-class trek. *Taxis-brousses* run daily between Andapa and Sambava (Ar10,000, 2½ hours), and will drop you at the park office en route.

Réserve Spéciale Anjanaharibe-Sud

Anjanaharibe, meaning 'Place of the Great God', is a rarely visited jewel of a reserve (www.anjanaharibe.marojejy.com; entry permit per day Ar45,000) of 172 sq km. It is vitally important for biodiversity conservation as it contains one of Madagascar's most diverse ecosystems thanks to its range of topography and elevation. Its waters feed the largest rice-producing area of the country, the lush Andapa Basin. The black indri is found here as well as the silky *sifaka* and white-fronted brown lemurs, and birds are legion. There are some fascinating plants such as the 'dinosaur' plant *Takhtajania perrieri,* described as a living fossil – it has been living on earth for 120 million years. Hot springs complete the picture. One of the last areas of untouched wilderness on the planet, Anjanaharibe Sud is hard going but hugely rewarding.

◉ Sights

Besides the natural wonders of the park itself, there is an excellent interpretation centre at the MNP office in Manantenina (with signs in English).

🏃 Activities

Viewing some of the rarest forest creatures, the black indri and the silky *sifaka*, is the main purpose of visiting the reserve. The 'living fossil' plant, *Takhtajania perrieri,* is a remarkable sight. There are hot springs near the camp. Hiking here is strenuous. The summit, Anjanaharibe Anivo, is not open to the public. Using Camp Indri as your base, there are two main trails.

Ranomafana Trail

Allow a full day for the Ranomafana Trail: it is only 4.3km from Camp Indri to the hot springs, but the going is quite tough. The trail passes through dense rainforest and then the small village of Andranomafana and crosses the Marolakana River before arriving at the hot springs. Some of these are too hot for comfort, but those where river water mixes with the spring are more comfortable. Locals use the springs to cure diseases. On the walk, you will most likely see white-fronted brown lemurs, and possibly indri and silky *sifakas.* Watch out for leeches.

Takhtajania Trail

The Takhtajania Trail climbs a ridge eastwards for 2½ hours from Camp Indri to a site where this primordial tree grows. Discovered in 1909 but not seen again until 1994, the tree grows to about 9m and has leathery, aromatic leaves and red flowers. You will also probably see black indris, silky *sifakas* and red-bellied lemurs. It's a moderately difficult trail through open forest and has splendid mountain views.

Expedition Costs

The entry fee is the same as for Parc National Marojejy (p178) and can also be paid at the MNP office (p179) in Mantenanina: Ar45,000 per person per day. You also need the following.

➡ Guide per day Ar60,000 if you provide their food; Ar70,000 if they bring their own.

➡ A local guide hired from Andapa or Befingotra village per day costs Ar60,000 if you provide their food; Ar70,000 if they bring their own. It's a requirement to hire this local guide.

➡ Cook per day Ar25,000 if you provide their food; Ar35,000 otherwise.

➡ Porters hired in Andasibe-Mahaverika or Befingrotra village per day Ar15,000.

Accommodation costs Ar15,000 per person per night in sheltered tents.

🛏 Sleeping

Camp Indri   CAMPGROUND €
(www.anjanaharibe.marojejy.com; tents per person Ar15,000) Built in 2015, Camp Indri has four covered tent shelters, a covered dining area, toilet and shower and running water. A covered picnic table is at the nearby river. Tents, mattresses and cooking utensils are provided. It's at 900m elevation and can be chilly. Several groups of indri live around the camp, as well as one group of silky *sifakas.*

ℹ Information

The MNP office (p179) is 60km from Sambava, and 40km from Andapa, in the village of Manantenina, and arranges entry permits as well as guides, porters and cooks.

ℹ Getting There & Away

From Andapa, you can take a *taxi-brousse* to Ambodipont (Ar10,000, 45 minutes) and then walk a further 3km to the village of Andasibe-Mahaverika, a total of about 20km. Alternatively, hire a 4WD to Andasibe-Mahaverika on a badly rutted road (Ar120,000, 1½ hours). Hire porters here.

The distance from Andasibe-Mahaverika to Camp Indri is a total of 15km; you can walk this in six hours. Or begin with a two-hour walk to the village of Befingotra where you can find lunch in a *hotely,* and hire a *moto-taxi* (motorbike taxi; per person Ar60,000, one hour) for part of the way. Porters are changed at Befingotra.

The last section of the journey is on foot for about three hours to Camp Indri.

To return, you'll have to do all this in reverse.

Eastern Madagascar

Why Go?

Eastern Madagascar is travel the way it used to be. There is a wildness here of primordial allure, from the misty mountains of Masoala, down the huge coastline with its pounding sea and overhanging palms, to the lush waterways of the Pangalanes Lakes. This part of the country is largely cut off from the rest, and from itself, by a degraded transport network, including some roads out of an engineer's nightmare. Travelling here requires a combination of plane, car, 4WD, motorbike, scooter, pirogue (dugout canoe), ferry, cargo boat, *taxi-brousse* (bush taxi) and motorboat. This inaccessibility results in isolated communities and, for the traveller, a constant sense of coming upon undiscovered locales, including entire national parks. There's no doubt it can be frustrating at times, but Eastern Madagascar produces more travellers' tales than anywhere else. If you value that, come here first.

Best Places to Eat

➜ La Véranda (p193)

➜ Chez Samson (p207)

➜ Idylle Beach (p204)

➜ Ocean 501 (p193)

Best Places to Stay

➜ Samaria (p205)

➜ Masoala Forest Lodge (p215)

➜ Libertalia (p206)

➜ Sahorana Lodge (p198)

➜ Hôtel Pangalanes Jungle Nofy (p190)

➜ Mantadia Lodge (p184)

When to Go
Tamatave (Toamasina)

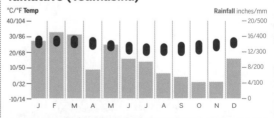

Jun–Oct Vanilla season; flights can be full in the northeast.

Jul–Sep Whale watching in the Baie d'Antongil; weather can be rough.

Dec–Mar Hold onto your hat, it's cyclone season.

Eastern Madagascar Highlights

❶ Parc National Andasibe Mantadia (p186) Waking up to the wail of the *indri*, one of Madagascar's largest lemurs.

❷ Île Sainte Marie (p199) Watching humpback whales breach and hearing them sing is a once-in-a-lifetime opportunity.

❸ Piscines Naturelles d'Ambodiatafana (p202) Sacred and stunning natural swimming pools with endless sand dunes to explore.

❹ Parc National Masoala-Nosy Mangabe (p213) Mountain rainforest tumbling into the sea and phenomenal biodiversity.

❺ Maison Blanche (p207) Enjoying breathtaking panoramic views with a sundowner on Île aux Nattes.

❻ Île aux Nattes (p207) Snorkelling, swimming and general beachcombing on this little slice of paradise.

❼ Lac Ampitabe (p189) Drifting on a solar-powered boat from Vohibola, taking in the birdlife and local folklore.

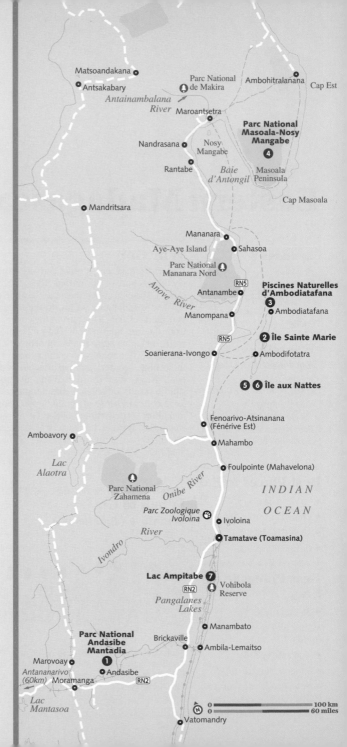

EAST OF ANTANANARIVO

This region's landscapes are gloriously diverse, from the wooded hills around Lac Mantasoa, to the major-attraction rainforest parks of Andasibe, and to the peaceful, tropical Pangalanes canals that follow the east coast. The climate is as varied as the topography. you'll need rain gear in the parks and swimwear on the coast.

Lac Mantasoa

☑ 034 / POP 10,000

This 20-sq-km artificial lake, built in 1931, is a good place for fishing, sailing and picnicking, and is a popular weekend retreat for Antananarivo residents. The hotels on the lakeside all offer boating, waterskiing, pedalos, fishing and more. The lake also holds a special place in history as being the site where Madagascar's industrial revolution started.

In 1833 Frenchman Jean Laborde built a country palace for Queen Ranavalona I, as well as carpentry and gunsmith shops, a munitions factory, an iron forge and a foundry. The primary aim was to supply the monarch with swords, arms and ammunition. Much of this was destroyed in 1851 when slaves rebelled, while other parts now lie underwater, but some notable buildings can still be seen and visited in the village of Mantasoa, offering a fascinating insight into Madagascar's heyday as an industrial powerhouse.

🛏 Sleeping

Domaine de l'Ermitage   HOTEL €€€

(☑ 020 42 660 54, 034 04 960 64; d from Ar125,000; 🖥 ⚊) This large hotel, set in beautiful gardens, has excellent facilities, with game rooms, a fireplace lounge and a host of water sports and activities (horse riding, trampolining, mountain biking etc) on offer. Though nice enough, the rooms themselves don't really equal the rest of the property. There is a very popular buffet lunch (Ar45,000) on Sunday.

ℹ Getting There & Away

Mantasoa village lies about 60km east of Antananarivo. If you're going by *taxi-brousse* (Ar3000), plan to spend the night here, as it is impossible to know whether you'll find a *taxi-brousse* heading back to Tana in the afternoon.

Moramanga

☑ 056 / POP 42,300

Running along the RN2 road, Moramanga is the largest town between Antananarivo and Tamatave on the east coast. It's an important commercial centre for local people but has little tourism value. However, you might have to pause here if you're heading to the Andasibe Parks on public transport. Take a pousse-pousse (rickshaw) around.

⊙ Sights

Musée de la Gendarmerie Nationale   MUSEUM

(Police Museum; ☑ 020 56 821 39; Camp Tristany; Ar10,000; ⊙ 8am-noon & 3-5pm Mon-Fri, 9-11am & 2-4pm Sat & Sun) Exhibits cannons, police uniforms, a vintage *taxi-brousse* and an enormous bunch of dried marijuana. There are also various traditional medicines and spells on displays.

🛏 Sleeping & Eating

Hotel Nadia   HOTEL €

(☑ 020 56 822 43; r Ar30,000) A basic budget option in the middle of the busy market, with its own cafeteria. Serviceable, but could be cleaner and the beds are as saggy as a hammock.

Bezanozano   HOTEL €€

(☑ 032 69 769 03; d from Ar80,000; ⚊) This sprawling complex is the best choice around here. The rooms are dated, but they're large and have balconies that peer down over a huge pool. The restaurant – which is about the best in town – serves Malagasy, European and Chinese fare and is where many tour groups stop for lunch.

Hôtel Restaurant Espace Diamant   HOTEL €€

(☑ 020 56 823 76; d Ar60,000) This spick-and-span hotel has a quiet garden setting and tiled rooms with big beds and a large restaurant.

Le Coq d'Or   INTERNATIONAL €

(☑ 020 56 820 45; mains from Ar12,000; ⊙ noon-3pm & 7-9pm Tue-Sat, noon-4pm Sun) A neat painted cafe off the main road, serving *soupe chinoise* (noodle soup with fish, chicken or vegetables), fried chicken and other Malagasy meals. Highly rated by locals.

ℹ Information

Regional Tourism Office (☑ 034 10 018 58; www.ortalma.org; Hôtel Bezanozano;

⊗8.30am-12.30pm & 2.30-5.30pm Mon-Fri, 8.30am-12.30pm Sat) This helpful office is located above the Bezanozano restaurant (p183), and covers Moramanga, the Andasibe Parks and Lac Alaotra.

❶ Getting There & Away

TAXI-BROUSSE

Taxis-brousses leave regularly from Antananarivo's eastern *taxi-brousse* station for Moramanga (Ar7000, 2¾ hours).

There are direct *taxi-brousse* connections from Moramanga to Andasibe (Ar2000, 1½ hours) every few hours. To get to Tamatave (Ar15,000, five to seven hours), you will need to wait until a vehicle coming from Antananarivo arrives with space.

TRAIN

At the time of research the Moramanga–Tamatave passenger train was out of action.

Andasibe

📞 056 / POP 12,000

The large village of Andasibe is surrounded by several protected forest parks and reserves whose unique, highly visible and generally very well habituated wildlife – as well as close proximity to the capital – have made this area rightfully popular with travellers. The largest park is the Parc National Andasibe Mantadia. This is actually the organisational union of two separate parks, the northern Parc National Mantadia and the much smaller Parc National Analamazaotra. To these are added Parc Mitsinjo, Réserve de Torotorofotsy and Mahay Mitia Ala (MMA). Back on the RN2 about 8km east of Andasibe lie two further parks: the Vohimana Forest and the Réserve de Maromizaha. Spend a few days in Andasibe exploring any of these parks and you are near-enough guaranteed some exciting lemur encounters.

🛏 Sleeping & Eating

MNP Campsite CAMPGROUND €

(📞033 49 402 65; camping per tent Ar10,000) Camping is available behind the Madagascar National Parks (MNP) office. One site has better toilets. You can also hire a tent (Ar10,000) if you reserve in advance.

Vohitsara Guest House GUESTHOUSE €

(📞034 60 899 69; vohitsara@hotmail.com; d/tr Ar30,000/50,000) This family-run operation,

on the edge of the village near the station, offers a varied selection of spick-and-span budget rooms with external showers and Malagasy food on request. For the rooms with the most character go for those in the old wooden building over the road from the main block.

Hôtel Les Orchidées HOTEL €

(📞020 56 832 05; hotelorchideeandasibe@yahoo.fr; d Ar50,000) An unusual place, the Hôtel Les Orchidées is the distinctive, stone building in the heart of the village. Not only does it offer very basic rooms, but it also doubles as the village nursery school, so don't expect much of a lie in and do expect to be a novel plaything for the children. With advance notice meals can be prepared.

Hôtel Feon'ny Ala BUNGALOW €€

(📞020 56 832 02, 033 05 832 02; www.feonnyala-hotel.com; s Ar48,000, bungalows s/d/f 84,000/from Ar90,000/108,000; 🛜) Whoever named this garden hotel 'Song of the Forest' was absolutely right: the site is virtually part of the forest in Parc National Analamazaotra (p186), so close that you can hear the *indris*. It always seems to be busy with a good crowd of travellers and the bar-restaurant is a convivial place to hang out.

The 60 thatched bungalows are comfortable enough and have hot showers, but unfortunately, they are so close together that you can't avoid listening in on your neighbour's conversations.

Hôtel Mikalo BUNGALOW €€

(📞034 11 817 85; s Ar62,000-72,000, d Ar72,600-94,200; 🛜) This hotel on the south side of the village has a roadside restaurant (set menu Ar25,000) that gets high marks for design, and the gardens are nice (pluck guavas straight from the tree). But sort carefully through the bungalows, which come in a variety of styles, as quality varies. It all comes across as a bit half-hearted.

★ Mantadia Lodge BOUTIQUE HOTEL €€€

(📞034 05 100 42; www.mantadialodge.com; d incl breakfast €105; ❄🛜❄) Spectacular new lodge high on a hill above Andasibe village, the 28 sharply decorated bungalows are the last word in Malagasy plush. Each has gnarled wooden floors and bed frames, dark slate tiling, cutting-edge art and weathered wooden decor. Each room has a private terrace with stunning mountain views.

Both the service and the Malagasy-French fusion food served in the restaurant are superb. Plus there's a spa and beautiful pool. Considering the quality it's great value and worth a splurge even if you're normally a die-hard budget traveller.

Andasibe Lemurs Lodge BUNGALOW €€€
(☑ 033 11 306 99, 032 11 306 99; d/bungalows Ar110,000/230,000; ✻ 🐾 🗷) A new resort-like hotel with a swimming pool that still needs a bit of time to grow into its surrounds, but otherwise it offers huge, comfortable bungalows with picture-frame jungle views or smaller, but equally comfortable rooms (cold showers only). It sits right beside the forest and you can lie in bed listening to the morning *indri* wail. The food is decent enough but the restaurant can be a bit soulless if there aren't many guests.

Andasibe Hotel LODGE €€€
(☑ 034 14 326 27; www.andasibehotel-resto.com; d/f Ar220,000/268,000; ✻ 🐾 🗷) This hotel on the west side of the village shines: it has huge rooms, with split levels, bold Asian styling and knockout views across a verdant rice paddy. The restaurant (menu Ar45,000) has creative French cuisine and there's a nice pool deck. Located on a forest lake, the hotel also offers kayaking.

Vakôna Forest Lodge LODGE €€€
(☑ 034 15 705 80, 033 02 010 01; www.hotelvakona. com; s/d incl breakfast €90/100; 🐾 🗷) This resort has everything – a lake with an island full of lemurs and a crocodile park (entry for both Ar25,000), an equestrian centre, a beautiful lodge, golf and squash, massage and a private airstrip. However, the bungalows are only average and it feels less like a safari lodge and more like a country club with animals as an amusing sideshow.

Be aware of the location 7km north of Andasibe: it's a long hike from the park office and you will probably opt for a transfer (Ar40,000).

❶ Information

There's no overall tourist information office for the Andasibe parks but guides are usually knowledgeable about the practicalities of visiting any of the parks as are some hotel staff.

For information specifically concerning the Parc Mitsinjo (p187), talk to the staff at the Association Mitsinjo (p187). For background information on the Vohimana Forest (p188) contact the French-Malagasy NGO **L'Homme et l'Environ-**nement (MATE, Man & the Environment; www. madagascar-environnement.org).

❶ Getting There & Away

From Tana, the best way to reach Andasibe is to take a *taxi-brousse* to Moramanga first, then another to Andasibe (Ar2500, one hour). Ask the driver to drop you at your hotel. Otherwise, you can take any *taxi-brousse* along the RN2 for 26km to the Andasibe junction at Antsapanana, then walk or hitch the 3km to the village itself.

If you're leaving Andasibe, you either have to return to Moramanga first, or wait for a *taxi-brousse* on the RN2. This can be difficult going east as *brousses* from Tana tend to be full. If you hire a car or taxi from Tana, keep in mind that you'll have to leave by 6am in order to hear the *indris*.

At the time of research the Moramanga–Tamatave passenger train was out of action

Parc National Andasibe Mantadia

☑ 056

Almost every visitor to Madagascar spends time at the Parc National Mantadia and for good reason. The thick, humid mountain rainforests of this park are filled with the hooting, grunting and wailing of 11 different species of lemur including the fabled *indris*. Many of the lemurs here are so well habituated to human visitors that they barely bother er to acknowledge approaching people. This makes for some wonderful wildlife encounters. This Unesco-protected area comprises

---

❶ PARC NATIONAL ANDASIBE MANTADIA

Best time to visit October to November when orchids are blooming.

Key highlight *Indris.*

Wildlife Diademed *sifaka,* Parson's chameleon, leaf-tailed gecko, paradise flycatcher.

Habitat Primary and secondary mid-altitude rainforest.

Gateway towns Andasibe.

Transport options *Taxi-brousse* or car.

Things you should know Parc National Analamazaotra can get very busy. Head to Mantadia or one of the other nearby parks for a quieter wildlife experience.

Andasibe Area Parks

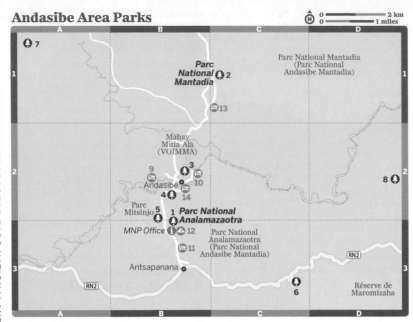

Andasibe Area Parks

two distinct parks. More accessible and fairly flat for easy walking is the 8-sq-km Parc National Analamazaotra, with its entrance and large information centre on the main road to Andasibe. Some 17km to the north lies the wilder, primary forest of 155-sq-km Parc National Mantadia. This is harder terrain but worth the effort.

◉ Sights

★**Parc National
Analamazaotra**   NATIONAL PARK
(Périnet; www.parcs-madagascar.com; entry permit per day adult/child Ar45,000/25,000; ⊙ticket office 6am-4pm) ✿ This is the most popular park within Parc National Andasibe Mantadia. The real draw of this reserve is the rare *indri*, Madagascar's largest lemur, whose unforgettable wail can be heard emanating from the misty forest throughout the day, most commonly in the early morning. There are about 60 resident family groups of two to five *indris* each.

In addition to the *indris*, you may also see woolly lemurs, grey bamboo lemurs, red-fronted lemurs, black-and-white ruffed lemurs and diademed *sifakas* (one of the largest lemur species). In 2005 the Goodman's mouse lemur was discovered here and identified as a distinct species. Eleven species of tenrec, the immense and colourful Parson's chameleon and seven other chameleon species are also found here. Over 100 bird species have been identified in the park, together with 20 species of amphibian. The park is also home to the endemic palm tree *Ravenea louvelii*, found nowhere else on the island.

Because the reserve is small, most of it can be covered in short walks, including two small lakes, Lac Vert (Green Lake) and Lac Rouge (Red Lake).

There are four organised walking trails, all of which are generally easy going. The easiest, most popular trail is the Circuit Indri 1 (for four Ar40,000, about two hours), which includes the main lakes and the territory of a single family of indris. The moderate Circuit Indri 2 (Ar50,000, three hours) visits the lakes and encompasses the patches of two separate families.

The Circuit Aventure (for four Ar60,000, four to six hours) does all of the above, plus some more strenuous walking. Join these circuits together for an 8km trail of about six hours. The Palmier Circuit (2km, one to two hours) is specially designed for children and takes in palms, orchids and two *indri* families.

The best time for seeing (and hearing) *indris* is early in the morning, from 7am to 11am. The park tends to fill up from July to October, Madagascar's tourist high season.

★ **Parc National Mantadia**   NATIONAL PARK
(www.parcs-madagascar.com; entry permit per day adult/child Ar45,000/25,000; ☺ 6am-5pm) Part of the Parc National Andasibe Mantadia, this park is about 17km north of Andasibe. Created primarily to protect the *indri*, Mantadia also hosts the black-and-white ruffed lemur. A quiet, beautiful area with numerous waterfalls and wonderful landscapes, it is undeveloped and seldom visited com-

pared to its popular neighbour to the south, so if you're here in high season it's well worth the detour to escape the crowds.

Established circuits include the easy 1km Circuit Rianasoa to see *indris*, orchids and a natural pool where you can swim (Ar40,000, one hour). This can be combined with the Sacred Waterfall for a 2km, two-hour moderate walk with some steep slopes (Ar80,000). There's also the moderately hard Circuit Tsakoka (Ar70,000, three hours), which is especially good for seeing frogs, birds and plants, and the Trekking Circuit (Ar100,000, 10 hours), a difficult trail of 15km, offering diverse altitudes and superb landscapes. If the weather has been wet (which it often is), watch out for leeches on the trails.

Permits and guides can be obtained at the MNP office (p188) in Parc National Analamazaotra. You'll need all your own camping equipment if you're planning to stay the night; the MNP campsite (tent sites free), just outside the park, has no facilities. To get to Mantadia from the MNP office, you will most likely need your own vehicle (Ar150,000 from Andasibe) or bicycle.

Parc des Orchidées   NATURE RESERVE
(Ar20,000; ☺ 7.30am-noon & 1.30-4pm) **FREE**
This little park is at its most attractive in October to December when the orchids are in bloom. By late summer it's almost completely dried up. There's no signage so you need a good guide to fully appreciate it. Even if the orchids aren't blooming the park is a good place to spot chameleons; in particular the dinosaur-like Parson's chameleon.

It's found on the main road between the MNP office (p188) and Andasibe.

WORTH A TRIP

PARC MITSINJO

Located on the main road opposite the MNP office (p188), **Mitsinjo** (Andasibe; Ar45,000) is a private reserve run by **Association Mitsinjo** (☎ 034 39 271 00; www.association mitsinjo.wordpress.com; Andasibe; ☺ 7am-9pm), set up by guides to promote conservation and community tourism. It's a great idea to add this to your itinerary before or after visiting Parc National Mantadia.

There are three circuits: a short circuit (guide per person Ar30,000), a medium circuit (Ar40,000) and a long circuit (Ar60,000). An excellent night hike within the actual forest (1½ hours, Ar20,000) gives you a much better chance of seeing the smaller nocturnal lemurs, sleeping chameleons and rare leaf-tailed lizards. You can also visit the reforestation area and plant a tree (one to two hours, Ar30,000); there's no separate entry fee. The Accrobranche (zipline) through the forest canopy was out of action at the time of research, but staff hope to get it up and running again during 2020.

For more information visit Mitsinjo's small handicrafts shop next to the Parc Mitsinjo office.

RESERVE DETOURS

Réserve de Torotorofotsy (Ar80,000) A varied and attractive landscape of wetlands, forests and small villages, this private reserve is known for its greater bamboo lemurs and excellent birdwatching. A visit here to see the birds, and perhaps the golden mantella frog, costs Ar80,000 per person for four to five hours.

Like Parc Mitsinjo 12km south, Torotorofotsy is managed by Association Mitsinjo (p187). Information is available at its handicrafts shop next to the Parc Mitsinjo office.

Mahay Mitia Ala (VOIMMA; Andasibe; ⊙6am-5pm) The Mahay Mitia Ala (VOIMMA) park, opened in 2011, is managed by a local association to promote biodiversity, conservation and local development. The species found here are the same as in nearby parks, including the indri and the elusive aye-aye. The main benefit of this park is accessibility. The trails are clear and wide, allowing better views of wildlife, and there are no steep hills such as exist elsewhere. The park is generally quieter than similar local parks.

Réserve de Maromizaha (Anevoka; Ar25,000) If you want real unadulterated wilderness then the Réserve de Maromizaha is what you're looking for. This 100-sq-km ecotourism reserve, about 8km southeast of the Parc National Mantadia (p187) is more the preserve of scientists and researchers than tourists and it offers a genuine wilderness experience. The area is home to 14 somewhat elusive and only partially habituated lemur species, including diademed *sifakas* and black-and-white ruffed lemurs, both of which are also found at Parc National Mantadia.

Vohimana Forest (Ar25,000) Established as a private reserve in 2001, this crucial 1.6-sq-km corridor links the Andasibe area parks with the forests of the south. At present facilities include around 20km of walking trails, from two hours to three days in length, taking in lemurs, birds and the pointy-nosed *Columma gallus* chameleon (not found elsewhere). There are no set guiding fees but expect to pay Ar60,000 for a half-day circuit.

❶ Information

The **MNP office** (⊙6am-4pm) for Parc National Andasibe Mantadia is located at the entrance of the Parc National Analamazaotra and contains a helpful interpretation centre. Entrance permits and guides are available here. The office also sells an informative booklet (Ar5000).

❶ Getting There & Away

Depending on where you're staying you could walk from your accommodation to the park gate. Otherwise ask staff at your accommodation to organise a car transfer.

Brickaville

🎵 058 / POP 190,000

Brickaville is a hot, sticky and ramshackle transit point between Antananarivo and Tamatave. It's also the main access town for the Pangalanes Lakes. With accommodation in the town being very basic it's best to try and get here early enough so that you don't end up stuck here for the night.

If you do, **Hôtel Capricorne** (d Ar35,000), on the main road, has fairly grotty rooms with en suite bathrooms that will pass muster. Staff are not used to foreigners.

❶ Information

BOA Bank (⊙1-4.30pm Mon, 8-11.45am & 2-6pm Tue-Fri) With ATM, on the main street.

❶ Getting There & Away

The taxi-brousse station is a short way north of the town centre on the main road. There are *taxis-brousses* from Moramanga (Ar12000, three hours), Antananarivo (Ar15,000, 5½ hours), Andasibe (Ar10,000, 2½ hours) or from Tamatave (Ar7000, 1½ hours).

PANGALANES LAKES

The Pangalanes Lakes are one of Madagascar's lightly visited natural wonders, where half the fun is getting around. Travel here is done largely by long, narrow metal canal boats, which ply the waters from end to end, leaking all the while. Cruising in this placid freshwater network is a fascinating journey through time and history, not to mention luxuriant vegetation.

In the villages of the Betsimisaraka people, traditional life goes on as ever. People cast nets, paddle by in pirogues (dugout canoes), dry eels in the sun and invariably wave a greeting. Fishing weirs appear at intervals, like gates across the waterway. The lakes themselves are picturesque, with nice beaches and no development apart from a handful of beach bungalows. With just a long and very narrow outer beach separating the lakes from the Indian Ocean, a brief walk takes you from placid waters to tempestuous sea.

Lac Ampitabe (Akanin'ny Nofy)

With an interesting village to visit, several fine hotels (including some well-hidden budget options), good lake and ocean beaches and two private reserves – one of which offers super-up-close lemur encounters while the other protects a patch of Madagascar's fast vanishing coastal forest, Lac Ampitabe well rewards anyone who makes the effort to get out here.

The lake is only accessible only by boat.

⊙ Sights

Vohibola Forest   NATURE RESERVE

FREE Vohibola is one of the last pieces of littoral forest in the country. There are three rewarding hiking trails and you might even get to see the *Calumma vohibola*, a chameleon discovered only in 2009. There's no entry fee, but guides cost around Ar5000 for a two-hour walk. Organise these through Chez Nolah (p190) in Andranokoditra village.

Palmarium Reserve   NATURE RESERVE

(Ankanin'ny; ☑ 033 14 847 34; Ar25,000; ☉ dawn-night) Very popular with tour groups, this private reserve is touted by some tour companies as 'the best place to photograph lemurs'. That might well be true because the representatives of the seven different lemur species (two of which are actually crossbreeds) found here are all incredibly tame. The whole experience is rather contrived with some species not even being native to this area and the forest itself is more of an extended hotel garden. That said, it's fun!

You can also do a night visit (Ar85,000) to a small island which is home to a couple of habituated aye-ayes.

Note that residents of the Palmarium Hotel (p190) get free entry to the reserve and pay Ar75,000 for the aye-ayes.

Andranokoditra   VILLAGE

The village of Andranokoditra is a popular half-day destination with tour groups staying at nearby lakeside hotels. It's an interesting enough little fishing village but the flow of tourists means you can expect to be trailed around by people trying to sell handicrafts and jewellery. It's a base for canal trips and the hiking trails in Vohibola.

𝕋 Activities

Solar-Powered Boats   BOATING

Environmentally friendly solar-powered boat trips through the lakes and canals can be organised through Chez Nolah (p190) in

---

THE DEAD ZONE

With the exception of Manakara, the southeast coast of Madagascar is basically a dead zone for travellers, unless you want pure 4WD adventure. Heading south from Brickaville, Vatomandry, Mahanoro and Nosy-Varika offer virtually no sights or attractions, with the exception of some waterfalls. In Mananjary the beach is used as a latrine and the market floods in heavy rains. After Manakara, the RN12 is paved as far as the frontier town of Vaingaindrano, and easily traversed save for a 30km stretch of unpaved road north of Farafangana. However, the unpaved 220km between Vaingaindrano and Fort Dauphin (Taolagnaro) is notoriously treacherous and should only be attempted in dry season with a trustworthy 4WD. The route contains 10 ferry crossings, five motorised and five hand-powered, and two nature reserves. Parc National Midongy du Sud, located 100km inland of Vaingaindrano, requires a difficult trip through dense jungle, and is only for specialists. Réserve Spéciale Manombo, 30km south of Farafangana, is the only worthwhile stop, home to a patch of coastal forest and the rare white-collared brown lemur. Swimming is dangerous along the entire coastline due to sharks and strong currents. If you do want to attempt the route allow at least two full days of travelling – when conditions are in your favour!

Pangalanes Lakes

Tamatave
(Toamasina)
(50km)

Vohibola
Forest

Lac
Ampitabe
Andranokoditra

Lac
Irangy

Lac
Rasoamasay

RN2

Lac
Rasobe

Manambato
4WD Track

Lac
Anjaraborona

INDIAN
OCEAN

Moramanga

Brickaville

Ambila-
Lemaitso

Pangalanes Lakes

the village of Andranokoditra. It's a wonderful, peaceful way to explore the region and there's plenty of time for birdwatching. Prices depend on the length of trip.

🛏 Sleeping

Chez Nolah
HUT €

(☑ 034 74 428 47, 034 16 308 31; d Ar20,000) If you want a real village immersion then this simple, family-run place has six thatch huts in the middle of Andranokoditra village. Each hut has a couple of beds with mosquito nets and there are shared bucket showers and toilets. The welcome is warm and meals cost Ar15,000.

★ Hôtel Pangalanes Jungle Nofy
BUNGALOW €€€

(☑ 034 47 931 58, 034 72 343 77; www.hotel pangalanes-junglenofy.com; d/family bungalows from Ar130,000/150,000; 🐾) The 10 massive and comfortable bungalows here are built into and around the trees and front an exquisite white-sand beach (albeit one with a few reed patches growing in the shallows). Check out the massive crocodile skulls mounted on the wall of the attractive thatch-roof beach bar and terrace restaurant (three-course meal Ar35,000).

Bush House
BUNGALOW €€€

(☑ 033 12 441 27, 020 22 248 47, 034 51 455 55; www.boogiepilgrim-madagascar.com/bush-house-pangalanes-channel-hotel; d bungalows from Ar132,000) 🌿 Of all the lakeside lodges, Bush House has the choice location in the heart of a sandy bay. The quality bungalows with cheery porches have an elevated location that affords views across the lake, with stairs winding down to the beach. There's also a hilltop viewpoint from where you can see the interesting landscape of lakes, peninsula and sea.

Activities are well managed, with lots of options; free kayaks are a plus. Bush House is accredited by Fair Trade in Tourism. Three-course menus cost Ar40,000.

Palmarium Hotel
BUNGALOW €€€

(☑ 034 13 934 21, 034 17 729 77; www.palmarium. biz; s/d/family bungalows Ar150,000/180,000/225,000) The Palmarium Hotel is adjacent to the private Palmarium Reserve (p189) on Lac Ampitabe and is accessible only by boat. The bungalows are expensive at this package-tour destination and they lack much privacy, but the lemurs that crash dinner

CANAL DES PANGALANES

The Canal des Pangalanes is one of the quiet wonders of Madagascar, a collection of natural and artificial waterways that stretches over 645km along the east coast from Foulpointe to Farafangana. It was constructed between 1896 and 1904, during the French colonial period, in an effort to create a safe passage for cargo boats to Tamatave; one look at the waves on the nearby Indian Ocean explains why.

Since then the navigability of the canal has ebbed and flowed like the tide. After WWII the canal was expanded and 30-ton barges could travel the 160km from Tamatave to Vatomandry. After a long period of silting in, renovations began in the 1980s, including a new barge network. Today the canal is slipping backwards again. Sections north of Tamatave, between Vatomandry and Mahanoro, and south of Mananjary have grown in. The remains of the old barge network are rotting by the pier in Tamatave. It all makes one wonder: could the depth of the canal be an economic barometer for Madagascar?

The best place to explore it today is actually in the south, near Manakara (p74).

are great company, and there is a nice bar to hang out in that knows how to make a decent mojito.

Rates include entry into the reserve. Set-menu meals are Ar50,000.

ⓘ Getting There & Away

Manambato is the main jumping-off point for Lac Ampitabe. From Manambato you have to charter a boat to your hotel; talk to the people at the beach. They will start negotiating at Ar200,000, and aren't all that keen on negotiating... Alternatively, wait until the next tour group shows up and see if they are going your way, as a single seat will be much cheaper (around Ar65,000).

Manambato

Manambato is primarily an access town for the Pangalanes Lakes, but it's also home to a lovely white-sand beach on the shore of Lac Rasobe.

🛏 Sleeping

Acacias　　　　　　　　　　BUNGALOW €€
(☏ 033 12 338 35; www.acaciasbungalows.com; s/d bungalows Ar50,000/90,000) Cute and good-value hexagonal-shaped, thatch-roof bungalows overlook pretty Lac Rasobe's beach. A switched-on management pays attention to the details and can organise boats to other destinations. Picnics packed on request.

ⓘ Getting There & Away

To get to Manambato, turn east off the RN2 30km north of Brickaville. It's a 7km sandy track. This track is rough but is feasibly possible in a normal 2WD vehicle.

Ambila-Lemaitso

Whichever way you go about it, the journey to the sleepy village of Ambila-Lemaitso is long, rough and excitingly adventurous. Once in Ambila-Lemaitso you will discover a go-slow tropical fishing village where whole days can pass by under the shade of a mango tree. The setting, astride the barrier beach, with its lake on one side, the roaring ocean on the other, and barely 50m in between, is captivating.

The main attraction here is Nirvana d'Ambila, which faces the ferry crossing at the end of the Brickaville piste. The clean and basic bungalows, with private bathrooms and hot water, have all been renovated, and the atmospheric restaurant features lots of fresh seafood.

🛏 Sleeping

Tropicana　　　　　　　　　　BUNGALOW €
(☏ 033 08 037 39; d bungalows Ar30,000) Very simple accommodation is available at Tropicana, but what the place lacks in luxury it makes up for with a million-dollar beach setting.

Nirvana d'Ambila　　　　　　BUNGALOW €€
(☏ 033 15 017 78, 034 15 736 91; nirvanabckvlle@gmail.com; d bungalows Ar70,000) Relaxed Nirvana d'Ambila faces the ferry crossing at the end of the Brickaville piste. The hotel enjoys a captivating location astride the barrier beach, with placid canal waters on one side and wild ocean surf on the other. The clean and basic bungalows, with private bathrooms and hot water, have all been renovated.

The atmospheric restaurant (breakfast Ar10,000, set menu Ar40,000) features lots of fresh seafood.

ⓘ Getting There & Away

The turnoff for Ambila-Lemaitso is on the RN2 a few kilometres north of Brickaville and just over the bridge (look for the faded sign for Hotel Nirvana). From this turn-off it's a 17km track which is in an absolutely terrible state and a meaty 4WD is required. Allow two to three hours to cover these few short kilometres. After heavy rain, it might be impassable. Once (if!) you get to the end of the track you will then need to cross the canal by hand-operated ferry (Ar8000) to Ambila-Lemaitso.

However, at the time of research, this vehicle ferry was out of action and there was no indication as to when it might get up and running again. For the moment you will have to cross the canal in a small boat and then walk 4km into the village. Either call Nirvana d'Ambila for a transfer, or ask around for a private car at the *taxi-brousse* station in Brickaville. Take this option if you intend to stay in Ambila-Lemaitso overnight.

TAMATAVE (TOAMASINA)

🔲 020 / POP 300,810

Madagascar's most important seaport, Tamatave is a hot, dusty and chaotic town full of decaying colonial buildings, roadside markets and throngs of pousse-pousse carts. The emphasis is on commerce, not tourism, apart from being an important transit point.

There are some bright spots amid the fading grandeur if you know where to find them, meaning that you can have a good time here for a day or two. It's a convenient spot to break the journey between Antananarivo and Île Sainte Marie, or to organise a trip down the Canal des Pangalanes.

◉ Sights

Place Bien Aimé   PLAZA
At Pl Bien Aimé, you'll find the remains of a once-grand park; a dozen magnificent banyan trees weep before a crumbling colonial mansion.

Bazary Kely   MARKET
(Little Market; Blvd de la Fidelité; ⊙from 7am) Bazary Kely sells fish and produce in the ruins of a commercial complex, west of the train station.

Bazary Be   MARKET
(Big Market; Rue Amiral Billard; ⊙from 6.30am) Tamatave's colourful Bazary Be sells fruit, vegetables, spices, handicrafts and beautiful bouquets of flowers (should you feel the need to brighten up your hotel room).

Place de Colonne   PLAZA
A monument to those killed in the 1947 uprising against the French, this plaza is in a sad state of disrepair.

Musée du Port   MUSEUM
(by donation; ⊙9am-4pm Tue-Sun) The small university museum at the entrance to the port constitutes barely 2½ rooms of farming tools, fishing implements, archaeological finds and tribal charms, along with poster displays on deforestation and local conservation projects. Some of the captioning is in English, including translations of some typically cryptic Malagasy proverbs.

Catholic Church   CHURCH
(Rue Amiral Billard) Landmark church in Tamatave. It's open to the public from shortly before to shortly after services.

🏃 Activities

For around Ar6000 you can swim at various hotels, including **Hôtel Neptune** (Blvd Ratsimilaho; Ar6000; ⊙8am-6pm) and **Sharon Hotel** (Blvd de la Liberation; Ar6000; ⊙8am-6pm).

☞ Tours

Tropical Service   TOURS
(🔲020 53 336 79; www.croisiere-madagascar.com; 23 Blvd Joffre) Top-end local tours, transfers and travel services.

Chrismiatours   BOATING
(🔲032 62 954 55; www.chrismiatoursmada.com; Blvd Joffre, Hôtel Eden) Wide variety of tours on the Canal des Pangalanes leaving from Tamatave. Tours last anything from a half-day to several days.

🛏 Sleeping

Hôtel Eden   HOTEL €
(🔲020 53 312 90; Blvd Joffre; r Ar30,000, without bathroom Ar20,000) This basic backpackers hotel is far from a Garden of Eden, but with a mix of shared and private bathrooms and helpful staff, it's a popular budget stay. Chrismiatours is based here, so it's a good place to organise a tour of the Canal des Pangalanes.

Hôtel Les Flamboyants HOTEL €€

(☑ 032 71 093 51, 020 53 323 50; hotelflamboyants @gmail.com; Blvd de la Libération; r with fan/air-con Ar45,000/50,000; ❄ 🛜) An old, but well-kept concrete-box hotel done moderately well, with air-conditioning that is welcome in summer. Rooms are large, and some have decent balconies (add an extra Ar5000), but the hot water struggles at times. The restaurant conjures up tasty meals.

Génération Hôtel HOTEL €€

(☑ 020 53 321 05; www.generationhotel-tamatave. com; Blvd Joffre; d Ar62,500-75,000; ❄ 🛜) At this slightly cluttered and dated hotel all rooms have balcony and fridge. Furnishings are old-style and the water coming out of the shower is quite salty. Staff don't seem to agree with smiling...

★**Hôtel Joffre** BOUTIQUE HOTEL €€€

(☑ 020 53 323 90; www.hoteljoffre-tamatave.com; Blvd Joffre; d Ar133,000-220,000; ❄ 🛜) A central location, attractive terrace cafe, excellent service and evocatively colourful rooms with eye-grabbing wall art, styled beds and bright, polished-tile bathrooms all help to make this the best-value hotel in Tamatave. The handicraft and textile shop in the lobby is a good place to bag a souvenir.

★**La Véranda** HOTEL €€€

(☑ 020 53 340 86; www.veranda-hotel-restaurant-tamatave.com; 5 Rue Lieutenant Bérard; d from Ar120,000; ❄ 🛜) Almost verging on being a boutique hotel, this is the best-value place to stay in town. Rooms here are smart and spacious; some have a balcony and even a bathtub, and there are many arty touches. The excellent restaurant operates on the ground floor, but is closed on Sundays and holidays so best bring some supplies!

Java Hotel HOTEL €€€

(☑ 034 12 252 53, 020 53 316 26; www.java-hotel-tamatave.com; 34 Blvd Joffre; d from Ar142,000; 🅿 🛜) An antiseptic business hotel, but given the competition, a bit of mouthwash feels refreshing. Rooms and hallways sparkle and the artwork hanging from the walls adds a bit of pop. Interior parking is another welcome touch, particularly in Tamatave. Discounts are possible. Le Verseau restaurant is on the ground floor.

Select your room carefully at weekends as it's close to a nightclub and some rooms can be noisy.

Calypso Hotel & Spa HOTEL €€€

(☑ 032 07 131 33, 020 53 304 59; www.hotel calypso.mg; Rue Lieutenant Noël; d incl breakfast from €129; ❄ 🛜 🏊) This is the top hotel in the city, and the only one with this level of polished international finish. It offers elegantly appointed rooms with glass showers and attractive island-style decor, a beautiful indoor pool, a gym, a spa and a posh restaurant. Clients are a mix of businesspeople and high-end tour groups.

🍴 Eating

★**La Véranda** INTERNATIONAL €

(☑ 020 53 340 86; www.veranda-hotel-restaurant-tamatave.com; Rue Lieutenant Bérard; mains from Ar9000; ⊗ 9am-midnight Mon-Sat; 🛜) The refined restaurant and terrace at La Véranda is a popular choice for French expats and visitors thanks to its wide-ranging menu of well-turned-out European and Malagasy dishes at very reasonable prices. The three-course set menu (Ar15,000) changes daily and is far too tempting to settle for less. Eat inside or on the lovely colonial-style terrace.

Adam & Eve Snack Bar CRÊPES €

(☑ 020 53 334 56; Blvd Joffre; mains from Ar8000; ⊗ 7am-10pm Tue-Sun) A popular budget option, this semialfresco bar and terrace cafe has a loyal following for its Malagasy dishes, zebu somasas, big crispy salads, ice cream and crêpes. Even if you're not eating it's a very enjoyable place to relax for an hour or so over one of the freshly squeezed juices.

Score SUPERMARKET €

(Ave de l'Indépendance; ⊗ 8.30am-1pm & 2.30-7pm Mon-Sat, to 12.30pm Sun) Self-caterers and treat-seekers should check out Score supermarket.

Shoprite SUPERMARKET €

(Ave de l'Indépendance; ⊗ 8.30am-7.30pm Mon-Sat, to 1pm Sun) Reasonably well-stocked supermarket.

★**Ocean 501** SEAFOOD €€

(☑ 032 64 147 43; www.ocean501.biz; Blvd Ratsimilaho Salazamay; mains Ar15,000-25,000; ⊗ 7-11pm) Laid-back beach-shack restaurant with beautifully prepared and well-presented seafood dishes. However, you'll be so focused on the waves lapping the sands of the beach right in front of you that you probably won't even notice the splashes of thought that have gone into each dish. It's a short way north of the town centre.

Tamatave (Toamasina)

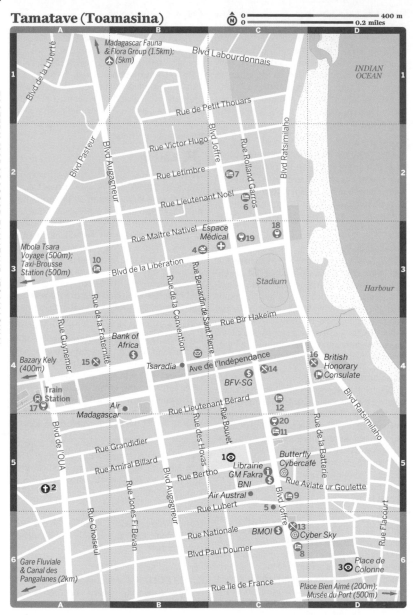

0 — 400 m
0 — 0.2 miles

Blvd de la Liberté

Madagascar Fauna & Flora Group (1.5km); (5km)

Blvd Labourdonnais

INDIAN OCEAN

Rue de Petit Thouars

Blvd Pasteur

Blvd Augagneur

Rue Victor Hugo

Blvd Joffre

Rue Rolland Garros

Blvd Ratsimilaho

Rue Letimbre

7

Rue Lieutenant Noël

6

Rue Maître Nativel

Espace Médical

19

18

4

Mbola Tsara Voyage (500m); Taxi-Brousse Station (500m)

10

Blvd de la Libération

Rue de la Convention

Rue Bernardin de Saint Pierre

Stadium

Harbour

Rue de la Fraternité

Rue Guynemer

Bank of Africa

Rue Bir Hakeim

Bazary Kely (400m)

15

Tsaradia

Ave de l'Indépendance

14

16 British Honorary Consulate

Blvd Ratsimilaho

BFV-SG

Train Station

17

Air Madagascar

Rue Lieutenant Bérard

Rue Bouvet

12

Blvd de l'IOUA

Rue Grandidier

Rue des Hovas

20

11

Rue de la Batterie

Rue Amiral Billard

Blvd Augagneur

Rue Bertho

1

Librairie GM Fakra

BNI

Butterfly Cybercafé

Rue Aviateur Goulette

Rue Jones Fl Bevan

Rue Choiseul

Air Austral

Rue Lubert

5

Blvd Joffre

9

Rue Nationale

BMOI

13 Cyber Sky

Rue Flacourt

2

Blvd Paul Doumer

8

Gare Fluviale & Canal des Pangalanes (2km)

3 Place de Colonne

Rue Île de France

Place Bien Aimé (200m); Musée du Port (500m)

La Terrasse   PIZZA €€

(020 53 302 41; Blvd Joffre; mains/menu Ar14,000/13,000; 7am-1am;) This hopping street-side bistro with tasty pizza and grills is the go-to lunch spot for people on the move. Street children gather around the edge of the terrace to beg for food which some people might find off-putting.

Tamatave (Toamasina)

🍷 Drinking & Nightlife

★ **Gare des Manguiers** BAR
(www.garedesmanguiers.mg; Araben'ny Fahaleovantana, Gare de Tamatave; ⊗noon-midnight) An old railway carriage has been converted into the most happening bar in Tamatave. It has monthly cocktail specials using seasonal fruits, plus there's regular live music and other events and decent food is served within the same complex.

Taxi Be Nightclub CLUB
(www.facebook.com/taxibeclubtmm; Blvd Joffre; ⊗9pm-4am) This large venue in the centre of town features videos, lighting effects and DJs.

Queens Club CLUB
(Blvd Joffre; ⊗9pm-3am) There's a laid-back ambience at this centrally located club, set in an old house with a veranda.

Neptune Nightclub CLUB
(☑020 53 322 26; www.hotel-neptune-tamatave. com; Blvd Ratsimilaho; ⊗from 10pm Mon-Sat) A fairly uninspring nightclub in the large Hotel Neptune on the seafront.

ⓘ Information

DANGERS & ANNOYANCES
Avoid walking at night, particularly alone. It's best not to carry valuables such as cameras around with you (but equally be cautious about leaving them unattended in cheap hotels). At night, take a tuk-tuk rather than a pousse-pousse.

EMBASSIES & CONSULATES
British Honorary Consulate (☑020 53 325 69; 2 Rue Lieutenant Berard, La Ligne Scandinave) Based out of La Ligne Scandinave shipping-line offices. It's open by advance appointment only.

INTERNET ACCESS
Butterfly Cybercafé (Blvd Joffre; per hour Ar3000; ⊗8.30am-noon & 2.30-6pm Mon-Fri, to noon Sat) A handful of computer terminals are available at this small internet cafe and computer-repair office.
Cyber Sky (Blvd Joffre; per hour Ar3000; ⊗8am-8pm Mon-Sat) Small internet cate.

MEDICAL SERVICES
Espace Médical (☑020 53 315 66; www. espacemedical.mg; Blvd de la Libération; ⊗24hr) The best clinic in the city has a 24-hour accident and emergency department.

MONEY
There are many banks in the centre with ATMs. There are also plenty of exchange bureaus.
Bank of Africa (BOA; Blvd Augagneur; ⊗8-11.30am & 2-4.30pm Mon-Fri)
BFV-SG (cnr Blvd Joffre & Araben'ny Fahaleovantena; ⊗7.30-11.30am & 2-4pm Mon-Fri)
BMOI (Blvd Joffre; ⊗8-11.15am & 1.45-4.15pm)
BNI (Blvd Joffre; ⊗8-11.30am & 2-4.30pm Mon-Fri) Takes MasterCard.

POST
Post office (Araben'ny Fahaleovantena; ⊗8-11.30am & 2-4.30pm Mon-Fri, 8-11.30am Sat)

TOURIST INFORMATION
Librairie GM Fakra (www.facebook.com/ librairie.gmfakra; Blvd Joffre; ⊗8am-noon & 2.30-6pm Mon-Fri, 8am-noon Sat) A few English news magazines, plus maps of the region and postcards.

❶ Getting There & Away

AIR

Air Austral (☎ 020 53 300 26; www.air-austral.com; Rue de Lattre de Tassigny; ⊙8-11.45am & 2-5.45pm Mon-Fri, 8-11.45am Sat) Flies daily except Sunday and Friday between Réunion Island and Tamatave (from €368).

Air Madagascar (☎ 020 53 323 56; Ave de l'Indépendance; ⊙8-11.45am & 2-5.45pm Mon-Fri, 8-11.45am Sat) Flies daily between Tamatave and Antananarivo (€227, one hour).

Tsaradia (☎ 020 23 444 44; www.tsaradia.com; Ave de l'Indépendance; ⊙8-11.30am & 2.30-5.30pm Mon-Fri, 8-10am Sat) Has twice-daily flights from Antananarivo to Tamatave (from €123, 45 minutes).

BOAT

To Île Sainte Marie If you are heading to Île Sainte Marie via Soanierana-Ivongo, your boat company will provide a shuttle service from Tamatave.

To the northeast Cargo boats without set schedules also ply the waters of the northeast. This type of travel is generally slow and uncomfortable, and potentially dangerous, particularly during cyclone season (December to March); always check forecasts and ask local advice before travelling. Those prone to motion sickness should not attempt it. Standards vary widely; cabins are sometimes available, but on most boats you can expect to be bedding down on deck, and you will need to bring your own food and water. If you're still interested, ask any pousse-pousse driver to take you to the bureau of boats going to Mananara or Maroantsetra. This is an obscure shed by the port that you will never find on your own.

PRIVATE 4WD

Taxi-brousse company **Mbola Tsara Voyage** (☎ 033 75 679 35; contact@mbolatsaravoyage.com; Blvd de la Liberation, taxi-brousse station; ⊙7am-7pm) rents private 4WDs for travel on the RN5. Published prices for car and driver from Tamatave include Mananara and Maroantsetra (Ar2 million) but with any luck, aggressive bargaining might reduce this.

PUBLIC TRANSPORT

➡ The **taxi-brousse station** (Blvd de la Liberation) at the northwestern edge of town serves Antananarivo, as well as points north as far as Soanierana-Ivongo (Ar10,000, four hours) and south as far as Mahanoro (Ar20,000, four hours).

➡ Minibuses and coaches run along the RN2 throughout the day to Moramanga (Ar15,000, seven hours) and Antananarivo (Ar20,000 to Ar23,000, at least seven hours). It is best to leave early to ensure that you reach your destination during daylight.

➡ If road conditions permit, you may be able to find a *camion-brousse* (truck) or similar large vehicle heading towards Mananara (Ar60,000) or Maroantsetra (Ar90,000, two to three days). A 4WD to Mananara or Maroantsetra will likely cost Ar2 million (one or two days).

❶ Getting Around

➡ Taxis between town and the airport (5km north of town) should cost around Ar25,000. Taxi rides within town are Ar3000 to Ar5000.

➡ Some local minibuses shuttle passengers around town for Ar300, if you can work out the routes; service 4 goes to the Bazary Kely (p192) and the port.

➡ To hire a car locally, ask at any hotel, restaurant or travel agency, or ask around at the *taxi-brousse* station. It may be more expensive if you want to take the vehicle beyond Foulpointe.

➡ Pousse-pousse drivers charge from Ar1000 per trip within the town centre. The drivers are fairly friendly, but agree on the fee before you climb in. Tuk-tuks are the same price and a much safer option at night.

NORTH OF TAMATAVE

☎ 020

While it's the beaches that are the big attraction in the area north of Tamatave, with the quiet sand-fringed coves of Mahambo being the best option, this region also holds other attractions including a tumbledown fortress in Foulpointe and an excellent zoo in Ivoloina. If you have your eyes set on the beaches and islands even further north then head to Soanierana-Ivongo, which is the ferry port for Île Sainte Marie. Beyond lies the daunting RN5 that can only be traversed by a reliable 4WD.

Parc Zoologique Ivoloina

The **Parc Zoologique Ivoloina** (☎ 032 05 103 07, 020 53 996 54; www.seemadagascar.com; adult/child Ar20,000/12,000; ⊙9am-5pm) is a very well-run zoo and botanical garden set on a lovely lake just north of Tamatave. The beautiful grounds of Ivoloina (ee-va-la-*ween*) cover 2.82 sq km and contain more than 100 lemurs from 10 different species, both caged and semiwild, as well as chameleons, radiated tortoises, tree boas and tomato frogs. The botanical garden contains more than 75 species of native and exotic plants, and a model farm designed to demonstrate sustainable agricultural methods. Visitors can enjoy four walking trails with booklets in English, a snack bar and an education centre. An optional guide is Ar10,000 for a basic two-hour tour, or Ar40,000 for a full day. Book in advance for a night tour (5.30pm) to see the nocturnal lemurs (Ar10,000).

ⓘ Getting There & Away

To reach the park from Tamatave, take the RN5 north, go 9km past the airport, and turn left on the unpaved road in front of the Ivoloina Bridge. Continue on until you see the park entrance sign (the trip takes half an hour). A charter taxi from town costs around Ar70,000 for a return trip; *taxis-brousses* leave to Ivoloina village (Ar7500) every hour or two. From Ivoloina village it's a scenic 4km walk to the park entrance.

Foulpointe (Mahavelona)

☑ 020 / POP 8000

Foulpointe (fool-*pwant*) has some smile-inducing white-sand beaches, and a strip of accommodation and dining. Although the town itself is quite nondescript if you're looking for a quick sun 'n' fun escape from Tamatave, this is a worthy option.

◉ Sights

Fort Manda FORTRESS

(guide fee Ar5000; ⊙9am-noon & 2.30-4.30pm) The evocative ruins of this 19th-century Merina fort, built for Radama I, are about 500m north of Foulpointe. Its walls, which are 8m high and 6m thick in places, are made from coral, sand and eggs. You can clamber about the ruins and from the highest points, there are gorgeous views over the Indian Ocean. A guide will show you around the site and explain the history and legends of the place.

In a case of mistranslation, the word Manda actually means 'fortress' in Malagasy, so the site is known as 'Fort Fortress'...

🛏 Sleeping

Le Grand Bleu BUNGALOW €€

(☑020 57 220 06, 034 07 220 06; www.grandbleu-tamatave.com; d bungalows from Ar80,000, 6-person villas Ar140,000; ✳🗑) The 'Big Blue' complex fronts directly onto the beach, and the rooms here come well equipped. If you're any judge of character, however, you'll forgo the air-con rooms for the subtler breezes of the cute wickerwork bungalows.

Manda Beach Hôtel HOTEL €€€

(☑034 11 220 00; www.mandabeach-hotel.com; d/bungalows from Ar100,000/148,000; ✳🗑🗑)

With its central pool, concrete rooms, tennis courts, Western music and long stretch of parasols on the sand, not to mention the nearby golf course, this place feels more like a beach motel in Florida than a hotel in Madagascar. Choose the beachfront bungalows over the industrial rooms. Menu Ar35,000; nonguests can use the pool for Ar10,000.

ⓘ Getting There & Away

Foulpointe lies 58km north of Tamatave. Minibuses depart from the Tamatave *taxi-brousse* station daily, generally in the mornings (Ar5000, 1½ hours).

For short hops, such as to Mahambo or Fenoarivo-Atsinanana, you can try flagging down just about any vehicle going in the right direction; hotel vehicles may be able to take you all the way to Tamatave, but you'll have to pay at least the equivalent of the *taxi-brousse* fare.

Several vehicles daily pass Foulpointe on their way between Tamatave and Soanierana-Ivongo. Heading south, when they pass Foulpointe depends on what time the ferry from Île Sainte Marie arrives at Soanierana-Ivongo. Heading north, wait by the road side before 9am to get to Soanierana-Ivongo in time for the best boats.

Mahambo

☑ 033 / POP 26,000

Mahambo is a coastal village with a safe swimming beach and luxuriant vegetation that comes right down to the shore in some places. For the moment its distance from the main road means it's a quiet and enticing place, and while facilities are expanding it

THE INFAMOUS RN5

The 240km of RN5 from Soanierana-Ivongo to Maroantsetra is probably the worst 'road' in Madagascar. The very idea of calling it a 'National Road' is so hysterical that only the sight of your ride floating on a couple of dugout canoes will stop you laughing.

The road has distinct stretches, each with its own set of difficulties.

➡ Soanierana-Ivongo to Manompana is essentially a swamp; the main stretch of the road is so bad that locals have done a special deviation for motorbikes. It is still phenomenally muddy but just about manageable.

➡ Manompana to Sahasao has a number of deep sandy stretches (sometimes you're on the beach, racing the waves): they're treacherous when dry but manageable when wet.

➡ Sahasao to Mananara is probably one of the hardest, with sections of sheer rock mixed with slippery red clay and steep gradients.

➡ Mananara to Maroantsetra is all about the river crossings: there are more than a dozen and only a handful of bridges. The rest need to be crossed by raft or diesel-powered ferries.

There have been plans to seal the road for years and the new president (elected in December 2018) has again promised to do so, but until then, it is likely to remain a very challenging trip. A construction company was rebuilding at least six bridges between Maroantsetra and Mananara at the time of research. Works are scheduled to be completed some time in 2020, which may see the return of regular *taxi-brousse* (bush taxi) service between the two towns.

Although there are *taxis-brousses* between Mananara and Tamatave (which stop at Soanierana-Ivongo), they are agonisingly slow: passengers frequently have to walk and help push the vehicle.

For now, the best, and quickest option, is to take a *moto-taxi* (motorcycle taxi). Motorbikes can pick up speed easily where the terrain allows, they're much more agile on narrow stretches of road and they can use small man-powered rafts on river crossings, which fill up much quicker than the lumbering, diesel-swilling ferries.

should still be some time before resort life starts to take over.

🛌 Sleeping

Zanatany　　　　　　　　　BUNGALOW €
(☏ 033 15 324 73; d/family bungalows Ar30,000/60,000; 🛜) This little restaurant in the centre of the village has the cheapest digs in town. It's very basic, but a good deal.

Ylang-Ylang　　　　　　　BUNGALOW €€
(☏ 033 76 659 96; www.facebook.com/hotel-ylang-ylang-mahambo-713286592104164; bungalows Ar60,000; 🛜) If you can't be on the beach, then this wonderfully scented garden with its well-kept row of wooden cottages is a fine substitute. Staff organise various excursions as well as surf lessons.

★**La Pirogue**　　　　　　　LODGE €€€
(☏ 033 08 768 10; www.pirogue-hotel.com; r/bungalows from Ar99,500; 🛜) This elegant resort has a fascinating reef-front location, a stunning and quiet soft sand beach and a beautiful garden setting complete with resident lemurs. The bungalows are delightful with local wood

carvings and deckchairs on the porch. There's a wonderful outside dining area with the sea lapping nearby, although the food is pricey.

Kayaks and pedalos are free for guests. Motorbikes (half-day Ar20,000) and quad bikes (30 minutes Ar50,000) are available, and fishing trips can be arranged.

🛈 Getting There & Away

Mahambo is 30km north of Foulpointe (Ar2500, 45 minutes) and about 90km from Tamatave (Ar6000, 2½ hours) on the RN5. If taking a *taxi-brousse*, ask the driver to drop you at the intersection (you'll see the hotel signs), then walk about 2km down the sandy track heading east.

Fenoarivo-Atsinanana

POP 18,000

Unless you have a great interest in cloves, or need to visit a bank, there's really no reason to come to this agricultural market town (usually just called 'Fenoarivo' or 'Fénérive').

But if you're looking for a great place to stay, **Sahorana Lodge** (☏ 034 17 074 47; www.

sahoranalodge.com; d from Ar65,000; ☺ mid-Sep–Apr; ☏) is a simply superb rustic-chic lodge in a delightful location a short way south of town. Each wooden and thatch cottage is immaculately well kept and all have breezy terraces with views out over fields of rice and crashing Indian Ocean waves. Delicious gourmet meals are another highlight and there's a quiet and gorgeous beach a short walk away.

❶ Getting There & Away

Taxi-brousse run frequently to Tamatave.

Soanierana-Ivongo

POP 22,000

The riverside port of Soanierana-Ivongo (son-ee-ran-*eevong*) is the most practical of places: you go there to get a boat to Île Sainte Marie, or stop here en route back from the island.

Le Fumet (☎033 42 875 80; d Ar45,000) on the southern outskirts of town is the only decent accommodation option in town. It has reasonably light bedrooms and a restaurant. It's set back from the beach so you'll be able to enjoy the sound of the crashing waves.

❶ Information

The crossing to/from Île Sainte Marie is dangerous, as the boats exit a shallow river mouth with incoming breaking waves. There have been several fatal accidents in the past. The danger is particularly pronounced between June and August, when water levels are low and the weather is bad.

❶ Getting There & Away

BOAT

➡ There are two main shuttle boats from Soanierana-Ivongo to Ambodifotatra on Île Sainte Marie: **Gasikara Be** (☎Soanierana-Ivongo 034 43 856 13, Tamatave 020 53 987 49; www.sainte-marie-tours.com; 40 Blvd Joffre, Tamatave; one way Ar70,000, with bus to/from Tamatave Ar80,000) and **Cap Sainte-Marie** (☎032 05 118 08, 020 53 351 48; www.cap-sainte-marie.com; one way Ar70,000, with bus to/from Tamatave Ar80,000). Both have a ticket office right by the waterside.

➡ You can buy a boat ticket only, or, if you're coming from/going to Tamatave, a boat ticket combined with a minibus transfer. The trip between Soanierana and Tamatave currently takes about six to seven hours.

➡ Boats leave Ambodifotatra at daybreak, arrive in Soanierana between 7am and 8am

and then wait for their respective shuttle buses to arrive from Tamatave to leave. The road between Tamatave and Soanierana being pretty average, boats tend to leave any time between 11am and 1pm. Crossing time is 1¼ hours.

➡ Another boat service that plies the north-eastern coast between Soanierana-Ivongo and Mananara (Ar135,000, five hours) three days a week from March to August and every day from September to February is **Melissa Express** (☎032 68 447 01, 033 37 838 68; melissa express1@gmail.com). There's a service all the way to Maroantsetra (Ar215,000, nine hours) twice a week from September to February. This is the only service of its kind on this coast but is subject to interruptions, particularly in June and July. The ticket office is by the waterside.

TAXI-BROUSSE

Taxis-brousses depart Tamatave for Soanierana-Ivongo and vice versa (Ar15,000, six to seven hours) around 6am every morning. However, they are not coordinated with boat departures. If you're intending to travel via Soanierana-Ivongo to get the boat to Sainte Marie, book your bus transfer with the boat company. For *taxis-brousses* going north, ask at the station: the road is in dreadful condition and vehicles were only going as far as Mananara at the time of research. The pickups usually leave full from Tamatave so finding a seat will be tricky.

ÎLE SAINTE MARIE

POP 26,460

The best thing about Île Sainte Marie is that it contains all the ingredients for a great holiday *and* great travel. This is a very long (57km), thin, lush and relatively flat tropical island surrounded by beaches and reef and spotted with thatched villages. The port of Ambodifotatra, a quarter of the way up the western coast, is the only sizeable town. South of here, the shore is lined with a great variety of hotels and resorts, which don't overpower the setting, culminating in the small island of Île aux Nattes, a postcard tropical paradise where you can easily imagine pirates coming ashore with treasure chests in tow. In contrast, the upper half of the island is quite wild, and its great length means that there is plenty of room for exploration.

❶ Getting There & Away

The sea is rough from March to July, especially in June and July. Boats sometimes don't run for several days at a time. Travellers on a tight schedule, who are not otherwise driving the

Île Sainte Marie

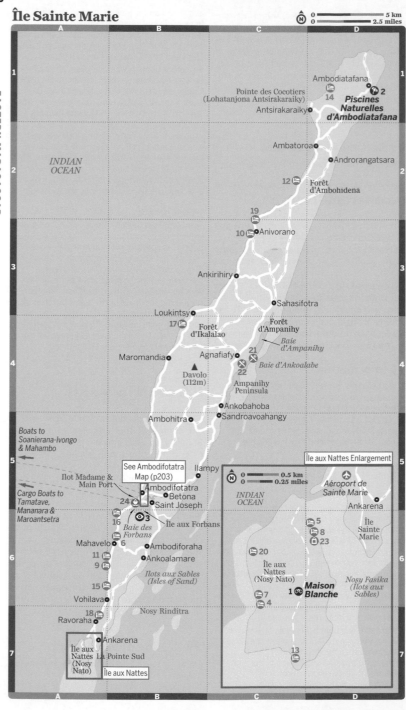

0 ___ 5 km
0 ___ 2.5 miles

A | **B** | **C** | **D**

INDIAN OCEAN

Ambodiatafana
14
Piscines Naturelles d'Ambodiatafana 2

Pointe des Cocotiers (Lohatanjona Antsirakaraiky)
Antsirakaraiky

Ambatoroa
Androrangatsara

12
Forêt d'Ambohidena

19
10 Anivorano

Ankirihiry

Sahasifotra

Forêt d'Ampanihy

Loukintsy
17
Forêt d'Ikalalao

Baie d'Ampanihy
21
22 *Baie d'Ankoalabe*

Maromandia

Agnafiafy

▲ Davolo (112m)

Ampanihy Peninsula

Ankobahoba
Sandroavoahangy
Ambohitra

Boats to Soanierana-Ivongo & Mahambo

Ilampy

Îlot Madame & Main Port

See Ambodifotatra Map (p203)

Ambodifotatra
Betona
Saint Joseph

Cargo Boats to Tamatave, Mananara & Maroantsetra

24
3
16
Baie des Forbans
Île aux Forbans

6

Mahavelo
Ambodiforaha
Ankoalamare

11
9

Îlots aux Sables (Isles of Sand)

15

Vohilava

18
Ravoraha

Ankarena
Île aux Nattes (Nosy Nato)
La Pointe Sud

Nosy Rinditra

Île aux Nattes Enlargement

0 ___ 0.5 km
0 ___ 0.25 miles

INDIAN OCEAN

Aéroport de Sainte Marie
Ankarena

Île Sainte Marie

5
8
23

20

Île aux Nattes (Nosy Nato)

Nosy Fasika (Îlots aux Sables)

Maison Blanche 1

7
4

13

Île Sainte Marie

coast road, should consider flying to/from
Tamatave or Antananarivo.

AIR

Tsaradia (Rue Dadare; ⊙9am-4pm Mon-Fri, to
noon Sat) has regular flights to Antananarivo
(one hour) and Tamatave (35 minutes); **Madagasikara Airways** (☑ 034 05 970 16, 032 05
970 10; www.madagasikaraairways.com; Aéroport de Sainte Marie) also flies to Tana twice a
week. Air Madagascar has direct flights to the
French island of Réunion (two hours).

BOAT

→ There are three main shuttle boats between
Île Sainte Marie and the main land: Gasikara Be
(p199) and Cap Sainte-Marie (p199), which sail
to/from Soanierana-Ivongo (1¼ hours),
and **El Condor** (☑ Tamatave 034 70 433 01,
île Ste Marie 034 70 433 02; www.bluemarine-
madagascar.com; Hôtel Mahambo Beach;
one way Ar100,000, with bus to Tamatave
Ar110,000), which sails to/from Mahambo
(three hours). All have ticket booths at the port.

→ You can buy a boat ticket only, or, if you're
travelling to/from Tamatave, a boat ticket
combined with a minibus transfer. The trip
between Tamatave and Soanierana currently
takes about six to seven hours (and three to
four hours to Mahambo).

→ If you're travelling to/from Tamatave, El
Condor is your best option; if you're travelling
to/from Maorantsetra or Mananara, then sail
to/from Soanierana-Ivongo. This is to minimise
your road travel on the east coast.

→ Boats leave Ambodifotatra at daybreak and
then wait for their respective shuttle buses to
arrive from Tamatave before returning to Sainte
Marie.

→ Cargo boats leave from a different port on
Ilot Madame, the tiny island at the entrance
to Baie des Forbans, sailing to Mananara,
Maroantsetra and Tamatave. There are no set
schedules for these; departures are often in the
evening or at night, and you will likely have to
wait several days for something to turn up.

❶ Getting Around

There is a good paved road on the western side
between the airport and the northern tip. The
remaining roads are dirt, rock or sand. All midrange and top-end hotels offer private transfers
from the port and the airport.

TO/FROM THE AIRPORT

The airport is at the southern tip of the island,
13km south of Ambodifotatra. A tuk-tuk costs
Ar15,000.

BICYCLE

Virtually every hotel and all kinds of other places
have bikes of varying quality for hire. The going
rate is from Ar20,000 per day. Once off the
paved road you need a mountain bike.

CAR & MOTORCYCLE

→ The whole food chain of motorised vehicles
– including cars, buggies, quads, motorcycles
and scooters – is available for hire.

→ Quads cost Ar300,000 per day, including fuel
and a guide; although pricey, they're a great
way to get off the beaten track and operators
have devised plenty of circuits to do just that.

EASTERN MADAGASCAR ÎLE SAINTE MARIE

DON'T MISS

PISCINES NATURELLES D'AMBODIATAFANA

In the north of Sainte Marie, near Ambodiatafana village, these **natural pools** (Ar10,000) are separated from the Indian Ocean by a granitic gate of about 100m. During each tide, the sea fills these natural basins by crashing against the rocks. The ocean is too rough to swim there from June to September but they're absolutely idyllic in spring and summer (October to February). There are phenomenal panoramic views of the island from the sand dunes at the back of the beach.

The beach and pools are sacred and there are many *fadys* (taboos) to respect so a guide is compulsory.

➜ Much cheaper is a motorbike, which you can hire for Ar50,000 per day (fuel not included). This is a particularly good option to go to the Ampanihy Peninsula (via Ilampy).

➜ For those who wish to putt-putt along sealed surfaces, you can pick up a scooter from around Ar40,000 per day, which is a lot of fun. Virtually every hotel has scooters for hire; you'll also find them on the main road in Ambodifotatra.

➜ If you wish to travel in a group, you can hire a car and driver through any high-end hotel; negotiations start at Ar250,000 per day.

TAXI-BROUSSE

There are just a handful of *taxis-brousses* on Île Sainte Marie, which are unlikely to be much use to travellers. There is at least one departure per day from Ambodifotatra to the northern tip (Ar8,000, two hours), and one departure to the pirogue crossing for Île aux Nattes at the southern tip (Ar2,000, one hour).

TUK-TUK

Tuk-tuks have become the default option for getting around Sainte Marie. They sit three (sometimes even four if the driver shares his seat) passengers; flag them anywhere on the road. Short trips will cost Ar2000 to Ar5000; longer trips, say from Ambodifotatra to the airport, the southern tip of the island or Loukintsy, cost Ar15,000 to Ar20,000.

Ambodifotatra

Ambodifotatra (am-bodi-*foot*-atr) is Île Sainte Marie's only real town and has all the island's practical facilities. You'll find everything you need to organise your stay, plus some interesting restaurants.

◎ Sights

Cimetière des Pirates CEMETERY
(Pirate Cemetery; Ar5000) This is a fascinating spot from which to contemplate the history of the island. The cemetery overlooks the Baie de Forbans just south of Ambodifotatra, the perfect pirate hang-out. Missionaries, and colonial and marine officers are also buried here, but you can clearly see the skull and crossbones on the grave of one English pirate. The crumbling piers used for ship repairs are visible from here, as is the small island of Île aux Forbans, where many pirates lived.

Access is via an isolated foot track, which crosses several tidal creeks and slippery logs about 10 minutes south of the causeway. 'Guides' have erected a hut at the start to collect a fee and do a guided tour (Ar15,000). They're not sanctioned by the local tourist office, however, and their actual knowledge and English is limited so we strongly recommend that you come here with someone who knows the history of the area. The tourist office and other local operators can arrange this. It's completely unique and worth the effort.

🏃 Activities

★**Crazy Lemur** ADVENTURE SPORTS
(☑ 032 04 816 56; www.crazylemur.fun) This multiactivity centre should be one of your first stops – whatever the time of year, your inclinations or budget, Crazy Lemur will have something for you to do. As well as being a renowned dive centre (it's PADI-accredited and was formerly known as the Lémurien Palmé), it has also diversified in recommending and booking activities with other operators (kitesurfing, climbing etc).

Fluent English spoken.

☞ Tours

Orpheu Todivelo TOURS
(☑ 0340179381, 0324008443; orpheu09@hotmail.fr) If you are looking to put together any type of itinerary on the island, a great guide to call is Orpheu. This dynamic young gentleman speaks fluent English, makes things happen and knows everyone. Formerly head of the tourism office, he now runs his own agency.

Ambodifotatra

N 0 —— 200 m
0 —— 0.1 miles

Ambodifotatra

Activities, Courses & Tours
1 Crazy Lemur B3

Sleeping
2 Hôtel Freddy B3
3 Hotel Hortensia A3
4 Idylle Beach A2
5 Les Palmiers B1

Eating
6 Choco Pain B4
   Crazy Lemur .... (see 1)
   Idylle Beach .... (see 4)
7 La Paillote B3
8 La Terrasse B3
9 Pizza Mama Santa B3

Drinking & Nightlife
10 Baramix/La Polina A2
11 La Banane B3

Information
12 Célamada B4
13 Office Régional de Tourisme
    Sainte Marie B3

Transport
14 Cap-Sainte Marie Ticket Booth B4
15 El Condor Ticket Booth B3
   Gasikara Be Ticket Booth .... (see 14)
16 Port Barachois B4

of humpback-whale season: there's a big parade, games, stalls, exhibitions, concerts and a conference, all to raise awareness about these enormous mammals.

🛏 Sleeping

Les Palmiers　　　　　　　　　　BUNGALOW €
(☑ 034 27 351 67, 032 04 960 94; hotel.palmiers@ yahoo.fr; d/family bungalows Ar50,000/90,000) A little compound up a path from the centre of town with simple, good-value bungalows with fans, hot water and well-equipped kitchens. Plus you'll get the company of the inimitable Séraphine, who's been running her bungalows for 20 years.

Hotel Hortensia　　　　　　　　　　HOTEL €
(☑ 034 01 403 69; Ave La Bigorne; d Ar41,000-56,000, family Ar61,000) Nice large balconies face the ocean at this spacious and reasonably priced two-storey hotel run by a friendly Malagasy family. Rooms facing the road are cheaper.

Hôtel Freddy　　　　　　　　　　HOTEL €
(☑ 032 83 079 50; billetfred@yahoo.fr; Rue Belgique; d/f Ar60,000/90,000; ❄ 🛜) This tip-top

✴ Festivals & Events

Whale Festival　　　　　　　　　　PARADE
(Festival des Baleines; www.festivaldesbaleines. com; ☉ mid-Jul) If you're on Île Sainte Marie in July, don't miss the Whale Festival. It's a huge event that celebrates the start

midrange hotel, run by the lovely Freddy, a Malagasy who worked for the French navy and decided to settle back home, does all the basics right. Rooms are clean and sizeable with hot water, a shared balcony, lots of light and even satellite TV (and air-con for a supplement of Ar20,000 per night).

Idylle Beach HOTEL €€€
(☑ 032 48 684 81; www.idyllebeach.com; r €40-55; ❄ ☎ ❄) A wonderful little place right by the sea, this hotel has road-side rooms and more expensive sea-view rooms. The rooms are small but worthy of the best boutique hotels in Europe when it comes to design and comfort. The casual yet sophisticated bar-restaurant (mains Ar27,000 to Ar50,000) with a creative, seasonal menu, is one of the best on the island.

✖ Eating

La Terrasse MALAGASY €
(Ave Bigorne; mains Ar7000-12,000; ❄ 11.30am-9.30pm) This is the place to come and get your fill of *poisson sauce coco* (fish in coconut sauce) or fried calamari. The open-air setting, right by the sea, and laid-back vibes are additional draws.

Choco Pain CAFE €
(patries Ar2000, sandwiches Ar6000; ❄ 4.30am-1pm) This little cafe is a boon for travellers catching the dawn departures of the boats to the mainland, as it opens at 4.30am. For those lucky enough to get a lie-in, come in for a midmorning coffee: the pastries are excellent. It also does cooked breakfasts and good sandwiches for a quick and cheap lunch.

★ Crazy Lemur CAFE €€
(mains Ar12,000-20,000; ❄ 8am-late) This activity centre (p202) doubles as a great cafe and bar, which serves informal meals (omelette and salad, burger and fries etc) on a lovely slice of beach: tables are set in the sand and under the palms.

Pizza Mama Santa PIZZA €€
(Ave La Bigorne; pizzas Ar11,000-18,000; ❄ 11.30am-9pm) Great wood-fired pizza and a lovely dining room. Portions are huge. Take-away available.

La Paillote EUROPEAN €€
(Ave La Bigorne; mains from Ar10,000; ❄ 8.30am-10pm; ☎) This *vazaha* (foreigner) hang-out entices with its very attractive open-air floor plan, street-front location (great for people-

watching) and broad menu, from pizza to langouste. Try the thick zebu fillets. English spoken.

★ Idylle Beach FUSION €€€
(www.idyllebeach.com; mains Ar27,000-34,000; ❄ 11.30am-10pm; ☎) This cool restaurant is without a doubt one of the best on the island: the fusion cuisine blends European and tropical influences to produce wonders such as tuna carpaccios or succulent zebu steak in green-pepper sauce. The desserts are phenomenal too. It is pricey, but a worthwhile treat.

♒ Drinking & Nightlife

La Banane BAR
(Ave La Bigorne; ❄ 5pm-late) The bar is the favourite hang-out of French retirees and the atmosphere can be seedy.

Baramix/La Polina CLUB
(Ar5000; ❄ 6pm-late Wed-Mon) This nightclub fills up at weekends.

❶ Information

MONEY
Bank of Africa (Ave La Bigorne; ❄ 8-11.45am & 2.30-4.45pm Mon-Fri) and **BFV-SG** (Ave de la Bigorne; ❄ 7.30-11.30am & 2-4pm Mon-Fri) both have ATMs and change currency.

POST
Post office (❄ 9am-noon & 2-4pm Mon-Fri) Sells stamps but is unlikely to be of other use.

TOURIST INFORMATION
Cétamada (☑ 032 12 090 31; www.cetamada. org; Port Barachois; ❄ 8am-5pm Jul-Sep) This association promotes conservation of the humpback whales that visit Sainte Marie between July and September. It has also established a code of best practice for whale-watching operators; accredited members can be found on its website.
Office Régional de Tourisme Sainte Marie (☑ 034 03 804 55, 034 48 441 98; www.sainte marie-tourisme.mg; Ave La Bigorne; ❄ 8am-4pm Mon-Sat) Has information about activities and guides on the island.

❶ Getting There & Away

Port Barachois in Ambodifotatra is where boats sail to/from the mainland (p201). This is where you'll find the ticket counters for the three boats that ply the route: **Gasikara Be** (❄ 4.30am-noon), **Cap-Sainte Marie** (❄ 4.30am-noon) and **El Condor** (❄ 4.30am-noon).

SHIVER ME TIMBERS

In the late 17th and 18th centuries Île Sainte Marie was the headquarters of the world's pirates, who enjoyed its proximity to maritime trade routes, its protected harbour (a great place to hide), its abundant fruit and its women. Legendary brigands including William Kidd once brought their boats here for repairs, and set up house on Île aux Forbans, near Ambodifotatra. At one point the pirate population topped 1000. Today the remains of several pirate ships still lie within a few metres of the surface in the Baie des Forbans, including Kidd's *Adventure*, and Captain Condent's famous *Fiery Dragon*, while the skull and crossbones can be seen engraved at the nearby pirate cemetery.

In May 2015, to great excitement, a 50kg silver bar was discovered off Île Sainte Marie by US explorer Barry Clifford, who claimed it was part of Kidd's long-lost treasure from the *Adventure*. It was presented to the Malagasy president with much fanfare. There was hope that tourism to the island would soar as more people searched for 'X marks the spot'. Next up, Unesco sent a team to investigate that scuppered this romantic tale: they say the silver bar is 95% lead, and definitely not old enough to be part of Kidd's bounty.

A tuk tuk to the airport or the pirogue crossing to Île aux Nattes is Ar15,000.

The **Total** (◔ 8am-6pm) petrol station on the southern edge of town will be handy if you rent a scooter or motorbike.

North of Ambodifotatra

Sometimes it's easy to forget, but north of Ambodifotatra lies three-quarters of the island. In terms of accommodation, almost all is on the west coast, which is more sheltered from cyclones. There is a good paved road to the northern tip, after which the road down the eastern side gets rough, and the real adventure begins.

It will take several enjoyable hours, but you can drive all the way to the Piscine Naturelles d'Ambodiatafana (p202), a natural pool at the northeastern tip of the island, where there are some basic bungalows. The Fanilo Albrand lighthouse lies to the southwest. From the ridge, Maroantsetra and Baie d'Antongil are sometimes visible.

🛏 Sleeping & Eating

Le Bon Endroit   GUESTHOUSE €
(☏020 57 906 62, 033 09 624 38; www.lebon endroit.net; d/f Ar40,000/60,000) This brilliant budget guesthouse is off the beaten track. The simple en suite bungalows occupy a rugged coral beach, and there's a convivial restaurant (mains Ar10,000). The emphasis is on free activities – snorkelling, kayaking, local walks, games on the big lawn etc.

Arnaud and Nouba, the Franco-Malagasy owners, are lovely hosts and a mine of information. Scooters available for hire.

★ **Samaria**   BUNGALOW €€€
(☏034 20 515 15; www.samaria-hotel.com; half board per person €48; 🕸) Few hotels on Sainte Marie have this idyllic a location – and this is an idyllic island! Set in expansive tropical gardens, Samaria has its own natural swimming pool and rocky outcrop with panoramic coastal views; it also happens to be an amazing snorkelling spot. There are just a handful of bungalows, each blending modern design and local materials.

The bar-restaurant is equally wonderful, with the same panoramic views, plunging sunsets and delicious fare. There are free kayaks and snorkelling gear for guests to use.

Les Tipaniers Lodge   BUNGALOW €€€
(☏034 15 528 96; www.tipaniers.com; d from Ar140,000; 🕸) If you'd like to get away from it all, you couldn't do better than this: located at the very northern tip of the island, Tipaniers is remote, stunning and yet surprisingly comfortable. It's basically your cliche desert island with mod cons: white-sand beach, swaying palms, turquoise water and eight pretty bungalows with big beds.

Tipaniers is a long way from everywhere – except the piscines naturelles (p202), to which you can walk in an hour or so. You can rent scooters etc but you'd be better off staying here to enjoy this unspoilt corner of the island, rather than using it as a base to explore the whole island. If you can, have two or three nights here and then another couple of nights elsewhere.

Hôtel Sainte Marie Lodge   BOUTIQUE HOTEL €€€
(☏034 19 059 52; www.hotel-saintemarie lodge-madagascar.com; d/ste incl breakfast €66/74; 🕸🛏) This elegant lodge on a large

piece of waterfront is a big step above the competition, with a charming ambience that is part safari lodge and part piano bar. The rooms are simple but comfortable and the suites are huge. The communal areas are sensational too, with lots of books and games. English is spoken. Minimum three-night stay.

Quads and other activities are available, including whale watching.

Masoandro Lodge   LODGE €€€
(☑034 44 416 28, 020 57 910 43; www.masoandro. mg; standard d bungalows €76, menu €17; ❄ ⚕ ≋) This beautiful wooden lodge is located on a hillside with great long-range views, and there's a fantastic pool area with an adjacent waterfall. It's well situated, on the road between Ambodifotatra and the northern tip, equally convenient for town and adventure. The nature bungalows have way more charm than the luxury ones and are half the price. Multiple excursions available.

South of Ambodifotatra

The area between Ambodifotatra and the airport contains most of the island's hotels and a variety of restaurants. The beach is narrow on this western shore, but on the other side, facing the Ilots aux Sables (Isles of Sand), lies a beautiful unspoilt stretch of tropical coastline. Walk across the small hill to the east of the airport.

🏃 Activities

Bora Dive & Research   DIVING
(www.boraresearch.com) This PADI-accredited diving centre is one of the best on the island. It offers everything from introductory dives to night dives, packages and courses. Prices start at Ar270,000 for a two-dive package. It also runs whale watching in winter. The dive centre is part of the Princesse Bora Lodge & Spa (p207).

🛏 Sleeping

La Baleine   BUNGALOW €
(☑032 40 257 18; www.hotel-la-baleine.com; d/f Ar50,000/100,000; ⚕) The beachfront bungalows are rather basic but the location is fantastic: a palm-fringed beach that is a prime spot for whale watching in winter. Service is friendly and attentive.

Chez Nath   HOSTEL €€
(☑034 41 754 28; brunococolodge@gmail.com; dm/d €7/20) This little hostel is a great find, a backpacker vibe with a touch of class. The bathrooms are lovely, an unusual treat at this price point. Best of all are the dorms (three or four beds), a boon for single travellers. It has a great restaurant-bar (mains Ar15,000 to Ar20,000), with regular events such as live music and beach BBQs.

Jardins d'Eden   BUNGALOW €€
(☑034 09 265 76; www.lesjardinsdeden-sainte-marie-madagascar.com; d bungalows Ar90,000; ⚕) Botanophiles will love this guesthouse with grand views, high up on a hill overlooking the pirate cemetery. The expansive gardens are full of exquisite plants and are a haven of cooler temperatures on hot summer days. Excellent Indian and Creole cuisine is served too. It's a shame the hotel keeps habituated lemurs however, a practice conservationists condemn.

★ Libertalia   BUNGALOW €€€
(☑034 18 997 27, 020 57 923 03; www.lelibertalia. com; d Ar198,000; ⚕≋) 🖉 The lascivious whistles of the house parrot welcome you to this popular hotel named after the mythical pirate kingdom. The setting is unique, with a small private island connected to the lovely beach by a great swimming dock. A sophisticated kitchen, friendly staff and special touches such as hydrophones for listening to the whales singing make for a winning proposition.

Owners Didier and Martine are founder members of Cétamada (p204) and can arrange whale-watching excursions, other boat trips and diving. Kayaks, mountain bikes, motorbikes and scooters are also available. Accepts credit cards.

Ravoraha   BOUTIQUE HOTEL €€€
(☑032 40 513 90; www.ravoraha.com; d incl breakfast from €40; ⚕) 🖉 The Buddha-bar-style decor is among the most elaborate on the island – everywhere you look there are brightly-coloured soft furnishings, statues, vintage lanterns and tropical flowers. The standard bungalows are rather small but the tree house and family bungalows are fantastic, as is the lagoon in front of the hotel.

Ravoraha is committed to minimising its environmental impact but maximising its social impact. It notably eschews the use of air-con, offers travellers the opportunity to take their rubbish back home thanks to its plastic compactor; it also asks travellers to rent scooters and bikes directly from local villagers and pays for all the school fees of the local primary school.

Les Villas de Vohilava   VILLA €€€

(☑ 020 57 900 16; www.vohilava.com; villas for 4 people from Ar288,000) These five large and very well-done beachfront villas, with two to three rooms, a kitchen and a chef, are designed for groups of four to 10 people (food supplies are not included). The attentive owner, Henri, ensures a quality stay. You can hire bikes and scooters, and kayaks are free. Whale-watching trips and other excursions can be arranged.

Princesse Bora
Lodge & Spa   LUXURY HOTEL €€€

(☑ 034 05 090 48; www.princessebora.com; d half board per person from €125; ❄❡❄) One of Madagascar's top resorts. Creative touches include an extraordinary spa with pirogue tubs and its own essential-oil laboratory, an extensive wine cellar with a private label, a nearby tropical nursery featuring the island's diverse species, huge bungalows with suspended wooden beds, enamel bathrooms and serpentine corridors reminiscent of a reef. There's also an arty pool and an elegant restaurant.

Set on a nice beach with comfortable sunloungers and outdoor showers, none of this comes cheaply, but this is one high-end property where you really do get what you pay for. The secret is the extraordinary Swiss family behind it, for whom the lodge is not just a business but a ruling passion extending well beyond the normal boundaries of tourism.

Hôtel Lakana   BUNGALOW €€€

(☑ 0324 45 434 45; www.sainte-marie-hotel. com; d bungalows Ar135,000-150,000; ❡) This hotel and restaurant is known for its bungalows on stilts over the sea, each with its own bathroom back on land. Smarter bungalows (with bathroom) are clustered in a well-tended garden.

✗ Eating

★ Chez Samson   SEAFOOD €€€

(☑ 020 57 914 01, 034 38 129 60; borahamazava@ yahoo.fr; Baie d'Ampanihy; menu Ar40,000) Samson trained as a chef in the best kitchens of Madagascar and he decided early on that the remote and stunning location of his restaurant would be no obstacle to fine dining. You're therefore guaranteed to be treated

to the most delicious (and fresh) seafood, salads and indulgent desserts, all beautifully presented and with views of the Baie d'Ampanihy.

The restaurant also has a couple of basic but tidy bungalows (Ar50,000) if you'd like to spend the night in this wonderful corner of the island.

Chez Nono   SEAFOOD €€€

(☑ 020 57 901 98; Baie d'Ampanihy; menu Ar30,000-40,000) A bungalow restaurant in a clearing overlooking the Baie d'Ampanihy. The food here is fresh from the sea, and fabulous. By fresh, we mean it has wicker baskets of live fish and mangrove crabs in the nearby creek, while the morning's catch of shrimp is still kicking. It also organises excursions around Baie d'Ampanihy. Call ahead to book.

☆ Entertainment

Casa à Nono   CLUB

(◷ Thu, Fri & bank holidays) The main party spot on Sainte Marie – it's near the airport.

Île aux Nattes (Nosy Nato)

What a lovely place this is. Île aux Nattes is a classic tropical island, with curving white beaches and overhanging palms, a turquoise sea with waves breaking over the reef, a gentle breeze and a lush green interior. While only a brief pirogue (dugout canoe) ride from the southern tip of Île Sainte Marie, there's a palpable sense of isolation and adventure. Numerous sand pathways open the way for exploration without the possibility of getting lost in an area only 2km across. So if you are suffering from visions of tropical paradise, here is your medicine.

◉ Sights

Wandering about and taking in the exquisite landscape is one of the best things to do on Île aux Nattes.

★ Maison Blanche   VIEWPOINT

(Ar3000 or a drink; ◷ 8am-6.30pm) No stay on the island would be complete without a sundowner at Maison Blanche: this atypical house has a rooftop terrace with 360-degree views of the island, Sainte Marie and the surrounding lagoon. It is jaw-droppingly beautiful and well worth the entry fee (or even better, a drink).

🏊 Activities

Most hotels provide snorkelling equipment for free; if you'd like to take things further, Sainte-Marie Plongée, on the northeast side of the island, has PADI-certified instructors; the best time for sea-based activities is August to February.

During whale season (July to September), the west coast is a prime viewing spot with whales breaching just off the beach. Most hotels organise whale-watching excursions; Cétamada (p204) has a list of accredited operators.

Sainte-Marie Plongée　　　　　DIVING
(☑032 29 898 54, 032 52 706 26; Baboo Village) This PADI-certified dive centre offers dives across around Île aux Nattes and Sainte Marie, as well as various other sea-based activities including whale watching in winter, kayaking and snorkelling.

🛌 Sleeping

⭐**Chez Sica**　　　　　BUNGALOW €
(☑032 42 478 86, 032 41 656 98; www.chezsica.com; Île aux Nattes; d/f Ar40,000/80,000) Wow. If you are looking for inexpensive accommodation, look no further: here it is. The hotel is like an open park beneath the palms, with an absolutely gorgeous location on a fringing reef. Most bungalows have a thatched porch with hammocks with dreamy views; bathrooms and toilets are shared. Guests also have access to a well-equipped communal kitchen.

The kitchen makes it a great budget choice for longer stays. Alternatively, the Beach Bar, run by the delightful Mariella, opens morning and evening for breakfast and drinks; delicious meals (Ar15,000 to Ar20,000) can also be prepared by local cook Judith (you'll need to order ahead).

A pirogue from Île Sainte Marie to Chez Sica costs Ar10,000, or you can walk (30 minutes) from the northern drop-off point.

Chez Tity　　　　　BUNGALOW €
(☑034 04 065 80; cheztity@gmail.com; d Ar40,000, without bathroom Ar35,000) A basic place, with surly welcome and slightly rundown bungalows.

⭐**Les Lémuriens**　　　　　BUNGALOW €€
(☑032 41 973 03; www.les-lemuriens.com; d/f €30/50, s/d without bathroom €10/20; 🖳) By far the prettiest hotel on Île aux Nattes, this little boutique number on the southern tip of the island is a gem: the bungalows are gorgeous, the food is excellent and the location on a curving beach fabulous. It's quite windy in winter (June to August) but at other times the free kayaking and snorkelling come into their own.

Whale-watching excursions are available in winter; the hotel is a member of Cétamada (p204). Transfers to/from the airport/port of Ambodifotatra cost Ar25,000/40,000.

La Maison Blanche　　　　　GUESTHOUSE €€
(☑032 40 084 32; www.ileauxnattes.net; d Ar60,000-90,000, f Ar110,000; 🖳) On such a small island, La Maison Blanche is an unusual proposition: accommodation that is not by the beach. Instead, its unique selling point is its phenomenal panoramic views, which you can enjoy from every room and the stunning rooftop terrace. Rooms are huge and beautifully decorated, with parquet floors, white walls and colourful soft furnishings.

Room No 1 (La Tête dans les Etoiles) is the size of a small flat and would be excellent for groups of friends or families. Meals are available on order. Note that access is via a very steep staircase.

Baboo Village　　　　　BUNGALOW €€€
(☑034 17 198 19; www.baboo-village.com; d/f €40/60; 🖳) At the northern tip of the island, Baboo Village enjoys a prime spot on the lagoon separating Île aux Nattes and Île Sainte Marie, an ideal place for swimming, snorkelling and generally revelling in the view (the loungers on the jetty are prime real estate). Note that seafront bungalows have private but separate bathrooms. Top restaurant too.

Sambatra　　　　　BUNGALOW €€€
(☑033 76 834 99; www.sambatrabeachlodge.com; d incl breakfast €55; 🖳) This South African–owned establishment brings something of the backpacker vibe to Île aux Nattes with its cool bar, beach dining room and movie and jam nights. The bungalows are very nicely done and all have hot water. The hotel is located on a west-facing beach with phenomenal sunsets.

Analatsara Eco-Lodge　　　　　BUNGALOW €€€
(☑032 02 127 70; www.analatsara.net; d incl breakfast €40-70; 🖳) This high-quality miniresort comes complete with local art, convivial communal spaces and a lovely beach. A couple of bungalows share a bathroom, others have their own. The standout is the tree house, with trapdoor entry. It's a shame the generator is so loud. We take issue with the

so-called 'animal hospital' for habituated lemurs, a practice decried by conservationists.

A six-person villa with housekeeper, chef and 16-hour electricity is €850 per week (food supplies not included). Transfer from the airport/tip of Sainte Marie to Analatsara costs €15/€10; alternatively it's a 30-minute walk from the northern drop-off point on Île aux Nattes. Credit cards accepted. Set menu (three courses and alcoholic drinks) is €22.

🛍 Shopping

Tsara Mora   FOOD & DRINKS

(⊙9am-5pm Sun-Fri, to noon Sat) A great little grocery store where you'll find picnic and store-cupboard essentials, as well as toiletries.

ⓘ Getting There & Away

A pirogue between the southern tip of Sainte Marie and Île aux Nattes is Ar2000. Hotels can organise transfers directly to the airport or Port Barachois in Ambodifotatra.

BAIE D'ANTONGIL & MASOALA PENINSULA

The remote Baie d'Antongil stretches from Mananara around Maroantsetra to Cap Masoala at the end of the Masoala Peninsula, a deep blue 'U' teeming with wildlife where mountainous forests tumble into the sea. Cut off from easy road access to the south, and with nothing but hiking trails elsewhere, this is a place whose only reliable contact with the outside world is the intermittent flights into Maroantsetra and seasonal ferries to Manana. But this isolation is precisely what makes it so special: Masoala is a Unesco World Heritage Site thanks to its exceptional biodiversity. If you're in need of natural wonder, this is the place to come.

ⓘ Getting There & Away

Baie d'Antongil is hard to reach. The main gateway is Maroantsetra, which you can fly to from Antananarivo.

From September to February, regular ferry services also link Maroantsetra with Mananara and Soaniera-Ivongo.

The RN5 from Maroantsetra to Mananara is in terrible condition, with more than a dozen river crossings; there is no regular *taxi-brousse* service and the only way to drive it is by motorbike. *Moto-taxis* do the trip in about six hours.

Mananara

POP 46,000

Mananara is a small, dusty and very out-of-the-way town set in a clove- and vanilla-producing area at the southern entrance to Baie d'Antongil. It's low on attractions but if you're travelling on the RN5, it's likely you'll have to stop over. On the plus side, you'll get the chance to visit Aye-Aye Island, which is the best place to see Madagascar's most reclusive and bizarre lemur.

👁 Sights

Aye-Aye Island   WILDLIFE RESERVE

(night tour Ar30,000) This small, privately owned island in the middle of the Mananara River is home to about 15 aye-ayes (and other lemurs). A sighting isn't guaranteed but this is where you stand the best chance of seeing them in Madagascar: the island means they're relatively contained and the coconut trees aren't so high that all you'll see is a brown blob and a pair of glinting eyes. Night tours can be organised, including transport (car and pirogue) at Chez Roger (p210).

Parc National Mananara Nord   PARK

(www.parcs-madagascar.com/aire-protegee/parc-national-mananara-nord; entry permits per day Ar45,000, guide per day Ar40,000) Parc National Mananara Nord is something of a misnomer: not only is the park located south of Mananara, its entrance is in Sahasoa, 30km from Mananara.

The remote 240-sq-km park encompasses some of the last remaining lowland rainforest in the country. An additional 10 sq km of islets and surrounding reefs are protected as a marine park, the largest being Nosy Atafana. The park itself isn't the most traveller-friendly: the two-hour terrestrial circuit requires four hours of hiking to get there. The **MNP office** (☏033 19 463 67, 034 40 146 07) is in Sahasoa, about 30km south of Mananara.

The park has two main circuits, one terrestrial and the other marine. The terrestrial circuit begins 6km south of the park office by foot. It takes four hours to get there, two to do the circuit, and another four to get back. You're advised to camp overnight in the park. The marine circuit includes a trip to Nosy Atafana, and costs an additional Ar120,000 to Ar150,000 for boat and fuel. The cost per person thus declines with the

Baie d'Antongil & the Masoala Peninsula

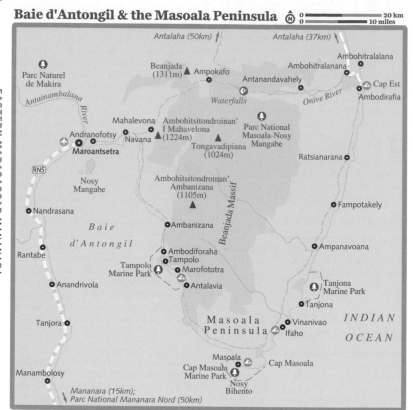

size of the group (maximum eight). A third circuit takes two full days and covers both land and sea. For any trip in the park, you'll need to be self-sufficient with food and water, and, if hiking, in good shape. Camping is Ar5000 per tent.

While lemurs are not always seen, Manarara Nord contains *indris,* brown lemurs, ruffed lemurs and aye-ayes, and is the only known habitat of the hairy-eared dwarf lemur. There is also a variety of geckos, including the endemic uroplatus and day geckos. Offshore there are dugong.

🛏 Sleeping

Chez Roger BUNGALOW €

(☑ 032 52 329 87, 033 08 769 22; d Ar40,000) This is the best place to stay if you want to visit Aye-Aye Island (p209). The rooms (and bathrooms) have seen better days, but service is very friendly and the restaurant does decent meals (Ar15,000 to Ar20,000 for a main).

Sahasoa Bungalows BUNGALOW €

(☑ 033 19 463 67, 034 40 146 07; d Ar20,000) These bungalows on a tropical-paradise beach in Sahasoa are right next to the Parc National Mananara Nord office. For meals, you'll need to hire a cook in the village and buy the main ingredient – fish or chicken – to put on top of your rice.

ⓘ Information

Bank of Africa (⊙ 8am-3.30pm Mon-Fri) Has an ATM.

ⓘ Getting There & Away

BOAT

The **Melissa Express** (☑ 032 68 447 01, 033 37 838 68; melissaexpress1@gmail.com) passenger boat operates along the coast between Maroantsetra and Soanierana-Ivongo with the following schedule.

➡ Mananara–Soanierana-Ivongo (Ar135,000, five hours, three times a week March to August, daily September to February). Passengers can also buy a ticket all the way to Tamatave: the Soanierana–Tamatave leg is done by *taxi-brousse*.

➤ Mananara–Maroantsetra (Ar80,000, three hours, twice a week September to February).

The service is subject to frequent weather-related interruptions, and the duration of travel is merely indicative. Don't travel by boat if you need to be anywhere by a certain time, or leave plenty of time.

Cargo boats sail all along the coast from Tamatave as far as Sambava. They take passengers although there are no set fares, routes or schedules, and no facilities on board. Bring sun protection (an umbrella is handy), food and water, and a sense of adventure. Note that people are often seasick.

MOTO-TAXI

Moto-taxis leave from the parcage close to the hospital. They charge Ar300,000 for the six-hour trip to Maroantsetra and Ar1 million for Soanierana-Ivongo, which can be done in a day.

TAXI-BROUSSE

Cooperative **Kofifen** (☑ 034 07 054 88) runs *taxi-brousses* between Mananara and Tamatave, stopping in Soanierana-Ivongo. The fare is Ar100,000 for a place in the cab (the vehicle on this route is a pickup truck). The trip takes at least two days.

There are no regular *taxi-brousse* services to Maroantsetra.

Manompana

POP 10,000

This small coastal village 38km north of Soanierana-Ivongo is where to head if you want to ditch beach tourism in favor of rural isolation. Attractions include the scenic Point Tintingue and the protected Ambodiriana Forest.

◉ Sights

Ambodiriana Forest NATURE RESERVE
(☑ 033 41 424 04; www.adafam.org; park permit Ar35,000, guide Ar20,000) Rare species flourish in this protected humid forest, including the mouse lemur, the candy cane palm (*Dypsis paludosa*) and a parasitic orchid (*Gastrodia madagascariensis*). The forest is managed by the association Adefa, which organises a day trip that takes in the reserve's three waterfalls. It's a shame the package is so expensive: on top of the permit and guide, you're required to take a spotter (Ar15,000), a pirogue (Ar18,000) and a picnic lunch for everyone (Ar10,000 per person).

🛏 Sleeping & Eating

Grez Grondin BUNGALOW €
(☑ 033 14 980 15, 034 06 925 85; Antanambe; d/f bungalows Ar40,000/80,000) Wherever you're from, arriving here is a delightful surprise: charming bungalows, a friendly owner and a stunning location, on a beach at the tip of a lagoon. The bungalows are simple but there is hot water, a rarity around here. Meals (three courses, Ar20,000) are fabulous too, especially the seafood (the owner is from Réunion). Call ahead to book meals.

Chez Gonneau BUNGALOW €
(☑ 034 68 880 61; www.sites.google.com/site/chezgonneau; Antanambe; d Ar40,000) This B&B is run by a French couple who were born and grew up in Madagascar; they've opened their family home to visitors, who can sleep in one of six bungalows nestled in the expansive grounds. Meals (Ar20,000 for three courses) are served and the owners can organise all manner of excursions, including at sea (they have a boat).

Au Bon Ancrage/Chez Wen Ki BUNGALOW €
(☑ 033 19 676 64; Manompana; d bungalows Ar25,000) Basic bungalows on the beach, with running water. No meals served.

❶ Getting There & Away

Manompana is on the *taxi-brousse* route between Mananara and Tamatave. They are often full but you may get lucky. Alternatively, plan ahead by calling the *taxi-brousse* station at either end the day before and booking your seat.

Maroantsetra

POP 27,000

Set at the apex of the Baie d'Antongil, near the mouth of the Antainambalana River, Maroantsetra is full of languid charm, and enjoys both river scenery and ocean views. It's a great place to spend a day before setting off to the protected areas of Masoala or Makira. Just be aware that Maroantsetra's climate is one of the wettest in Madagascar, particularly from May to September.

◉ Sights

Maroantsetra is set in the most beautiful location and although it has few sights per se, you would be strongly advised to do a 'tour de ville', basically a guided tour of town. These usually take in coconut groves, vanilla/clove plantations, the boatyards along the

EASTERN MADAGASCAR MANOMPANA

canal and the MNP interpretation centre. The tours are your best chance of spotting Maroantsetra's tomato frog, a big bright-red frog found nowhere else on earth except Maroantsetra's back gardens. MNP (p216) and top-end hotels offer these tours (allow Ar70,000 for the guide).

CPALI AGRICULTURAL CENTRE
(Conservation Through Poverty Alleviation, International; ☑ 032 04 452 46; www.cpali.org) This worthy NGO works with rural farmers living on the edge of biodiversity hotspots to develop sustainable livelihoods that support both people and ecosystems. Its main activity is the production of wild silk made from the cocoons of local silkworms. At the facility in Maroantsetra, you can visit the workshop where the cocoons are processed into innovative textiles. You can purchase artefacts in the small shop; visits are free but donations encouraged. Call ahead.

🛏 Sleeping

Bungalows Vanga BUNGALOW €
(☑ 032 64 412 41, 034 79 638 05; r Ar25,000) These beachside bungalows are a great budget option: right by the beach, with gorgeous views of Nosy Mangabe, but with cold bucket showers only and a fair walk from town. The hotel will cook meals (Ar8000 to Ar10,000 for mains) if you order in advance.

Masoala Resort BUNGALOW €€
(☑ 032 11 075 51, 033 15 051 52; www.masoala resort.com; d garden/sea view Ar85,000/105,000; ❄ 🛜 🏊) This hotel occupies a fine location, with a grand view of Nosy Mangabe. Although the bungalows feel somewhat dated, they are spotless, spacious and comfortable. Each has its own decking area, from where you can take in the lovely tropical surroundings. Service is attentive and the restaurant serves delicious, wholesome meals (Ar45,000 for two generous courses).

Manager Franck has planted a small botanical trail, with typical local plants such as clove and tamarind; he's also dug a wildlife pond, which teems with wildlife, including Maroantsetra's rare and endemic tomato frog.

Le Coco Beach BUNGALOW €€
(☑ 032 04 807 58; cocobeachotelmaroantsetra@ yahoo.fr; d Ar60,000; ❄ 🛜) The atmospheric bungalows, set in a coconut grove by the river, are reasonably priced for Maroantsetra but the whole place feels a little unloved.

There is wi-fi in the reception area. No restaurant on-site.

Manga Beach Hotel HOTEL €€€
(www.mangabeach-madagascar.com; d/tr Ar129,000/165,000; ❄ 🛜) This hotel feels slightly out of place in Maroantsetra. The large concrete building and plain rooms feel out of touch with the thatched-roof bungalows and tropical vibe of the area. That said, the rooms are huge and undeniably comfortable, with large beds and good mattresses. There is a bar-restaurant, with a huge terrace overlooking the canal.

 Eating

Vivanette MALAGASY €
(Ar7000-15,000; ⊙ 7am-9pm) This open-air restaurant-bar, right on the canal by the bridge, is a great spot for a quick meal or beer with a side order of sea breezes. The fare is simple but well cooked: *mi sao* (noodle stir-fry), soups, kebabs, fried fish etc.

Florida Snack CHINESE €
(dishea Ar4000-8000; ⊙ 7am-9pm) This Chinese-run cafe serves the usual Malagasy fare, along with Chinese favourites such as spring rolls and sweet and sour dishes. It also has delicious homemade yoghurts.

Restaurant Ravinala MALAGASY €€
(Ar8000-18,000; ⊙ 7am-9pm) Along with the usual assortment of stir-fries and grilled fish, Ravinala also serves decent pizzas.

🍺 Drinking & Nightlife

Chez Binina BAR
(⊙ 4pm-late) A typical Malagasy bar, open-air with a BBQ at the front churning out *masikita* (small kebabs). This is a nice place to stop for a drink, watch some football and enjoy Maroantsetra's good vibes.

Super Goût BAR
(⊙ 2pm-late) A friendly bar that comes into its own on *vendredi joli* (aka Friday night), with karaoke and music in general.

🛈 Information

Bank of Africa (⊙ 8am-2.30pm Mon-Fri) and **BNI** (⊙ 1-4.30pm Mon, 8-11.45am & 2-4pm Tue-Fri) both have branches with ATMs.

🛈 Getting There & Away

Maroantsetra is one of the most isolated towns in Madagascar. The RN5 between Soanierana-Ivongo and Maroantsetra is so bad that *taxi-brousse* have stopped running from Maroantsetra to Mananara.

The air and boat options aren't much better: there are flights to Tana only and boat services to Mananara between September and February only.

AIR

➤ Tsaradia flights connect Maroantsetra twice a week with Antananarivo (just once from January to March).

➤ Weather may affect plane schedules, particularly during the rainiest months (winter and summer).

➤ Flights fill up quickly during vanilla season (July to October) so book ahead.

BOAT

➤ The **Melissa Express** (Ar80,000; ⊙ 8-11.30am & 2.30-4.30pm Mon-Fri) passenger boat runs between Maroantsetra and Mananara (three hours, which then runs on to Soanierana-Ivongo) twice a week between September and February. Fare is Ar80,000. The service is subject to frequent weather-related interruptions, and the duration of travel is merely indicative.

➤ Cargo boats sail from Maroantsetra to Île Sainte Marie, Tamatave, Antalaha and Mananara. They take passengers although there are no set fares, routes or schedules, and no facilities on board. Bring sun and rain protection (an umbrella is handy), food and water, and a sense of adventure. Note that people are often seasick.

MOTORCYCLE

The only reliable option out of Maroantsetra by road for the time being is a *moto-taxi*. It costs Ar300,000 to go to Mananara (six hours) and Ar1.6 million to Soanierana-Ivongo (two days, although you may want to make it three for comfort). The fares include all boat/bridge crossings as well as the food and accommodation allowance for the driver.

A few tips for travelling by *moto-taxi*:

➤ This is very tough going – be prepared to get wet, walk, help push the bike through a swamp or out of a rut.

➤ You *will* get wet and muddy – it rains a lot around here, there are rivers to cross, rafts to get on and off etc. Make sure you have waterproof trousers, a waterproof jacket and gumboots. It's also a good idea to line the inside of your bag (even though the drivers will provide a plastic sheet for the outside).

➤ Consider hiring a separate bike for luggage: this is for your comfort as well as your security.

➤ Make sure you agree on the timing of the itinerary with your driver: *moto-taxis* are obsessed with getting from A to B in the quickest time

possible and find the concept of leisurely travel hard to grasp.

Be Leonor (☑ 032 43 812 42, 034 13 696 24; www.facebook.com/norbe), the president of the local *moto-taxi* association, is warmly recommended; unfortunately he doesn't speak English. Otherwise ask at **Bar Taxi Moto** (☑ 032 52 553 45) close to the market.

PRIVATE 4WD

Because of the appalling condition of the road, finding even a private 4WD is very difficult, not to mention costly (Ar4 million to Ar6 million). Local tour operators (p215) can help you find a vehicle.

❶ Getting Around

➤ The airport is about 8km southwest of town. The journey to town by tuk-tuk is Ar10,000 per person.

➤ Tuk-tuks zoom about town; most trips will cost Ar2000 to Ar3000 per person.

Parc National Masoala-Nosy Mangabe

The magical Masoala (mash wala) is the site of a 2100-sq-km national park containing one of the best primary rainforests in the country. The bulk of the park is on the mainland peninsula but it also encompasses the small island of Nosy Mangabe (p214) off Maroantsetra and an isolated pocket around Cap Est, the country's easternmost point. There are also three protected marine areas: Tampolo Marine Park on the peninsula's southwestern coast, Cap Masoala Marine Park at the tip of the peninsula and Tanjona Marine Park on the southeastern coast.

◉ Sights

The national park is famous for its fauna and flora; its landscapes, with rainforest-covered mountains tumbling into the sea, are unrivalled too.

★ **Parc National Masoala-Nosy Mangabe** NATIONAL PARK

(www.parcs-madagascar.com/aire-protegee/parc-national-masoala-nosy-mangabe; entry permit per day 45,000, compulsory guide per day Ar100,000) This 2100-sq-km national park contains one of the best primary rainforests in the country. It is famous for its vegetation, which includes rare hardwoods, bamboos, and dozens of species of fern, palm and orchid. Ten lemur species are found here, along with several tenrec and mongoose species, 14 bat species, 60 reptile species and about 85 bird species. It also encompasses three protected marine areas. The reserve is only accessible by boat, or on foot if you are hiking.

The park's headquarters (p216) are in Maroantsetra, where you can get permits and guides. There is also a park office in Antalaha on the east coast.

★ **Nosy Mangabe**   NATIONAL PARK
(www.parcs-madagascar.com/aire-protegee/parc-national-masoala-nosy-mangabe; entry permit per day Ar45,000, compulsory guide day/overnight trip Ar70,000/100,000) Part of Parc National Masoala-Nosy Mangabe, this thickly forested and mountainous tropical island is one of the crown jewels of the Antongil Bay. With huge soaring canarium trees arising from flying buttress roots, a rusty shipwreck piercing one side, waterfalls, a yellow sickle-shaped beach, foreign inscriptions and the omnipresent sound of the jungle, it is quite possibly the closest thing to a Robinson Crusoe experience you'll get. It rains a lot, though, so be prepared.

Reptiles and amphibians thrive thanks to the lack of predators, including the leaf-tailed gecko, one of nature's most accomplished camouflage artists. You'll also find several species of chameleon, many frogs and several harmless species of snake, including the Madagascar tree boa. It is also home to various lemurs, including the elusive aye-aye, which was introduced here in 1967 to protect the species from extinction. It is highly unlikely you'll see one, but you'll no doubt see the white-fronted brown lemur, who like hanging out by the camp,

and with a bit of luck, the black and white ruffed lemur too.

There are a handful of well-maintained trails: a popular option takes you to the summit of the island. Another leads to Plage des Hollandais, a beach with rocks bearing the scratched names of some 17th-century Dutch sailors. From July to September, you can see whales offshore.

The island is usually included in itineraries combining Masoala (either as a picnic stopover or an overnight stay) but you could also visit as a day trip from Maroantsetra.

MNP runs a very well-equipped beachside **campground** (camping per tent Ar5000) with shelters, picnic tables, a kitchen, showers and flush toilets. It's an idyllic spot.

Entry permits can be obtained at the MNP office (p216) in Maroantsetra. Boat transfers can be arranged through your guide; the trip takes 30 to 45 minutes.

🏃 Activities

There are excellent opportunities at Parc National Masoala-Nosy Mangabe for hiking, sea kayaking, snorkelling and swimming. The entire peninsula is exceptionally wet, however, particularly during June and July, when river levels are highest. October to December are somewhat drier and best for hiking. July to September is whale season, when humpback whales come to the bay to give birth and mate: they can be seen from the coast and on boat transfers from Maroantsetra.

Hiking

This is a hiker's paradise. If you are staying in the lodges around Ambodifohara, there are many short trails that you can take. There are also three main long-distance trails for serious hikers: guiding fees for these routes are set, even if you decide to do it in fewer days. Park permits are not included; note that some stretches of the routes are not actually in the park itself so you won't need a permit for every day. The MNP office (p216) will advise you.

➡ Maroantsetra to Antalaha passes through rice paddies and gentler terrain. It is the easiest but also the least interesting. A guide for five days is Ar800,000.

➡ For forest lovers, the Maroantsetra to Cap Est route (up to eight days) is more interesting, particularly the spectacular Cascade (waterfall) Bevontsira, but also more challenging, with tough terrain, river crossings, mountains and (shudder) leeches. A guide is Ar1.2 million.

➡ Finally, you can walk the entire rim of the peninsula, from Maroantsetra to Antalaha via Cap Masoala and Cap Est. This journey takes up to 15 days. A guide is just over Ar2 million.

You'll need to bring all your food and camping equipment with you. Contact local operators to organise a package including cook, porters and camping equipment.

All long-distance hikes are fairly demanding and involve muddy stretches. At certain times of the year you may have to wade through rivers. Ask at the MNP office or with guides about trail conditions.

☞ Tours

All lodges in the park can organise packages including guides, park permits and boat transfers as well as accommodation on a full-board basis. If you'd like to mix things up however, either by adding a couple of days of hiking to or from the park, having the opportunity to camp, staying in village accommodation, or combining Masoala with other nearby protected areas such as Makira, try the following.

Ecolodge Chez Arol (p216) As well as having a lodge in Masoala, the Malagasy and French owners also have a small lodge in Makira and can organise varied itineraries in the area.

Elysée Velomasy (☏ 032 49 512 64, 033 14 829 43; elyseeguide@yahoo.fr) One of the best guides in the area Elysée is fluent in English and the president of the local guides' association. He is knowledgeable, kind and reliable and can organise anything from a standard trip to multiday hikes, taking your budget constraints into consideration.

Mada Expeditions (☏ 032 86 614 68, 032 77 266 42; www.mada-expeditions.com) This tour operator offers circuits across Madagascar but one of its fortes is Masoala, where it has a small lodge at Cap Masoala. It runs multiday hikes and kayak trips on the peninsula.

Sobeha Tour (☏ 032 50 615 26; www.sobeha.com) The founder of this tour operator, Fredel Mamindra, is from Maroantsetra and although his agency offers the gamut of circuits on the island, his home region has a special place in his heart. The

agency is one of the few operators that organises circuits on the RN5.

The companies all can provide camping equipment and arrange cooks, porters, supplies and guides as well as transport logistics such as boats, pirogues etc.

🛏 Sleeping

Chez Maman'iMela   BUNGALOW €
(d Ar60,000) This is the most authentic (and cheapest!) option in Masoala. Maman'iMela has four impeccable bungalows (with electricity) at the heart of the village of Ambodifohara: two are en suite (bucket showers and flush) and two share bathroom and toilet. The only way to book Chez Maman'iMela is through your MNP guide; you'll also have to bring a cook for your meals.

If you add accommodation, the cost of the cook and food supplies, you're looking at Ar150,000 or less per person per day (depending on the number of people in your group), far less than other types of accommodation in the park.

★ **Masoala Forest Lodge**   LODGE €€€
(☏ 032 05 415 86; www.masoalaforestlodge.com; per person 3 nights, all-inclusive €1990; ⊙ late Apr-Dec; 🕿) 🏊 Staying here is akin to a high-end safari, including luxury tents (with hot water). Located on a 100,000-sq-metre forest reserve, there are just seven palm-thatched tents up in the trees. The owners, Pierre and Maria Bessler, have been here for more than 15 years and poured their heart into this little haven: service is truly stellar and the experience unique.

There are activities galore – from wildlife walks to snorkelling, kayaking, boat trips and more. Meals are sumptuous too, with teatime and nightly drinks around the fire thrown in as well. The minimum program for a three-night stay is all inclusive (private flights from Antananarivo to Maroantsetra, boat transfer, park permits, meals and activities). Packages are also available for four, seven, 10 and 11 nights.

Tampolodge   LODGE €€€
(☏ 032 55 636 04, Italy +39 36 63 54 13 02; tampolodge@yahoo.fr; d bungalows full board per person Ar350,000; 🕿) This lodge has a great location, on a fantastic arc of beach split by the alluring S-bend of the Tampolo river. Accommodation is in basic bungalows with cold water, but with large bathrooms. Daniele, the Italian manager, likes nothing

better than to cook up a storm for his clients (a mix of fine Italian and Malagasy fare).

The lodge is equipped with solar panels for electricity and also has wi-fi. Boat transfer from Maroantsetra costs Ar450,000 per person with an additional Ar60,000 per day spent in the park. Park permits and guiding fees are additional (although the lodge can arrange them for you).

Ecolodge Chez Arol   LODGE €€€

(📋 032 40 889 02, 033 12 902 77; www.arol-ecolodge.com; per person full board €85-135) 🍴 Set in expansive grounds right on the edge of the forest, Arol offers thatched-hut bungalows with hot water. Run by a local Malagasy and his French business associate, it is one of the oldest lodges in the area and offers a range of excellent packages combining nature as well as culture. Prices are all inclusive (transport, guide, activities etc).

The lodge actively supports the local community: it helped install a micro hydro-turbine to provide electricity for the village and supports the local school. Electricity comes courtesy of said micro hydro-turbine and solar panels.

🛈 Information

The park headquarters is located at the **MNP office** (📋 032 04 627 70; www.parcs-madagascar. com/aire-protegee/parc-national-masoala-nosy-mangabe; ⊙ 8am-4pm) in Maroantsetra. The guides here are well organised, and many speak English.

Hikes can also be arranged at the MNP office in Antalaha or in Ambodirafia, near Cap Est, although fewer guides there speak English.

Guides are mandatory and cost Ar100,000 per day (and Ar60,000 for your last day, when you'll get the boat back to Maroantsetra); there are set fees for multiday hikes.

🛈 Getting There & Away

The park is only accessible by boat (which is pricey – allow around Ar450,000 per person, although this is often included in packages), or on foot if you are hiking. All the accommodation options in the reserve organise boat transfers.

Understand
Madagascar

History

In the grand scheme of history, Madagascar is a baby: although the country has existed in its current form for nearly 100 million years, humans only set foot on the island a few thousand years ago, a marked difference to nearby East Africa, which is generally seen as the cradle of humanity. Like its neighbours on the mainland, however, its modern history has been shaped by colonialism, and the struggles to shake off its long shadow.

Arrivals from Asia & Europe

In 2015 underwater explorers pulled an ingot from a shipwreck off the coast of Île Sainte Marie, claiming it was part of the long-lost treasure of infamous Scottish pirate Captain William Kidd. UN investigators quickly dismissed the claim, however: the ingot was a mere block of lead, not silver.

Considering that human beings evolved on the African continent just across the Mozambique Channel, their arrival in Madagascar was comparatively late (between 2500 and 4000 years ago) and by a rather circuitous route. Anthropological and ethnographical clues indicate that Indo-Malayan seafarers may have colonised the island after migrating in a single voyage, stopping en route at various points in the Indian Ocean. Their coastal craft possibly worked their way along the shores of India, Arabia and East Africa, trading as they went, before finally arriving in Madagascar. Linguistic clues also support this theory, as elements of Sanskrit have been identified in the Malagasy language.

This theory was challenged in 2018, however, when scientists from the Zoological Society London found elephant bird fossilised bones with cut marks. The bones were dated to about 10,000 years ago, suggesting that humans were living on Madagascar much earlier than initially thought.

Asian settlers brought with them the food crops of their homelands, such as rice. This Asian influence was tempered over the years by contact with Arab and African traders, who plied the seas of the region with their cargoes of silk, spices and slaves. Gradually the Asian culture of the new settlers was subsumed into a series of geographically defined kingdoms, which in turn gave rise to many different Malagasy tribes.

Marco Polo was the first European to report the existence of a 'great red island', which he named Madagascar, after possibly having confused it with Mogadishu in Somalia. But Arab cartographers had long known the island as Gezirat Al-Komor, meaning 'island of the moon' (a name later transferred to the Comoros). It wasn't until 1500 that the first Euro-

TIMELINE	11th century BC	5th century AD	15th century
	Elephant bird fossilised bones bearing cut marks and dated 10,000 BC suggest humans were present on the island.	Madagascar is settled by Indo-Malayans who migrate by sea from the distant shores of Indonesia and Malaysia. They bring with them agricultural, linguistic and cultural traditions.	Arabic script brought by Muslim immigrants is adapted to Malagasy language. Sorabe (Great Writings) is the preserve of a selected few and used only for high-profile documents.

peans set foot on Madagascar, when a fleet of Portuguese vessels arrived. The Dutch and British tried to establish permanent bases at various points around the coast, only to be defeated by disease and less-than-friendly locals.

More successful were the efforts of buccaneers from Britain, France and elsewhere, who, from the end of the 17th century onwards, made Madagascar a base from which they attacked merchant ships sailing between India and Europe.

'No Frontier but the Sea'

As Malagasy trade with Europe grew during the 18th century, several rival kingdoms began to vie for dominance. The Menabe people under Andriamisara I founded a capital on the banks of the Sakalava River, from which the modern-day Sakalava tribe took its name. Meanwhile on the east coast, Ratsimilaho – the son of an English pirate and a Malagasy princess – succeeded in unifying rival tribes into a people that became known as the Betsimisaraka. In central Madagascar, a certain Chief Ramboasalama took the snappy name Andrianampoinimerinandriantsimitoviaminandriampanjaka (Andrianampoinimerina for short), meaning 'Hope of Imerina', and unified the Merina into a powerful kingdom that soon came to dominate much of Madagascar.

In 1810 Andrianampoinimerina was succeeded by his equally ambitious son Radama I, who organised a highly trained army that conquered Boina (the main Sakalava kingdom in northwestern Madagascar), the Betsimisaraka peoples to the east, the Betsileo to the south and the kingdom of Antakàrana in the far north, whose warrior princes preferred suicide or exile to surrender. Unable to take the Sakalava kingdom of Menabe by force, Radama prudently married Princess Rasalimo, daughter of the

SORABE

Sorabe ('Great Writings'; from the Arabic word *sora*, 'to write', and the Malagasy *be*, meaning 'big') is an early written form of Malagasy using Arabic script. The earliest Sorabe manuscripts were written sometime after the 15th century under the influence of Muslim traders (academics disagree on whether they were from the Arabian Peninsula or what is now Indonesia) who wanted to reproduce pages of the Koran. Sorabe was later used to write histories and genealogies, astrologers' predictions and various works on traditional medicine. Knowledge of the script was primarily the preserve of specially trained scribes known as *katibo*. Most Sorabe manuscripts are in the possession of the Antaimoro and Antambohoaka tribes in southeast Madagascar, although the oldest-surviving example is conserved in a library in Paris.

1500	1600	Late 18th century	1817
Portuguese sailors under the command of Diego Dias become the first Europeans to set foot on Madagascar; Dias names the island Ilha de São Lourenço.	Malagasy kings do a brisk trade in slaves with African, European and Arab traders. It is estimated that up to 150,000 slaves were exported during the 17th century.	Merina chief Ramboasalama assumes the throne at Ambohimanga and unifies the various Merina peoples into a powerful kingdom.	Radama I enters into diplomatic relations with Great Britain, beginning a period of British influence that carries on well into the 19th century. Missionaries convert the Merina court to Christianity.

Menabe king, thereby fulfilling a vow made by his father that the Merina kingdom would have 'no frontier but the sea'.

His empire building complete, Radama I set about courting European powers, especially Great Britain. The London Missionary Society (LMS) soon arrived with a contingent of Welsh missionaries who began converting the Merina court and educating children in schools.

In 1828 Radama died at the tender age of 36. His successor was his widow Ranavalona I, who promptly set about reversing Radama's policies. Ties with European powers were almost severed, and those who refused to abandon Christianity (a European import) were hurled over the cliffs outside the Rova in Antananarivo (Tana). During her 33 years in power, Ranavalona elevated torture and execution to new plateaus of inventiveness. She was said to be sexually insatiable and had a stream of lovers.

French Conquest & Colonialism

Ranavalona died in 1861, understandably unlamented by what remained of her subjects. Her son Radama II succeeded her. He was a reformer and he rescinded most of his mother's policies and welcomed back the Europeans.

In May 1862, however, Radama II was assassinated. Rainilaiarivony, the king's assassin, took the post of prime minister and married Radama's widow, who took the title Rasoherina I. He quickly issued an edict stating that the queen could act only with the consent of her ministers – effectively leaving the real power to him, her husband.

Rasoherina survived until 1868 and was succeeded by Ranavalona II, who died in 1883 and was succeeded by Ranavalona III. Prime Minister Rainilaiarivony married both queens and became the principal power behind the throne, building a magnificent residence in Antananarivo.

By the late 19th century, British interest in Madagascar had begun to wane, and French influence had increased. That influence turned into outright aggression in 1883, when French warships occupied major ports and forced the Malagasy government to sign a treaty declaring the island a French protectorate. Further demands ensued, and in 1894 the French accused the Merina government of tyranny and demanded the capitulation of Queen Ranavalona III. When she rejected their demands, a French army marched on Antananarivo, taking the capital in September 1895.

On 6 August 1896, Madagascar was officially declared a French colony. A year later Queen Ranavalona III was sent into exile in Algeria and the Merina monarchy was abolished.

1828	1835	1840s	1861
Ranavalona I becomes queen, commencing a 33-year reign. She declares Christianity illegal and denounces European influence, with the exception of French industrialist and engineer Jean Laborde.	The Bible is published in Malagasy, following the London Missionary Society's transliteration of the language in Roman alphabet. Until then, Malagasy had been written in the Arabic script Sorabe.	Jean Laborde kickstarts Madagascar's industrial revolution by building an industrial complex in Mantasoa complete with brickworks, blast furnaces, an arms and munitions factory, and textile mills.	Ranavalona dies and Radama II becomes king, abolishing forced labour and reinstating freedom of religion. Missionary activity begins to expand and Christianity becomes the predominant religion of Madagascar.

Malagasy Nationalism & Independence

In the early 20th century Madagascar's new rulers abolished slavery, although it was replaced with an almost equally exploitative system of taxes. Land was expropriated by foreign settlers and a coffee-based import and export economy developed. With economic growth and an expanding education system, a new Malagasy elite began to emerge, and resentment of the colonial presence grew in all levels of society. Several nationalist movements evolved among the Merina and Betsileo tribes, and strikes and demonstrations became more frequent.

Nationalist leader Jean Ralaimongo began the Malagasy independence movement in the 1930s, but his campaign was cut short by the outbreak of WWII. During the first half of WWII, the French in Madagascar came under the authority of the pro-Nazi Vichy government. But the Allies, fearing the Japanese could use Madagascar as a base to attack shipping, launched a seaborne attack and captured the town of Diego Suarez. Antananarivo and other major towns also fell to the British after months of fighting, but were handed back to the Free French (those who fought on the side of the Allies in WWII) of General de Gaulle in 1943.

Postwar Madagascar experienced a nationalist backlash, with resentment towards the French culminating in a rebellion in March 1947. The rebellion was eventually subdued after an estimated 90,000 Malagasy were killed. During the 1950s, nationalist political parties were formed, the most notable being the Parti Social Démocrate (PSD) of Philibert Tsiranana, and reforms paved the way to independence.

On 14 October 1958, the Malagasy Republic was proclaimed, becoming an autonomous state within the French Community. After a period of provisional government, a constitution was adopted in 1959 and full independence was achieved on 26 June 1960, with Tsiranana the country's first president.

After the euphoria, however, discontent with the country's ongoing ties with France and its poor economic performance grew. Following uprisings in 1971 and 1972, Tsiranana was forced to resign and hand over power to his army commander, General Gabriel Ramanantsoa.

The Third Republic

In February 1975, after several coup attempts, General Ramanantsoa stepped down and was replaced by Colonel Richard Ratsimandrava, who was assassinated within a week of taking office. The rebel army officers who had announced the military takeover were quickly routed by officers loyal to Ramanantsoa, and a new government headed by Admiral Didier Ratsiraka, a former foreign minister, came to power.

HISTORY MALAGASY NATIONALISM & INDEPENDENCE

The word for zebu cattle in Malagasy is *hen'omhy*, which is of Bantu origin. Linguists have established that all Malagasy words used for domestic animals have African roots, confirming the fact that African migrants who settled on the island brought with them the prized animals.

1862	1896	1930s	1939–1945
Radama II is assassinated by Rainilaiarivony, who becomes prime minister and marries Radama's widow, Rasoherina I. He will also marry the next two queens, Ranavalona II and Ranavalona III.	Madagascar becomes a French colony. Governor General Joseph Gallieni declares French the official language and sets about destroying the power of the Merina and removing all British influence.	A Malagasy independence movement begins to gather momentum, fuelled by resentment of the French colonials by a growing, educated middle class and led by nationalist leader Jean Ralaimongo.	Madagascar is under the authority of the pro-Nazi Vichy French government. Fearing the Japanese could use the island as a base, the Allies attack and capture several towns.

Ratsiraka attempted radical political and social reforms in the late 1970s, severing all ties with France and courting favour with former Soviet-bloc nations.

In March 1989 Ratsiraka was returned for a third seven-year term in an election that some regarded as questionable. It sparked riots, and 1991 was marked by widespread demonstrations demanding the president's resignation. The country ground to a halt as a result of general strikes and riots, and protests left dozens dead.

In late October 1991 an agreement was signed with opposition politicians in preparation for popular elections and the birth of the so-called 'Third Republic'. However, Ratsiraka still refused to step down. In July 1992, there was an attempted civilian coup, but the rebels failed to gain popular support and were forced to surrender.

Elections were finally held in 1993 and resulted in victory for opposition candidate Professor Albert Zafy, ending Ratsiraka's first 17 years

JEAN LABORDE

One of the few Europeans Queen Ranavalona tolerated was a French engineer, Jean Laborde (he was thought to be her lover). Laborde was shipwrecked on the east coast of Madagascar in 1831, at a time when Ranavalona was busy sending Europeans packing. Laborde's engineering skills didn't go unnoticed, however, and Ranavalona, ever the cunning ruler, sensed an opportunity. She granted Laborde large tracts of land and access to unlimited forced labour if he could provide her with weapons that would, in turn, expedite the job of getting rid of foreigners.

Laborde set to work and within a few years he had not only built an arms and munitions factory in Mantasoa (about 60km east of Antananarivo), but a complete industrial complex, too, with blast furnaces to produce cast iron, puddling mills to produce wrought iron, a steel plant, glassworks, brickworks, a cement plant and textile mills. As Malagasy novelist Naivo put it, Mantasoa had 'risen from the ground by the will of a single individual and the industry of a multitude'. He also built a summer palace for Ranavalona in Ambohimanga and contributed to a host of engineering projects, from roads to bridges.

As Ranavalona became more and more tyrannical, Laborde decided to take part in a plot to overthrow her in 1857. The coup failed and Laborde was banned from the island. The 1200-or-so labourers who had slaved on the Mantasoa industrial complex took the opportunity to rebel and torched the place – the few buildings left standing can still be viewed in Mantasoa.

Laborde was invited back in 1861 by Radama II, Ranavalona's son, and was made France's first consul to the Merina court by Napoleon III. Laborde died in 1878 in Madagascar and is buried in Mantasoa, on a hill overlooking what was once the engine of Madagascar's industrial revolution.

1947	26 June 1960	1975	Late 1970s
A rebellion led by Joseph Raseta and Joseph Ravoahangy is brutally suppressed by the French. Thousands of Malagasy are killed and the rebellion's leaders are sent into exile.	Madagascar gains full independence from France in a peaceful transition. Philibert Tsiranana is elected president, though in effect the French still run the country and maintain military bases.	General Gabriel Ramanantsoa steps down after coup attempts; his followers appoint Admiral Didier Ratsiraka as leader. Ratsiraka adopts Soviet-style ideology and cuts ties with France, leading to economic decline.	Ratsiraka pushes his nationalist agenda. French is no longer taught in primary schools and he decrees that towns must be known by their Malagasy names.

in power. After trying to sack his prime minister, Zafy was unexpectedly impeached by his parliament in July 1996 for abuse of authority. New presidential elections were called in November 1996 and, to the surprise of everyone, including international monitors, Ratsiraka (who had been in exile in France for the previous 19 months) won.

Reform & New Optimism

Self-made millionaire Marc Ravalomanana began his path to success by pedalling around his home town on a bicycle selling pots of homemade yoghurt. By the time he became mayor of Antananarivo in 1999, his company, Tiko, was the biggest producer of dairy products in Madagascar.

Ravalomanana announced his candidacy for the presidency of Madagascar, under the banner of his TIM party (which stands in Malagasy for 'I Love Madagascar'), in December 2001 and went head to head with Didier Ratsiraka. Upon hearing the results, both men insisted they had won, and a bitter six-month struggle for power ensued. As Ravalomanana swore himself in as president, Ratsiraka declared a state of emergency and imposed martial law.

The military eventually swung towards Ravalomanana, tipping the balance of power, and in April 2002 the Malagasy High Constitutional Court declared Ravalomanana the outright winner. By August Ravalomanana's administration had received endorsement from the UN, then won a convincing majority in elections for the National Assembly. Ratsiraka refused to accept that the game was over, but left for exile in France anyway.

Ravalomanana quickly set about his reform agenda, introducing a new currency (the ariary). Foreign investors were cheered by a major hike in economic growth and wooed by laws that provided tax breaks and allowed foreigners to own land.

Ravalomanana comfortably won a second term in office in 2006. On the back of his electoral success, he organised a referendum to change the constitution, with many of the amendments conferring on him more power (notably the option of standing for two more terms). The referendum scraped by, but the opposition was outraged by what they saw as an increasingly autocratic government.

The Coup & the Long Transition

In 2008 Ravalomanana made three decisions that antagonised the last of his supporters. In July he signed a lease with Korean company Daewoo Logistics for 13,000 sq km of arable land for commercial farming, a sacrilege in a country where land is generally perceived as belonging to ancestors.

Criminal suspects under Queen Ranavalona I were forced to drink a strong poison called *tangena*. If they vomited profusely enough, they were declared innocent. Most died.

The novel *Beyond the Rice Fields* by Malagasy author Naivo vividly describes the ordeal.

HISTORY REFORM & NEW OPTIMISM

1991	1996	2001	2006
Economic decline ignites widespread strikes and protests. The 'Third Republic' calls for elections but Ratsiraka refuses to step down. Opposition leader Albert Zafy is eventually elected president in 1993.	Among widespread accusations of criminal activities, President Zafy is impeached for abuse of power and general elections are called. Ratsiraka is returned to power and becomes president again in 1997.	Former yoghurt peddler Marc Ravalomanana swears himself in as president. Ratsiraka declares martial law, and violent protests ensue. Ravalomanana is declared the winner after a six-month showdown.	Marc Ravalomanana is swept to office for a second term as president. Encouraging economic growth leads the World Bank to wipe US$20 billion from Madagascar's national debt.

In October he bought a second presidential plane. Not only was this perceived as outlandish in a poor country such as Madagascar, but the source of the financing was obscure, which led a number of international donors to withhold their funding in protest.

And finally, in December, Ravalomanana closed the TV and radio station Viva, owned by the then mayor of Antananarivo and now president, Andry Rajoelina. Rajoelina rallied opponents under his new TGV party and mass demonstrations took place in December and January. On 7 February 2009, the army opened fire on protesters gathered in front of the presidential palace, killing 37 and injuring around 200. With international pressure mounting, Ravalomanana finally handed his resignation to the army on 17 March 2009 and fled to South Africa. Within a few hours, the army had swiftly passed all powers to Rajoelina, who was sworn in as president of the High Transitional Authority (Haute Autorité de Transition; HAT).

The events were widely condemned by the international community as a coup. They refused to recognise Rajoelina as Madagascar's legitimate leader and turned off whatever international-aid taps were left.

This had devastating consequences for Madagascar: international aid represented 75% of public expenditure, so public services dwindled to the bare minimum. The expulsion of Madagascar from the US-sponsored African Growth Opportunity Act (AGOA) also led to the collapse of the textile and other export-oriented industries, with the loss of 100,000 jobs. Between 2009 and 2014, the proportion of people living on less than US$2 a day went from 60% to 90% of the population.

The HAT had initially promised elections within 24 months, but it took more than two years just to draft the road map meant to get Madagascar out of the crisis. At the center of the disagreement was who would be able to run for president (Rajoelina was keen, the international community wasn't) and the return of Ravalomanana from exile.

It took another two years to organise the polls (during which Rajoelina successively renounced, revived and finally withdrew his candidacy) and in December 2013, Hery Rajaonarimampianina was finally elected president.

When Rainilaiarivony assassinated Radama II, he strangled him with a silken cord to avoid the *fady* (taboo) over the shedding of royal blood.

Not Hery Good

The 2013 presidential elections were a necessary first step for Madagascar to turn the page of the transition, but they proved insufficient to get the country back to where it was in 2008. Rajaonarimampianina, or Hery as he was widely known, had been elected with little popular support and no party, and he struggled to get a majority in parliament and pass reforms. His tempestuous relationship with the legislative body

February–March 2008	March 2009	September 2011	October 2013
Cyclone Ivan crashest into the island, killing nearly 100 people and leaving more than 330,000 without homes.	Antananarivo mayor Andry Rajoelina overthrows Ravalomanana in an army-backed coup. The UN and the EU refuse to recognise the new government, and international donors withhold all aid.	A road map negotiated under the auspices of the international community lays out the way out of the crisis: elections without the main protagonists and return of political exiles.	First round of the long-awaited presidential elections. There are 33 candidates. President Hery Rajaonarimampianina is elected in the second round on 20 December.

came to a head in 2015 when the national assembly tried to impeach him and organised a vote of no-confidence against the prime minister (both narrowly failed).

Hery's mandate was marked by a general increase in corruption, a sluggish return to form for the economy (it only hit the 5% GDP growth mark in 2018, a 'magic number' it had coveted since the return to democracy in 2013) and the adoption of controversial media and electoral laws, which respectively infringed on press freedom and failed to address issue of transparency in political financing.

Perhaps one of the most positive outcomes of his tenure was the signing in 2016 of an Extended Credit Facility with the International Monetary Fund (IMF), which set the country on the path of essential structural reforms and brought in much-needed financing.

It wasn't enough to save him, however: Hery got just 8.8% of the votes in the first round of the presidential elections in October 2018, a record low for an incumbent president; the run-off was fought between Ravalomanana and Rajoelina, the 2013 duel that had never happened. Rajoelina won and in January 2019 was sworn in.

Nationalist leader Jean Ralaimongo became a slave at the age of seven. He was freed in 1898, when the colonial government abolished slavery. After serving with the French during WWI, he stayed in France and met the young Ho Chi Minh, from whom he got many of his communist ideologies.

HISTORY NOT HERY GOOD

June 2015	July 2016	May 2018	December 2018
President Hery Rajaonarimampianina narrowly escapes impeachment by parliament after the Constitutional Court rules in his favour.	The International Monetary Fund approves a $304.7-million Extended Credit Facility over 3½ years to boost economic growth and encourage structural reforms.	The government reverses an earlier decision to introduce new electoral laws, thereby ending weeks of protests in which two people were killed.	Andry Rajoelina is elected president after defeating Marc Ravalomanana in the second round. Hery Rajaonarimampianina, the incumbent, comes a distant third.

Malagasy Life

Traditions and beliefs hold an important place in Malagasy life, influencing everything from the orientation of houses to who you should vote for. This isn't to say Malagasy society is static: economic development, population growth and globalisation are changing the country, although more slowly than many would like.

Behaviour & Etiquette

Above Part of a *famadihana* ('turning of the bones') ceremony in Antsirabe (p65)

On arrival in Madagascar your first impression is likely to be of a polite but rather reserved people. This apparent timidity is a reflection of *fihavanana*, which means 'conciliation' or 'brotherhood'. It stresses avoidance of confrontation and achievement of compromise in all walks of life. It is unseemly to discuss some subjects, such as personal problems, even with close friends. Likewise, searching or indiscreet questions are avoided at all costs.

Politeness in general is very important to the Malagasy, and impatience or pushy behaviour is regarded as shocking. Passengers queuing for a flight, for instance, will place their tickets in a neat row on the check-in desk or put their luggage in an orderly line before patiently awaiting their turn.

The welcoming of strangers and the traditions of hospitality are held sacred throughout Madagascar. It is considered a household duty to offer food and water to a guest, no matter how poor the inhabitants are themselves. In return, travellers should always honour this hospitality by accepting what has been offered to them.

Population & Language

Malagasy people are divided into 19 tribes, whose boundaries are roughly based on old kingdoms. Tribal divisions are still evident between ancient enemies such as the Merina and the Antakàrana. Also important is the distinction between Merina highlanders, who have more prominent Asian origins and are associated with the country's aristocracy, and so-called *côtiers* (literally, 'those from the coast'), whose African influences are more pronounced and who are often looked down on by the Merina. In Antananarivo, well-off *côtières* (women from the coast) often straighten their hair to avoid discrimination against their coastal origins.

The main tribal groups are Merina, who make up 27% of the population, Betsimisaraka (15%), Betsileo (12%), Tsimihety (7%), Sakalava (6%), Antaisaka (5%) and Antandroy (5%). There are also small groups of Indian, Chinese, Comorian and French living on the island.

This ethnic patchwork is matched by a hotchpotch of dialects. The official Malagasy language of newspapers and schools is based on the Malagasy of the Merina people, but each region has its own dialect. Vocabulary and accents vary to the extent that people from different provinces struggle to understand one another.

If you see a young Malagasy man wearing a comb in his hair, he's advertising his search for a wife.

FAMADIHANA

On the crest of a hill, a grove of pine trees whispers gently. In the shade, trestle tables are spread with sticky sweetmeats and bowls of steaming rice. A band plays a rollicking, upbeat tune as the stone door of a family tomb is opened. Old ladies wait at the entrance, faces dignified under their straw hats. Middle-aged men indulge in lethal homemade rum, dancing jerkily to the rhythms of the band.

One by one the corpses are brought out of the tomb, wrapped in straw mats and danced above the heads of a joyful throng. The bodies are rewrapped in pristine white burial *lambas* (scarves), sprayed with perfume and meticulously labelled by name with felt-tip pens. Everyone wants to touch the ancestors and talk to them. A period of quiet follows, with family members sitting by the head of the dead in silent communication, weeping but happy at the same time. The air is charged with emotion.

Then it's time to feast, celebrate and gossip with all the relatives, all the while checking in on the ancestors, filling them in on the action, making sure they are part of the festivities.

Then the bodies are danced one more time around the tomb, a few traditional verses are read out and the stone is sealed with mud for another seven years.

Famadihana ceremonies take place between July and September in the *hauts plateaux* (highlands) region from Antananarivo south to Ambositra. These days it's generally OK to attend one, as long as your visit is arranged through a hotel or local tour company. On no account should you visit without an invitation and never take photos unless specific permission has been granted.

Malagasy Ethnic Groups

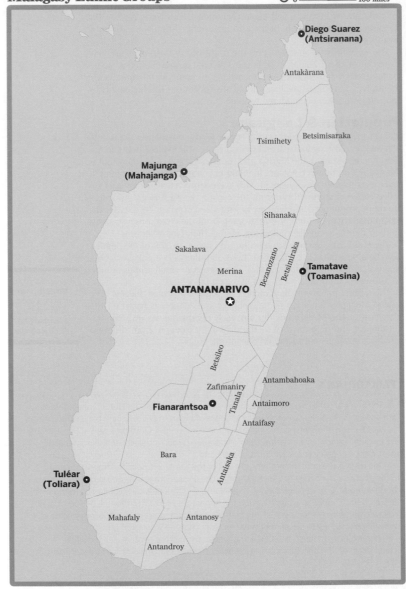

0 — 200 km
0 — 100 miles

Diego Suarez
(Antsiranana)

Antakàrana

Tsimihety

Betsimisaraka

Majunga
(Mahajanga)

Sihanaka

Sakalava

Bezanozano

Betsimiraka

Merina

Tamatave
(Toamasina)

ANTANANARIVO

Betsileo

Antambahoaka

Zafimaniry

Tanala

Antaimoro

Fianarantsoa

Antaifasy

Bara

Antaisaka

Tuléar
(Toliara)

Mahafaly

Antanosy

Antandroy

Religion & Beliefs

About half of Madagascar's population adheres to traditional beliefs, while the efforts of proselytising Europeans during the 19th century have resulted in the other half worshipping at Catholic and Protestant churches. A small, but growing, proportion is Muslim. In recent years, evangelical churches have become popular, too, with charismatic preachers,

Statue of the Virgin Mary overlooking Fianarantsoa (p76)

inspirational singing and dancing, and unusual venues (from stadiums to town halls).

The church and politics have gone hand in hand for many years, too. Former president Marc Ravalomanana was vice-president of the FJKM, the largest Protestant church in Madagascar, for many years, while the Catholic Church officially endorsed coup leader Andry Rajoelina when he took power in 2009 (a decision it then regretted). Religious leaders have also been involved in reconciliation efforts to turn the page on the transition years.

Christian Malagasies often retain great respect for traditional beliefs, which are rooted in reverence for one's ancestors and their spirits. Among most tribes, this is manifested in a complex system of *fady* (taboos) and burial rites, the best known of which is the ceremonial exhumation and reburial known as *famadihana* (literally, 'the turning of the bones'), practised mostly in the Highlands.

Malagasies invoke spirits for protection, fertility or good health at sacred sites, be it a baobab tree, a forest waterfall or a royal tomb. You'll recognise these sites from the offerings – zebu horns, *lamba* (white cotton or silk) scarves, small denominations of money, blood, honey, sweets etc. Praying and offering ceremonies are popular Sunday family outings and are often accompanied by a picnic.

Concepts of time and date also have a great influence. Malagasies strongly believe in *vintana* (destiny), which determines the most auspicious date for activities (building a house, planting a new crop etc) or events (such as circumcisions, weddings and funerals). Each day of the week has its connotations: Wednesday and Friday are good for funerals; Saturday, which is associated with nobility, is considered good for celebrations. To make sure they choose the most favourable date for an

A common ritual after the death of a family member is for the entire family to go down to a local river and wash all their clothes, an event you'll often see from the roadside, with clothes drying along the riverbanks.

occasion, Malagasies will consult a *mpanandro* (astrologer) for guidance on *vintana*.

Every ceremony is invariably accompanied by the slaughter of a zebu, more than one if the family is wealthy or influential in the community. The blood and the horns are valuable offerings and the meat is shared by those attending, the hump (which is brown fat) being the most sought-after part.

The complex set of beliefs of the Malagasy has been constructed through the assimilation of diverse influences. The funeral rites of many tribes, for example, have Austronesian roots, while the status of cattle is thought to have African roots. Belief in *vintana*, on the other hand, is thought to originate from Islamic cosmology.

Family Life & Home

The family is the central tenet of Malagasy life and includes not only distant cousins, but also departed ancestors. Even urban, modern Malagasies, who reject the belief that ancestors have magic powers, regard those who are no longer alive as full members of the family. *Famadihanas* are an opportunity to communicate with ancestors. Families spend a great deal of time and money on family reunions, and *taxis-brousses* (bush taxis) are often full of individuals visiting relatives.

Malagasy homes are arranged according to astrological principles: the northeast corner is the noble and auspicious part of the house, and doors always face west. Many Malagasies think life on earth is temporary, whereas life after death is permanent, so families will favour lavish tombs and keep a modest house.

Marriage is a pretty relaxed institution and divorce is common. Children are seen as the primary purpose of marriage and essential to happiness and security. The idea that some people might choose not to have children is greeted with disbelief.

Women

Women are a dynamic force in Malagasy society. They are very active in the workplace and are represented at every echelon of society, from street vendor to politician, school teacher to entrepreneur. Women are also regarded as the head of the domestic sphere, even if they also go out to work.

Women tend to marry and have children young: 16 or younger is typical in rural areas, while 20 is about average in urban areas, where women are more likely to go through secondary and superior education. A woman will generally move to her husband's village. Polygamy exists but is not commonplace.

Sexually, Malagasy society is fairly liberated. Women can dress quite provocatively, and they can be quite forward with sexual advances to men, including foreigners. Prostitution is rampant in a number of areas, and travellers should be aware that sex tourism is heavily punished.

FADY

••

Fady is the name given to local taboos designed to respect the ancestors. *Fady* can take innumerable forms and vary widely from village to village. It may be *fady* to whistle on a particular stretch of beach, to walk past a sacred tree, to eat pork, or to swim in a certain river.

Although foreigners will be excused for breaking *fady*, travellers should make every effort to respect these taboos. The best thing to do is to ask locals for information, and be particularly careful on sacred sites and in the vicinity of tombs or burial sites.

Top Zebu Market (p83), Ambalavao

Bottom Woman knitting outside a home, Majunga (Mahajanga; p119)

Economy

Most Malagasies bemoan the fact that their country, despite having so much going for it, has failed to develop economically. Political instability and economic mismanagement are primarily to blame. Madagascar therefore remains one of the world's poorest countries. It ranked 161 out of 189 countries in the 2018 Human Development Index of the UN Development Program (UNDP). Its GDP in 2018 was US$12.1 billion (136 out of 205 countries on the World Bank's ranking), lower than that of Afghanistan, Armenia and Yemen.

Madagascar's economy is mainly subsistence agriculture, with rice, cassava, bananas and maize as the main food crops. The principal cash crops are vanilla, lychee, cloves and cocoa, with vanilla earning a substantial percentage of foreign exchange. Madagascar also exports nickel, cobalt and ilmenite (titanium ore) from two large-scale mining projects (one in Fort Dauphin in the south, the other in Ambatovy near Moramanga). The manufacturing industry is experiencing strong growth, with textile and seafood processing leading the charge.

Although the EU is one of Madagascar's most important trading partners, China is becoming increasingly important: in a 2016 survey by Afrobarometer, 27% of Malagasies said China was the country with the greatest influence over Madagascar, second only to France (42%).

The share of adults with an account at a financial institution or mobile money service in Madagascar has increased from 9% in 2014 to 18% in 2017, but it is still far below the sub-Saharan African average of 43%.

Although Madagascar signed the 2018 Kigali declaration setting up the African Continental Free Trade Agreement, it was yet to ratify it (making it effective) at the time of going to print. In fact, Madagascar does surprisingly little trade with its continental neighbors, a missed opportunity given the size of these economies (South Africa notably).

Urban & Rural Life

Any visitor to Madagascar will notice the huge disparities in development between rural and urban areas. This is due to several factors: physical isolation (road density in Madagascar is just 5.4km per 100 sq km, which is low: Zambia for instance has 6.9km per 100 sq km and Kenya 28.4km per 100 sq km, and the roads that do exist are in poor condition);

VANILLA

The vanilla plant was introduced to Madagascar from Mexico by French plantation owners over the course of the 19th century. They named it *vanille* (*lavanila* in Malagasy), from the Spanish *vainilla* or 'little pod'. It is a type of climbing orchid, *Vanila planifolia*, that attaches itself to trees. Each flower must be hand-pollinated, which makes vanilla production extremely labour intensive. The vanilla seeds grow inside long pods hanging from the plant, which are collected and cured in factories.

Madagascar produces about 80% of the world's vanilla. The plant grows most abundantly in northeastern parts of the country, particularly the SAVA region (comprising Sambava, Andapa, Vohémar and Antalaha), where the hot and wet climate of the coast is ideally suited for its cultivation.

Madagascar's vanilla made headlines in 2017 when prices rocketed to $635 a kilo (more than silver), 30 times more than in 2013. The spike was due to a combination of factors: in March 2017, cyclone Enawo struck the island and destroyed much of that year's crop. Growers have since struggled to match demand as it takes three to four years for a new plant to produce vanilla pods. Prices have since oscillated between $500 and $600 a kilo.

This spike in prices has created 'vanillionaires' and led to 'vanilla wars' with theft, violent robberies, trafficking and even murders taking place, all in order to gain a share or even control of this most lucrative market.

Vanilla drying, Mananara (p209)

climate (the southern half of the country is arid and the east coast is prone to cyclones and floods, both of which affect agricultural productivity); and access to electricity (13%, one of the lowest in Africa), which is essential for business activity. All in all, agriculture is the livelihood for 80% of the population but contributes less than 20% of GDP. This explains why poverty (defined as people living under $1.90 a day) has shifted so little: it inched back from 77.7% in 2014 to 75.1% in 2018.

On virtually every indicator (schooling, access to water and sanitation, malnutrition etc), rural populations fare worse than their urban counterparts. Surveys have found that poverty is not only more generalised in rural areas, it's also deeper, with people facing chronic and severe malnutrition: 49% of children under the age of five suffer from stunting (impaired growth and development due to poor nutrition), one of the highest rate in the world.

> Many Malagasy surnames start with the honorary prefix 'Ra', the equivalent of 'Mr'. Similarly, many kings' names started with 'Andriana', a term that roughly translates as 'noble'.

Sport

Malagasies love watching international football (soccer; the English Premier League, in particular) and rugby (the French and European leagues, notably). National team Les Barea took part in its first African Cup of Nations in 2019, where it made it to the quarter finals and got a hero's welcome for its performance.

Where Malagasies punch above their weight is in the rather niche sport of pétanque (played with metal balls on dirt ground). A French import, it's become a case of the student outdoing (or certainly equalling) the teacher: Madagascar won the Pétanque World Championship in 1999 and 2016, and has won numerous international opens, so don't be surprised to see the game played up and down the country, on the beach, in village squares, or wherever there is a flat enough bit of ground.

Arts

Madagascar has a rich and diverse artistic tradition that goes far beyond the wonderful quality displayed in popular souvenirs – music, literature, poetry and storytelling are especially prolific genres. Discovering and appreciating it can be tough for those who speak neither French nor Malagasy, so make a point of asking your guide, or enthusiastic anglophone locals, to introduce you to their favourites.

Literature

Two excellent collections of Malagasy writing are *Voices from Madagascar: An Anthology of Contemporary Francophone Literature*, edited by Jacques Bourgeacq and Liliane Ramarosoa, which contains Malagasy writing in French and English; and *Hainteny: The Traditional Poetry of Madagascar* by Leonard Fox, with translations of beautiful Merina poems charting love, revenge and sexuality.

The earliest Malagasy literature dates from historical records produced in the mid-19th century. Modern poetry and literature began to flourish in the 1930s and 1940s. The best-known figure was the poet Jean-Joseph Rabearivelo, who committed suicide in 1947 at the age of 36, reputedly after the colonial administration decided to send a group of basket weavers to France to represent the colony instead of him.

Modern-day literary figures include Michèle Rakotoson, Johary Ravaloson, David Jaomanoro, Elie Rajaonarison, Jean-Luc Raharimanana and Naivoharisoa Patrick Ramamonjisoa, who goes by the pen name of Naivo. Most of their works are published in French; *Beyond the Rice Fields*, by Naivo, is the first ever Malagasy novel to be translated into English.

Oral Traditions

Hira gasy are popular music, dancing and storytelling spectacles held in the central highlands of Madagascar. Brightly clad troupes of 25 performers compete for prizes for the best costumes or the most exciting spectacle. An important part of *hira gasy* is *kabary*, in which a performer delivers an oratory using allegory, double entendre, metaphor and simile. *Hira gasy* has long been used to deliver important information, or raise awareness of certain topics (health, politics, environmental issues, respecting family values etc). Unfortunately, unless you are fluent in Malagasy, you're unlikely to agree with the proverb that says, 'While listening to a *kabary* well spoken, one fails to notice the fleas that bite one'. All the same, it is a cultural event well worth seeing.

More accessible are the songs and dances after the *kabary*. Dancers are dressed in bright gowns called *malabary*, and women also wear the traditional *lamba* (scarf). The competition winner is decided by audience members, who throw small denominations at their favourite troupe.

The interesting film *Quand les Étoiles Rencontrent la Mer* (When the Stars Meet the Sea), directed by the Malagasy Raymond Rajaonarivelo, is the story of a young boy born during a solar eclipse.

Music

Most traditional Malagasy music revolves around favourite dance rhythms: the *salegy* of the Sakalava tribe, with both Indonesian and Kenyan influences; *watsa watsa* from Mozambique and the Congo; the *tsapika*, originating in the south; and the *sigaoma*, similar to South African music.

The most widely played traditional wind instrument is the *kiloloka*, a whistle-like length of bamboo capable of only one note. Melodies are played by a group of musicians, in a manner similar to a bell ensemble.

PIERRE-YVES BABELON/SHUTTERSTOCK ©

Top *Hira gasy* performance, Antananarivo (p41)

Bottom Traditional Antandroy graves (p236), decorated with carved wooden stele

**Arts
Perfor-
mances**

Hira gasy
(Antananarivo)

Zegny'Zo festival
(Diego Suarez)

Donia festival
(Nosy Be)

Grill du Rova
(Antananarivo)

Institut Français
Madagascar
(Antananarivo)

The tubular instrument you'll see on sale at tourist shops and craft markets is a *valiha*, which has 28 strings of varying lengths stretched around a tubular wooden sound box (generally made of bamboo). It resembles a bassoon, but is played more like a harp and originates from Southeast Asia. The most famous performer of *valiha* is Justin Vali, a household name in world-music circles.

Apart from at special events such as the Donia festival in Nosy Be, or *hira gasy* performances, traditional Malagasy music can be hard to find and it is often restricted to rural areas.

Malagasy pop music is usually a cheesy blend of guitar rock, rough-and-ready rap and hip-hop, and soulful ballads, a genre best represented by national treasure Poopy (she was awarded the Malagasy equivalent of an MBE in 2014 for her long and distinguished career). Current big names include AmdondronA, Mage 4 and Black Nadia.

Perhaps Madagascar's most successful band ever is the folk-pop Mahaleo, led by charismatic frontman (and presidential hopeful in 2018) Dama. In the same vein, you'll find singer-songwriters Nogabe Randriaharimalala, Lala Njava and Nicolas Vatomanga.

For more traditional sounds, Jerry Marcos, a master of *salegy*, is guaranteed to have you shaking your stuff like there's no tomorrow.

Contemporary Malagasy artists are relatively easy to see in Antananarivo, where there are numerous venues (look in the newspapers on Friday for event details, or the free listings available in hotels and restaurants).

Architecture

Each region of Madagascar has its own architectural style and building materials. The Merina and Betsileo of the *hauts plateaux* (highlands) live in distinctive red-brick houses. The typical Merina home is a tall, narrow affair with small windows and brick pillars in the front that support open verandas. The Betsileo dispense with the pillars and trim their houses with elaborately carved wood.

Coastal homes are generally constructed of lighter local materials, including *ravinala* (literally 'forest leaves'; also known as travellers' palm) and raffia palm. Houses in humid areas are generally raised to promote ventilation and avoid insects.

Death being considered the passage to eternal life, tombs are often more elaborate than everyday dwellings. In the highlands, tombs are grand affairs: rectangular brick pavilions, often whitewashed, decorated with colourful geometric shapes. In the west, the Sakalava decorate their tombs with erotic sculptures (increasingly rare because of looting), whilst in the south Antandroy and Mahafaly people decorate theirs with *aloalo*, ornate carved wooden steles topped with zebu horns. The carvings can be figurative or abstract.

Textiles

Textiles have always played a huge part in Malagasy society, with some types of cloth even being imbued, it is believed, with supernatural powers. The Merina used cocoons collected from wild silkworms (endemic to the island, and which are harvested in the wild rather than farmed) to make highly valued textiles called *lamba mena* (red silk). The silks were woven in many colors and pattern combinations and, in the past, had strong links with royal prestige, expressed by the color red. Worn by the aristocracy in life and death, *lamba mena* were also used in burial and reburial ceremonies.

Lamba are still used in funeral rites and you'll see red-and-white cloths tied to sacred trees across the country as tokens of gratitude to ancestors for fulfilled prayers.

Madagascar has a couple of high-profile photographers. Pierrot Men (www.pierrotmen.com), whose signature black and white images have been turned into postcards and posters, and Rajisolo (www.rijasolo.com), a photojournalist for press agency AFP, whose images regularly make it to Western media. The new Musée de la Photo in Antananarivo is another photography highlight.

Malagasy Cuisine

Food is taken seriously in Madagascar, where French, Chinese and Indian influences have blended with local eating traditions into an exciting and often mouth-watering cuisine. Regional variations are many, with a variety of fruit, vegetables and seafood dictating local tastes and recipes.

Where to Eat

What you eat in Madagascar will largely depend on *where* you eat. *Hotelys* or *gargottes* are small, informal restaurants found in every city and town. They are cheap and serve no-frills, typical Malagasy fare such as *romazava* (beef and vegetable stew), *poulet sauce* (chicken in tomato sauce) or grilled fish, with a mountain of rice for bulk. The quality ranges from rough to delicious. The tastier Malagasy food is often served in private homes, and what better excuse to make friends with the locals!

Restaurants, which range from modest to top-end establishments, serve various types of cuisines, including fancier versions of Malagasy standards. Quality is invariably good, sometimes outstanding. Many restaurants offer a *menu du jour* (three-course set menu), or a *plat du jour* (daily special), which are generally good value. Prices for the set menu are usually around Ar15,000 to Ar25,000. For à la carte menus, the average price of a main course is Ar12,000 to Ar25,000.

Note that in most tourist areas, hotels have the best (and sometimes only) restaurants, which means you'll eat most of your meals there.

A number of Madagascar's signature dishes, such as *romazava* (beef and vegetable stew) or *ravitoto* (pork stew with manioc greens), used to be the preserve of the nobility. They were served in *tatao* or *hanim-pitoloha*, a banquet of seven dishes prepared to celebrate the royal bath on the Malagasy New Year.

Best Madagascan Restaurants

➡ Mad Zebu (p131) A trained Michelin-starred chef in the middle of nowhere: totally unexpected and spectacularly good.

➡ Toko Telo (p46) Run by the chef of a cooking school, this is the best place in Tana to try genuine local cuisine.

➡ La Table d'Alexandre (p156) French gastronomy with a tropical twist in a setting worthy of *Out of Africa*.

➡ Chez Madame Chabaud (p124) A Majunga institution serving fabulous fusion cuisine (and mean cocktails).

➡ Chez Samson (p207) High-brow cuisine in the mangrove forest of Île Sainte Marie. As amazing as it sounds.

NATIONAL FAVOURITES

Romazava A beef stew in a ginger-flavoured broth. It contains *brêdes mafana*, a green leaf reminiscent of Indian *saag* in taste that will make your tongue and lips tingle thanks to its anaesthetic properties!

Ravitoto Another well-loved Malagasy dish, it is a mix of fried beef or pork with shredded cassava leaves and coconut milk; truly delicious.

Pizza Just like Europeans and Americans, Malagasies have succumbed to pizzas! They are a popular treat among middle-class families and you'll find an inordinate number of pizza joints (often with takeaway) in every large town and city.

Romazava (beef and vegetable stew; p237)

Malagasy Classics

Eating rice three times a day is so ingrained in Malagasy culture that people sometimes claim they can't sleep if they haven't eaten rice that day. In fact, the verb 'to eat' in Malagasy, *mihinam-vary*, literally means 'to eat rice'.

Rice is eaten in a broth for breakfast (*vary amin' anana*); for lunch and dinner it is generally accompanied by a helping of meat, such as *hen'omby* (boiled zebu), *hen'ankisoa* (pork), *hen'akoho* (chicken) or *hen'andrano* (fish). Common preparations include *ravitoto* (stew – usually beef or pork – with manioc greens and coconut), *sauce coco* (a delicious coconut curry, usually with chicken, fish or seafood) and the nondescript *sauce* or *ritra* (generally a tomato-based affair; served with anything from chicken to fish).

To keep things interesting, the Malagasies have developed an arsenal of aromatic condiments, such as *sakay* (a red-hot pepper paste with ginger and garlic), *pimente verde* (a fiery green chilli) and *achards* (hot pickled fruit, such as tomato, lemon, carrot or mango, used as relish – you'll see bottles of the stuff sold by the roadside).

Rice Alternatives

The most common alternative to rice is a steaming bowl of *mi sao* (fried noodles with vegetables or meat), or a satisfying *soupe chinoise* (clear noodle soup with fish, chicken or vegetables), dishes that show the Asian origins of the Malagasy.

Poorer rural communities supplement their rice diet with starchy roots such as manioc or corn.

If you're invited to a Malagasy celebration, bring a present (a small amount of money or a bottle of rum). Hold your wrist with the opposite hand when passing food or drinks.

The growth of a rice plant is described in Malagasy using the same words as those for a woman becoming pregnant and giving birth.

Seafood

Given that Madagascar is an island, it's hardly surprising that seafood features prominently on the menu. Prices are so low that all but those on the tightest budgets can gorge themselves at whim on fish, freshwater crayfish, prawns, lobster and even tiny oysters (from Morondava). Adhering to the motto that less is more, seafood is often cooked simply, grilled or fried, or in *sauce coco*.

The African Cookbook by Bea Sandler has some good recipes from Madagascar.

Vegetarians & Vegans

The Malagasy don't find vegetarianism difficult to understand, and they are often more than happy to cater for special diets if you give them enough notice. If you eat eggs, you will have no problem as any restaurant can whip up an omelette. If you don't, getting enough protein could be a problem, as beans and lentils are not widely available.

Snacks & Munchies

One of the first things you'll notice on arriving in Madagascar is the dizzying variety of snacks available at street stalls. Savoury snacks include meat samosas (called *sambos*), small doughnuts called *mofo menakely* and *masikita* (tiny zebu kebabs).

The log-like cake you'll see sold on roadsides is *koba*, a concoction of ground peanuts or pistachios, rice flour and sugar, wrapped tightly in banana leaves, baked and sold in slices. *Hotelys* also make delicious sweet doughnuts, which they serve with a cup of black coffee.

In towns and cities you'll also find plenty of patisseries selling cakes, croissants, pastries and meringues. Baguettes can be bought from every street corner, although the quality is often poor.

Gourmet Cuisine

Madagascar has developed a unique strand of haute cuisine that blends Malagasy and French influences and makes the best of local ingredients. Among our favourites are zebu steak with green pepper sauce and *frites* (fries), roast chicken with vanilla mashed potatoes, and grouper in pink peppercorn sauce with sautéed potatoes. Desserts are equally exciting, with chocolate cakes and vanilla custard, crêpes and local fruit jams, exotic sorbets and ice cream.

Gourmet cuisine is served up and down the country in better restaurants and is an absolute highlight of any trip to the red island.

Hot Drinks & Soft Drinks

Most Malagasies like to accompany a rice meal with a drink of rice water. This brown, smoky concoction, known as *ranovola* or *ranon'apango*, is made from boiling water in the pot containing the burnt rice residue – definitely an acquired taste. That said, it is the safest water to drink in *hotelys* since it has been boiled.

Despite the fact that coffee is grown in Madagascar, only the most up-market establishments offer espresso or good filter coffee. Elsewhere you'll have to content yourself with (often quite bitter) black coffee and learn to love condensed milk. Tea is better; TAF-brand teabags are excellent.

Soft drinks (Coke, Pepsi, Fanta) are sold at every bar under the Malagasy sun. Madagascar also produces its own sodas, including the synthetic-tasting Bonbon Anglais ('English sweet', a lemonade).

Far and away the best sweet drinks, however, are the *jus naturels* (freshly squeezed fruit juices). Local wonders include *corossol* (soursop), *grenadelle* (passionfruit), papaya, mango and whatever is in season. In

When you order a beer, you'll generally be asked 'PM ou GM?' Moderately thirsty travellers will opt for PM or *petit modèle* (small model, 330mL); parched visitors will quench their thirst with a GM or *grand modèle* (large model, 660mL).

THE MIGHTY ZEBU

Zebu cattle not only provide status and transport, they are also well known for their excellent meat. Zebu beef is prepared in much the same way as European cattle beef – in stews, kebabs (known locally as *masikita*, often tiny in size) and as succulent steak.

Zebus are synonymous with status and wealth (a zebu costs €500 to €800, a huge amount of money for a Malagasy family); zebu meat is therefore the festive food par excellence. Zebus will be slaughtered for weddings, *famadihanas* (exhumation and reburial ceremonies), circumcisions and other important festivals or events.

The hump, which is brown fat, is a delicacy (it used to be the preserve of the nobility). It is seldom served in restaurants, but it is a must at Malagasy celebrations, where it is served grilled or in kebabs.

coastal areas, street vendors sell green coconuts, which they will split open so that you can drink the vitamin-packed juice.

Although Malagasy wines still have some way to go to rival regional counterparts, the Vin Blanc Doux from Clos Malaza is generally held to be the best local vintage.

Boozy Delights

The most popular Malagasy beer is Three Horses Beer (universally known as THB). Up a notch in the alcoholic stakes is the island's rum. Most bars and restaurants offer *rhum arrangé* – rum in which a variety of fruits and spices have been left to soak. Common flavours include lemon, ginger, cinnamon, lychee and vanilla; these alcoholic concoctions generally line the back of the bar in an array of demijohns worthy of an apothecary. *Rhum arrangé* is drunk neat as an aperitif or an after-dinner liqueur.

Although illegal, moonshine (generally known as *toaka gasy*) is widely available. Its alcohol content will blow your socks off, so go easy on the shots. In eastern Madagascar the local tipple of choice is *betsa-betsa* (fermented sugar-cane juice), while in the north, *trembo* (palm wine) is popular.

Madagascar's small wine industry is centred on Fianarantsoa. You'll probably want to try a glass out of curiosity, but it's definitely not the island's forte. Imported French and South African wine is served in better restaurants throughout the country.

Celebrations & Customs

A Malagasy proverb says 'the food which is prepared has no master'. In other words, celebrating in Madagascar means eating big. Weddings, funerals, circumcisions and reburials are preceded by days of preparations. Extended family, friends and often passers-by, too, are invited to share the food, usually a combination of meat dishes (note that turkey is considered a meat for special occasions), vegetables and, of course, a mountain of rice. At Malagasy parties, copious quantities of home-brewed rum are consumed and helpless drunkenness is entirely expected.

Environment

Madagascar is the world's fourth-largest island, after Greenland, Papua New Guinea and Borneo. Its incredibly diverse landscapes and unique wildlife are a product of history: cast adrift from Africa about 165 million years ago, Madagascar took with it a cargo of animals and plants that have been evolving in isolation ever since.

The Land

In the Beginning

What is now the island of Madagascar was once sandwiched between Africa and India as part of the supercontinent Gondwana, a vast ancient land mass that also included Antarctica, South America and Australasia.

Gondwana began to break apart about 180 million years ago, but Madagascar remained joined to Africa at the 'hip' – in the region of modern East Africa – for another 20 million years. About 88 million years ago the eastern half of Madagascar broke off, moving northward to eventually become India, by which time modern Madagascar had drifted to its present position. Since then, Madagascar has remained at its present size and shape, geographically isolated.

The Natural History of Madagascar by Steven Goodman and Jonathan Benstead provides the most comprehensive overview of the island's precious natural heritage.

The Eighth Continent

Madagascar measures 1600km on its longest axis, aligned roughly northeast to southwest, and 570km from east to west at its widest point. Almost the entire island is in the tropics, albeit well south of the equator, with only the southern tip protruding below the Tropic of Capricorn. The 5000km-long coastline features many long, sweeping sandy beaches, with coral reefs and atolls offshore in some areas, and is dotted with around 250 islands, of which Nosy Be and Île Sainte Marie are the largest. It is such epic numbers that have earned Madagascar the nickname 'the eighth continent'.

A chain of mountains runs down the eastern seaboard, forming a steep escarpment and trapping moisture that helps create the island's rainforests, which are rich in biodiversity. There is no modern volcanic activity on the island, although volcanoes previously erupted in the central highlands.

The Eighth Continent: Life, Death and Discovery in the Lost World of Madagascar by Peter Tyson is a scientific travelogue that guides readers through the island's unique natural history and biodiversity.

LOST GIANTS

When humans first arrived, Madagascar supported many animals much bigger than contemporary species: hippopotamuses, aardvarks, gorilla-size lemurs and giant flightless birds, similar to modern African birds such as the ostrich, roamed the island. With the arrival of humans, many of the larger animals, which no doubt provided a ready supply of protein, were wiped out. Over the last 1000 years, scientists estimate that 16 species of lemur, plus tortoises, the hippopotamuses, giant aardvarks, the world's largest bird (the 3m-high elephant bird *Aepyornis*) and two species of eagle have become extinct.

Forests

Rainforest, Parc National Masoala-Nosy Mangabe

Dry deciduous forest, Parc National Ankarafantsika

Spiny forest, Arboretum d'Antsokay

The island's highest point is 2876m Maromokotro, an extinct volcanic peak on the Tsaratanana massif, followed by the 2658m Pic Imarivolanitra (formerly known as Pic Boby) in Parc National Andringitra.

Mineral Beauty

Going east from the western coastline, limestone is replaced by sandstone, which rises into majestic formations in places such as Parc National Isalo.

Northern and western Madagascar host impressive limestone karst formations – jagged, eroded rocks that contain caves, potholes, underground rivers and forested canyons rich in wildlife such as crocodiles, lemurs, birds and bats. Karst is known locally as *tsingy* and is protected within one of Madagascar's three Unesco World Heritage Sites, Parc National Bemaraha, as well as in the Réserve Spéciale Ankarana and Parc National Tsingy de Namoroka.

Wildlife

Madagascar's 80-million-year isolation has allowed its wildlife to take a remarkable evolutionary turn. Undisturbed by outside influences and human beings (who 'only' arrived 2000 years ago), the various fauna and flora followed their own interpretation of the evolution manual. The result is that 70% of animals and 90% of plants found in Madagascar are endemic.

As well as being completely unique, their sheer variety is staggering: Madagascar hosts 5% of all known animal and plant species. Habitat degradation threatens much of this incredible natural wealth, though, and habitat conservation is now a priority.

Fauna

Lemurs

Madagascar's best-known mammals are the lemurs, of which there are 111 species. As well as being entertaining to watch (they are primates after all, and therefore distant cousins of ours), it's hard to overrate how

---

WILD EXPECTATIONS

Many first-time visitors naturally associate Madagascar with two things – Africa and wildlife – leading to visions either of East African game parks, or of zoo-like rainforests. The reality is quite different. First, there are no plains full of roaming beasts here. In fact, there are no wild animals larger than a small dog.

Outside the parks, the most common impression is of the *absence* of wildlife. You can drive for days through the spiny forest in the south, for example, and see virtually nothing but a few domesticated zebu. Likewise, along the lush wetlands of the Canal des Pangalanes there are hardly any birds. There are many reasons for this, beginning with the impact of hunting and deforestation, which has decimated animal populations. But even the great biological diversity in the forests is not always obvious. Some animals are nocturnal, or shy of humans, or simply rare. The broad-nosed gentle lemur, for example, was thought to be extinct until it was rediscovered in Ranomafana in 1972. It was observed again in the late 1980s and is only occasionally seen today. Many fascinating animals, such as the world's smallest chameleon, are simply tiny. And rainforest is, by its very nature, a fairly effective shield for its inhabitants.

So when seeking out this country's wildlife, it is best to adjust your focus to a smaller scale, look carefully around you, be patient and hire a good guide. It can be challenging to spot that bamboo lemur in the canopy, but that's what makes it so rewarding when you do.

Tsingy peaks, Parc National Bemaraha (p131)

unique they are: Madagascar's lemurs are found nowhere else on earth, which also explains why primatologists class Madagascar in a category of its own, the other three being Africa, Southeast Asia and the Americas.

Lemurs are divided into five families: the beautifully marked *sifakas* and *indris* (of which only one species is extant), all known for their leaping abilities; a family of small, nocturnal mouse lemurs that includes the world's smallest primates; the 'true' lemurs, such as the ring-tailed and ruffed lemurs; the sportive lemurs; and, most remarkable of all, the bizarre, nocturnal aye-aye, which extracts grubs from under bark with its long, bony middle finger.

Other Mammals

Madagascar has many species of small mammals, such as bats, rodents and tenrecs. Tenrecs are related to shrews and fill a similar niche as tiny hunters of the leaf litter. Among their diverse forms are shrew tenrecs, the hedgehog-like spiny tenrecs and even an otter-like aquatic species.

There are six species of carnivores – all are mongooses and civets – including the ring-tailed mongoose, the fanaloka and the puma-like, lemur-eating fossa.

Madagascar's waters harbour rich marine life – dolphins, dugongs and humpback whales. Whales come to Madagascar to give birth and mate during winter months.

Birds

Madagascar has the highest proportion of endemic birds of any country on earth: of the 209 breeding species, 51% are endemic. A large percentage of birds are forest-dwelling and therefore under pressure from land clearing.

The BBC's seminal three-part series *Madagascar*, narrated by Sir David Attenborough, makes for an inspirational introduction to the great island. More sobering is the Forests episode of the Netflix *Our Planet* series, also narrated by Attenborough, which shows the destruction of the dry Menabe forests in the southwest.

GOING, GOING...BACK AGAIN!

The last century saw several Malagasy bird species pushed perilously close to the brink of extinction. Waterbirds have fared particularly badly: the Alaotra grebe was last seen in the 1980s and was declared extinct in 2010.

All three of the country's endemic duck species are rare. One, the Madagascar pochard, had last been observed in 1994, when a female was rescued by a conservation worker from a fisherman's net on Lac Alaotra. The rescuer kept the bird alive in a bath in the hope that a mate would be found, but it succumbed and the Madagascar pochard was presumed extinct. But in 2006 the unthinkable happened: nine adult Madagascar pochards were discovered with young on a remote lake in the Alaotra basin in northern Madagascar.

In a desperate effort to save the species from extinction, the Durrell Wildlife Conservation Trust, the Wildfowl and Wetlands Trust (WWT), the Peregrine Trust and the government of Madagascar recovered eggs about to hatch and set up an emergency captive-breeding program, with the long-term aim of reintroducing the rare duck to its habitat. The program has managed to rear 114 birds and in December 2018, 21 were released on Lake Sofia in northern Madagascar after a period of acclimatisation.

In April 2018, Malagasy authorities seized 10,000 rare radiated tortoises in a smuggler's house near Tuléar. A few months later, another 7000 were found in the nearby town of Betioky. All were bound for the pet trade in Asia. Traffickers received a six-year prison sentence and a $26,000 fine.

Among Madagascar's unique bird families are the mesites – skulking, babbler-like birds thought to be related to rails; the spectacular ground-rollers, including a roadrunner-like species unique to the spiny forests; the tiny, iridescent asities, similar to sunbirds and filling a similar niche; and the vangas, which have taken several strange twists as they evolved to fill various forest niches. There are a number of predators, including the highly endangered Madagascar serpent eagle and fish eagle, and nocturnal species as well.

Most species are resident (ie nonmigratory), although a few are seasonal migrants to East Africa. Waterbirds are rather poorly represented in Madagascar because there are comparatively few large bodies of water. Some of the best concentrations are in the Mahavy-Kinkony Wetland Complex on the west coast. The richest habitat by far for birds (and all other terrestrial life forms) is the rainforest of the eastern seaboard, although many of these species are rare and poorly known.

Reptiles & Amphibians

There are 346 reptile species on Madagascar, including most of the world's chameleons, ranging from the largest – Parson's chameleon, which grows to around 60cm – to the smallest, the dwarf chameleons of the genus *Brookesia*, which fits on your thumbnail! You might also spot the king of camouflage, the leaf-tailed gecko, and the amazingly colourful Labord's chameleon. Equally attractive are some of Madagascar's 300 species of amphibians, including spectacularly coloured frogs such as the bright-red tomato frog and iridescent Malagasy poison frogs.

Amazingly, the verdant forests support not a single snake species harmful to people. Among the many beautiful snakes are the Madagascar boa and the leaf-nosed snake. In contrast the Nile crocodile is just as dangerous here as it is in Africa and it kills people every year.

Best Whale Watching

Baie d'Antongil

Île Sainte Marie

Anakao

Nosy Be

Ifaty

Five of the world's seven species of marine turtle can be found in Madagascar (all endangered, some critically). The country is also home to several species of tortoise, many of which are endangered. With its distinctive and ornate shell, the ploughshare tortoise is the most threatened because of poaching (a shell can fetch US$50,000): there are just 50 individuals left in the wild. In a desperate attempt to stem the illegal trade in ploughshare shells, the Durrell Wildlife Conservation Trust (which runs

a captive breeding program at Parc National Ankarafantsika) and the
government decided in 2015 to deliberately deface all remaining animals'
shells in order to make them less attractive to poachers.

Invertebrates

As you might expect from somewhere that has such thriving wildlife, the
bugs in Madagascar are out in force. It is thought there are some 100,000
species of insect on the island. Among the most charming specimens are
hissing cockroaches, scorpions, giraffe-necked weevils, tarantulas, giant
millipedes, stick insects and the incredible flatid bug, which looks more
like a giant bit of paper confetti than an insect.

Fish

Freshwater fish face tremendous pressure owing to silting of rivers
through erosion. A survey by the International Union for Conservation of
Nature (IUCN) found that 34% of freshwater fish species in Madagascar
were faced with extinction.

Marine life is incredibly diverse, but similarly vulnerable to erosion
run-off, notably the country's beautiful coral. Madagascar has the world's
fifth-largest coral reef, but overfishing, pollution, climate change and
sediment from soil erosion have greatly impacted its health.

Madagascar harbors a number of sharks, which, depending on your
point of view, is either great (conservationists, fishers, some divers) or
scary (swimmers, surfers, the other divers). Risks of attacks are particularly high on the east coast, less so in areas where fringing corals protect
the shores. Their numbers have dwindled dramatically, however, especially in the southwest, because of demand for shark fins.

Flora

Madagascar's plants are no less interesting than its animals and its flora
is incredibly diverse. About 15,000 species are known to science, including the bizarre octopus trees, several species of baobab and a pretty flower that is used to treat leukaemia.

> The Malagasy have nicknamed baobabs 'roots of the sky', after their scraggly branches. Legend has it that God made the baobab the most beautiful tree on earth. The devil was so jealous that he decided to plant baobabs upside down so that he could view them from hell!

ENVIRONMENT WILDLIFE

ICONIC TREES

The photogenic Allée des Baobabs in western Madagascar has done much for the popularity of this giant tree. Madagascar is home to seven of the world's eight baobab species,
of which six are native and endemic (the seventh species is that found on mainland Africa, the eighth in Australia).

The trees stand out for their size (up to 30m high), huge trunks (one of the largest in
the country is in Majunga, with a circumference of 21m), old age (many are thought to
be several centuries old) and signature scraggly branches, which are in full view over the
winter months, when baobabs have lost their foliage. The trees store water in their trunks
and are therefore well adapted to dry environments.

Another of Madagascar's iconic plants – it is, technically, not a tree – is the *ravinala*, or
travellers' palm, named so after the large quantities of rainwater it can store at the base
of its leaves. *Ravinala*, which is native to the island, has many uses in Madagascar. The
leaves are dried and used for building roofs in traditional houses, and bundles of dried
leaves are sold by the roadside everywhere in northern and eastern Madagascar. Done
well, a *ravinala* roof can last 10 years. The tough stems are often used to make beautiful
ceiling or wall panels. The wood from the trunk is also used for various building purposes.

Perhaps as a nod to its durability, Air Madagascar chose the *ranivala* tree as its
emblem.

Parc National Masoala (p213)

The island's vegetation can be divided into three parallel north–south zones, each supporting unique communities of plants and animals: the hot, arid west consists of dry spiny desert or deciduous forest; the central plateau *(hauts plateaux)* has now been mostly deforested; and the wettest part of the country, the eastern seaboard, supports extensive tracts of rainforest. Mangrove forests grow in sites along the coast, particularly near large estuaries. All of these habitats have suffered extensive disturbance.

Arid Landscapes

The spiny desert is truly extraordinary. Dense tangles of cactus-like octopus trees festooned with needle-sharp spines are interspersed with baobabs whose bulbous trunks store water, allowing them to survive the dry season. The baobabs' large, bright flowers are filled with copious amounts of nectar, often sipped by fork-marked lemurs. About 60 species of aloe occur in Madagascar, and many dot the spiny desert landscape.

Dry deciduous forests are a feature of the western half of the country, although they do not look quite as bare as their northern-hemisphere counterparts in the depths of winter. The thinner winter foliage does make it prime bird- and lemur-watching time, however.

The rosy periwinkle, a flower endemic to Madagascar, has been a source of alkaloids that are 99% effective in the treatment of some forms of leukaemia.

The Highlands

The vast areas of blond grassland of the *hauts plateaux* are actually the result of extensive felling by humans. The boundary of the sole remaining patch of natural forest, at Parc National Zombitse-Vohibasia, stands in forlorn contrast to the degraded countryside surrounding it.

Growing among the crags and crevices of Parc National Isalo are nine species of *Pachypodia*, including a tall species with large, fragrant yellow-white blossoms, and the diminutive elephant-foot species that nestle in cliff crevices on the sandstone massif.

Rainforest

Madagascar's eastern rainforests once covered the entire eastern seaboard and still support the island's highest biodiversity, most of which is found nowhere else on earth. Giant forest trees are festooned with vines, orchids and bird's-nest ferns (home to tree frogs and geckos).

There are 1000 species of orchid in Madagascar, more than in all of Africa, and more than 60 species of pitcher plants are found in swampy parts of rainforests. Insects are attracted to the nectar of these carnivorous plants, but are trapped by downward-pointing spines along the inside of the 'pitcher' and are eventually dissolved and absorbed by the plant.

Environmental Issues

Madagascar faces tremendous environmental challenges, none greater than deforestation. Just like every other country, Madagascar is also going to have to contend with the effects of climate change on its unique biodiversity.

Deforestation

Around 90% of Malagasy households rely on firewood and charcoal for their domestic energy needs. This reliance has put immense pressure on Madagascar's forests, as has the need for agricultural and grazing land (slash-and-burn, or *tavy* in Malagasy, is widespread). A 2019 study by French Agricultural Research Center for International Development (Cirad) found that Madagascar had lost 44% of its forest cover since the 1950s and that the rate of deforestation had accelerated since 2005. Even more concerning is the fact that 46% of remaining forests are highly fragmented, with 46% of the forest now less than 100m from a cleared or open area.

Mangroves are similarly affected: a 2019 WWF survey found that since 1995, Madagascar had lost 24% of its mangroves and that the trend had accelerated since 2015.

The impact of deforestation on such a large scale is catastrophic for Madagascar's wildlife. A 2015 report from IUCN found that 114 of the country's mammal species were threatened – the second-highest number for any country in the world.

In 1994 there were 50 known species of lemur. By 2006, thanks to extensive research, the number had gone up to 71. Today there are 111 and primatologists say that new species are still being discovered.

Asian common toads are thought to have arrived in Madagascar on a shipping container in the early 2010s. Conservationists are extremely concerned about the impact they could have on endemic fauna: a 2018 study found that no predators on the island could withstand the toxins secreted in its skin.

THE WAILING INDRI

The wondrous *indri* has been described as looking like 'a four-year-old child in a panda suit'. It's famous for its eerie cry, a whooping siren that can be heard over a kilometre away. It is used mainly to define a particular group's territory, though there are also distinct mating and alarm calls. *Indris* are active on and off throughout the day, beginning about an hour after daybreak, which is usually the best time to see them. Despite the incredible cacophony of sound that comes out of the forest, each individual only calls for about four or five minutes per day.

Indris eat complex carbohydrates, and therefore need to spend much of their day in a sedentary manner digesting their food. They spend most of their time high in the forest canopy, feeding, sleeping and sunning themselves. Their powerful hind legs make them capable of 7m horizontal leaps from tree to tree, and they are perfectly balanced despite their stump-like tails. *Indris* are very sensitive to any change in environment, which is the main reason for their endangered status – not only does deforestation threaten their habitat, but no *indri* has ever survived in captivity, as they simply stop eating and die.

ILLEGAL ROSEWOOD LOGGING

In April 2000 Cyclone Hudah tore through the Masoala Peninsula in northeast Madagascar. The storm left a trail of devastation in its wake: satellite images revealed that around 3% of the forest was severely damaged. Although rosewood (known locally as *bola bola*) exploitation had been banned, then president Marc Ravalomanana exceptionally allowed fallen trees to be sold as timber. Little did he know that this would open the floodgates of illegal logging.

In 2009 the transitional authorities decided to make rosewood export legal in a bid to generate new revenue streams (foreign donors had withheld their funding because of the unconstitutional change of power). The traffic, driven by demand for luxury furniture and musical instruments from China and the US (a rosewood bed sells for US$2 million in China) spiralled out of control. The worst-affected areas were the northeastern national parks of Marojejy and Masoala and the adjoining Makira forest (now a protected area).

In 2009 an investigation by Madagascar National Parks, the environmental NGO Global Witness and the US Environmental Investigation Agency uncovered the scale of the pillaging. The report revealed that 100 to 200 trees were being taken down every day, a bounty worth US$80,000 to US$460,000. It also found that the police and officials at every level of the forestry sector had colluded with traffickers.

The Malagasy authorities reacted by forbidding all precious wood exports in April 2010. Its implementation has remained symbolic, however, with *bola bola* traffic continuing unabated. Even the addition of rosewood and ebony to the Convention on International Trade in Endangered Species (CITES) and an international embargo since 2013 did little to stem the flow. Logs of rosewood have continued to find their way to China via Zanzibar, Tanzania, Kenya and Hong Kong. In 2014 Singapore authorities seized nearly 30,000 rosewood logs valued at $50 million – one of the largest wildlife seizures ever in the history of CITES.

The trade has been devastating not only because of the deforestation it causes, but also because of the accompanying trafficking it has brought (animal poaching, gold prospecting etc). Rosewood trees are now critically endangered: there are no seed-bearing trees left outside of national parks (rosewood grows slowly and takes 40 to 50 years to reach this stage).

Focus has now shifted to the vexing question of what to do with the stockpiles of precious timber in government custody. The government is intent on selling it to bring in revenue but conservationists argue that this would fuel rather than curb illegal felling of precious timber. Instead they argue that rosewood and other precious timber should be granted the highest protection status under CITES, Appendix 1, which bans all trade of listed species.

Deforestation has also led to an increase in soil erosion. During the rainy season, Madagascar's laterite soils 'bleed' into the country's streams and rivers. The red earth saturates coastal waters, threatening fragile marine ecosystems, including precious coral reefs. Landslides have also become more common during the rainy season, damaging roads, rail tracks and people's homes.

Natural Resource Exploitation

Madagascar has immense natural wealth: minerals, rare earth metals, coal, gemstones and precious woods. There are already a couple of large-scale mines in operation – one exploiting nickel and cobalt in Ambatovy near Moramanga, and another one mining ilmenite (titanium ore) and zircon (a gemstone) near Fort Dauphin (Taolagnaro).

Madagascar may also have large deposits of oil and gas – its proximity to Mozambique and Tanzania, where large reserves were discovered over the past few years, suggest this is likely, although prospecting is still at an early stage. Only one on-shore block has so far been confirmed as being commercially viable (a heavy oil deposit in western Madagascar).

Common tenrec mothers can give birth to 25 infants at one time, the most of any mammal in the world.

Top Deforestation (p247) is a major environmental issue in Madagascar

Bottom Madagascar's lemurs (p251) are found nowhere else on earth.

MARCELLA MIRIELLO/SHUTTERSTOCK ©

LEMURS IN PERIL

Few people realise quite how endangered lemurs are. According to the International Union for Conservation of Nature (IUCN), they are now the most threatened mammal group on earth, with 94% of all species threatened with extinction (up from 64% in 2005).

This sorry state of affairs is down to several factors: deforestation, which has squeezed their natural habitat; poaching (for wildlife trade) and hunting (from impoverished local communities); and the 2009–13 political crisis, which not only saw a complete breakdown of the rule of law in protected areas, but also led a number of donors to suspend their funding for environmental conservation.

Lemurs are also at risk of climate change, which could shrink their habitat even further, and shift it by hundreds of kilometres in some cases.

Thankfully, the situation is now well documented and an internationally supported strategy is in place to protect lemurs. At its heart is the involvement of local communities and greater financial support for conservation efforts.

Prospecting in the extractive sector virtually ground to a halt during the transition years (2009–13), but with the return to political stability in 2014, many are keeping a watchful eye on developments. The Malagasies are understandably keen to make the best of their natural wealth, but with this expectation comes great anxiety about the environmental impact of such projects. Madagascar was suspended from the Extractive Industries Transparency Initiative (EITI) during the transition but was reintegrated in June 2014. It was suspended again in 2018–19 for failing to comply with reporting requirements but the new government, appointed after the 2019 parliamentary elections, has vowed to make full compliance a priority.

Madagascar's seas also suffer from overfishing. Human population growth and lack of food and employment alternatives in the south have pushed marine ecosystems to the brink. A number of NGOs are currently working with coastal communities to improve their livelihood's sustainability and have developed successful Locally Managed Marine Protected Areas.

Stakeholders in southwest Madagascar launched an ambitious action plan in early 2019 to move the region's octopus fishery towards Marine Stewardship Certification (MSC). Sustainable fishing practices would not only protect marine resources, but also guarantee long-term employment for those depending on this activity for their livelihood.

Madagascar is the only country outside of the UK where the prestigious Royal Botanic Gardens, Kew keeps a permanent presence. It has notably worked on the island's palms, documenting around 200 species.

What You Can Do

➡ Offset your air miles to Madagascar with carbon credits.

➡ Carefully consider your purchase of precious wood items.

➡ Never buy lemurs, tortoises or other protected species, no matter how sorry they look. Instead, report any mistreatment of animals to the police or the nearest Madagascar National Parks (MNP) office.

➡ If you buy gemstones, make sure you buy them from an established dealer and get an export permit.

MILEHIGHTRAVELER/GETTY IMAGES ©

Wildlife Guide

When Madagascar broke away from Africa some 160 million years ago, its cargo of primitive animals evolved in some novel directions, free from the pressures felt on other land masses, such as human hunters. The result is one of the most important biodiversity hotspots in the world, on land as well as sea. You'll need a good guide, patience and a little bit of luck, to appreciate it in all its glory.

Above Giraffe-necked weevil. (p274)

1. Ring-tailed lemur 2. Black & white ruffed lemur 3. Red ruffed lemur 4. Mongoose lemur

Colourful Typical Lemurs

Lemurs are an extraordinarily diverse group of prosimians (primate ancestors) found only in Madagascar. 'Typical' lemurs are long-tailed, monkey-like animals with catlike faces, prominent ears and prehensile hands with separate fingers and toes.

Ring-Tailed Lemur

These sociable lemurs forage on the ground in groups of 13 to 15, searching for fruit, flowers, leaves and other vegetation in spiny and dry deciduous forest. Habituated troops live at Réserve d'Anja. *Length 95–110cm; weight 2.3–3.5kg.*

Black & White Ruffed Lemur

This species' social behaviour is complex: males and females may occupy separate territories, or live in mixed social groups. They are easily seen at the Andasibe area parks. *Length 110–120cm; weight 3.1–3.6kg.*

Red Ruffed Lemur

Like other ruffed lemurs, this species primarily eats fruit, is highly vocal and sometimes hangs by its hind feet while feeding. It is found only in lowland primary rainforest on the Masoala Peninsula. *Length 100–120cm; weight 3.3–3.6kg.*

Mongoose Lemur

Recognisable by their piercing orange eyes and strongly marked bibs, mongoose lemurs live in pairs with their offspring. They tend to be more secretive than other 'typical' lemurs, but can be readily seen at Parc National Ankarafantsika. *Length 75–83cm; weight 1.1–1.6kg.*

1. Crowned lemur 2. Common brown lemur 3. Red-bellied lemur
4. Black lemur

ANNA VESELOVA/SHUTTERSTOCK ©

Plain Typical Lemurs

Many lemurs are plainly marked with mousy brown or grey colours that make them inconspicuous in the shaded forests where they live. Lemurs don't need strong social markings because they rely on scent to mark territories and signal their readiness to breed.

Crowned Lemur

Male and female crowned lemurs have different colourations. They live in dry deciduous forest and rainforest in northern Madagascar. Habituated troops can be seen at Réserve Spéciale Ankarana. *Length 75–85cm; weight 1.1–1.3kg.*

Common Brown Lemur

Living in groups of three to 12, these lemurs are active during the day but may be partly nocturnal in the dry season. Common at the Andasibe area parks. *Length 100cm; weight 2–3kg.*

Black Lemur

Males are dark brown or black, while females vary from golden brown to rich chestnut with flamboyant white ear and cheek tufts. They're easily seen in Parc National Lokobe. *Length 90–110cm; weight 2–2.9kg.*

Red-Bellied Lemur

You can tell male red-bellied lemurs from females by the white 'teardrops' of bare skin under their eyes. See them at Parc National Ranomafana, especially from May to June. *Length 78–93cm; weight 1.6–2.4kg.*

Eastern Lesser Bamboo Lemur

The most common of the bamboo lemurs is widespread in eastern rainforests at Parc National Ranomafana and the Andasibe area parks. *Length 56–70cm; weight 0.7–1kg.*

 1. Decken's sifaka **2.** Coquerel's sifakas **3.** Diademed sifakas
4. Indri

KKAPLIN/SHUTTERSTOCK ©

Sifakas & Indris

Also known as simponas, *sifakas* are prodigious leapers that move rapidly by propelling themselves from tree to tree with their elongated back legs. Many are attractively marked and easily seen at national parks where troops have been habituated. *Indris* and *sifakas* are members of the same family.

Verreaux's Sifaka

This beautiful lemur is famous for balletic bounds across clearings, leaping sideways on its strong back legs. The species is restricted to dry deciduous forest in the south and is easily seen at Parc National Isalo. *Length 90–110cm; weight 3–3.5kg.*

Coquerel's Sifaka

These attractive *sifakas* commonly travel in groups. They're restricted to dry deciduous forest in Madagascar's northwest, such as Parc National Ankarafantsika. *Length 93–110cm; weight 3.7–4.3kg.*

Decken's Sifaka

Protected by a strong local *fady* (taboo), these little-known *sifakas* sometimes live in towns in western Madagascar. They're common in Parc National Bemaraha. *Length 92–110cm; weight 3–4.5kg.*

Diademed Sifaka

Arguably the most beautiful of all lemurs, this species is almost the same size as the *indri*. It's widely distributed on the eastern seaboard but is best seen at the Andasibe area parks. *Length 94–105cm; weight 6–8.5kg.*

Indri

Known locally as *babakoto*, the *indri* is the largest lemur and has the strongest voice, which can travel 3km through the forest. *Indris* can leap up to 10m between tree trunks, and they travel in family groups of two to six while foraging, mostly for leaves. See them at the Andasibe area parks. *Length 69–77cm; weight 6–9.5kg.*

1. Grey mouse lemur 2. Weasel sportive lemur 3. Aye-aye

Common Nocturnal Lemurs

Approximately half of all lemur species are nocturnal. The nocturnal species are the smallest lemurs, and include mouse lemurs (the smallest of all primates), dwarf lemurs and sportive lemurs. The aye-aye is classified in its own family and even among lemurs stands out as unique.

Gray Mouse Lemur

Like most mouse lemurs, this species can be very common in suitable habitats, which include deciduous dry forest, spiny forest and secondary forest. It is typically active in the lower tree layers, although it moves very quickly and often retires from torchlight soon after being spotted. Mouse lemurs eat insects, fruit, flowers and other small animals, and are preyed upon by forest owls. *Length 25–28cm; weight 58–67g.*

Aye-Aye

With its shaggy, grizzled coat, bright-orange eyes, leathery bat-like ears and long, dextrous fingers, the aye-aye is a strange-looking animal and the subject of much superstition. The middle digit of each forehand is elongated, and is used to probe crevices for insect larvae and other morsels. Aye-ayes are difficult to see but widely distributed in rainforests and dry deciduous forests. Your best chance to see one is on Aye-Aye Island. *Length 74–90cm; weight 2.5–2.6kg.*

Weasel Sportive Lemur

Found in rainforests of east-central Madagascar, these lemurs have dense woolly fur and spend the night munching on leaves, often staying for hours in the same tree. Males are solitary and highly territorial, while females remain with their offspring. *Length 30–35cm; weight 0.5–1kg.*

Rare Nocturnal Lemurs

Nocturnal lemurs are hard to find and may require the assistance of expert guides to spot. Some are thought to be highly endangered, while so little is known about others that their numbers and distribution have not been accurately determined.

Milne-Edwards' Sportive Lemur

Long, powerful back legs enable the eight species of sportive lemur to leap from tree to tree, balanced by their long tails. They sleep during the day in holes in trees and emerge after dark to feed. This species lives in dry deciduous forest in the west and northwest and can generally be seen at Parc National Ankarafantsika. *Length 54–58cm; weight 1kg.*

Western Avahi

The nine species of avahi have dense fur that gives them a woolly appearance, hence their alternative name of 'woolly lemurs'. Their diet consists of a large variety of leaves and buds, and families huddle together during the day in dense foliage in the forest canopy. Woolly lemurs can be found in both humid and dry forests. *Length 59–68cm; weight 0.9–1.3kg.*

Pygmy Mouse Lemur

Owing to its size and nocturnal habits, this very small lemur went undetected for more than 100 years until it was rediscovered in 1993. It has been found in dry forests at Parc National Bemaraha and Réserve Forestière de Kirindy, but almost nothing is known of its history, whether it's threatened or if new populations will be found. *Length 12–13cm; weight 43–55g.*

1. Milne-Edwards' sportive lemur 2. Western avahis 3. Pygmy mouse lemur

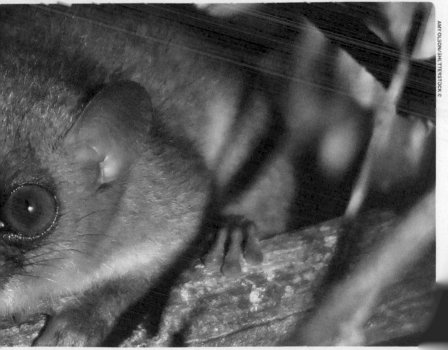

ANGELA N PERRYMAN/SHUTTERSTOCK ©

1. Fossa 2. Fanaloka 3. Ring-tailed mongoose

Carnivorous Mammals

Although lemurs are the undoubted highlight, Madagascar has many other types of native land mammal, including eight predators, dozens of bats and rodents, and tenrecs (primitive, shrew-like animals that have evolved into at least two-dozen forms, including spiny and aquatic species). A few of the island's unique carnivores are highlighted here.

Fossa

The legendary fossa is a solitary and elusive predator of lemurs and other animals. It is extremely agile and cat-like, even descending trees head first. It is reputed to follow troops of lemurs for days, climbing trees to pick them off as they sleep at night. Fossas were the villains in the animated film *Madagascar*. They are regularly spotted at Réserve Forestière de Kirindy. *Length 140–170cm; weight 5–10kg.*

Fanaloka

Also known as the Malagasy or striped civet, the nocturnal, fox-like fanaloka is found in eastern and northern rainforests. It hunts mostly on the ground but can climb well, eating rodents, birds and other animals. During the day it sleeps in tree hollows and under logs. It can be found at Parc National Ranomafana. *Length 61–70cm; weight 1.5–2kg.*

Ring-Tailed Mongoose

This attractive mongoose is widespread and active by day, and is therefore probably the easiest carnivore to spot. Family parties communicate with high-pitched whistles as they forage for small animals, including reptiles, birds and eggs, insects, rodents and even small lemurs. Generally seen at Parc National Ranomafana and Réserve Spéciale Ankarana. *Length 60–70cm; weight 0.7–1kg.*

Omnivorous Mammals

Most of Madagascar's mammals feed off insects, berries, fruit and seeds. Some focus on certain foodstuff; others vary their diets according to which foods are available at different times of the year. Many bats play an important role in disseminating seeds and pollinating flowers.

Hedgehog Tenrec

Nocturnal hedgehog tenrecs forage by sniffing out insects and their larvae and fallen fruit among leaf litter. During the day they shelter in tunnels under logs or tree roots. They are found in many habitats, including forests near Antananarivo and in Parc National Montagne d'Ambre. *Length 16–22cm; weight 180–270g.*

Madagascar Flying Fox

Flying foxes roost upside down in big, noisy colonies, like most bats, but use trees rather than caves as roosting sites. Colonies can number up to a thousand individuals and great flocks take to the wing at dusk, fanning out across the countryside to feed on fruit. A colony of this species is a permanent fixture at Réserve Privée de Berenty. *Length 23–27cm; wingspan 1–1.2m; weight 500–750g.*

Giant Jumping Rat

Madagascar's largest rodent is strictly nocturnal. Pairs live in burrows with their offspring, foraging for seeds and fallen fruit after dark. They generally move on all fours but also hop on their hind legs. They were formerly more widespread but now live in a relatively small area of dry deciduous forest in western Madagascar; the only place where you may see them is Réserve Forestière de Kirindy. *Length 54–58cm; weight 1.1–1.3kg.*

1. Madagascar flying fox **2.** Hedgehog tenrec **3.** Giant jumping rat

2

1. Madagascar bee-eater **2.** Madagascar kingfisher **3.** Madagascar kestrel **4.** Madagascar hoopoe

Birds of the Open Country

Madagascar's birds are unusual: many evolved in isolation and 80% of the country's species are found nowhere else in the world. Sadly, many of these are now rare or endangered and others have become extinct within the last 100 years or so.

Madagascar Bee-Eater

Best seen in full sunlight, loose flocks of these graceful birds forage for flying insects over open country. They nest in hollows in river banks and road cuttings. *Length 23-31cm.*

Madagascar Kingfisher

A flash of orange usually gives this bird away when it dives into water for small fish and tadpoles. Otherwise, it sits still for long periods and could be overlooked. It is common everywhere near fresh water, especially mangrove forests. *Length 15cm.*

Madagascar Kestrel

Madagascar has comparatively few birds of prey but this is a common species. It is often seen hovering over grasslands near highways before swooping down to catch small animals. *Length 25-30cm.*

Madagascar Hoopoe

In flight this extraordinary bird shows off its stripes and looks like a huge butterfly. Its crest can be fanned but normally lies flat. It is common across the island, especially in dry deciduous forest. *Length 32cm.*

Sickle-Billed Vanga

This crow-sized bird lives in noisy flocks that move through forests making nasal *waa waa waa* calls, and probes for food under bark and crevices with a long, down-curved bill. It's common at Parc National Ankarafantsika. *Length 32cm.*

1. Madagascar paradise-flycatcher **2.** Helmet vanga **3.** Blue vanga
4. Nelicourvi weaver

Rainforest Birds

Madagascar's rainforests support the island's highest bird diversity; birdwatching in this environment can be both challenging and extremely rewarding. Long, quiet spells can be suddenly broken by a frenetic 'wave' of feeding birds composed of a dozen or more different species that will have you flipping through your field guide trying to identify them before they disappear into the foliage.

Madagascar Paradise-Flycatcher

Females of this large, active rainforest flycatcher are rufous with a black head, while males sport 12cm tail streamers and may be rufous, white or black, or a combination of all three. They're common at Parc National Ranomafana. *Length 18–30cm.*

Helmet Vanga

The helmet vanga looks like no other bird – its extraordinary, bright-blue bill is incongruously large, almost toucan-like, and thought to act as a resonator when it calls in the forest. Restricted to intact rainforests of the Masoala Peninsula. *Length 29cm.*

Blue Vanga

The stunning vanga is unmistakable and common in a variety of forest types across the island. Vangas can be conspicuous birds that travel in pairs or small groups, often in the company of other forest birds. *Length 16cm.*

Nelicourvi Weaver

Most weavers are found in grasslands, but this rainforest species often associates with flocks of greenbuls while foraging in the forest. Both sexes have yellow heads but females lack the striking black mask of males. *Length 15cm.*

DAVE STAMBOULIS/ALAMY STOCK PHOTO ©

1. Nile crocodiles **2.** Parson's chameleon **3.** Radiated tortoise
4. Tomato frog

Reptiles & Amphibians

Reptiles are usually overlooked, but chameleons are among Madagascar's most famous animals – for good reason. They have a fantastic ability to change their colors, and have eyes that swivel independently of each other on raised cones, and sticky tongues that shoot out to catch prey.

Nile Crocodile

Crocodiles are found in freshwater habitats, including the Tsiribihina River, and in the cave system of Réserve Spéciale Ankarana. *Length up to 5m.*

Parson's Chameleon

The world's largest chameleon prefers rainforests and lives in the forest canopy. Males have a massive casque (helmet-like structure) and two blunt 'horns'. *Length up to 40cm, in rare cases up to 69cm (males); females are smaller.*

Radiated Tortoise

Confined to dry forests in southern Madagascar, this striking tortoise is endangered due to poaching. It is the subject of an intensive conservation program and is being bred in captivity at Arboretum d'Antsokay. *Length 40cm; weight 15kg.*

Pygmy Leaf Chameleon

This chameleon is one of the world's smallest vertebrates. It can be found on Nosy Be, where it hunts among leaf litter and on low branches. *Length 28mm (males), up to 33mm (females).*

Tomato Frog

This bizarre frog is restricted to northeastern Madagascar (Maroantsetra specifically) and is endangered because of the pet trade. Females are larger and brighter than males, and both sexes exude sticky mucus when threatened by a predator. *Length 6cm (males), up to 10.5cm (females).*

1. Humpback whale **2.** Hawksbill sea turtle **3.** Clown triggerfish
4. Bicolour parrotfish

Fish & Coral-Reef Animals

Coral reefs and marine environments are among Madagascar's most overlooked and relatively unstudied treasures. The island's southwest coast alone has the fifth-largest coral-reef system in the world. While reefs in the southwest have suffered massive damage from coral bleaching, scientists were stunned to discover on a recent survey that the reefs of the northeast coast are remarkably healthy and have the highest coral diversity in the western Indian Ocean.

Hawksbill Sea Turtle

These attractive coral-reef sea turtles were once abundant in the waters around Madagascar but are now critically endangered because of pollution (plastic bags, which they mistake for jellyfish), loss of nesting sites, fishing malpractice (floating nets) and hunting. *Length 1m.*

Humpback Whale

Whale watching is a popular activity at the Baie d'Antongil and Île Sainte Marie when several hundred humpbacks arrive from Antarctica in June and linger with their calves until September. *Length 12–16m.*

Clown Triggerfish

This exceptionally colourful reef fish has a stout orange-lipped mouth adapted for crushing sea urchins and clams. When threatened, they wedge themselves among rocks with their rigid fins. *Length 25–50cm.*

Bicolour Parrotfish

This large, endangered species of shark feeds exclusively on plankton. The distinctive spot patterns are unique to each individual. Researchers recently found that a small population clusters seasonally around Nosy Be in the northwest. *Length 9–13m.*

Comet moth

Insects & Other Invertebrates

Madagascar's forests support thousands of fascinating and unusual invertebrates. Most are inconspicuous and easily missed, but you will also encounter clouds of brilliant butterflies, huge moths and bizarre beetles.

Comet Moth

These stunning yellow moths with long dangling tails are bigger than your hand. Their habitat is threatened but fortunately the legendary moths are being successfully bred in captivity. *Wingspan up to 22.5cm; tail length 20cm.*

Flatid Leaf Bug

Looking at first glance like clusters of tiny fuchsia flowers, colonies of adult leaf bugs have evolved in this way as protection against predators. Their young, known as nymphs, look like pieces of lace or lichen attached to branches. *Length 5mm.*

Giraffe-Necked Weevil

This bizarre little beetle with an outrageously long neck is found only on the small tree *Dichaetanthera cordifolia*. They are quite common in Parc National Ranomafana and the Andasibe area parks. 'Necks' on males are much longer than on females. *Length 2.5cm.*

Madagascar Hissing Cockroach

Strangely, this flightless cockroach has become a popular pet outside its native Madagascar. In the wild it lives in rotting logs, where females give birth to live young. Females are gregarious but males are solitary. When disturbed, both sexes can emit a hissing sound by forcing air through their spiracles (breathing pores) as a defence mechanism, although rival males also hiss to assert dominance. *Length 12.5cm.*

Parks & Reserves

Many visitors come to Madagascar for its amazing parks and reserves, and rightly so: they often are the highlight of a trip. Madagascar's efforts to set aside so much of its land for protection deserves to be saluted and supported: poaching, financing and sustainable management remain challenges, although the government seems determined to tackle them.

A Brief History

Although protected areas in Madagascar have existed since the 1950s, the environmental movement began in earnest in 1985 with an international conference of scientists, funding organisations and Malagasy government officials. Biologists had long known that the country was an oasis of amazing creatures and plants, but the clear felling and burning of forests all over the island was threatening these treasures. Concerned international donors and the Malagasy government joined together to plan a major conservation program.

By 1989 Madagascar had a national Environmental Action Plan, which offered a blueprint for biodiversity action for the next 15 years. The first step was to create a national park system, called the Association Nationale pour la Gestion des Aires Protégées (Angap; National Association for the Management of Protected Areas), and then set Angap to work on creating new parks and training staff. The last phase of the program, which started in earnest in the noughties, aimed to develop sustainable tourism in the country's protected areas.

Although not perfect, great strides have been achieved in the country's protected areas since 1985. Angap changed its name to Madagascar National Parks (MNP; www.parcs-madagascar.com) in 2009 and it now manages 43 protected areas covering around 20,000 sq km. In total, Madagascar now has more than 60,000 sq km of land (and sea) under protection.

Best
Protected
Areas for
Lemurs

Réserve d'Anja

*Réserve de
Nahampoana*

*Parc National
Ranomafana*

*Parc National
Mantadia*

WORLD HERITAGE SITE IN DANGER

In 2007 Unesco declared the eastern-seaboard Rainforests of the Atsinanana a World Heritage Site. The site includes six rainforest national parks: Parc National Marojejy, Parc National Masoala-Nosy Mangabe, Parc National Zahamena, Parc National Ranomafana, Parc National Andringitra and Parc National Andohahela. Unesco acknowledged the importance of these forests in maintaining Madagascar's high levels of biodiversity.

But in July 2010 the World Heritage committee decided to move the Rainforests of the Atsinanana to its List of World Heritage in Danger because of illegal logging and hunting of endangered species. The committee noted that 'despite a decree outlawing the exploitation and export of rosewood and ebony, Madagascar continues to provide export permits for illegally logged timber'.

Unesco urged Madagascar to respect the legislation, but as of 2019 there was still no sign that the rainforests of Atsinanana would be moved off the red list any time soon because of continued trafficking, wildlife poaching and illegal mining.

Fragile Gains

Lords and Lemurs by Alison Jolly is a history of the Réserve Privée de Berenty that skilfully weaves together the stories of the spiny desert Tandroy people, three generations of French plantation owners, lemurs and lemur-watchers.

At the World Parks Congress in Durban in 2003 (an event organised every 10 years by the International Union for Conservation of Nature), then president Marc Ravalomanana announced a bold plan to triple the extent of Madagascar's protected areas. Amazingly, the country achieved its goal, a feat that president Hery Rajaonarimampianina proudly announced in November 2014 at the World Parks Congress in Sydney.

Despite this achievement, the picture inside Madagascar's protected areas isn't all rosy. National parks in the northeast of the country such as Marojejy and Masoala have been subject to severe illegal logging of precious hardwoods (rosewood in particular) during the transition (2009–13), and despite the return to constitutional rule in 2014, the illegal trafficking has continued. Others such as Ankarana, Ranomafana and Isalo have struggled to contain mining rushes, notably for sapphires.

The government faces two more challenges: the sustainable management of protected areas (notably their financing, which is largely supported by international donors) and how to translate conservation efforts into economic development. Although local communities receive (in theory) 50% of park admission fees, the government and conservation organisations alike are keen to see conservation play a wider role in Madagascar's economic growth.

Undaunted, the president called on the international community at the 2014 Sydney conference to help Madagascar meet these challenges and set his country another goal: to triple the extent of marine protected areas by the next World Parks Congress (likely to be held in 2024).

Sustainable Conservation

Enlightened conservationists know that for conservation programs to succeed in poor developing nations, local people must be involved.

From the beginning, the needs of the people living in and around the parks were incorporated into park management plans. Money from park admission fees is used to build wells, buy vegetable seeds, help with tree nurseries, rebuild schools and build small dams to facilitate paddy, rather than hillside, rice cultivation.

Tourism has also fostered employment opportunities in villages around major national parks, with rangers, guides, porters and those working in guesthouses and restaurants all benefiting.

CARBON FOR SALE

The Parc Naturel de Makira in eastern Madagascar is the country's largest protected area and home to 1% of the world's biodiversity. In an effort to make the park financially sustainable, the government of Madagascar and the Wildlife Conservation Society (www.wcs.org) set up a REDD+ carbon credit scheme (REDD+ stands for Reducing Emissions from Deforestation and Forest Degradation Plus Conservation).

The idea is to assign financial value to the carbon stored in trees and to compensate the institution or community (in developing countries only) protecting the forested areas. Deforestation is thought to contribute around 20% of greenhouse gas emissions, so finding incentives to avoid it is an important climate-control mechanism. It's also a good way to 'make conservation pay', with 50% of carbon revenues used to benefit communities directly.

In September 2013, the government announced that more than 700,000 credits had been approved for sale, which would save 32 million tonnes of CO_2 from reaching the atmosphere. But the scheme hit a snag in 2016 and sales were suspended. As of the time of writing however, there were signs that they would resume under the new administration.

Top Granite boulders, Réserve d'Anja (p82)

Bottom Rainforest, Parc National Ranomafana (p71)

MADAGASCAR'S NATIONAL PARKS & RESERVES

PARK	FEATURES
Parc National Andohahela (p113)	Three types of forest: humid, transition and dry
Parc National Andringitra (p85)	Rugged granite peaks, fantastic trails and scenery
Parc National Ankarafantsika (p126)	Diverse landscapes, from dry forest to canyon and lakes
Parc National Bemaraha (p131)	Spectacular limestone pinnacles, Unesco World Heritage Site
Parc National Isalo (p91)	Sandstone mountains, gorges with natural swimming pools
Parc National de Kirindy-Mite (p141)	Sand dunes, dry forest, brackish lakes, mangroves
Parc National Lokobe (p154)	Primary forest on an isolated peninsula
Parc National Marojejy (p178)	Remote peaks, lush rainforest, canyons
Parc National Masoala-Nosy Mangabe (p213)	Primary rainforest, mangroves and protected marine areas
Parc National Mantadia (p187)	Pristine forest, excellent local guides, well-marked trails
Parc National Marin de Nosy Tanikely (p156)	Tiny tropical island surrounded by shallow reefs
Parc National Montagne d'Ambre (p170)	Humid forest, old French botanical gardens, waterfalls
Parc National Ranomafana (p71)	Secondary rainforest, forested slopes, waterfalls
Parc National Zombitse-Vohibasia (p96)	Southwestern Madagascar's last island of dense, dry forest
Réserve d'Anja (p82)	The mountain-size 'three sisters' boulders; forest
Réserve Forestière de Kirindy (p139)	Dense, dry deciduous forest
Réserve Spéciale Ankarana (p171)	Tsingy (limestone pinnacles), caves, dry forest
Réserve Spéciale Cap Sainte-Marie (p112)	Stark, windswept cape, Madagascar's southernmost point

Every organisation involved in conservation has dedicated funding and projects to raise awareness about the importance of biodiversity and to improve the livelihoods of communities living on the edge of protected areas. Activities include income-generating projects, training for park rangers and field assistants, school outreach programs, reforestation etc.

But the most successful examples are those where local communities are directly involved in the management of the protected area. The Réserve d'Anja is a great example. It is run and managed by village association Anja Miray, whose 250 members are local residents, and it attracts around 14,000 visitors a year, more than many national parks.

The many Locally Managed Marine Areas (LMMA) are another shining example of protected areas where local communities own, manage and enforce the protection of their coastline and seabed. A 2015 study of LMMAs in southwest Madagascar found that, over a period of eight years, short-term bans on octopus fishing had helped stocks recover and doubled fishermen's incomes during the fishing season thanks to bigger

ACTIVITIES	WILDLIFE	BEST TIME TO VISIT
Hiking, camping, birdwatching	Spiny iguanas, birds, including harrier hawks	Apr-Dec
Trekking, climbing	Ring-tailed lemurs, orchids	Oct-Nov
Hiking, birdwatching, lemur watching, boat trips	129 species of birds, 8 species of lemur	Year-round
Climbing, hiking, pirogue trips	Lemurs, birds, reptiles	Apr-Oct
Hiking, swimming	*Sifakas*, ring-tailed lemurs, *Pachypodium*	May-Oct
Hiking, birdwatching, pirogue trips	Birds, including flamingos	May-Nov
Hiking, lemur watching, pirogue trips	Black lemurs, boa constrictors, birds, including owls	Year-round
Trekking on the Marojejy Massif, lemur watching	Silky *sifakas*, reptiles, amphibians, millipedes	Aug-Nov
Trekking, sea kayaking	Ruffed lemurs, brown lemurs, humpback whales, orchids	Aug-Jan
Hiking, lemur watching, birdwatching	Lemurs (including the *indri*), abundant birdlife, reptiles, orchids	Oct-Nov
Snorkelling, swimming, walking	Turtles, coral, numerous species of fish	Year-round
Hiking, birdwatching, lemur watching	Brookesia chameleons, amphibians, lemurs	Year-round
Hiking, lemur watching, birdwatching	Lemurs, birds, insects, orchids	Sep-Dec
Hiking, birdwatching	85 species of birds, lemurs	May-Oct
Hiking, climbing, lemur watching	Ring-tailed lemurs	Year-round
Hiking, night walks, lemur watching	Fossas, giant jumping rats, lemurs	Year-round
Hiking, caving, birdwatching, night walks	Bats, 11 species of lemur, birds (including flycatchers)	Jun-Dec
Hiking, camping, searching for elephant-bird eggshells	Radiated tortoises, spider tortoises, whales offshore	May-Oct

catches – a win-win situation. There are now 65 LMMAs in Madagascar, covering about 11% of the country's seas.

Scientific Research & Parks

The biodiversity that Madagascar's parks and reserves protect is of great interest to scientists, and many of the country's protected areas host research programs in primates, biodiversity, endemicity, the effects of climate change, deforestation and much more.

The Institute for the Conservation of Tropical Environments set up the ValBio research centre next to Parc National Ranomafana. The Wildlife Conservation Society manages Parc Naturel de Makira, the largest protected area in Madagascar. The Durrell Wildlife Conservation Trust has had a captive tortoise breeding centre at Parc National Ankarafantsika for nearly 25 years and is fighting to save the Menabe Antimena Protected Area in the southwest. The German Primate Centre has been researching Réserve Forestière de Kirindy's lemurs since 1993. WWF is

NATIONAL PARK ADMISSION FEES

	PROTECTED AREAS	ADMISSION (AR/DAY)
King parks	Ankarana, Isalo	65,000
main parks	Andohahela, Ankarafantsika, Bemaraha, Lokobe, Montagne d'Ambre, Nosy Hara, Ranomafana	55,000
other parks	Ambohitantely, Analamazaotra, Analamerana, Andringitra, Baie de Baly, Beza-Mahafaly, Cap Sainte-Marie, Kirindy Mite, Mananara Nord, Manombo, Manongarivo, Mantadia, Marojejy, Masoala-Nosy Mangabe, Mikea, Sahamalaza, Tsimanampesotse, Tsingy de Namoroka, Zahamena, Zombitse-Vohibasia	45,000

working on wildlife corridors between protected areas, and American scientists from Harvard, Montclair State University and the Californian Academy of Sciences are looking at ways to increase insect consumption and improve chicken rearing in the northeast in order to reduce the consumption of endangered bushmeat (notably lemurs).

These are just a handful of projects taking place in the country's protected areas, but they highlight their importance to the scientific community, a fact that is, sadly, not always well explained to visitors.

Visiting Protected Areas

Admission Fees

National park admission prices for foreign nationals depend on the park's category. The fee is per day. Children pay Ar25,000 per day in all parks.

Admission to other protected areas varies between Ar10,000 and Ar60,000 per day for an adult. Children generally pay a nominal fee.

Guides

Guides are compulsory in all MNP protected areas (national parks, special reserves and strict nature reserves), but not always in other protected areas. You don't need to book a guide in advance: just turn up at the MNP office on the day (or the day before if you'd like to discuss itineraries) and you will be assigned a guide who matches your request (guides work in rotation).

In 1986 scientists 'rediscovered' the greater bamboo lemur (previously thought extinct) in what is now Parc National Ranomafana. They also discovered a new species, the golden bamboo lemur. So extraordinary were these findings that they led to the creation of the park.

Unfortunately, there can be big variations in the level of knowledge about fauna and flora from one guide to another. All MNP guides speak French, and an increasing number now speak English.

Fees vary depending on the park and the length of walks, but in any case they are generally clearly displayed at the reserve or park entrance. A charge of Ar40,000 for half a day's walk is about average.

Camping

Almost all national parks have designated camping areas. The locations are invariably atmospheric, but facilities vary from pretty good to really basic.

Don't be put off if you haven't come equipped for camping: all you really need is a warm sleeping bag and some toilet roll. Some parks rent tents, cooking utensils etc and if they don't, they will usually know a local outfit that does. You can also hire porters and cooks (who can usually sort out supplies for you). Just drop by the MNP office to reserve everything the day before you need to set off.

Survival Guide

Directory A–Z

Accessible Travel

Madagascar has few facilities for travellers with disabilities. This, combined with a weak infrastructure in many areas of the country, may make travel here difficult.

Wheelchair users will struggle with the lack of surfaced paths; visually impaired travellers should be especially careful of open drains and irregular pavements.

Public transport is very crowded and unable to accommodate a wheelchair unless it is folded up. Private vehicle rental with a driver is commonplace, however, and would offer a good alternative. Make sure you talk through any special requirements with the agency at the time of booking.

In Antananarivo and most of the provincial capitals, there are hotels with either elevators or accommodation on the ground floor. While most bungalow accommodation – a common type of lodging in Madagascar – is generally on the ground floor, there are often steps up to the entrance, and inner doorways can be too narrow for a wheelchair. Few bathrooms are large enough to manoeuvre a wheelchair in, and almost none have any sort of handles or holds.

The good news, however, is that one organisation in France has developed a fully accessible circuit along the RN7. All the hotels on the circuit have built dedicated accessible bungalows or rooms, travel is in a specially equipped vehicle and circuits in national parks are offered in *Joëlette* (a one-wheeled, all-terrain chair held by two people). Contact **Dominique Dumas** (☑ +33 6 63 76 57 91; d.dum2@wanadoo.fr) for more information.

Organisations that provide information on world travel for the mobility impaired include the following:

Mobility International USA (www.miusa.org)

Society for Accessible Travel & Hospitality (www.sath.org)

Accessible Travel Online Resources

Download Lonely Planet's free Accessible Travel guides from http://lptravel.to/AccessibleTravel.

Bargaining

Bargaining is commonplace in markets, when buying souvenirs and when negotiating taxi fares. It isn't in restaurants, bars or hotels.

When haggling, try to get a reference price from locals as a guide but bear in mind that many Malagasy think it is fair that foreigners should be charged more than locals for the same goods or service.

Customs Regulations

Travellers are allowed to leave the country with the following:

➡ 2kg of vanilla (dried)

➡ 1kg of hallmarked jewellery with receipts

➡ 1kg peppercorn or coffee Precious stones and woods must come with conformity and export certificates. If the retailer doesn't provide it to you, inquire at the customs desk at the airport.

For a full list of regulations, check Douanes Malgaches (Malagasy Customs; www.douanes.gov.mg).

ADDRESSES IN MADAGASCAR

Addresses in Madagascar are complex affairs – locals don't tend to go by street names and there's no standard system. Sometimes we include addresses for places on prominent streets, but if the street is not well known, we simply give the area of town where you'll find the place, or a description of how to locate it. If in doubt, ask around locally.

Electricity

Type C
220V/50Hz

Type E
220V/50Hz

Embassies & Consulates

Australian High Commission The Australian High Commission in Mauritius has consular responsibility for Madagascar.

EATING PRICE RANGES

The following price ranges refer to the price of a main course.

€ less than Ar12,000 Food stalls, *hotelys* or *gargottes* (informal Malagasy eateries). Rice dishes are the staple, and there is also a huge variety of fritters.

€€ Ar12,000 to Ar25,000 Restaurants, some of which are very fancy. A small increase in price, but a big jump in quality: zebu steaks, grilled seafood and vegies, which are often delicious.

€€€ more than Ar25,000 Expect haute cuisine, elaborate presentation, decadent wine or rum selections and elegant surroundings.

Canadian Consulate Canadian nationals should contact the High Commission of Canada in Pretoria, South Africa.

Comorian Embassy (Map p50; 020 22 658 19, 032 08 865 57; Rue Docteur Théodore Villette, Isoraka; 9am-noon Mon-Fri)

French Embassy (Map p50; 020 22 398 98; www.mg.ambafrance.org; 3 Rue Jean Jaurès, Ambatomena; 8am-4pm Mon-Fri) There are also representatives In Diego Suarez (Antsiranana), Majunga (Mahajanga) and Tamatave (Toamasina).

German Embassy (Map p42; 020 22 238 02, www.antananarivo.diplo.de; 101 Rue Pasteur Rabeony, Ambodiroatra; 7am-12.30pm & 1-4pm Mon-Thu, 7am-1pm Fri)

Irish Embassy (www.dfa.ir/mozambique) The embassy in Mozambique has consular responsibility for Madagascar.

Netherlands Consulate (Map p58; 020 23 682 31; nl.mg@moov.mg; Villa Christina No 88, Lotissement Bonnet, Ivandry)

South African Embassy (Map p58; 020 22 494 82, 020 22 433 50; www.dirco.gov.za/madagascar; Rue Ravoninahitriniarivo, Ankorondrano; 7.30am-4.30pm Mon-Thu, to 1.30pm Fri)

UK Embassy (Map p42; 020 22 330 53; www.gov.uk/world/organisations/british-embassy-antananarivo; 9th fl, Tour Zital,

rue Ravoninahitriniarivo, Ankorondrano; 7.45am-3.45pm Mon-Thu, to 1.45pm Fri)

US Embassy (Map p58; 020 23 480 00; https://mg.usembassy.gov; Point Liberty, Andranoro, Antehiroka; 7.30am-5pm Mon-Thu, to 1.30pm Fri)

Food

Eating in Madagascar is a treat: food is generally good and excellent value.

The majority of restaurants in Madagascar fall In the midrange category and standards are often excellent. Meal times are as follows:

➡ Breakfast: 6am to 9am

➡ Lunch: 11.30am to 2.30pm

➡ Dinner: 6.30pm to 9.30pm

Insurance

A travel-insurance policy to cover theft, loss and medical problems is essential. Some policies specifically exclude dangerous activities, which can include diving, motorcycling or even hiking.

Check that the policy covers an emergency flight home. This is an important consideration for Madagascar, given the cost of air tickets to most destinations.

Worldwide travel insurance is available at www.lonelyplanet.com/travel-insurance. You can buy, extend and claim online anytime – even if you're already on the road.

Internet Access

Virtually every hotel (even budget ones) now offers complimentary wi-fi, even if only in the reception area. The same is true for midrange and top-end restaurants. The connection is generally good enough for emails, but can struggle with more demanding applications such as Skype/FaceTime or downloads.

Internet cafes can be found in major towns and cities. Connection speeds are usually OK. Prices range around Ar50 per minute.

If you have a smartphone, an excellent alternative is to buy a local SIM card and a 4G package: Ar25,000 will buy you 1GB of data. The mobile coverage is excellent, so you should be connected reliably, except in very remote areas.

Legal Matters

Malagasy authorities take sex tourism very seriously – offenders risk five to 10 years in jail and forced labour. Sentences are particularly severe when minors are affected.

The use and possession of marijuana and other recreational drugs is illegal in Madagascar, including the stimulant *khat* (even though the latter is widely and openly consumed in the north).

If you are arrested, ask to see a representative of your country.

LGBT Travellers

Homosexuality is legal in Madagascar, but not openly practised. The age of consent is 21.

Overt displays of affection – whether the couple is of the same or opposite sex – are considered to be culturally inappropriate.

Maps

Regional maps and street maps of provincial capitals are produced by Foiben Taosarintanin'i Madagasikara (FTM). FTM maps can be fairly dated but are generally accurate, although they can be hard to find (normally in bookshops for around Ar20,000).

Carambole publishes detailed maps of Antananarivo, which are widely available at bookshops and cost about Ar15,000.

Topographical maps are hard to find in Madagascar, so buy one before you leave home.

Money

Madagascar changed its currency from the Malagasy franc (FMG) to the ariary (Ar) in 2005. But despite having had several years to get used to the new currency, many Malagasies still count in FMG (one ariary is worth five FMG), so it is essential you clarify which currency a price is being quoted in, particularly in rural areas.

The highest denomination is Ar20,000; for travellers, it means that changing just €300 will produce a hefty wad.

There seems to be a national shortage of change, so make you sure you always have small denominations handy.

Some hotels (often at the higher end of the range) will accept payments in foreign currency.

ATMs

You'll find ATMs in all major towns and cities. All will accept Visa. BNI Madagascar and Société Générale (BFV-SG) ATMs also accept MasterCard. Withdrawals from ATMs are capped at Ar300,000.

Credit Cards

Visa credit cards are accepted at all upmarket hotels, restaurants and shops and many midrange establishments, as well as Air Madagascar/Tsaradia offices.

MasterCard can be used at some ATMs, but only a small number of outfits will accept payments with it.

Some places levy a commission of about 5% to 8% for credit-card payments.

Visa and MasterCard can be used at most banks to obtain cash advances of up to Ar10 million; commission rates go as high as 5%, depending on the bank.

Money Changers

The main banks are Bank of Africa (BOA), BNI Madagascar, Banky Fampandrosoana'ny Varotra-Société Générale (BFV-SG) and Banque Malgache de l'Océan Indien (BMOI).

All banks will readily exchange euros; US dollars are generally accepted, too. Other currencies will be harder to exchange outside major cities.

Most banks will refuse €100 or US$100 notes (for fear of counterfeit), so bring small denominations only. The opposite is true of money changers and on the black market.

Upmarket hotels often have currency-exchange facilities, but check how competitive their rates are.

Tipping

The following is just a guide, especially when it comes to tipping guides (be they guides in national parks or your driver), where it all comes down to how pleased you are with their services. To put things in perspective, the minimum wage (for those lucky enough to be employed) is Ar133,000 a month. A teacher would earn about Ar200,000 a month.

Taxis, bars	Not expected
Porters	Small note (Ar200 or Ar500)
Restaurants	5% of the bill
National park/ local guides	10% of the fee
Driver guide	Ar5000 to Ar20,000 a day

Opening Hours

Shops geared towards tourists tend to open longer at the weekend.

Banks (Tana) 8am to 4pm Monday to Friday

Banks (rest of the country) 7.30am to 11.30am & 2pm to 4.30pm Monday to Friday

Bars 5pm to 11pm

Restaurants 11.30am to 2.30pm & 6.30pm to 9.30pm

Shops 9am to noon & 2.30pm to 6pm Monday to Friday, to noon Saturday

Post

There are post offices located in every town and city. The postal service is slow, but generally OK for postcards and letters. Parcels, however, seem to be regularly stolen and Malagasies never send valuables through the post. Instead, use an international courier such as **DHL** (☎020 22 428 39; www.dhl.com), which has offices in Tana, Diego Suarez, Antsirabe and Tamatave.

Top-end hotels sometimes sell stamps as well as postcards.

Public Holidays

Government offices and private companies close on the following public holidays. Banks are generally also closed the afternoon before a public holiday.

New Year's Day 1 January

Insurrection Day 29 March; celebrates the rebellion against the French in 1947

Easter Monday March/April

Labour Day 1 May

Ascension Thursday May/June; occurs 40 days after Easter

Pentecost Monday May/June; occurs 51 days after Easter

National Day 26 June; Independence Day

Assumption 15 August

All Saints' Day 1 November

Christmas Day 25 December

Safe Travel

Crime

Tourists have been attacked in a number of isolated spots, including Batterie Beach near Tuléar, Montagne des Français and Parc National Montagne d'Ambre near Diego Suarez, Réserve Spéciale de l'Ankarana in the north and Mont Passot in Nosy Be.

Always enquire with local guides and hotels about security on excursions.

Natural Disasters

Cyclone season runs from December to March. The east coast is the most affected but cyclones can also hit the west coast. Heed local warnings and seek advice at the time for transport and activities.

Robbery

Vehicles travelling at night have been subject to attacks over the past few years. *Taxis-brousses* (bush taxis) are now therefore required to travel in convoy at night, but private vehicles should avoid being on the road after dark

---

MADAGASCAR'S CULTURAL CALENDAR

Alahamady Be (March) The low-key Malagasy New Year.

Santabary (April/May) The first rice harvest.

Fisemana (June) A ritual purification ceremony of the Antakàrana people.

Sambatra (June to December) Circumcision festivals held by most tribes between June and September, and in November and December in the southwest.

Famadihana (July to September) The 'turning of the bones'.

(many drivers will, in fact, refuse to drive at night).

Following the spate of attacks around the *tsingy* (limestone pinnacle formations) of Parc Nacional Bemaraha, private vehicles must now travel in convoy with an armed escort between Belo-sur-Tsiribihina and Bekopaka (the gateway to the national park).

Telephone

The country code for Madagascar is ☏+261. Phone numbers have 10 digits.

Landline numbers start with ☏020; mobile numbers start with ☏032, 033 or 034.

To call out of Madagascar, dial ☏+00 before the country code.

If you don't have a mobile phone, phone services (including fax) are offered at some post offices, upmarket hotels and internet cafes.

Mobile Phones

Mobile-phone coverage, including 3G/4G, is excellent in Madagascar. The main networks are Telma (www.telma.mg), which is government owned, Airtel (www.airtel.mg) and Orange (www.orange.mg). Some remote areas only have coverage from one network.

SIM cards are very cheap (Ar500 to Ar2000) and can be bought from the mobile networks' offices.

You can buy credit at literally every street corner in towns and cities and in grocery shops in the form of electronic credit or scratch cards (Ar1000 to Ar100,000). A national/international SMS costs around Ar120/340.

National calls cost around Ar720 per minute.

International calls from mobile phones cost Ar870 to Ar4770 per minute.

WhatsApp is increasingly popular.

Toilets

➡ Western-style flush toilets are common in midrange and top-end hotels and restaurants.

➡ Elsewhere you may find sit-down loos but will have to flush with a bucket; squat toilets are common in rural areas.

➡ Malagasy plumbing struggles to handle toilet paper, so you'll often see small bins next to toilets instead.

Tourist Information

Madagascar's tourist offices (www.madagascar-tourisme.com) range from useless to incredibly helpful. They will generally be able to provide listings of hotels and restaurants in the area and, in the best cases, help you organise excursions or find a guide.

MNP (www.parcs-madagascar.com) offices are generally excellent (with a couple of exceptions) when it comes to logistics and practical advice, but they often have little in the way of maps or literature.

Visas

To obtain a visa, travellers will need to provide a return

plane ticket, have a passport valid for at least six months after the intended date of return and have one free page in the passport for the visa stamps.

Visas of up to 90 days can be purchased at the airport upon arrival.

➠ 30-day visas cost €35
➠ 60-day visas cost €40
➠ 90-day visas cost €50

Longer or different types of visas must be arranged before travel – note that application times can be long.

The government is introducing an e-visa system (www.evisamada.gov.mg) whereby travellers will be able to apply and pay for their visas online, although this wasn't operational at the time of research.

Always check with your country's embassy on the latest conditions and fees.

Volunteering

More people are showing interest in volunteering for community-enhancement and scientific research projects in Madagascar.

Lonely Planet does not endorse any organisation that we do not work with directly. Travellers should investigate

any volunteering option thoroughly before committing to a project.

The following organisations regularly take on volunteers, although most placements require payment.

SEED Madagascar (✒London +44 20 8960 6629; www.madagascar.co.uk) Based in the Anosy region in southeastern Madagascar, this charity works on poverty alleviation and environmental conservation through sustainable development initiatives. Volunteering opportunities focus on conservation fieldwork. Placements run from two to 10 weeks and require donations (£795 to £2495).

Blue Ventures (✒London +44 20 7697 8598; www.blueventures.org) Based in London, with a field site in Andavadoaka,

this organisation coordinates teams of volunteer divers to survey the southwestern reef and promote marine conservation, notably through the creation of locally managed marine conservation areas. Volunteering stints range from three to 12 weeks; prices vary depending on the level of diving qualification (£2650 for six weeks is a good guide).

Peace Corps (www.peacecorps.gov) The US government's volunteering program (whose mission is 'to promote world peace and friendship') is very active in Madagascar, where it has around 140 members. Placements are usually two years and volunteers usually end up speaking fluent Malagasy by the end of their stint. The scheme is open to American nationals over 18 years.

Transport

GETTING THERE & AWAY

The vast majority of travellers arrive in Madagascar by air, with only a smattering of intrepid travellers making the crossing from southern Africa or neighbouring Indian Ocean islands. Cruise ships are increasingly popular too, although passengers usually only alight for day trips and excursions.

Flights, cars and tours can be booked online at lonelyplanet.com/bookings.

Entering Madagascar

If you are coming from a yellow-fever-infected country, you will be asked for a yellow fever vaccination certificate.

Air

Opening Madagascar's skies to competition over the last few years has increased the number of destinations serving the country and has significantly decreased airfares. It's still going to be a one or two stopover job for most travellers, but at least you have more options about where you break the journey.

Airports & Airlines

Long-haul international flights come into Ivato airport, 20km north of Antananarivo (Tana), and Nosy Be (notably charter flights). Most regional airports also handle flights to/from Réunion, Mauritius, the Comoros and South Africa. Note: departure tax is included in the price of a plane ticket.

Air Austral (Map p50; ☑020 22 303 31; www.air-austral. com; 23 Ave de l'Indépendance) French carrier linking Réunion and Mauritius with several cities in Madagascar.

Air France (Map p58; ☑020 23 230 23; www.airfrance.mg; Tour Zital, Rte des Hydrocarbures, Ankorondrano; ☺8.30am-5pm Mon-Fri) French carrier with up to five flights a week between Paris and Antananarivo.

Air Madagascar (Map p50; ☑020 22 510 00; www. airmadagascar.com; 31 Ave de l'Indépendance; ☺7.30am-7pm Mon-Sat) The national carrier has direct flights from France (Paris and Marseille), Thailand, Guangzhou (China), South Africa (Johannesburg) and neighbouring Indian Ocean islands.

Air Mauritius (www.airmauritius. com) Flies between Mauritius and Tana six times a week.

Air Seychelles (www.air seychelles.com) Flies between Tana and Mahé twice a week.

Ethiopian Airlines (www. ethiopianairlines.com) Flies between Addis Ababa and Tana and Nosy Be four times a week.

Kenya Airways (www.kenya-airways.com) Two flights a day between Nairobi and Tana.

South African Airlink (www. flyairlink.com) Daily flights between Johannesburg and Tana and two weekly flights between Johannesburg and Nosy Be.

Turkish Airlines (www.turkish airlines.com) Flies between Istanbul and Antananarivo four times a week.

Sea

Yachts regularly sail to Madagascar to/from South Africa, Mozambique, Mayotte, Réunion and Mauritius, and travellers may be able to join the crossing as crew members. Your best options to find a boat are online forums, word of mouth and asking around at ports (Nosy Be in particular).

Tours

The following European, American and Australian tour operators offer trips to Madagascar, whether tailor-made or as part of a group:

Adventure Associates (www. adventureassociates.com; Australia) Runs two trips a year to Madagascar.

Baobab Travel (www.baobab.nl; Netherlands) Offers a south and east circuit.

Cortez Travel & Expeditions (www.air-mad.com; USA) Well-established operator with an agency in the USA and one

CLIMATE CHANGE & TRAVEL

Every form of transport that relies on carbon-based fuel generates CO_2, the main cause of human-induced climate change. Modern travel is dependent on aeroplanes, which might use less fuel per kilometre per person than most cars but travel much greater distances. The altitude at which aircraft emit gases (including CO_2) and particles also contributes to their climate change impact. Many websites offer 'carbon calculators' that allow people to estimate the carbon emissions generated by their journey and, for those who wish to do so, to offset the impact of the greenhouse gases emitted with contributions to portfolios of climate-friendly initiatives throughout the world. Lonely Planet offsets the carbon footprint of all staff and author travel.

in Madagascar. Offers organised tours as well as customised trips.

Madagaskar Travel (www.madagaskar-travel.de; Germany) General and specialist fauna-and-flora itineraries.

Natural High Safaris (www.naturalhighsafaris.com; UK) Specialises in top-end itineraries, including dedicated family itineraries.

Priori (www.priori.ch; Madagascar) Cultural and wildlife tours, run by a Swiss national who is a long-time Madagascar resident.

Rainbow Tours (www.rainbowtours.co.uk; UK) Specialist and general-interest guided trips to Madagascar; highly recommended by travellers.

Wildlife Worldwide (www.wildlifeworldwide.com; UK) Specialist wildlife-viewing tours, including some led by wildlife photographer Nick Garbutt.

Zingg Event Travel (www.zinggsafaris.com; Switzerland) Individual and group circuits.

GETTING AROUND

Air

Flying within Madagascar can be a huge time saver, considering the distances and state of the roads. There is a good network of internal flights, with useful inter-regional routes. All major cities and towns are connected to the capital.

The frequency of flights does vary between seasons.

Certain routes, such as Morondava–Toliara (Toliara) during the high season (May to September) and all flights to/from Sambava during the vanilla season (June to October), are often fully booked months in advance. Plan ahead for cheap fares and to avoid disappointment.

Flights usually cost between €80 and €300, depending on the route, fare conditions and how far in advance you book.

Airlines in Madagascar

Shop around for best fares and availability.

Tsaradia (www.tsaradia.com) A subsidiary of Air Madagascar, this is the main domestic airline. You can book flights directly from its website (which accepts major credit cards) or from its offices (there is one in every major city).

Madagasikara Airways (www.madagasikaraairways.com) Started flights in late 2015: it flies between Tana and all major cities (except Maroantsetra) and also has some inter-regional routes. Its flights aren't as frequent as those of Tsaradia.

Bicycle

A mountain bike is normally essential if cycling in Madagascar. Inner tubes and other basic parts are sometimes available in larger towns.

The terrain varies from very sandy to muddy or rough and rocky.

It's usually no problem to transport your bicycle on *taxis-brousses* (bush taxis) or trains.

You'll find mountain bikes for hire (around Ar20,000 per day) in most large towns and tourist hotspots such as Île Sainte Marie (Nosy Boraha) and Nosy Be.

Boat
Cargo Boat

In parts of Madagascar, notably the northeast and southwest coasts and Canal des Pangalanes, cargo boats (sometimes called *boutres*) are the primary means of transport. Cargo boats have no schedules and leave with the tides. There are no amenities, so passengers travel on deck, where they are exposed to the elements.

Capsizing occurs regularly, so don't get in if the seas are rough, or if the boat is overcrowded. Some precautions to keep in mind:

➡ Always check the forecast and ask local advice before setting off.

➡ Make sure there are life jackets on board.

➡ Bring plenty of water (and food) and sun protection (hat and cream).

➡ Don't travel at sea during the cyclone season between January and March.

Pirogue

Engineless pirogues or *lakanas* (dugout canoes),

Major Domestic Air Routes

whether on rivers or the sea, are the primary means of local transport where roads disappear.

Pirogues can easily be hired, along with a boatman; bear in mind that the ride can be quite rough.

Bus

Premium bus services are a great, affordable alternative to slow/dangerous *taxis-brousses* and expensive internal flights. Vehicles are regularly serviced, they have functioning air-con, only take the right number of passengers, leave on time, serve meals and even have dedicated departure/arrival lounges away from chaotic *taxi-brousse* stations.

They only ply the main (profitable) routes between Tana and major cities, however. The main operators:

Cotisse Transport (☑032 11 027 10; www.cotisse-transport. com)

Gasy'Car VIP (www.gasycarvip. com)

Malagasy Car (☑032 03 188 88; www.malagasycar.com)

Car & Motorcycle

Due to the often difficult driving conditions, most rental agencies make hiring a driver compulsory with their vehicles.

Of Madagascar's approximately 50,000km of roads, less than 20% are sealed, and many of those are riddled with potholes the size of an elephant. Routes in many areas are impassable or very difficult during the rainy season.

The designation *route nationale* (RN) is sadly no guarantee of quality.

➡ Driving in Madagascar is on the right-hand side.

➡ Police checkpoints are frequent (mind the traffic spikes on the ground) –

always slow down and make sure you have your passport and the vehicle's documents handy.

➡ If you see a zebu on the road, slow right down as it can panic, also, there may be another 20 in the bushes that haven't yet crossed.

Car Hire

If you insist on driving yourself, note the following rules:

➡ You must have an International Driving Licence.

➡ You must be aged 23 or over and have had your licence for at least a year.

➡ Wearing a seatbelt is mandatory.

You'll find petrol stations of some kind in all cities and towns. For longer trips and travel in remote areas, take extra fuel with you.

Spare parts and repairs of varying quality are available in most towns. Make sure to check the spare tyre (and jack) of any car you rent before setting out.

Charter Taxi

An alternative to hiring a car and driver (difficult in areas where there is little tourism) is chartering a taxi or a *taxi-brousse*, whether for one or several days. Here are some tips to make the best of it:

➡ Enquire at the *taxi-brousse* stand, or ask your hotel for the going rate for your journey.

➡ Be sure to clarify such things as petrol and waiting time.

➡ Check that the vehicle is in decent shape before departing.

➡ For longer, multiday journeys, check that the driver has the vehicle's documents and a special charter permit (indicated by a diagonal green stripe).

➡ Prepare a contract that you and the driver will sign stipulating insurance issues, the agreed-upon fee (including whether or not

petrol is included) and your itinerary.

Motorcycle

Motorcycles can be hired by the half- or full day at various places in Madagascar, including Tuléar, Nosy Be and Île Sainte Marie.

Chinese motorbikes are increasingly replacing the well-known Japanese brands.

Wearing a helmet is compulsory; it should be provided in the rental.

Hitching

Hitching is never entirely safe in any country in the world, and we don't recommend it. Travellers who do decide to hitch should understand that they are taking a small but potentially serious risk. People who do choose to hitch will be safer if they travel in pairs and let someone know where they are planning to go.

Traffic between towns and cities is thin and most passing vehicles are likely to be *taxis brousses* or trucks, which are often full. If you do find a ride, you will likely have to pay about the equivalent of the *taxi-brousse* fare.

Along well-travelled routes, or around popular tourist destinations, you can sometimes find lifts with privately rented 4WDs.

Local Transport

Charette

In rural parts of Madagascar, the *charette,* a wooden cart drawn by a pair of zebu cattle, is the most common form of transport. Fares are entirely negotiable.

Pousse-Pousse & Cyclo-Pousse

The colourful pousse-pousse (rickshaw) is a popular way to get around in some cities. Fares vary between Ar500 and Ar2000 for a

CAR & DRIVER Q&A

In Madagascar, the road-transport system is such that most rental cars come with a mandatory driver, making the choice of both a critical decision in your travel planning. Here are the key issues to consider.

Do I Need a 4WD?

It depends on your route. If you're sticking to the RN7 between Tana and Tuléar (Toliara), you don't need a 4WD. Two-wheel-drive vehicles are cheaper to rent and run, so this is an important cost consideration. Discuss your itinerary with the car-hire company.

How Do I Find a Good Driver?

Go through an agency (p294), your hotel or a word-of-mouth recommendation. Either way, it is essential you shop around. Talk to the driver ahead of time. Make sure you speak a common language and that the driver has experience in your region. If you're not hiring through a reputable agency, take a look at the car, particularly if you are going on a long journey. See how well the driver takes care of it. If you are out of the country, ask him to send you pictures.

How Much Does a Car & Driver Cost?

The car and driver are one package (this includes the driver's food and board allowance). Fuel is generally extra, although not always. Prices for a car are typically Ar100,000 to Ar150,000 per day. Prices for a 4WD vary from Ar180,000 to Ar280,000 per day depending on the model of the vehicle (and the area where you're going to). Some drivers will charge by the road surface – dirt or sealed – regardless of the car. Prices also decrease with long-term rentals of 10 days or so. This is negotiable, but a 10-day 4WD rental typically ranges from Ar150,000 to Ar220,000 per day. Also, the renter is responsible for paying to return the vehicle to where it began, which involves both a daily rental fee plus fuel. Finally, make sure you clarify whether or not extras, such as toll roads and ferry crossings, are included as they can add up quickly.

How Can I Pay?

If you go through an agency, you may be able to pay by card or bank transfer. Otherwise you'll have to go through Western Union or pay cash. Whatever method you opt for, it's customary to pay 30% to 50% at booking, and the rest at the end of the trip.

---

ride, depending on distance. When it's raining and at night, prices increase. Some travellers may feel uncomfortable being towed around by someone in this fashion, but remember that this is the driver's living, and your patronage will be most welcome to them.

Another variation of the pousse-pousse is the cyclo-pousse, in which the cab is attached to a bicycle. They're quicker than pousse-pousse, so fares tend to be slightly more expensive.

Taxi-Brousse

The good news is that taxis-brousses are cheap and go everywhere. The bad news is that they are slow, uncomfortable, erratic and sometimes unsafe.

Despite the general appearance of anarchy, the taxi-brousse system is actually relatively well organised. Drivers and vehicles belong to transport companies called coopératives (co-operatives). Coopératives generally have a booth or an agent at the taxi-brousse station (called gare routière or parcage), where you can book your ticket.

Although the going can be slow, taxis-brousses stop regularly for toilet breaks, leg stretching and meals (at hotelys – small roadside places that serve basic meals).

There are national and regional services (called ligne nationale and ligne régionale). They can cover the same route, the difference being that on national services the taxis-brousses go from A to B without stopping and only squeeze three people to a row. On regional services, people hop on and off along the way, and there are four people per row, so tickets are cheaper. Make sure you stipulate which service you'd like when booking your ticket.

SEATS & LUGGAGE

➡ Most *taxis-brousses*, notably the Mercedes Sprinter minibuses used for long journeys, stick to the number of seats in the vehicle. This is less true of *bâchés* (small, converted pick-ups) and *camions-brousses* (generally large trucks, used for long-distance trips).

➡ The two front seats beside the driver are usually the most spacious and most sought after. They are, however, the most dangerous in the event of an accident since there are no seatbelts.

➡ Seats at the back of the Mazda minibuses will be very uncomfortable for anyone taller than 1.65m and downright impossible for anyone taller than 1.85m (but they'll be fine in the much more spacious Sprinter vehicles).

➡ You can buy more than one seat.

➡ Specific seats can be booked, but you'll have to book at least the day before at the *taxi-brousse* station.

➡ Luggage goes on the roof under a tarpaulin and is tightly roped in.

➡ *Taxis-brousses* leave when full, which can take an hour or a day. If you'd like to speed up the process, buy the remaining seats.

➡ The choice of a *taxi-brousse* will often come down to joining the next vehicle to leave, which will be packed to the roof, or holding out for a decent seat in a later *taxi-brousse*.

COSTS

➡ Fares for all trips are set by the government and are based on distance, duration and route conditions. Ask to see the list of official fares; it is generally displayed in cooperative booths.

➡ *Never* buy your ticket from a tout – always get it from the cooperative booth at the *taxi-brousse* station, or from the driver if in doubt. In any case, get a receipt.

➡ Prices are the same for locals and foreigners. However, fares can vary between vehicle types

and the service (regional/ national).

➡ Children under five travel free (but must sit on a parent's lap).

SAFETY

The larger German minibus *taxis-brousses* are generally in pretty good condition, which can't be said of the smaller minibuses, and definitely doesn't apply to the ancient Peugeots or *bâchés* plying rural areas. The one thing to watch out for is smooth tyres. General safety advice is not to travel after dark, but on longer routes it simply can't be helped. Note, however, that *taxis brousses* are required to travel in convoys at night.

Tuk-Tuks

The ubiquitous yellow tuk-tuks (motorised rickshaws) are starting to overcome pousse-pousse in popularity. They fit three people in the cab and generally work on a flat-fare basis (Ar500 to Ar1000). You can charter them for longer journeys (to go to the airport or the port for instance).

TAXI-BROUSSE GLOSSARY

The term *taxi-brousse* (literally 'bush taxi') is used generically in Madagascar to refer to any vehicle providing public transport. When you buy your *taxi-brousse* ticket, therefore, you could be about to climb into anything from a pick-up truck to a rumbling juggernaut with entire suites of furniture tied to its roof.

The most common guise of the *taxi-brousse* is the 14-seater Japanese minibus (Mazda especially). On longer routes (eg Tana to Morondava or Tana to Tuléar), Mercedes Sprinter minibuses are increasingly popular: they seat 18 people and are the most spacious and comfortable of the lot (comparable to a low-cost European airline).

For shorter journeys (eg Diego Suarez to Joffreville) and in rural areas, ancient Peugeot 504s or 505s are the go. They are smaller and therefore fill quicker, and also tend to fill more than their theoretical number of seats (three at the front and four or five at the back).

A *bâché* is a small, converted pick-up truck, which usually has some sort of covering over the back and benches down each side. *Bâchés* are used on shorter, rural routes and are hideously uncomfortable.

The *camion-brousse* is a huge 4WD army-style truck, fitted with a bench or seats down each side, although the majority of passengers wind up sitting on the floor, on top of whatever supplies the truck is carrying. They are used for particularly long or rough journeys. Small Tata trucks now ply long-distance off-road journeys such as Tana to Fort Dauphin – they're more comfortable than the army trucks but agonisingly slow.

ROAD SOLIDARITY

Public-transport options are few and far between in remote areas – and sometimes nonexistent during the six months of the rainy season. If you've hired a 4WD to travel through remote areas, you'll see many locals hitching for a lift to the next town or village – you (and the driver) may be keen to help out, but some car-hire companies forbid drivers from accepting hitchhikers because of security concerns. Note, too, that villagers reuse water bottles to store chutneys and juices and will often ask whether you have any spare (to the cry of 'Eau Vive! Eau Vive!'), so don't throw them away.

Tours

Madagascar's many tour operators can organise anything from a three-week discovery trip to more specialist tours such as mountain-bike excursions, walking tours, wildlife-viewing trips, and cultural and historic tours. All have English-speaking guides and/or drivers.

Following is a nonexhaustive list of reliable companies that can arrange excursions throughout Madagascar. They can all arrange a car and driver, too, if you want to organise your itinerary yourself.

Asisten Travel (☏020 22 577 55; www.asisten-travel.com)

Boogie Pilgrim (Map p42; ☏020 22 248 47; www.boogie pilgrim-madagascar.com; Tana Water Front, Bâtiment Trio Property, Ambodivona; ⏰office 8am-noon & 1-5pm Mon-Fri)

Espace Mada (☏034 05 828 45; www.madagascar-circuits. com)

Evasion Sans Frontière (☏020 22 616 69; www.evasionsans frontiere.com)

Mad Cameleon (☏020 22 630 86; www.madcameleon.com)

Malagasy Tours (☏020 22 356 07; www.malagasy-tours.com)

Mikaia Rasolofomanana (☏034 02 693 27; mikaia samoel@gmail.com)

Ortour (☏032 07 704 64; www.ortour.com)

Ramartour (☏020 22 487 23; www.ramartour.com)

Sobeha Tour (☏032 50 615 26; www.sobeha.com)

Tany Mena Tours (☏020 22 326 27; www.tanymena-tours. com)

Travelers of Madagascar (☏034 19 633 03; www. travelersofmadagascar.com)

Za Tours (☏020 22 424 22; www.zatours-madagascar.com)

Train

The Malagasy rail system, known as the Réseau National des Chemins de Fer Malgaches (RNCFM), is made up of over 1000km of tracks, but is used mostly by freight transport. The FCE (Fianarantsoa-Côte Est) operates trains between Fianarantsoa and Manakara.

Health

As long as you stay up to date with your vaccinations and take some basic preventive measures, you'd have to be pretty unlucky to succumb to any serious health hazards while in Madagascar.

BEFORE YOU GO

Get a check-up with your dentist and your doctor six to eight weeks before coming to Madagascar to ensure you are up to date with immunisations, to discuss malaria prophylaxis, and to make sure tooth decay won't turn into an abscess while you're away.

Insurance

Find out in advance whether your insurance plan will make payments directly to providers or will reimburse you later for overseas health expenditures (most medical facilities and doctors in Madagascar expect payment upfront).

It's vital to ensure that your travel insurance will cover the emergency transport required to get you to a good hospital – in South Africa or Réunion (a French territory), or all the way home – by air and with a medical attendant if necessary. Not all insurance plans cover this, so check the contract carefully.

Medical Checklist

It's a good idea to carry a medical and first-aid kit with you. Following is a list of items you should consider packing. Contact-lens wearers should also make sure

they have spares and plenty of lens solution.

➡ Adhesive or paper tape

➡ Antibacterial ointment for cuts and abrasions

➡ Antibiotics (if travelling off the beaten track)

➡ Antidiarrhoeal drugs (eg loperamide)

➡ Antihistamines (for hay fever and allergic reactions)

➡ Anti-inflammatory drugs (eg ibuprofen)

➡ Antimalaria pills

➡ Bandages, gauze and gauze rolls

➡ Condoms

➡ Insect repellent for the skin

➡ Insect spray for clothing, tents and bed nets

➡ Iodine tablets (for water purification)

➡ Oral rehydration salts

➡ Paracetamol (acetaminophen) or aspirin

➡ Scissors, tweezers and safety pins

➡ Steroid cream or hydrocortisone cream (for rashes)

➡ Sunblock (very difficult to find in Madagascar)

➡ Syringes and sterile needles (if travelling off the beaten track)

➡ Tampons (hard to find outside of the capital)

➡ Thermometer

Resources

It's a good idea to consult your government's travel

health website before departure, if one is available. The following websites can help:

Australia (www.smartraveller.gov.au)

Canada (www.phac-aspc.gc.ca)

United Kingdom (www.fitfortravel.nhs.uk)

United States (www.cdc.gov/travel)

World Health Organization (WHO; www.who.int)

IN MADAGASCAR

Availability & Cost of Healthcare

Getting Treated

Pharmacies For minor problems such as cuts, bites, upset stomachs or colds, pharmacies should be your first port of call in Madagascar. Pharmacists are, on the whole, well trained. Pharmacies are clean and well stocked, and there is an efficient on-call rotation in most towns and cities (generally displayed in the window). Most drugs and bandages cost the same or a little less than in developed countries (generic drugs are used more widely).

Medical centres & hospitals For more serious conditions, you will need to go to a medical centre or a hospital. Public hospitals are, on the whole, poorly equipped and underfunded, but they are sometimes the only option available (note that patients often have to buy medicine, sterile dressings, intravenous fluids etc from the local pharmacy). There are good

REQUIRED & RECOMMENDED VACCINATIONS

The World Health Organization (www.who.int) recommends the following vaccinations as routine (many are administered as part of standard childhood immunisation programs, but adults may need a booster):

➡ BCG (tuberculosis)

➡ Diphtheria, tetanus and pertussis (DTP)

➡ Haemophilus influenzae type b (HIB) – this is the leading cause of bacterial meningitis

➡ Hepatitis B

➡ Human papillomavirus (HPV)

➡ Measles, mumps and rubella (MMR)

➡ Pneumococcal disease

➡ Polio

➡ Rotavirus

Madagascar had a very serious measles epidemic in 2018–19; vaccination is therefore highly advisable. Vaccinations for the following are also recommended:

➡ Hepatitis A

➡ Typhoid

Rabies is endemic in Madagascar, but vaccination is only recommended for visitors who will be spending extensive periods of time in remote areas.

Many vaccines don't ensure immunity until two weeks after they are given, so visit a doctor four to eight weeks before departure.

Ask your doctor for an International Certificate of Vaccination or Prophylaxis (otherwise known as ICVP or 'the yellow card'), listing all the vaccinations you've received.

medical centres in touristy areas such as Nosy Be, and good private facilities in Antananarivo. For anything serious, however, you will need to be evacuated to Réunion or South Africa.

Dentists There are dentists across Madagascar, and their standard of care varies.

Standards

Healthcare standards vary a lot from one practitioner to another and from one hospital to the next: standards are pretty good in Antananarivo, but patchy outside the capital. If you find yourself in need of medical assistance, contact your embassy or consulate for a list of recommended practitioners or establishments in your area.

Your insurance company may also have advice.

Infectious Diseases

Despite the intimidating list of infectious diseases in Madagascar, most are extremely rare among travellers. However, if you do experience unusual symptoms for more than three days, seek medical advice.

Cholera

Spread through Contaminated drinking water.

Symptoms & effects Profuse watery diarrhoea, which causes debilitation if fluids are not replaced quickly.

Prevention Cholera is usually only a problem during natural or artificial disasters, eg cyclones, war, floods or earthquakes. An oral cholera vaccine is available, but it is not particularly effective. Boil drinking water, or drink bottled water.

Dengue Fever

Spread through Mosquito bites.

Symptoms & effects Feverish illness with headache and muscle pains similar to those experienced with a bad, prolonged attack of influenza.

Prevention Avoid mosquito bites by covering up and wearing repellent during outbreaks. Seek medical advice if flu-like symptoms persist.

Diphtheria

Spread through Close respiratory contact with an infected person.

Symptoms & effects A temperature and a severe sore throat. Sometimes a membrane forms across the throat, and a tracheotomy may be needed to prevent suffocation.

Prevention Vaccination (DTP) is recommended and lasts 10 years.

Hepatitis A

Spread through Contaminated food (particularly shellfish) and water.

Symptoms & effects Jaundice and prolonged lethargy. First symptoms include dark urine and a yellow colour to the whites of the eyes. Sometimes a fever and abdominal pain might be present.

Prevention Vaccination is available and recommended.

Hepatitis B

Spread through Infected blood, contaminated needles and sexual intercourse.

Symptoms & effects Jaundice and occasionally liver failure.

Prevention Vaccination is available and recommended.

HIV

Spread through Infected blood, contaminated needles and sexual intercourse.

Symptoms & effects Attacks the body's immune system.

Prevention HIV prevalence in Madagascar is very low (0.2%, similar to Western European countries), so risk to travellers is minimal, but the same precautions apply here as at home: never have unprotected sex and make sure all hospital equipment is sterile.

Malaria

Spread through Bite of the female *Anopheles* mosquito.

Symptoms & effects The early stages of malaria include headaches, fever, generalised aches and pains, and malaise, which could be mistaken for flu. Other symptoms can include abdominal pain, diarrhoea and a cough. If not treated, the disease can progress to jaundice, reduced consciousness and coma, followed by death.

Prevention Malaria is present throughout Madagascar, although the risks of contracting the disease are higher on the coast (particularly in the east) than in the highlands. It is recommended that all travellers take prophylaxis: there is a variety of drugs available nowadays, ranging in price, regime and secondary effects. Atovaquone/proguanil (Malarone), doxycycline and mefloquine (Lariam) seem to be the most commonly prescribed – discuss your options with a medical professional. It is essential you seek medical help if you suffer from a persistent high fever during your stay or in the six weeks afterwards, as hospital treatment is essential.

Measles

Spread through Inhaling droplets coughed or sneezed by an infected person; the disease is highly infectious.

Symptoms & effects Cold-like symptoms (runny nose, sneezing, coughing), sore or red eyes, high fever, blotchy rash that starts on the head or upper neck. Measles can lead to serious complications including pneumonia or encephalitis.

Prevention A vaccine is available and offers lifelong protection.

Plague

Spread through Bite from infected fleas carried by rodents, handling infected animals (rodents, rabbits and cats in particular), or inhaling droplets from coughs of infected individuals.

Symptoms & effects Pneumonic plague is the most common type of plague in Madagascar. Sufferers will experience shortness of breath, blood-stained sputum and, in the worst cases, septicaemia (blood poisoning) and respiratory failure.

Prevention Plague occurs in small but regular outbreaks in remote areas of Madagascar. There is no vaccine. Travellers are very unlikely to be affected, but as a precaution, never handle animals and use insect sprays to avoid flea bites.

Poliomyelitis

Spread through Contaminated food and water.

Symptoms & effects Polio can be carried asymptomatically (ie showing no symptoms) and can cause a transient fever. In rare cases it causes weakness or paralysis of one or more muscles.

Prevention The vaccine is given in childhood and should be boosted every 10 years.

Rabies

Spread through Bite or lick on broken skin by an infected animal.

Symptoms & effects Rabies causes acute encephalitis (inflammation of the brain). It is always fatal once the clinical symptoms start, which might be up to several months after an infected bite.

Prevention A preventive vaccine of three injections exists, which

gives a person bitten by an infected animal more time to seek medical help. If you have not been vaccinated, you will need a course of five injections within 24 hours of being bitten.

Schistosomiasis (Bilharzia)

Spread through Flukes (minute worms) that are carried by a species of freshwater snail; the snails shed the flukes in slow-moving or still water. The parasites penetrate human skin during paddling or swimming and migrate to the bladder/bowel.

Symptoms & effects Transient fever and rash, and blood in stools or urine. In chronic cases, schistosomiasis can cause bladder cancer or damage to the intestines.

Prevention Avoid paddling or swimming in suspect freshwater lakes or slow-running rivers. A blood test can detect antibodies if you suspect you have been exposed, and treatment back home is then possible in specialist travel or infectious-disease clinics.

Tuberculosis (TB)

Spread through Close respiratory contact and, occasionally, infected milk or milk products.

Symptoms and effects TB can be asymptomatic, only being picked up on a routine chest X-ray. Alternatively, it can cause a cough, weight loss or fever, sometimes months or even years after exposure.

Prevention The BCG vaccination is recommended for those mixing closely with locals, although it gives only moderate protection.

TAP WATER

It is not safe to drink water from taps anywhere – including the most expensive hotels. Bottled water (Ar1800 to Ar4000) is available throughout the country. If you can get clear water from a tap or well, water-purifying tablets are a good option. Avoid ice in drinks unless it's been made from filtered water. To save on plastic, consider investing in a portable water filter/steriliser such as SteriPen (about US$100) or LifeStraw (about US$30).

TRAVELLER'S DIARRHOEA

Although it's not inevitable that you will get diarrhoea while travelling in Madagascar, it's very likely. Diarrhoea is the most common travel-related illness: figures suggest that at least half of all travellers to Africa will get diarrhoea at some stage. Sometimes dietary changes, such as increased spices, are the cause. To avoid diarrhoea, eat fresh fruits and vegetables only if they have been cooked or peeled, and be wary of dairy products that might contain unpasteurised milk. Although freshly cooked food can often be a safe option, plates or serving utensils might be dirty, so you should be highly selective when eating food from street vendors (and make sure that cooked food is piping hot all the way through). If you develop diarrhoea, drink plenty of fluids, preferably an oral rehydration solution containing lots of salt and sugar. A few loose stools don't require treatment, but if you start having more than four or five loose stools a day for more than a couple of days, you could start taking an antibiotic (usually a quinoline drug, such as ciprofloxacin or norfloxacin). If diarrhoea is bloody, persists for more than 72 hours or is accompanied by fever, shaking chills or severe abdominal pain, you should seek medical attention.

Typhoid

Spread through Food or water contaminated by infected human faeces.

Symptoms & effects Usually a fever or a pink rash on the abdomen. Sometimes septicaemia can occur.

Prevention A vaccine is available and gives protection for three years.

Environmental Hazards

Heat Exhaustion

Causes Heavy sweating and excessive fluid loss with inadequate replacement of fluids and salt.

Symptoms & effects Headache, dizziness and tiredness.

Prevention & treatment Aim to drink sufficient water to produce pale, diluted urine. To replace salt loss, drink oral rehydration fluids or plenty of savoury and sweet liquids (soup, fruit juice etc).

Heatstroke

Causes Occurs when the body's heat-regulating mechanism breaks down because of extreme heat, high humidity, dehydration and physical exertion.

Symptoms & effects An excessive rise in body temperature, irrational and hyperactive behaviour and, in the most serious cases, loss of consciousness.

Prevention & treatment Acclimatisation to different climate conditions is the best way to prevent heatstroke. Cool the person down with water and keep them in a cool, dark place. Treatment is similar to that for heat exhaustion, but emergency fluids (intravenous) may be needed for extreme cases.

Insect Bites & Stings

Causes Mosquitoes, fleas, scorpions, bedbugs and spiders.

Symptoms & effects Aside from the fact that some bugs can transmit diseases, insect bites or stings can cause irritation, infections, blisters and pain. Scorpion stings can be very nasty (fever is common), and sometimes fatal in people with heart conditions, so seek medical help if you're stung.

Prevention & treatment Avoiding getting bitten or stung is obviously the best way to go: wear trousers and long sleeves in the evenings as well as insect repellent. Where sand bugs can be an issue, such as the *mokafui* at Andilana Beach on Nosy Be, sunscreen with insect repellent is a good idea. In Ankarana, where scorpions are rife, don't sit on large rocks or logs, and if you camp, check your shoes in the morning and take great care when folding your tent. Antihistamine or steroid creams can help relieve itching from the more benign bites. Painkillers can be effective in dealing with painful bites. If you have a severe allergy (anaphylaxis) to bee or wasp stings, carry an adrenaline injection or similar with you as you won't find any outside of major cities.

Leeches

Causes Leeches are a type of worm that feed on the blood of hot-blooded animals (humans included). They're found in hot, humid areas, all along the east coast and particularly in the northeast.

Symptoms & effects Leeches produce an anaesthetic when they bite so you won't feel anything. Bites bleed profusely, however, since leeches use an anticoagulant to get the blood flowing whilst they feed.

Prevention & treatment The best way to prevent being bitten is to cover up and use insect repellent. Leeches are extremely persistent and in some areas, getting bitten is virtually unavoidable. Don't worry if you do get bitten, and don't try to pull the leech off: it'll fall off after 20 to 30 minutes of feeding.

Traditional Medicine

Although Western medicine is available in larger cities and towns, *fanafody* (traditional medicine or herbal healing) plays an important role in Madagascar, particularly in rural areas where there are few alternatives. *Ombiasy* (healers) hold considerable social status.

Language

Madagascar has two official languages: Malagasy and French. Malagasy is the everyday spoken language while French is often used for business and administrative purposes, and in the more upmarket sectors of the tourism industry. Unless you travel on an organised tour, stick to big hotels in major towns or speak Malagasy, some basic French will help you get by comfortably in the cities. In rural areas, where knowledge of French is less widespread, you may need to learn a bit of Malagasy too.

FRENCH

The sounds used in French can almost all be found in English. There are a couple of exceptions: nasal vowels (represented in our pronunciation guides by o or u followed by an almost inaudible nasal consonant sound m, n or ng), the 'funny' u (ew in our guides) and the deep-in-the-throat r. Bearing this in mind and reading our pronunciation guides as if they were English, you'll be understood just fine.

Note that French has two words for 'you' – use the polite form *vous* unless you're talking to close friends or children, in which case you'd use the informal *tu*. Of course, you can also use *tu* when a person invites you to do so.

All nouns in French are either masculine or feminine, and so are the adjectives and articles *le/la* ('the') and *un/une* (a) that go with the nouns. We've included masculine and feminine forms where necessary, separated by a slash and indicated with 'm/f'.

WANT MORE?

For in-depth language information and handy phrases, check out Lonely Planet's *French Phrasebook*. You'll find it at **shop.lonelyplanet.com**, or you can buy Lonely Planet's iPhone phrasebooks at the Apple App Store.

Basics

Hello.	*Bonjour.*	bon·zhoor
Goodbye.	*Au revoir.*	o·rer·vwa
Excuse me.	*Excusez-moi.*	ek·skew·zay·mwa
Sorry.	*Pardon.*	par·don
Yes.	*Oui.*	wee
No.	*Non.*	non
Please.	*S'il vous plait.*	seel voo play
Thank you.	*Merci.*	mair·see

How are you?
Comment allez-vous?   ko·mon ta·lay·voo

Fine, and you?
Bien, merci. Et vous?   byun mair·see ay voo

You're welcome.
De rien.   der ree·en

My name is ...
Je m'appelle ...   zher ma·pel ...

What's your name?
Comment vous appelez-vous?   ko·mon voo· za·play voo

Do you speak English?
Parlez-vous anglais?   par·lay·voo ong·glay

I don't understand.
Je ne comprends pas.   zher ner kom·pron pa

Accommodation

Do you have any rooms available?
Est-ce que vous avez des chambres libres?   es·ker voo za·vay day shom·brer lee·brer

How much is it per night/person?
Quel est le prix par nuit/personne?   kel ay ler pree par nwee/per·son

Is breakfast included?
Est-ce que le petit déjeuner est inclus?   es·ker ler per·tee day·zher·nay ayt en·klew

campsite	*un camping*	un kom·peeng
dorm	*un dortoir*	un dor·twar
guesthouse	*une pension*	ewn pon·syon

| hotel | *un hôtel* | un o·tel |
| youth hostel | *une auberge de jeunesse* | ewn o·berzh der zher·nes |

a ... room	*une chambre ...*	ewn shom·brer ...
single	*à un lit*	a un lee
double	*avec un grand lit*	a·vek un gron lee

with (a)...	*avec ...*	a·vek ...
air-con	*climatiseur*	klee·ma·tee·zer
bathroom	*une salle de bains*	ewn sal der bun
window	*fenêtre*	fer·nay·trer

Directions

Where's ...?
Où est ...? — oo ay ...

What's the address?
Quelle est l'adresse? — kel ay la·dres

Could you write it down, please?
Pourriez-vous l'écrire, s'il vous plaît? — poo·ryay·voo lay·kreer seel voo play

Can you show me (on the map)?
Pouvez-vous m'indiquer (sur la carte)? — poo·vay·voo mun·dee·kay (sewr la kart)

at the corner	*au coin*	o kwun
at the traffic lights	*aux feux*	o fer
behind	*derrière*	dair·ryair
in front of	*devant*	der·von
far (from)	*loin (de)*	lwun (der)
left	*gauche*	gosh
near (to)	*près (de)*	pray (der)
next to ...	*à côté de ...*	a ko·tay der...
opposite ...	*en face de ...*	on fas der ...

SIGNS

Entrée	Entrance
Femmes	Women
Fermé	Closed
Hommes	Men
Interdit	Prohibited
Ouvert	Open
Renseignements	Information
Sortie	Exit
Toilettes/WC	Toilets

| right | *droite* | drwat |
| straight ahead | *tout droit* | too drwa |

Eating & Drinking

What would you recommend?
Qu'est-ce que vous conseillez? — kes·ker voo kon·say·yay

What's in that dish?
Quels sont les ingrédients? — kel son lay zun·gray·dyon

I'm a vegetarian.
Je suis végétarien/ végétarienne. — zher swee vay·zhay·ta·ryun/ vay·zhay·ta·ryen (m/f)

I don't eat ...
Je ne mange pas ... — zher ner monzh pa ...

Cheers!
Santé! — son·tay

That was delicious.
C'était délicieux! — say·tay day·lee·syer

Please bring the bill.
Apportez-moi l'addition, s'il vous plaît. — a·por·tay·mwa la·dee·syon seel voo play

I'd like to reserve a table for ...	*Je voudrais réserver une table pour ...*	zher voo·dray ray·zair·vay ewn ta·bler poor ...
(eight) o'clock	*(vingt) heures*	(vungt) er
(two) people	*(deux) personnes*	(der) pair·son

Key Words

appetiser	*entrée*	on·tray
bottle	*bouteille*	boo·tay
breakfast	*petit déjeuner*	per·tee day·zher·nay
children's menu	*menu pour enfants*	mer·new poor on·fon
cold	*froid*	frwa
delicatessen	*traiteur*	tray·ter
dinner	*dîner*	dee·nay
dish	*plat*	pla
food	*nourriture*	noo·ree·tewr
fork	*fourchette*	foor·shet
glass	*verre*	vair
grocery store	*épicerie*	ay·pee·sree
highchair	*chaise haute*	dewn shay zot
hot	*chaud*	sho
knife	*couteau*	koo·to
local speciality	*spécialité locale*	spay·sya·lee·tay lo·kal

lunch	déjeuner	day·zher·nay
main course	plat principal	pla prun·see·pal
market	marché	mar·shay
menu (in English)	carte (en anglais)	kart (on ong·glay)
plate	assiette	a·syet
spoon	cuillère	kwee·yair
wine list	carte des vins	kart day vun
with	avec	a·vek
without	sans	son

Meat & Fish

beef	bœuf	berf
chicken	poulet	poo·lay
cod	morue	mo·rew
herring	hareng	a·rung
lamb	agneau	a·nyo
mackerel	maquereau	ma·kro
mussel	moule	mool
oyster	huître	wee·trer
pork	porc	por
salmon	saumon	so·mon
seafood	fruit de mer	frwee der mair
shellfish	crustacé	krew·sta·say
squid	calmar	kal·mar
trout	truite	trweet
turkey	dinde	dund
veal	veau	vo

Fruit & Vegetables

apple	pomme	pom
apricot	abricot	ab·ree·ko
asparagus	asperge	a·spairzh
beans	haricots	a·ree·ko
beetroot	betterave	be·trav
cabbage	chou	shoo
cherry	cerise	ser·reez
corn	maïs	ma·ees
cucumber	concombre	kong·kom·brer
grape	raisin	ray·zun
lemon	citron	see·tron
lettuce	laitue	lay·tew
mushroom	champignon	shom·pee·nyon
peach	pêche	pesh
peas	petit pois	per·tee pwa
(red/green) pepper	poivron (rouge/vert)	pwa·vron (roozh/vair)
pineapple	ananas	a·na·nas
plum	prune	prewn
potato	pomme de terre	pom der tair
pumpkin	citrouille	see·troo·yer
spinach	épinards	eh·pee·nar
strawberry	fraise	frez
tomato	tomate	to·mat
vegetable	légume	lay·gewm

Other

bread	pain	pun
butter	beurre	ber
cheese	fromage	fro·mazh
egg	œuf	erf
honey	miel	myel
jam	confiture	kon·fee·tewr
oil	huile	weel
pasta	pâtes	pat
pepper	poivre	pwa·vrer
rice	riz	ree

KEY PATTERNS

To get by in French, mix and match these simple patterns with words of your choice:

Where's (the entry)?
Où est (l'entrée)? oo ay (lon·tray)

Where can I (buy a ticket)?
Où est-ce que je peux (acheter un billet)? oo es·ker zher per (ash·tay un bee·yay)

When's (the next train)?
Quand est (le prochain train)? kon ay (ler pro·shun trun)

How much is (a room)?
C'est combien pour (une chambre)? say kom·buyn poor (ewn shom·brer)

Do you have (a map)?
Avez-vous (une carte)? a·vay voo (ewn kart)

Is there (a toilet)?
Y a-t-il (des toilettes)? ee a teel (day twa·let)

I'd like (to book a room).
Je voudrais (réserver une chambre). zher voo·dray (ray·ser·vay ewn shom·brer)

Can I (enter)?
Puis-je (entrer)? pweezh (on·tray)

Could you please (help)?
Pouvez-vous (m'aider), s'il vous plaît? poo·vay voo (may·day) seel voo play

Do I have to (book a seat)?
Faut-il (réserver une place)? fo·teel (ray·ser·vay ewn plas)

salt	sel	sel
sugar	sucre	sew·krer
vinegar	vinaigre	vee·nay·grer

Drinks

beer	bière	bee·yair
coffee	café	ka·fay
(orange) juice	jus (d'orange)	zhew (do·ronzh)
milk	lait	lay
red wine	vin rouge	vun roozh
tea	thé	tay
(mineral) water	eau (minérale)	o (mee·nay·ral)
white wine	vin blanc	vun blong

Emergencies

Help!
Au secours!　　o skoor

I'm lost.
Je suis perdu/perdue.　zhe swee·pair·dew (m/f)

Leave me alone!
Fichez-moi la paix!　fee·shay·mwa la pay

There's been an accident.
Il y a eu un accident.　eel ya ew un ak·see·don

Call a doctor.
Appelez un médecin.　a·play un mayd·sun

NUMBERS

1	un	un
2	deux	der
3	trois	trwa
4	quatre	ka·trer
5	cinq	sungk
6	six	sees
7	sept	set
8	huit	weet
9	neuf	nerf
10	dix	dees
20	vingt	vung
30	trente	tront
40	quarante	ka·ront
50	cinquante	sung·kont
60	soixante	swa·sont
70	soixante-dix	swa·son·dees
80	quatre-vingts	ka·trer·vung
90	quatre-vingt-dix	ka·trer·vung·dees
100	cent	son
1000	mille	meel

Call the police.
Appelez la police.　a·play la po·lees

I'm ill.
Je suis malade.　zher swee ma·lad

It hurts here.
J'ai une douleur ici.　zhay ewn doo·ler ee·see

I'm allergic to ...
Je suis allergique ...　zher swee za·lair·zheek ...

Shopping & Services

I'd like to buy ...
Je voudrais acheter ...　zher voo·dray ash·tay ...

Can I look at it?
Est-ce que je　es·ker zher
peux le voir?　per ler vwar

I'm just looking.
Je regarde.　zher rer·gard

I don't like it.
Cela ne me plaît pas.　ser·la ner mer play pa

How much is it?
C'est combien?　say kom·byun

It's too expensive.
C'est trop cher.　say tro shair

Can you lower the price?
Vous pouvez baisser　voo poo·vay bay·say
le prix?　ler pree

There's a mistake in the bill.
Il y a une erreur dans　eel ya ewn ay·rer don
la note.　la not

ATM	guichet	gee·shay
	automatique	o·to·ma·teek
	de banque	der bonk
credit card	carte de crédit	kart der kray·dee
internet cafe	cybercafé	see·bair·ka·fay
post office	bureau de poste	bew·ro der post
tourist office	office de tourisme	o·fees der too·rees·mer

Time & Dates

What time is it?
Quelle heure est-il?　kel er ay til

It's (eight) o'clock.
Il est (huit) heures.　il ay (weet) er

It's half past (10).
Il est (dix) heures　il ay (deez) er
et demie.　ay day·mee

morning	matin	ma·tun
afternoon	après-midi	a·pray·mee·dee
evening	soir	swar
yesterday	hier	yair
today	aujourd'hui	o·zhoor·dwee
tomorrow	demain	der·mun

Monday	lundi	lun·dee
Tuesday	mardi	mar·dee
Wednesday	mercredi	mair·krer·dee
Thursday	jeudi	zher·dee
Friday	vendredi	von·drer·dee
Saturday	samedi	sam·dee
Sunday	dimanche	dee·monsh

Transport

boat	bateau	ba·to
bus	bus	bews
plane	avion	a·vyon
train	train	trun

I want to go to ...
Je voudrais aller à ...   zher voo·dray a·lay a ...

Does it stop at (Amboise)?
Est-ce qu'il s'arrête à   es·kil sa·ret a
(Amboise)?   (om·bwaz)

At what time does it leave/arrive?
À quelle heure est-ce   a kel er es
qu'il part/arrive?   kil par/a·reev

Can you tell me when we get to ...?
Pouvez-vous me   poo·vay·voo mer
dire quand   deer kon
nous arrivons à ...?   noo za·ree·von a ...

I want to get off here.
Je veux descendre   zher ver day·son·drer
ici.   ee·see

first	premier	prer·myay
last	dernier	dair·nyay
next	prochain	pro·shun

a ... ticket	un billet	un bee·yay ...
1st-class	de première classe	der prem·yair klas
2nd-class	de deuxième classe	der der·zyem las
one-way	simple	sum·pler
return	aller et retour	a·lay ay rer·toor

aisle seat	côté couloir	ko·tay kool·war
delayed	en retard	on rer·tar
cancelled	annulé	a·new·lay
platform	quai	kay
ticket office	le guichet	ler gee·shay
timetable	l'horaire	lo·rair
train station	la gare	la gar
window seat	côté fenêtre	ko·tay fe·ne·trer

I'd like to hire a ...	Je voudrais louer ...	zher voo·dray loo·way ...
4WD	un quatre-quatre	un kat·kat
car	une voiture	ewn vwa·tewr
bicycle	un vélo	un vay·lo
motorcycle	une moto	ewn mo·to

child seat	siège-enfant	syezh·on·fon
diesel	diesel	dyay·zel
helmet	casque	kask
mechanic	mécanicien	may·ka·nee·syun
petrol/gas	essence	ay·sons
service station	station-service	sta·syon·ser·vees

Is this the road to ...?
C'est la route pour ...?   say la root poor ...

(How long) Can I park here?
(Combien de temps)   (kom·byun der tom)
Est-ce que je peux   es·ker zher per
stationner ici?   sta·syo·nay ee·see

The car/motorbike has broken down (at ...).
La voiture/moto est   la vwa·tewr/mo·to ay
tombée en panne (à ...).   tom·bay on pan (a ...)

I have had an accident.
J'ai eu un accident.   zhay ew un ak·see·don

I have a flat tyre.
Mon pneu est à plat.   mom pner ay ta pla

I've run out of petrol.
Je suis en panne   zher swee zon pan
d'essence.   day·sons

I've lost my car keys.
J'ai perdu les clés de   zhay per·dew lay klay der
ma voiture.   ma vwa·tewr

MALAGASY

Malagasy has around 18 million speakers. It belongs to the Malayo-Polynesian branch of the Austronesian language family and is unrelated to other African languages – its closest relative is a language from southern Borneo. Over the centuries Malagasy has

PLACE NAMES

Although most people continue to use French place names in Madagascar, since the time of independence places have been known officially by their Malagasy names. The following list may help alleviate confusion.

Malagasy	*French*
Ambohitra	Joffreville
Anantsogno	St Augustin
Andasibe	Périnet
Andoany	Hell-Ville
Antananarivo	Tananarive
Antsiranana	Diego Suarez
Fenoarivo	Fénérive
Iharana	Vohémar
Mahajanga	Majunga
Mahavelona	Foulpointe
Nosy Boraha	Île Sainte Marie
Taolagnaro	Fort Dauphin
Toamasina	Tamatave
Toliara	Tuléar

incorporated influences from Bantu (particularly in some of the west coast dialects) and Arabic. It has also been influenced by English and French – first in the 19th century by British and French missionaries, and later as a result of colonisation by the French in the first half of the 20th century. Malagasy was first written using a form of Arabic script. Its modern Latin-based alphabet was developed in the early 19th century.

The pronunciation of Malagasy words is not always obvious from their written form. Unstressed syllables can be dropped and words pronounced in different ways depending on where they fall in a sentence. If you read our pronunciation guides as if they were English, you'll be understood. Note that dz is pronounced as the 'ds' in 'adds'. The stressed syllables are indicated with italics.

Basics

Hello.	*Manao ahoana.*	maa·*now* aa·hon
Goodbye.	*Veloma.*	ve·*lum*
Good night.	*Tafandria mandry.*	taa·faan·*dri* maan·dri
Yes.	*Eny.*	e·ni
No.	*Tsia.*	tsi·aa
Please.	*Azafady.*	aa·zaa·*faad*
Thank you.	*Misaotra.*	mi·*sotr*
Sorry.	*Miala tsiny.*	mi·*aa*·laa tsin

Mr	*Ingahy*	in·*gaa*
Mrs	*Ramatoa*	raa·maa·*tu*
Miss	*Ramatoakely*	raa·maa·*tu*·kel

How are you?
Manao ahoana ianao? maa·*now* aa·ho·ni·aa·now
Fine, and you?
Tsara, ary ianao? tsaar aa·ri·*aa*·now
What's your name?
Iza no anaranao? i·zaa nu aa·*naa*·raa·now
My name is ...
... no anarako. ... nu aa·*naa*·raa·ku
Do you speak English?
Miteny angilisy mi·*ten* aan·gi·*lis*
ve ianao? ve i·aa·now
I don't understand.
Tsy azoko. tsi aa·zuk

Accommodation

Where's a ...? *Aiza no misy ...?* ai·zaa nu mis ...

campsite	*toerana filasiana*	tu·e·raan fi·laa·*si*·naa
guesthouse	*tranom- bahiny*	traa·num· baa·hin
hotel	*hôtely*	o·tel
youth hostel	*fandraisana tanora*	faan·*drai*·saa· naa taa·nur

Do you have a ... room?	*Misy ... ve ato aminao efitra iray ...?*	mis ... ve aat·waa·*mi*·now e·fi·traa i·rai ...
single	*ho an' olon-tokana*	waan u·lun·to·*kaa*·naa
double	*misy fandriana lehibe*	mis faan·*dri*·naa le·hi·be
twin	*misy fandriana kely*	mis faan·*dri*·naa kel

How much is it per night/person?
Ohatrinona isan' o·trin i·saan
alina/olona? aa·lin/u·lun
Can I camp here?
Mahazo milasy maa·*haa*·zu mi·*laas*
eto ve aho? e·tu ve ow

Directions

Where's the ...?
Aiza ...? ai·zaa ...
What's the address?
Inona ny adiresy? i·nu·naa ni aa·di·*res*

Can you write it down, please?

Mba afaka	mbaa *aa*·faak	
soratanao ve	su·raa·*taa*·now ve	
izany azafady?	*i*·zaan aa·zaa·*faad*	

Can you show me (on the map)?

Afaka asehonao	aa·faak aa·se·u·*now*	
ahy (eoamin'ny	waa (e·uaa·min·*ni*	
sarintany) ve?	saa·rin·*taan*) ve	

How far is it?

Hafiriana avy eto?   haa·fi·ri·naa *aa*·vi et

How do I get there?

Ahoana no lalako	ow·o·naa nu *laa*·laa·ku
mankany?	*maa* kaan

Turn left/right.

Mivilia ankavia/	mi·vi·*li* aan·kaa·vi/
ankavanana.	aan·kaa·*vaa*·naan

It's ...   ... *ilay izy.*   ... *i*·lai iz

behind ...	ao ambadiky	ow aam·*baa*·di·ki
	ny ...	ni ...
in front of ...	man*o*loana	maa·nu·*lo*·naa
	ny ...	ni ...
near	akaiky ny	aa·*kai*·ki ni
next to ...	manaraka	maa·naa·*raa*·kaa
	ny ...	ni ...
on the corner	eo an-jorony	e·waan·*dzu*·run
opposite ...	mifanatrika ...	mi·*faa*·naa·trik ...
straight	mandeha	maan·*de*
ahead	mahitsy	maa·*hits*
there	eo	e·u

Eating & Drinking

Can you recommend a ...?	Afaka manoro ahy... tsara ve ianao?	aa·faa·kaa maa·nur waa ... tsaar ve *i*·aa·now

bar	bara	baa·raa
dish	sakafo	saa·kaaf
place to eat	toerana hisakafoanana	tu·e·raan i·saa· kaa·fu·aa·naan

I'd like ..., please.	Mba mila ny ..., azafady.	mbaa *mi*·laa ni ... aa·zaa·*faad*
the bill	fakitiora	faak·ti·ur
the menu	lisitra sakafo	lis·traa saa·kaaf
a table for (two)	latabatra ho an' (olon-droa)	laa·*taa*·baa·traa waan (u·lun·*dru*)
that dish	iny sakafo iny	in saa·*kaa*·fu in

cup of coffee/tea ...	kafe/dite iray kaopy ...	kaa·*fe*/di·te i·rai kop ...
with milk	misy rorono	mis *ru*·nun
without sugar	tsy misy siramamy	tsi mis si·*raa*·maam

Could you prepare a meal without ...?	Mba afaka manao sakafo tsy misy ... ve ianareo?	mbaa aa·faak maa·now saa·kaaf tsi mis ... ve i·aa·naa·re·u
eggs	atody	aa·*tud*
meat stock	hena	he·naa

Do you have vegetarian food?

Manana sakafo	maa·naa·naa saa·kaaf
tsy misy hena ve	tsi mis ho naa ve
ianareo?	i·aa·naa·re·u

beer	labiera	laa·bi·er
bottle	tavoahangy	taa·vu·haan·gi
breakfast	sakafo maraina	saa·kaaf maa·rai·naa

NUMBERS

1	isa/iray	i·saa/i·rai
2	roa	ru
3	telo	tel
4	efatra	e·faatr
5	dimy	dim
6	enina	e·nin
7	fito	fit
8	valo	vaal
9	sivy	siv
10	folo	ful
20	roapolo	ru·aa·pul
30	telopolo	te·lu·pul
40	efapolo	e·faa·pul
50	dimampolo	di·maam·pul
60	enimpolo	e·ni·pul
70	fitopolo	fi·tu·pul
80	valopolo	vaa·lu·pul
90	sivifolo	si·vi·ful
100	zato	zaat
1000	arivo	aa·riv

coffee	kafe	kaa·fe
cold	mangatsiaka	maan·gaa·tsik
dairy products	ronono	ru·nun
dinner	sakafo hariva	saa·kaa·fu aa·ri·vaa
drink	zava-pisotro	zaa·vaa·pi·su·tru
eggs	atody	aa·tud
fish	trondro	trun·dru
food	sakafo	saa·kaaf
fork	forisety	fu·ri·se·ti
fruit	voankazo	vu·aan·kaaz
glass	vera	ve·raa
hot	mahamay	maa·mai
hungry	noana	no·naa
knife	antsy	aant·si
lunch	sakafo atoandro	saa·kaaf waa·tu·aan·dru
meat	hena	he·naa
milk	ronono	ru·nun
nuts	voanjo	vu·aan·dzu
plate	lovia	lu·vi
restaurant	hôtely fisakafoana	o·te·li fi·saa·kaa·fu·aa·naa

seafood	hazan drano	haa·zaan·draa·nu
spoon	sotro	su·tru
sugar	siramamy	si·raa·maam
tea	dite	di·te
thirsty	mangetaheta	maan·ge·taa·he·taa
vegetarian	tsy misy hena	tsi mis he·naa
waiter	mpandroso sakafo	paan·dru·su saa·kaaf
(boiled) water	rano (mangotraka)	raa·nu (maan·gu·traak)
wine	divay	di·vai
without ...	tsy misy ...	tsi mis ...

Emergencies

Help!
Vonjeo! — vun·dze·u

I'm lost.
Very aho. — ve·ri ow

Where are the toilets?
Aiza ny trano fivoahana? — ai·zaa ni traa·nu fi·vu·aa·haan

Call the doctor/police.
Antsoy ny dokotera/polisy. — aant·su·i ni duk·ter/po·lis

It hurts here.
Marary eto. — maa·raa·ri e

I'm allergic to (penicillin).
Tys mahazaka (penisilina) aho. — tsi maa·haa·zaa·kaa (pe·ni·si·lin) ow

Shopping & Services

I'm looking for ...
Mitady ... aho. — mi·taa·di ... ow

How much is it?
Ohatrinona? — o·trin·naa

Can you write down the price?
Mba afaka soratanao ve ny vidiny? — mbaa aa·faa·kaa su·raa·taa·now ve ni vi·din

What's your lowest price?
Ohatrinona ny vidiny farany? — o·trin·naa ni vi·din faa·raan

There's a mistake in the bill.
Miso diso ny fakitiora. — mis di·su ni faak·tu·raa

I'd like a receipt, please.
Mba mila resiò aho, azafady. — mbaa mi·laa re·si·u ow aa·zaa·faad

It's faulty.
Tsy marina io. — tsi maa·ri·ni·u

Can I have my ... repaired?
Afaka amboarina ve ny ... -ko? — aa·faa·kaamb·waa·rin ve ni ... ·ku

When will it be ready?
Rahoviana no vita?   row·*vi*·naa nu *vi*·taa

I'd like to change money.
Mba te hanakalo   mbaa te haa·naa·*kaa*·lu
vola aho azafady.   *vu*·laa ow aa·zaa·*faad*

market	*tsena*	tsen
mobile phone	*paoritabila*	por·*taa*·bi·laa
internet cafe	*sibera*	*si*·ber
pharmacy	*farimasia*	faa·ri·*maa*·si
post office	*paositra*	*po*·si·traa
tourist office	*biraon' ny vahiny*	bi·*row*·ni *vaa*·hin

Time & Dates

What time is it?
Amin'ny firy izao?   aa·min·*ni*·fi *ri*·zow

It's (two) o'clock.
Amin'ny (roa) izao.   aa min *ni* (ru) *i*·zow

Half past (one).
(Iray) sy sasany.   (rai) si *saa*·saan

Quarter past (one).
(Iray) sy fahefany.   (rai) si faa·*he*·faan

Quarter to (eight).
(Valo) latsaka fahefany.   (vaal) *laat*·saa·kaa faa·*he*·faan

At what time ...?
Amin'ny firy ...?   aa·min·*ni* fir ...

At ...
Amin'ny ...   aa·min·*ni* ...

yesterday	*omaly*	*u*·maal
today	*androany*	aan·*dru*·aan
tomorrow	*rahampitso*	raa·haam·*pits*
Monday	*Alatsinainy*	aa·laat·*si*·nain
Tuesday	*Talata*	taa·laat
Wednesday	*Alarobia*	aa·laa·*ru*·bi
Thursday	*Alakamisy*	aa·laa·*kaa*·mis
Friday	*Zomà*	zu·*maa*
Saturday	*Asabotsy*	aa·saa·*buts*
Sunday	*Alahady*	aa·laa·*haad*

Transport

A ... ticket (to Toliary), please.
Tapakila ... (mankany Toliary) iray, azafady.   taa·paa·*kil* ... (*maa*·kaan tu·*li*·aar) *i*·rai aa·zaa·*faad*

one-way	*mandroso*	*maan*·drus
return	*miverina*	mi·*ve*·rin

Is this the ... to (Toamasina)?
Ity ve ny ... mankany (Toamasina)?   *i*·ti ve ni ... maa·*kaan* (to·*maa*·sin)

boat	*sambo*	saamb
bus	*aotobisy*	o·*to*·bis
plane	*roaplanina*	ro·*plaan*
train	*lamasinina*	laa·*maa*·sin

bus stop	*fijanonana*	fid·zaa·*nu*·naan
economy class	*kilasy faharoa*	ki·*laa*·si faa·*haa*·ru
first class	*kilasy voalohany*	ki·*laa*·si vu·aa·*lu*·haan
train station	*gara*	*gaa*·raa

How long does the trip take?
Hafiriana ny dia?   haa·fi·*ri*·naa ni di

Is it a direct route?
Tsy mijanojanona ve?   tsi mi·dzaa·nu·dzaa·nu·naa ve

How long will it be delayed?
Hafiriana ny fahatarany?   haa·fi·*ri*·naa ni faa·haa·*taa*·raan

How much is it to ...?
Ohatrinona ny ...?   o·*trin*·naa ni ...

Please take me to (this address).
Mba ento any amin' (ityadiresy ity) aho azafady.   mbaa *en*·tu aa·ni aa·min (tiaa·di·*res* ti) ow aa·zaa·*faad*

I'd like to hire a car/4WD.
Mba te hanarama fiara/4x4 aho azafady.   mbaa te haa·naa *raa*·maa fi·aar/kaat·*kaat* raa ow aa·zaa·*faad*

Is this the road to (Antsirabe)?
Ity ve ny lalana mankany (Antsirabe)?   *i*·ti ve ni laa·laan maa·*kaan* (aan·tsi·raa·*be*)

bicycle	*bisikileta*	bis·ki·*le*·taa
highway	*lalambe*	laa·*laam*·be
motorcycle	*môtô*	mo·*to*
oil (engine)	*menaka*	me·*naa*·kaa
park (car)	*fijanonana*	fid·zaa·*nu*·naan
petrol	*lasantsy*	laa·*saant*·si
tyre	*kodiarana*	*ku*·di·aa·raan

QUESTION WORDS

When?	*Oviana?*	o·*vi*·naa
Where?	*Aiza?*	*ai*·zaa
Who?	*Iza?*	*i*·zaa
Why?	*Nahoana?*	naa·*hon*

GLOSSARY

andriana – noble
Antaimoro – east coast tribe from the region around Manakara; also the name given to a type of handmade paper
Antakarana – tribe from northern Madagascar
ariary – Madagascar's unit of currency
aye-aye – rare nocturnal lemur

bâché – small, converted pick-up truck
baie – bay
Basse-Ville – lower town
be – 'big' in Malagasy; denotes larger parts of a town
Betsileo – Madagascar's third-largest tribe after the Merina and the Betsimisaraka
Betsimisaraka – Madagascar's second-largest tribe
boutre – single-masted dhow used for cargo

camion-brousse – large truck used for passengers
cassava – root vegetable also known as manioc
Creole cuisine – a blend of African, Asian and European influences

fady – taboo, forbidden
famadihana – exhumation and reburial; literally 'the turning of the bones'
fossa – local name for the striped civet

gare routière – bus station
gargote – cheap restaurant
gasy – Malagasy (pronounced 'gash')
gîte – rustic shelter

Haute-Ville – upper town
hauts plateaux – highlands; the term is often used to refer to Madagascar's central plateau region

hira gasy – music, dancing and storytelling spectacles
hotely – small roadside place that serves basic meals

Imerina – region ruled by the Merina
indri – largest of Madagascar's lemur species

kely – 'small' in Malagasy; often used to denote a township or satellite town

lac – lake
lalana – street
lamba – white cotton or silk scarf

maki – Malagasy term for a lemur
Merina – Madagascar's largest tribe, centred in Antananarivo
MNP – Madagascar National Parks
mora mora – 'slowly, slowly' or 'wait a minute'; often used to mean the Malagasy pace of life

nosy – island
Nouvelle-Ville – new town

parc national – national park
parcage – *taxi-brousse* station
pic – peak
pirogue – dugout canoe
pousse-pousse – rickshaw

ravinala – literally 'forest leaves'; also known as travellers' palm, the most distinctive of Madagascar's palm trees
réserve spéciale – special reserve (often similar to a national park)
RN – route nationale; national road (often still no more than a track)
rova – palace

Sakalava – western tribe
sambatra – mass circumcision ceremony
SAVA – region comprising Sambava, Andapa, Vohémar (Iharana) and Antalaha
sifaka – a type of lemur, known in French as a 'propithèque'

taxi-be – literally 'big taxi'; also known as a 'familiale'
taxi-brousse – bush taxi; generic term for any kind of public passenger truck, car or minibus
tenrec – small mammal resembling a hedgehog or shrew
THB – Three Horses Beer; Madagascar's most popular beer
tilapia – freshwater perch (fish)
tsingy – limestone pinnacle formations; also known as karst

vazaha – foreigner or white person
Vezo – nomadic fishing subtribe of the Sakalava, found in the southwest
via ferrata – mountain route equipped with fixed cables, stemples, ladders and bridges.

ylang-ylang – bush with sweet-smelling white flowers used to make perfume

Zafimaniry – a subgroup of the Betsileo people who live in the area east of Ambositra, and are renowned for their woodcarving skills
zebu – a type of domesticated ox found throughout Madagascar; it has a prominent hump on its back and loose skin under its throat

Behind the Scenes

SEND US YOUR FEEDBACK

We love to hear from travellers – your comments keep us on our toes and help make our books better. Our well-travelled team reads every word on what you loved or loathed about this book. Although we cannot reply individually to your submissions, we always guarantee that your feedback goes straight to the appropriate authors, in time for the next edition. Each person who sends us information is thanked in the next edition – the most useful submissions are rewarded with a selection of digital PDF chapters.

Visit **lonelyplanet.com/contact** to submit your updates and suggestions or to ask for help. Our award-winning website also features inspirational travel stories, news and discussions.

Note: We may edit, reproduce and incorporate your comments in Lonely Planet products such as guidebooks, websites and digital products, so let us know if you don't want your comments reproduced or your name acknowledged. For a copy of our privacy policy visit lonelyplanet.com/privacy.

OUR READERS

Many thanks to the travellers who used the last edition and wrote to us with helpful hints, useful advice and interesting anecdotes:

A Adam Weier, Alberto Feriotti, Alison & Rodney Woodcock **C** Christoph Schuhmacher, Christopher Vinegra **D** David Halpern, Declan Gilmurray **E** Elisa Janszen **G** Gabriela Opas, Giuliana Dangelo, Grégoire Ludo **J** Jon Hildebrandt **K** Katrina Froese, Katy Tanis **L** Lukas Gschnitzer **M** Margaret Donnelly, Maria Clara Vigna, Marie Didone, Mark Rowlatt, Marta del Alamo, Micky Schepers **P** Peter Lindholst **R** Roberto Aureli **S** Simon Davies

WRITERS' THANKS

Anthony Ham

My debt to the people of Madagascar is a long one. Above all, thanks to Joachin (Zo) Randriamanefa, a wonderful driver and companion on the road. Thanks also to Touissant, Patricia Bejark, Roberto Crioce, Dari Maria Merzegora, Mikaia Samoela, Eli Todimana, Naina, Leonie and Ainonavela and Serge Nirina Rajaobelina. At Lonely Planet special thanks to Matt Phillips and Emilie Filou. For getting me places, thanks as always to Nikki Chamberlain. To my Valentina, Carlota, Marina, and to Jan, much love and gratitude.

This book is dedicated to my father, Ron.

Stuart Butler

First and foremost I would like to thank my wife, Heather, and children, Jake and Grace, for their patience while I criss-crossed Madagascar working on this project. Secondly, I would like to thank Roberto of Travellers of Madagascar for supplying an ever reliable car and Tony for driving so well and being such great company on the road. Thank you also to Matt Phillips for giving me the opportunity to work on this project.

Emilie Filou

Thanks to Patricia Rajeriarison for her friendship and great tips; Elysée Velomasy for being such a well of knowledge in Masoala; Be Léonor

for his indefatigable driving on the RN5; Mariella and Judith for their exquisite company on
Île aux Nattes; my amazing fellow writers for
the many tips; Moon, Loli and Gabi for step-
ping in with childcare duties; and of course,
to Adolfo, Sasha and Pablo for putting up with
my absences.

Helen Ranger

Misaotra to all the friendly Malagasy people
I so enjoy meeting, particularly the Madabest
team in Diego Suarez and smiley driver Vévé
who made travelling so much smoother;
baie dankie to Marcine on Nosy Komba for
her island insights and *merci bien* to Olivier
and Julie, writers of the French edition, who
brightened things up in Sambava, Diego and
Nosy Be. Fellow writers Emilie, Anthony and
Stuart, and Destination Editor Matt Phillips,
were a pleasure to work with, as always.

ACKNOWLEDGEMENTS

Climate map data adapted from Peel MC, Finlayson
BL & McMahon TA (2007) 'Updated World Map of
the Köppen-Geiger Climate Classification', *Hydrol-
ogy and Earth System Sciences*, 11, 1633–44.

Cover photograph: Panther chameleon, Ingo Arndt/
Nature Picture Library ©

THIS BOOK

This 9th edition of Lonely
Planet's *Madagascar* guidebook was curated by Anthony
Ham, and researched and
written by Anthony, Stuart
Butler, Emilie Filou and Helen
Ranger. The previous edition
was researched and wriiten by
Anthony, Emilie and Helen, and
the 7th edition was researched
and written by Emilie and Paul
Stiles. This guidebook was
produced by the following:

Destination Editor Matt
Phillips
Senior Product Editor
Elizabeth Jones
**Regional Senior Cartogra-
pher** Diana von Holdt
Product Editor Amanda
Williamson

Book Designer Fergal Condon
Assisting Editors Carly Hall,
Victoria Harrison, Kellie Lang-
don, Charlotte Orr
Cover Researcher Naomi
Parker
Thanks to Imogen Bannister,
James Hardy, Karen Hen-
derson, Kate James, Wibowo
Rusli, Brana Vladisavljevic

Index